Rolf Jucker · Jakob von Au
Editors

High-Quality Outdoor Learning

Evidence-based Education Outside
the Classroom for Children, Teachers
and Society

Editors
Rolf Jucker
SILVIVA–Swiss Foundation
for Nature-based Learning
Zürich, Switzerland

Jakob von Au
Englisches Institut Heidelberg
Heidelberg, Germany

Outdoor Teaching and Education
for Sustainable Development
University of Education
Heidelberg, Germany

ISBN 978-3-031-04110-5   ISBN 978-3-031-04108-2   (eBook)
https://doi.org/10.1007/978-3-031-04108-2

This Springer imprint is published by the registered company Springer Nature Switzerland AG
The registered company address is: Gewerbestrasse 11, 6330 Cham, Switzerland

This volume has been made possible by the generous support of SILVIVA, Switzerland (https://www.silviva.ch).

Contents

Health and Well-Being for Pupils and Teachers

Outdoor Learning Fosters Twenty-First Century Competencies

Teacher Competencies in Focus

International Perspectives and Case Studies

Contents

Outdoor Learning—Why It Should Be High up on the Agenda of Every Educator

Introduction

Rolf Jucker and Jakob von Au

1 Why is High Quality Education so Crucial Today?

Whether you like Greta Thunberg or not, it is very difficult to argue with her analysis that we need immediate urgent action to stop, mitigate and adapt to climate change—that "empty words" are simply not enough (Thunberg, 2020).

Why are we starting a volume on outdoor learning with this provocative statement? Is this going to be some missionary, ideologically driven, radical environmentalist manifesto?

We would argue—on the contrary. There are several converging fundamental insights at play here which we need to focus on so that you, as a reader, can fully appreciate and critically evaluate what we are trying to do with this book.

A note on terminology: We are fully aware that there is a wide variety of terms used for what concerns us here: nature-based learning, school-based outdoor learning, real world learning, Education Outside the Classroom, Draußenschule in German (based on *uteskole* (Norway) and *udeskole* (Denmark)), *utomhuspedagogikk* (Sweden) etc. Platonet is at present trying to find an internationally accepted term (https://www.outdoorplaycanada.ca/plato-net/). We decided, for this volume, to use the broader term 'outdoor learning', since we believe that the value and benefits of this approach apply to learning out in the real world generally, not just for schools but also for other types of formal, non-formal and informal learning. However, we have deliberately not standardised the terminology because this can obscure the rich, diverse practices which feed what we showcase here. So it was the chapter author's choice to use whatever terminology they preferred.

R. Jucker (✉)
Stiftung SILVIVA, Jenatschstrasse 1, CH-8002 Zürich, Switzerland
e-mail: rolf.jucker@silviva.ch

J. von Au
Englisches Institut Heidelberg, Brechtelstrasse 27/2, 69126 Heidelberg, Germany
e-mail: vAu@englisches-institut.eu

© The Author(s) 2022
R. Jucker and J. von Au (eds.), *High-Quality Outdoor Learning*,
https://doi.org/10.1007/978-3-031-04108-2_1

1.1 Complex World with Many Mutually Reinforcing Challenges

Maybe climate science and the Covid-19 pandemic have managed to help us appreciate a fundamental fact about our world: it mostly consists of complex systems, which can be defined as follows:

> A complex system is a system composed of many components which may interact with each other. Examples of complex systems are Earth's global climate, organisms, the human brain, infrastructure such as power grid, transportation or communication systems, social and economic organizations (like cities), an ecosystem, a living cell, and ultimately the entire universe.[1] Complex systems are systems whose behaviour is intrinsically difficult to model due to the dependencies, competitions, relationships, or other types of interactions between their parts or between a given system and its environment. (Wikipedia—Complex system, 2021)

Most serious challenges facing human society today are complex, systemic problems, often mutually reinforcing each other:

> Crises in the natural world have reached a critical level. Inaction now threatens the very existence of human society: the Intergovernmental Panel on Climate Change (IPCC) warns that averting the most serious consequences of climate change requires a radical overhaul of the global economy, while the OECD argues biodiversity loss is among the top global risks to society. Importantly, the intersection between these crises deepens their effects. For example, deforestation is a major cause of biodiversity loss while also being the second largest source of anthropogenic greenhouse gas emissions. Meanwhile, growing inequality, the changing nature of work, and continued human rights violations are just some of the major risks facing global society and the financial sector that supports it. (ShareAction, 2020, 4; see also UNESCO, 2020, 6)

We don't want to bore you with a litany of problems. However, the above discussion highlights two points which are important for us here:

1. There is no serious disagreement with the scientific consensus that almost anything of importance to human society is complex (including education and learning).
2. We can therefore not adequately approach such issues with simplistic, Twitter-sized soundbites, but only with appropriate systemic understanding.

1.2 Humans Are Stretched to Their Limits to Understand the World They Live in

The above sounds pretty straightforward. So let us just engage in such systemic learning and understanding, here with a focus on outdoor learning…

Or can we? As Jucker has shown in his book *Can We Cope with the Complexity of Reality?* (2020; see also Glasser, 2019), our human perception and cognition—as it evolved over time—is placing serious limitations on our individual capacity to

---

[1] Even teams in organisations are complex systems which necessitates a high understanding of systems in order to lead them successfully (Mautsch and Metzger, 2019, 141–160).

understand the world around us. As Kahneman (2012) amongst others has shown, our normal, automated mode of interaction with the world—in Kahneman's terminology "System 1", others call it "old brain" (Hawkins, 2021)—is efficient for everyday life, but highly flawed and hampered by a whole host of biases which interfere with objective, reflective, reasoned attempts to figure out what is going on (i.e. what Kahneman terms "System 2").

Or to put it more bluntly: From psychology and brain research we know that our personal experience, our personal knowledge, our memory, and even what we call our autonomous, inner 'I' or self are highly unreliable, often illusionary constructions of our brain. All of this is subject to a variety of perceptual distortions, psychological biases, and unreflected cultural prejudices (Jucker, 2020, 17–53). Only very rarely can we base reliable solutions on them:

> Every-day thinking does not understand itself, is therefore uncritical and, if at all, only partially able to come to true statements. (…) Without a critical theory of itself and without a theory of the nervous system, everyday thinking (…) believes that it understands the material things in the world directly as they are (naïve realism). (…) Its implicit meta-theory is equal to the one in magical and religious world-views and is the source of resistance against the scientific world-view of adults. (Obrecht, 2009, 56; translation by the authors)

This poses a fundamental philosophical problem: given both that our evolutionary machinery severely restricts our understanding of the world,[2] and that we are dependent on a sound understanding of reality, if we want to successfully interact with it, what do we do?

Recent experiences, such as Covid-19, and a historical reflection on how reliable knowledge is created show us that we can only generate a meaningful understanding of the world if we can reliably distinguish between fact and fake news. For this, we need verification processes that only science can offer: openness, a culture of error and reversibility in the case of new findings, verification of results by different methods, reproducibility, verification by others, and evidence.

Humanity's knowledge about reality, collectively acquired over decades, is therefore always more important than our personal, inevitably distorted mental model of it, which our brain is constantly constructing (Hawkins, 2021). This is the reason why state-of-the-art solutions to complex problems can never be provided by individuals, but only collectively, by teams, based on the best available knowledge (see Frith, 2007, 187). As a result, we must learn to take collectively verified knowledge (on climate change, for example) seriously and to mistrust our fallible pre-concepts, far too often guided by our personal interests, biases and prejudices. In other words, we need reasoned, evidence-based approaches:

---

[2] This is the case even on very basic levels. The human ear can perceive a limited range of the entire sound spectrum (usually from 20–20'000 Hz, while some animals can hear from as low as 7 Hz to as high as 100'000 Hz (Wikipedia – Hearing range, 2021). Moreover, the human eye can only see what is called visible light, which represents a "very small portion of the electromagnetic spectrum". Human vision ranges from 380 to 760 nm, whereas the entire spectrum ranges from Gamma rays at 1 pm (1 trillionth of a meter) to extremely low frequency radio waves at 100'000 km (Wikipedia—Electromagnetic spectrum, 2021).

The deliberate application of reason [is] necessary precisely because our common habits of thought are not particularly reasonable. (Pinker, 2018, 9)

1.3 Learning and Education is the Basis for Understanding and Change

If we take the fallibility of human perception and cognition together with the complexity of our world, then it emerges that understanding this world hinges on learning. This is the case for two reasons:

First, despite the limitations of human cognition, we are in for a chance: the way our brain works allows for continuous learning and correction of mistakes. In constant interaction with the real world, with experiences and things we learn, our brains correct and adapt the models of the world we base our understanding on (Hawkins, 2021; Frith, 2007). In other words, our brain is constantly learning, and there is no upper limit to what and how much we can learn (Bjork et al., 2013; Brown et al., 2014).

Second, contrary to the widespread opinion that it is enough to just pick one (however absurd) opinion and assume it is equally valid as any other, humanity has developed reliable processes since the Enlightenment that allow us to distinguish opinion from knowledge. When we use reason or System 2-thinking (Kahneman, 2012), and link it to a scientific approach (see Jucker, 2020, 37–43), "we can *learn* through criticism of our mistakes and errors, especially through criticism by others, and eventually also through self-criticism" (Popper, 1999, 84, italics in the original; see also Hawkins, 2021; Frith, 2007, 183; Rovelli, 2018, 132).

Therefore, it seems clear that we all need the best available, life-long learning, if we want to be able to both understand the world we live in and to be in the position to interact with and change it in ways which are meaningful, just and sustainable. To link back to Greta Thunberg's provocation at the beginning: we all need to be in a position to move from (often empty) words to action.

You might think you are in the middle of a highbrow discussion, which has not much applicability to normal people and particularly school kids. However, for good reason most foundational texts for education bills or national curricula in democratic countries state something like the following:

In compulsory education pupils develop fundamental knowledge and skills as well *as a cultural identity which enables them (...) to find their place in society and the workplace.* (Grundlagen für den Lehrplan 21, 2010, 8; emphasis added)

The inter-cantonal Commission of Education Ministers of the French- and Italian-speaking parts of Switzerland affirms that the *transmission of fundamental values of communal life in a democratic society* as well as the acquisition of a sound general education is the corner stone of compulsory education for all. (CIIP, 2003, 1; emphasis added)

So it seems that the core of the enlightenment, as declared by Immanuel Kant, is still the basis for education:

Enlightenment is humanity's emergence from her self-imposed immaturity. (Kant, 1784)

A democracy (and the self-determination of the people in a community) can only function if the people involved in this process have the skills and competencies to act maturely in the spirit of Kant. Where people cling to the lips of authoritarian or religious leaders or (social) media to be told how to understand the world and what to do, this is certainly not the case. Therefore, the greatest challenge facing our education systems—it seems to us—is how to accompany children, young people, and adults into the self-determined maturity referred to by Kant more than 200 years ago.

2 What is the Importance of Outdoor Learning in This Context?

2.1 Education Systems Are Complex—A Call for Modesty

Therefore the question arises: What does and does not work in education, if we look at it scientifically and not through the lenses of our goals, wishes and assumptions? It is clear that learning and teaching are multi-factorial processes, in other words highly complex systems. On the one hand, there are a host of underlying conditions and parameters from the macro to the micro level (see Fig. 1).

In the classroom, this includes things such as cultural and regional context, type of school, composition of class, school and class climate. With regard to teachers, we are looking at professional knowledge, technical, diagnostic, didactic and leadership competencies, cross-curricular and subject specific quality of teaching and teaching materials. With regard to students, these conditions and parameters include perception and interpretation of the teaching, family context (social class, richness of language environment, culture, familiarity with education, parenting, socialisation), the individual learning potential (previous knowledge, languages spoken, intelligence, learning and memory strategies, motivation to learn, willingness to make an effort, perseverance, self-confidence), and the use of learning time in class and in extracurricular activities (Hasselhorn & Gold, 2017, 237).

On the other hand, teaching and education are always only offers for learners: if and how this offer is taken up, is very much dependent on the learners and can therefore never be fully controlled by the educator:

In addition to the quantity and quality of the learning opportunities offered, the cognitive, motivational and emotional learning conditions of the pupils determine whether and how a learning opportunity is actually used. (Hasselhorn & Gold, 2017, 236; translation by the authors)

We would argue that we have not yet quite managed the 'evidence-based turn' in education. Far too much of our educational practice is still based on tradition, reproduction of our own educational experiences, fashionable trends and pseudo-scientific

Fig. 1 Factors influencing a person at different levels

approaches. However, at least since Hattie (2008) we have a growing base to rely on if we are looking for broadly evidence-based strategies to make educational interventions work. Remember: evidence-based very often means counter-intuitive, as demonstrated by almost all of the history of science. Therefore, you will find quite a few surprises in Hattie's 252 influences related to student achievement (Waack, 2019), compared to your preconceived ideas about what might work. But it is certainly worth integrating these findings into what we do in any educational intervention.

For our purposes, we can focus on a few which stand out, also supported by other research. Firstly, the value of a good teacher cannot be overestimated. There has been a strong tendency, coupled with an oversimplified understanding of constructivism, that you do not really need teachers anymore, because learning happens in the learner. However, research clearly shows that this is not the case. Having a good teacher is undeniably central for student achievement, and it is far from trivial. Pedagogical and psychological research has highlighted the complex and demanding social, pedagogical and didactic-professional qualities, which characterise a good teacher (Weinert, 1996). Research into excellence has also reinforced this understanding and thoroughly debunked the myths around talent and genius. In order to learn and to succeed in any domain with a high level of competence requires a lot of dedication and years of practice (Brown et al., 2014, 18; Ericsson & Pool, 2016, 96, 207), in other words, "effortful learning", akin to "System 2"-learning. It also requires a good dose of so-called non-cognitive skills (such as "self-discipline, grit, and persistence" [Brown et al., 2014, 199]) as well as tutors who give feedback in order to push and stretch learners not too much, but also not too little outside their comfort zone (Ericsson & Pool, 2016, 108).

In addition, it seems that collective learning is more effective—something everybody knows who floated his/her own 'fantastic' idea in a team, only to witness that afterwards this idea had matured into something clearly better, more complex and meaningful through the collaborative process (Rovelli, 2016, 6; Frith, 2007, 175; Rippon, 2019, 114; Dennett, 2017, 24, 378; Glasser, 2007).

We are left with a clear obligation to modesty and even humility. The insight that education and learning are complex systems means that we will only master them reasonably well if we face up to this complexity. Simplifications simply won't help and the 'one-size-fits-all' guru-solution for everything does not exists. We must develop reliable immune responses to simple answers or black-and-white solutions. Not just in politics, but also in education and learning, we still largely have to do our homework and start acting based on evidence, not ideology or mission. Which begs the question: Are we ready to look at our educational practice with more humility, openness, willingness to learn and culture of error?

Furthermore, any educational intervention is at the very best only a small puzzle piece that contributes to human development and learning. Learning offers are only necessary, never sufficient, elements for the transformation towards a dignified, liveable future. We need not only in education, but also on all other levels of the system (politics, cultural values, economic system, incentives and disincentives, media, families, identity construction, etc.), manifold, scientifically well supported interventions. But these interventions, in turn, will not be sustainable if they are not undertaken with an open, Popperean scientific mindset. They need to be based on a democratic foundation and oriented towards freedom and responsibility. They need to be informed by the precautionary principle. And finally, they need to be in touch with, as well as in acceptance of, complex, non-linear, systemic reality (Meadows, 2009, 181).

This clearly also applies to outdoor learning. As with any other educational approach, we should therefore be very careful not to overestimate its potential impact and not to raise our expectations too highly.[3] It is certainly not the magic wand to solve all educational problems, let alone the rest of humanity's predicatments.

---

[3] Just two very different examples: a) There is a tendency in outdoor learning circles to overrate personal experience. However: "The world we perceive is a simulation [by our brain] of the real world." (Hawkins, 2021, 175) This has consequences: "If you rely only on your personal experiences, then it is possible to live a fairly normal life and believe that the Earth is flat, that the moon landings were faked, that human activity is not changing the global climate, that species don't evolve, that vaccines cause diseases, and that mass shootings are faked." (ibid., 180)

b) We need to keep effect sizes in view. Mygind et al. write: "(…), it remains that sociocultural factors, such as percentage English learners, socioeconomic disadvantage, or presence of credentialed teachers, have a stronger bearing on healthy child development. In other words, within the socioecological totality of a child's world, green space may play a role, but sociocultural factors will be decidedly more important." (2021, 23)

2.2   Outdoor Learning—A Sober Assessment

Even though research into outdoor learning can be traced back to at least after World War II, its quality is still not anywhere near standards routinely used in other scientific fields (see chapter How to Raise the Standards of Outdoor Learning and Its Research in this volume; Mygind et al., 2019), if we understand science as "a social process that rigorously vets claims" (Oreskes, 2019, 141).

A recent, very thorough meta-study on the effectiveness of outdoor learning found only 13 studies—among a pool of 7830—that lived up to reasonable (not even high) methodological research standards (Becker et al., 2017). Studies in this area frequently suffer from poor study design and lack of methodological rigour in addition to representing very small numbers of participants. The duration of the inter-vention studied is often short; they tend to reflect special teaching situations rather than regular teaching; and they are generally neither randomized nor reproducible. Importantly, they mostly raise serious questions about the relationship, read influ-ence, of researchers on the participants. Very often, they have a circular design—in other words, they tend to validate the initial hypothesis with notoriously unreliable, subjective self-reporting of the participants. Attempts to triangulate the collected data (*thick description*) or even to use objective measuring tools (such as measuring movement with an accelerometer rather than asking teachers if and how far pupils moved) are very rare indeed. Finally, the conclusions drawn are often not linked to the data (on the limited quality of research in the area, see also Mygind et al., 2019, 2021). So far, so bad. We may be forgiven to continue to dream about double-blind studies in education for a viable, dignified future. Nevertheless, despite these many challenges, there are bright spots of progress, such as some excellent papers in the volume *The Natural World as a Resource for Learning and Development* (Kuo and Jordan (eds.), 2019; see chapter A Coordinated Research Agenda for Nature-Based Learning in this volume) and the methodologically sound and very carefully executed TEACHOUT study in Denmark (Nielsen et al., 2016[4]; see *Udeskole*—Pupils' Phys-ical Activity and Gender Perspectives and Pupils' Well-Being, Mental and Social Health in this volume).

2.3   Outdoor Learning—Its Specific Contributions to Learning for a Viable Future

Despite these clear limitations in terms of the established scientific quality of outdoor learning research and practice, there are a number of factors—particularly in the light of the above discussion about complexity and how learning works in humans—which seem to indicate that outdoor learning is not just a very important contribution to

---

[4] For a list of the publications of the project see: https://nexs.ku.dk/english/research/sport-individual-society/research-groups/physical-activities-during-school-and-leisure/gn-projects/gn-projects-completed/teachout-english/ Publications. Retrieved August 16, 2021.

the UN-proclaimed Sustainable Development Goal No. 4 ("Ensure inclusive and equitable quality education and promote lifelong learning opportunities for all"; United Nations, n.y.; see Jucker and von Au, 2019), but to high quality education in general.

If we take a systemic look at today's society, we are, as we have seen, confronted with various challenges: Climate and biodiversity crisis, democracy in times of social media and an increasingly digital world, integration and diversity, social, physical and mental health of students as well as teachers.[5] In order to master these challenges, we need resilient, healthy, mature people who can deal appropriately with the increasing complexity of the world and who can master the corresponding learning processes in high quality. We need 'deepened social maturity', in accordance with Kant.

If we look at children in this framework and ask ourselves what they need and what is good for them, then the following becomes apparent: Children have a right to the best possible development and nourishment of their potential. They have, as Carl Sagan beautifully said, a right to "wonder and scepticism" Sagan (1995), to diverse possibilities of perceiving, experiencing and exploring the world, i.e. to a successful understanding of the world. They have a right to the best possible learning processes, to experience self-efficacy, and to become competent at social learning.

Taking this social and child-centred view together, what is needed?

- Rich, diverse, dynamic and motivating learning spaces, learning opportunities and learning encounters,
- Enabling contact with the world and nature, understanding of the world and nature, understanding of the relationship between humans and the world/nature,
- Competence building for systemic thinking, understanding and acting,
- Experience of self-efficacy and transformation,
- Highest possible quality of teaching and learning experiences.

This is where learning in and with nature comes in. Outdoor learning supports successful learning on a very fundamental level.

First, some central aspects of learning appear in a new light, based on the progress made in brain and learning research in the last decades. As opposed to a computer hard drive whose storage capacity becomes exhausted, there seems to be no known limits to the human capacity for learning (Ericsson & Pool, 2016, 9, 40–41). Rather, we know now that the more we learn, the more connections we establish among different learnings, and the more we increase our capacity to advance understanding and our ability to learn (Ericsson & Pool, 2016, 43; Dirnagl & Müller, 2016, 260–261). The more we learn, the better we get at integrating and understanding issues, complex experiences, and abstract concepts such as Einstein's General Theory of Relativity—in other words central concepts about how the world works (Bjork et al., 2013; Brown et al., 2014, 76, 199).

If we combine this insight with the finding that real, three-dimensional, multi-sensorial experiences activate a multitude of brain regions and faculties, leading to

---

[5] Teachers in Switzerland, for example, have disproportionately high stress and burn-out levels (Sidler and Hunziker, 2016; Studer and Quarroz, 2017).

deepened connections among these regions and consequently to more resilience with regard to mental processes (Shaw, 2016, 251–252; Frith, 2007, 126–127; Dirnagl and Müller, 2016, 260–285; Brown et al., 2014, 167–168, 208–209), it seems inevitable to draw the following conclusion:

> Learning that activates as many senses as possible (seeing, smelling, touching,[6] hearing, moving, …), which takes place in dynamic, real-world learning environments, and which demands social interaction *and* self-guided involvement of the learners (Shaw, 2016, 139), is likely to be very effective. In addition, research shows that learning the same content while in motion, as opposed to being stationary, is more effective and evokes better long-term results (Dirnagl and Müller, 2016, 260).[7] If learners—and this does not only apply to children— are moving about, can touch things, view them from different perspectives, can smell, taste, and hear them, learning is more profound, more resilient and yields better long-term recall.

Second, mounting evidence indicates that real-world learning outside the classroom contributes to unlocking the full potential of learners. Since learning in and with nature takes place outside, in real, often unpredictable situations, which require quick comprehension, reaction, dialogue among each other, reflection and solution orientation, learning with nature contributes specifically to the competencies that we humans increasingly need in order to deal with the challenges we face in the twenty-first century (see chapter Rediscovering the Potential of Outdoor Learning for Developing 21st Century Competencies and chapter Fostering 21st Century Skills Through Autonomy Supportive Science Education Outside the Classroom in this volume). In the context of education for a viable future, learning outside is therefore well placed to help children and adults connect to all life and nurture the self-confidence and sense of agency that are necessary to take on the formidable responsibility of shaping humanity's common destiny. Learning in nature can also stimulate our innate desire to understand the world around us, thus increasing both motivation and our willingness to communicate and share with others.

Third, there is another reason why education—whether inside a classroom, in the community, at the workplace, in a research lab, or out in nature—is an indispensable tool for the change we need to an open, fair, just and sustainable future. Education can open up time and space to engage in "System 2" reasoning (Kahneman, 2012). It allows us to take the time needed to really understand an issue, with the help of outside experts, teachers and peers, texts, experiments, projects and much more.

---

[6] "Touch is not optional for human development. We have the longest childhoods of any animal – there is no other creature whose five-year-old offspring cannot live independently. If our long childhoods are not filled with touch, particularly loving, interpersonal touch, the consequences are dramatic." (Linden, 2016, 4).

[7] Bearing in mind that human learning is fundamentally tied to movement (Hawkins, 2021, 34–35).

Education therefore allows us to run 'living labs' in order to try out and find solutions to the urgent questions mentioned above and to nurture a resilient immune response to ideological beliefs, religious dogmas, and fake news.

This much we can glean from the available, general research on learning, education and change. However, if we dig into the specific research on learning in nature—even when bearing in mind the limitations outlined in 2.2 above—we can summarise: learning in and with nature is overall effective learning, as it cumulatively promotes learning processes and health on different levels (see Mann et al., 2021):

- *Academic learning success*: better recall of learning content, improved language competence (reading, writing, talking to adults, vocabulary), better solving of complex, interconnected tasks, better reasoning and analytical skills.
- *Social competencies*: strengthened social interaction, cohesion and trust between teachers and students, positive socio-emotional development, bearing in mind that a functioning learning community between teachers and students is a central condition for successful learning.
- *Self-competencies*: Increased intrinsic motivation and willingness to learn,[8] higher concentration, fewer disciplinary problems, high self-efficacy experience through discovery, experience-based and action-oriented learning, building a sense of identity, develop pro-social behaviour and personal executive functioning through risk-taking.
- *Physical and mental health*: Teachers and learners are significantly more in motion,[9] which makes learning more successful and makes learning content available in the long term, training of gross and fine motor skills, easier access to daylight[10] and fresh air than in classrooms, emotional and behavioural problems as well as hyperactivity are significantly reduced, especially in boys.
- *Real-world learning*: Rich and meaningful learning in real-world situations, different learning spaces serve the diverse learning needs of children in a variety of ways, which is more and more important in increasingly diverse classes.
- *twenty-first century skills*: Communication, cooperation, conflict resolution, creativity, critical thinking, resilience, self-regulation, dealing with the unexpected and complexity thinking are fostered.
- *Familiarity with nature*: Being close to nature and constructively dealing with the destruction of nature leads to increased environmental awareness and sustainable

---

[8] A very interesting research result, not specifically linked to outdoor learning, is that teachers with a high motivation to continuously learn and improve their own professional competencies impact positively on the motivation of their students (Dresel et al., 2013).

[9] The most recent figures: compared to in-door classes, outdoor learning means up to 41.8 min less sedentary time, up to 36.4 min more light and up to 11.48 min more moderate to vigorous physical activity per school day (Bølling et al., 2021).

[10] As discussed in chapter How Daylight Controls the Biological Clock, Organises Sleep, and Enhances Mood and Performance and chapter Outdoor Learning and Children's Eyesight, this has important implication for myopia prevention. A recent review from China stated: "To prevent myopia at younger ages, measures must be implemented, such as conducting school classes outdoors, incorporating more outdoor activities into the school curriculum, and providing additional outdoor programs for children on weekends." (Zhang and Deng, 2020)

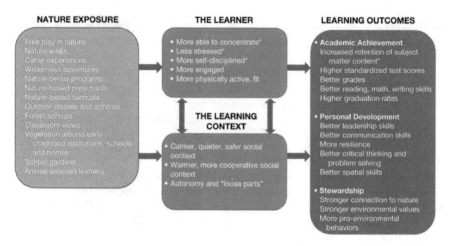

Fig. 2 Nature-based learning: exposures, probable mechanisms, and outcomes (from: Kuo, Barnes and Jordan, https://doi.org/10.1007/978-3-031-04108-2_3)

action (see chapter Childhood Nature Connection and Constructive Hope in this volume).

As a comparison with Hattie's list of factors for successful learning shows (see above, Waack, 2019), learning in and with nature cumulatively promotes many important foundations that make successful learning possible in the first place. In this way, learning in nature also supports children whose integration in the classroom is often a challenge (Fig. 2).

We believe that it is this *cumulative, fundamental fostering of learning in multiple dimensions* which is the core contribution of outdoor learning to high quality learning. Kuo, Barnes and Jordan (see chapter Do Experiences with Nature Promote Learning? Converging Evidence of a Cause-And-Effect Relationship in this volume) have summarised this well in Fig. 2:

This cumulative fostering of high-quality learning also qualifies outdoor learning as an approach to support SDG 4 and Education for Sustainable Development (ESD), irrespective of theme or topic. The Scottish *Curriculum for Excellence through Outdoor Learning* expresses this well:

> *Curriculum for Excellence* offers opportunities for all children and young people to enjoy first-hand experience outdoors, whether within the school grounds, in urban green spaces, in Scotland's countryside or in wilder environments. Such experiences motivate our children and young people to become successful learners and to develop as healthy, confident, enterprising and responsible citizens. Well-constructed and well-planned outdoor learning helps develop the skills of enquiry, critical thinking and reflection necessary for our children and young people to meet the social, economic and environmental challenges of life in the twenty-first century. Outdoor learning connects children and young people with the natural world, with our built heritage and our culture and society, (…). (Learning & Teaching Scotland, 2010, 7)

In fact, since all change rests on learning and outdoor approaches boost learning, it can even support the implementation of all the other 16 SDGs. Contrary to the often very conceptual and abstract discussions and propositions in ESD, outdoor learning is a very practical, easily implementable tool to enhance high quality learning directly. Particularly in terms of transforming teaching practice for learners in the best possible way, we believe that outdoor learning has a lot more direct implications and also chances of success, particularly since outdoor learning is at best an add-in approach which requires very little extra resources—a fact which is very important with a view to teacher acceptance and equitable access to high-quality learning, particularly in poor communities (see Bentsen et al., 2021).

However, as mentioned above, learning in and with nature is not the panacea for solving all problems in school. It is one of many useful, evidence-based, effective ways to support teachers and school teams in their daily work. But since outdoor learning, as understood here, is an add-in (directly enhancing and supporting high-quality curriculum-based work) and not an add-on (requiring additional time and resources *beyond* curriculum-focused teaching) approach,[11] it is not a question of burdening the school with yet another task beyond the curriculum, but rather of supporting its core business, namely teaching and learning.

Our understanding of outdoor learning in this volume is the following:

- curriculum-based teaching&learning activities outside the classroom but in school hours
- setting-sensitive, problem-based, experiential education
- pupil-led, teacher-facilitated learning
- inclusion of PA not as a goal but as a means to pedagogical and didactical ends
- regular activities on a weekly or biweekly basis. (Bentsen et al., 2021, 3)

3 Why This Book and Its Very Specific Approach?

We have now provided you with some of the evidence and many substantiated claims regarding the value and the specific contributions outdoor learning can make in a time where high-quality learning might never have been more important.

However, you might be quite justified to ask: why yet another volume on this? We have had the wonderful *Frontiers* volume, edited by Ming Kuo and Cathy Jordan (2019), we have all the papers from the TEACHOUT project available (see Footnote 4 above), we have the excellent books, edited by Sue Waite (2017 and 2019), and then there is *The SAGE Handbook of Outdoor Play and Learning* (Waller et al., 2017)—amongst others.

---

[11] Add-in is already good, but maybe we also have to think about subtractive solutions. There is interesting research which shows that the constant exposure to additive solutions makes them cognitively far more accessible: "It thus seems that people are prone to apply a 'what can we add here?' heuristic (a default strategy to simplify and speed up decision-making). This heuristic can be overcome by exerting extra cognitive effort to consider other, less-intuitive solutions." (Meyvis and Yoon, 2021, 189) The authors conclude that we need "to guard against the default tendency to add." (ibid., 190)

There are several reasons why we are convinced that this book is unique and serves a very specific purpose quite unlike any of the others. It should help launch and sustain discussion, debate and finally implementation of outdoor learning on a broad scale, on different systemic levels.

Our aim is clearly not to produce a straightforward scientific volume with research papers never published before. The volume is *not* directed at specialist researchers—they know their field inside out, know where to go for new research and have access to all the papers they need through their institutional access systems. Producing such a book takes far too long to be of interest to cutting-edge researchers. The volume is also *not* aimed at the average teacher who is looking for practical guidance on how to implement outdoor learning. This market is quite saturated in different countries (see, as examples, Waite et al., 2020; SILVIVA, 2018 and 2019).

We aim for another audience in that we try to bridge the gap between these two worlds. We provide you with a reader or compendium, mixing the carefully selected, best internationally available, highest-quality evidence with new, original contributions:

- In Part I (chapters A Coordinated Research Agenda for Nature-Based Learning, Do Experiences with Nature Promote Learning? Converging Evidence of a Cause-And-Effect Relationship, Refueling Students in Flight: Lessons in Nature May Boost Subsequent Classroom Engagement, Childhood Nature Connection and Constructive Hope, and How to Raise the Standards of Outdoor Learning and Its Research) you find the very best in terms of the scientific case for outdoor learning. This ranges from a holistic reflection on which research is needed, to the succinct provision of the evidence, in broad and narrow perspectives, to quality criteria for this research. It gives you a very good feel for how far the field has advanced in recent times, despite the limitations mentioned above.
- Part II (chapters *Udeskole*—Pupils' Physical Activity and Gender Perspectives and Pupils' Well-Being, Mental and Social Health) gives you a unique insight into a high-quality flagship research project: the TEACHOUT study from Denmark, from which we publish two summary papers.
- Part III (chapters Some Impacts on Health and Wellbeing from School-Based Outdoor Learning, How Daylight Controls the Biological Clock, Organises Sleep, and Enhances Mood and Performance and Outdoor Learning and Children's Eyesight) is specifically focussing on mental, physical and social health. Outdoor learning has unique contributions to make here (also touched upon already in Part II), both for pupils and teachers. We approach this both from an inside perspective from top-outdoor learning specialists in the UK, but also from the outside: we have asked two internationally recognised specialists who have no connection or vested interest in outdoor learning, to assess its health potential from their professional perspective: chronobiology and health in the built environment respectively.
- Part IV (chapters Rediscovering the Potential of Outdoor Learning for Developing 21st Century Competencies and Fostering 21st Century Skills Through Autonomy Supportive Science Education Outside the Classroom) is providing arguments and evidence for the claim put forward in this introduction that outdoor learning is

important for fostering the competencies all of us need to come to terms with the challenges of the twenty-first century.

- Part V (chapters Research and Documentation of Outdoor-Based Teaching in Teacher Education—The EOT Project, Bonding with the World: A Pedagogical Approach and *Udeskole*—Regular Teaching Outside the Classroom) homes in on one aspect which is almost religiously mentioned in every single recommendation on outdoor learning of the last decade: if we don't nurture and develop the necessary competencies of teachers (and teacher trainers for that matter) to teach outdoor learning to a high standard, it will not be embedded across school systems anytime soon.
- Part VI (chapters International Views on School-Based Outdoor Learning, Natural Connections: Learning About Outdoor-Based Learning, Outdoor School in Germany. Theoretical Considerations and Empirical Findings, Investigating Experiences of Nature: Challenges and Case-Analytical Approaches and Creating a Forest for Learning) finally both broadens and focusses our perspectives. From a fascinating international insight into outdoor learning we turn to nation-wide and individual case-studies, which provide the richness and depth of the territory which we have mapped out before.

By providing a veritable 'best-of' of recently published and new articles on the impact of outdoor learning, offering sound evidence, but also a rich tapestry of limitations and challenges, of exciting insights and success stories, we give you the learning tools to make outdoor learning 'doable' in your context.

We are not going to walk you through each individual chapter—we have provided abstracts for this reason. But just as a teaser, and really only *pars pro toto*, we give you a distinct flavour of our selection approach. Chapter Refueling Students in Flight: Lessons in Nature May Boost Subsequent Classroom Engagement, written by Ming Kuo, Matthew H.E.M. Browning and Milbert L. Penner, is really far too long and a reprint, you might say. Why do we still include it? In our view this paper is a perfect example of really carefully carried out, thoughtfully reflected research which can very well serve as a template for others to either do their own research or model their practice on it. Chapter How to Raise the Standards of Outdoor Learning and Its Research is a summary of a rather oldish paper. Again: why include it? Just the summary gives such a rich diet of why scientific rigour on the part of the researchers, and conceptual clarity on the part of education providers (i.e. the need for a Theory of Change) is so crucial, that it might well be declared compulsory reading for every researcher and every teacher and educator in the field.

Through this unique approach, we are able to present a rich, varied picture of reasons and insights into outdoor learning which is aimed at those interested readers, who want to go beyond the merely practical and are not specialists enough to dive on a daily basis into hard-core science papers. It is for those people who need a more than superficial understanding of the issues at stake, because they shape education, as policy makers, civil servants, directors of teacher training universities, teacher trainers, head teachers, and parents sitting on boards of educational authorities. It is furthermore aimed at teachers with an interest in developing their professional competencies and at professional educators, coaches and multipliers who train staff of educational NGOs.

In addition, the volume not only focusses on outdoor learning as an educational approach. It has itself an educational aim. We are very much aware of the fact that the intended audiences are broad and that this poses problems in terms of style. However, we were driven by a twofold educational intent. On the one hand, we have encouraged contributors to have readability in mind. We also aimed to enhance the 'way into the texts' with an abstract (unfortunately only in the online open access version), a bio statement about the authors, photos of the authors and a short recommended reading list of their preferred three titles in the field. On the other hand, given the need for an evidence-based approach, we aim to encourage and 'push' our audiences to really dare and plunge into 'proper' scientific texts: in Denmark, for example, continuous professional development training for outdoor teachers deliberately forces teachers to read scientific papers as is, with no 'translation'. If we are serious about the above-mentioned insight that we cannot understand our world, and act meaningfully in it, without adequate scientific understanding, than all of us need to develop both the courage and the competencies to read and understand scientific writing.

This really is the background to our 'idiosyncratic' approach: since we want to enhance the understanding and acceptance of outdoor learning, we need to provide a variety of approaches. We do know that every single target audience we aim for is in itself very varied again, from those who really need a simple 'translation' to those who quite happily dig into 'real science'. We are convinced that we offer a suitable variety of texts for this 'natural' spread of readers—from chapters where the authors support readers by explaining scientific terms in footnotes to chapters which read like essays rather than a paper in *Science* or *nature*.

If you walk away from reading parts or the whole of this book with a deepened and broadened understanding of outdoor learning—i.e. a "System 2" understanding—then we have achieved our aim.

4   Vision—What is Needed?

Given the systemic approach we pursued and our target audiences, all the recommendations we present here are intended for multiple stakeholders. For example, if we identify research which is dearly needed, then not just researchers should feel called upon, but also politicians who can allocate the money and teacher training institutions who might benefit from the results. In fact, if these groups of people were to cooperate right from the very start, this would in all likelihood not just improve the validity of the research, but also bridge the science-practice gap and make sure that up-to-date results and insights are actually taken up by the practitioners in the field—a notorious problem we are confronted with in all areas of education. We therefore encourage you to read the following in this spirit, and, if in doubt, feel responsible!

It is for good reason that we have included Cathy Jordan and Louise Chawla's A Coordinated Research Agenda for Nature-Based Learning as the very first chapter after the introduction. This piece is valuable for a wider audience not just for the very thorough and systemic perspective it takes (looking at learning outcomes, differential effects, the mechanisms by which nature and learning are linked, and the implications for policy and practice, see chapter A Coordinated Research Agenda for Nature-Based Learning, Table 1). It can also serve as a template for broad and inclusive processes, involving many different stakeholders, with the aim to arrive at the best possible result as well as launching a continual, focused process of future research. Jordan and Chawla have identified three domains for the latter:

1. learning outcomes, including understanding how learning in nature compares with learning in classrooms, preschools and child care centers, and how outcomes may vary by age, gender, socioeconomic background, ethnic background, individual differences, or special needs;
2. the mechanisms that explain relationships between nature and learning; and
3. how to most effectively apply research to policy and practice (chapter A Coordinated Research Agenda for Nature-Based Learning).

We have also seen above that research in the area in general could benefit from a serious reflection on research quality, including learning from other fields of research where standards are much higher—as mentioned, TEACHOUT has here been a trailblazer (Nielsen et al., 2016 and chapter *Udeskole*—Pupils' Physical Activity and Gender Perspectives and chapter Pupils' Well-Being, Mental and Social Health but also see chapter How to Raise the Standards of Outdoor Learning and Its Research). In the meantime, a number of systematic reviews on the effects of outdoor learning have been published which have reconfirmed some serious limitations regarding the quality or diligence of some research in the area (see, for example, Becker et al., 2017; Mygind et al., 2019, 2021; Dankiw et al., 2020). Be it sample size, mistaking correlation for causation, overestimating effect size, a narrow focus which excludes a systemic understanding of the hierarchy of factors influencing learning, understating the ambiguity of findings, insufficient quality of the models used, etc.—these aspects found in some research has lead one recent systematic review to conclude for the area they looked at: "The empirical evidence must currently be considered limited." (Mygind et al., 2021, 22) Another systematic review on the impacts of immersive nature-experiences on mental, physical and social health of children had to state repeatedly: "The quality of the evidence was considered low owing to risk of bias and imprecision due to small sample sizes." (Mygind et al., 2019).

Therefore, there is clearly plenty of room for improvement in the quality and scope of outdoor learning research. A recently published research protocol, co-written, amongst others, by four authors represented in this volume (Jeff Mann, Tonia Gray, Son Truong and Rowena Passy), has pointed out one particular area of concern, despite the mounting evidence "for developmental and well-being benefits on children and adolescents" through outdoor learning:

> The effect of Outdoor Learning on academic metrics remains under-researched. Indeed, many outdoor educators lament one of the key factors limiting Outdoor Learning from taking a

greater role in mainstream education is the paucity of evidence demonstrating its impact on
academic curriculum performance. (Mann et al., 2021, 3)

But let's not just look at research but a wider perspective. Even if we take all the
limitations mentioned above into account,[12] the collected evidence and arguments
in this volume (and much of the wider work it was nourished by) clearly points
to the insight that outdoor learning has an important role to play in an education
system, which wants to be 'fit4future'. Because of its 'add-in' approach, i.e. "direct
integration with curriculum time and aims", but also due to "extensive teacher accept-
ability, the whole-population application (…) and low associated costs" (Bentsen,
2021, 5), outdoor learning might indeed be one of the keys unlocking the potential
that high-quality learning can offer to our kids. If we look to places where really
game-changing, substantial learning takes place, which makes learners truly grow,
it is almost always focussed, motivated, real-world learning for a purpose (see Ericsson & Pool, 2016). Outdoor learning can be a stepping stone for such learning
journeys, because it nourishes important elements of successful learning: it keeps
the motivation high, it nurtures the social bond between teachers and learners, it takes
place in movement and interaction—you can complete your list of favourites while
reading this book.

However, what is needed that this vision of an education which develops not just
at best the potential of all kids, but also secures a viable future for humankind, moves
from "empty words" into action?

One of the most impressive examples of an attempt to systemically integrate
outdoor learning regularly into the compulsory school system has been Denmark. It
is also a particularly interesting case, because the progress of this implementation has
been regularly measured (Barfod et al., 2016, 2021; Bentsen et al., 2010). The latest
survey noted that "the curve is flattened", i.e. that the percentage of schools practicing
regular outdoor learning, is not increasing by much anymore (it lies at "approximately
one-fifth of general schools in Denmark" in 2019). But two results are interesting:
within these schools "the number of classes using regular EOtC (Education Outside
the Classroom) increases significantly" and "one third of all special-needs schools
work with regular EOtC" (Barfod et al., 2021, 5). So maybe we should be looking
at saturation and how to deal with it, and at circumstances, where outdoor learning
can provide an even bigger benefit, such as in special-needs schools.

Apart from maybe Scotland it is very rare to find such a systemic, concerted
effort as in Denmark to really transform schooling. The way our Danish colleagues
have simultaneously used national networks, teacher training, peer-to-peer learning,
research, influencing policy and much more, can certainly serve as a role-model for
many other countries. At the height of the Covid-19 pandemic, which had "fostered
the interests in using the outdoors during both school and leisure time" (Barfod
et al., 2021, 5), due to the ease for distancing and lower infection rates, the Danish

---

[12] Let's be fair: many of the limitations have also to do with the fact that outdoor learning as broadly
understood as it is here is a nascent field and similar limitations plague much more established
educational interventions.

Prime Minister, on primetime TV, urged all Danish School to teach outdoors whenever possible—something other countries can only dream of (except maybe Austria, where the Education Ministry issued a similar suggestion).

In Switzerland, we have certainly tried hard to emulate the lead of Denmark. SILVIVA, the Swiss Foundation for Nature-based Learning, has initiated an ambitious national, trilingual project with the aim that every pupil in Switzerland can profit from the multiple benefits of outdoor learning during their school career—and their teachers as well. Based on the insights presented in chapter How to Raise the Standards of Outdoor Learning and Its Research, SILVIVA has drawn up a Theory of Change to facilitate the transformation into an education system, where resilient, healthy children, youth and adults unlock their potential and learn to deal competently with a complex world—individually and collectively. Using an approach that is systemic, supportive, embedding, cooperative and participatory, using iteration, ideation, adaption and error tolerance, SILVIVA aims to use all the international and national knowhow as well as personnel and financial resources of its own and a broad range of partner organisations to sustainably anchor outdoor learning on all levels of the Swiss education system. Copying the Danish lead and inspired by the holistic approach presented in chapter International Views on School-Based Outdoor Learning (see Fig. 1), SILVIVA is focusing on building up local, regional and national networks; online platforms providing resources, exchange and support; encouraging necessary research; embedding outdoor learning in initial and continuous teacher training (a crucial, still very much under-researched and supported approach, see chapter Research and Documentation of Outdoor-Based Teaching in Teacher Education—The EOT Project); making it part of head master professional qualifications and supporting its integration into school culture and school development plans. Embedding means a shift and project, to institutional anchoring in an organisation (be it a school, educational authority, teacher training institution or a research department). Encouraged by the *National Curriculum Outdoors* series (Waite et al., 2020) it has become clear that an important driver for embedding are teaching materials (which are influencing teaching practice more than curricula) and increasingly national tests, but also national and international surveys (such as PISA) and software assessing student achievement. Once again encouraged by best practice in other countries, SILVIVA is also focussing very much on raising the visibility, legitimacy and acceptance of outdoor learning on all systemic levels, from national to regional decision makers, to parents and the general public, using a broad range of communication, coaching and training tools.

We are not elaborating on this to showcase Switzerland—it is some way behind other countries in many respects. Nevertheless, we are mentioning it because we are convinced of the importance of integrated, systemic approaches to fostering outdoor learning—an activity manual and a few courses for teachers will not do the trick.

There is also another important dimension to consider here. Research on successful social change, such as peoples' professional practice, clearly shows that this happens best in mutually reinforcing learning communities. When people know each other, can practice new behaviours together, can share and look over each other's shoulders, then new things, such as outdoor teaching, are not only recognised as good, but are effectively integrated into one's own professional practice. For other schools and teachers, this practice is then evidence that this could be useful and an incentive to try it too. By building up such pockets of good, tried and tested practice new approaches such as outdoor learning can truly spread and get systemically embedded. Centola has carefully researched such change mechanisms: "Successful social change is not about information; it's about norms." (Centola, 2021, 11) In Sociology, it is now accepted that "social networks are the crucial factor for social change." (ibid., 30) Centola therefore speaks of the need for "strong ties", "wide bridges" and "complex contagions" (i.e. multiple, reinforcing 'infections') to change social norms and established behaviour: you don't change unless you see people you know and trust adopt the new practice, multiple times:

> None of the major behavioral or social changes that have happened in the last half-century have spread the way viruses do. They have spread not through *reach* but through the phenomenon that, for years, network scientists believed to be the great enemy of effective contagion: *redundancy*. (…) Redundancy will not help to spread the measles. You can't get infected twice—it takes only one contact to do it. But when it comes to a new idea, the experience of being exposed to it from two, three, or four people within your network of strong ties—*that* changes the idea into a norm. It changes how you think and feel about it. And that is the overlooked power of redundancy. (Centola, 2021, 49)

You cannot force-feed people to change. You need a "System 2"-approach: slow, reflected, careful, testing, adapting, changing, improving—precisely the reason for the broad variety of arguments, approaches, styles and reflection we present in this volume, to help you adopt a "complex contagion" approach to embedded outdoor learning. This will help to make sure that words do turn into action.

So far, so good. We have role-models, tried and tested approaches, a growing body of sound evidence which testifies to the multiple reinforcing benefits of outdoor learning for academic learning, social interaction, personal development and well-being, mental, physical and social health, creativity, and much more. So we can get to work and we truly hope that this book will serve as a toolbox for you to do so.

However, if you think back to the beginning of this chapter there remains one hard nut to crack. Given what we know about our evolutionary machinery as well as the limits to our perception and cognition, systemic thinking, understanding, and action does not come to us easily—on the contrary, because "laziness is built deep into our nature" (Kahneman, 2012, 35). Systemic understanding is an extreme version of a "System 2"-task: difficult, effortful, counterintuitive, and strenuous. Speaking to many experienced educators and experts, it seems to us that there are hardly any tried and tested, effective educational interventions which help children, youth and adults to train and competently learn systemic understanding, and then even make it their preferred path of reflection, whatever the issue at hand. If you know of such learning interventions, which ideally have been validated by research, by all means get in touch with us.

The trouble really is that systemic understanding is rich in prerequisites: you need to understand systems at a profound level, so that you are capable of grasping any other system that might be thrown your way in sufficient depth; you need to understand fundamental principles of life (i.e. evolution, physics, chemistry, biology, sociology, economics), so that the most flawed preconceptions about life are cleared up; you need to understand the evolutionary machinery of human perception and cognition (including the fundamental principles of how the brain and learning work), so that a realistic self-assessment is at least possible; you need to have at your disposal various tools and methods which help you to move from System 1 into System 2, so that a distanced, self-reflective, self-critical, careful, intersubjective understanding can be generated, based on the best available evidence; you need a willingness to learn and change and a fostered culture of error (Carl Sagan's "wonder and skepticism"); and finally, you need to translate all of the above into concrete, real-life action. In other words, we all need to become change agents who accomplish the art of "skilful muddling", as Harold Glasser aptly calls it (2019, 64). In essence, what we are talking about is reapplying Kant's quest for "humanity's emergence from her self-imposed immaturity" (Kant, 1784) to today's challenges.

Given the challenges we face as a species, establishing such systemic learning interventions should have a very high priority. We have started dreaming of concocting a cook-book (of whatever format) for complexity learning which fills this gap. The idea is to collect functioning examples on all levels, presented in such a way, that everybody can cook them, i.e. replicate them. Please do get in touch if you would like to be part of a team to find out.

Let us end on this reflective note:

> The main message today has to be, with [Svenja] Flaßpöhler: *differentiation*. Unless we all become a lot more accurate, evidence-based, and work with up-to-date knowledge rather than System 1 easy answers, assumptions, old mental models, traditions or beliefs, we will hardly make headways towards the open, just, free and democratic vision I developed at the beginning [of the book]. (…) We need to encourage System 2 – slow, serious, careful and systemic analysis, thinking and action – any time over System 1. (…) Maybe this just means that we as educators have to truly embody, live with every cell in our body, the scientific approach: always be open to learn. History teaches us that traditional explanations mostly don't work, and, in time, get replaced: So, we need to have an open mind and be prepared to throw them out if evidence comes to the fore to disprove them (even if they are dear to us or our System 1)! Ericsson and Pool, in their study on excellence (2016), have shown that we all can do this: there is no genetic predisposition which makes this only available to some; a democratic message I find heartening and liberating. (Jucker, 2020, 103–106)

Recommended Further Readings

1. Capra, Fritjof, and Pier Luigi Luisi (2014). *The Systems View of Life. A Unifying Vision.* Cambridge: Cambridge University Press.
2. Shaw, Julia (2016). *The Memory Illusion. Remembering, Forgetting, and the Science of False Memory.* London: Random House Books..
3. Jucker, Rolf (2020). *Can We Cope with the Complexity of Reality? Why Craving Easy Answers Is at the Root of our Problems. Reflections on science, self-illusions, religion, democracy and education for a viable future.* Newcastle upon Tyne: Cambridge Scholars Publishing. https://www.cambridgescholars.com/product/978-1-5275-4851-0

Acknowledgements RJ would like to thank SILVIVA Foundation, its team and board for the continued, unconditional support and for the innovative, co-constructive development of the national project to systemically integrate outdoor learning into Swiss compulsory schooling. SILVIVA also made this volume possible in the first place, by providing the financial support for editing and writing this book, as well as for the Open Access fee, translation and printing costs. Thank you so much! Another special ¡Muchas gracias! is due to Harold Glasser. Our multi-hour discussions and your incredibly gentle and sharp mind have pushed me beyond boundaries I even didn't know were there. Lastly, I want to thank my co-editor Jakob von Au very much indeed—the collaboration on this and the parallel German volume (von Au & Jucker (2022). *Draußenlernen Neue Forschungsergebnisse und Praxiseinblicke für eine Bildung für nachhaltige Entwicklung.* Bern: hep. https://www.hep-ver lag.ch/draussenlernen) has been incredibly enriching. It has also regularly refuelled me when things were getting tough.

References

Barfod, K., Ejbye-Ernst, N., Mygind, L., & Bentsen, P. (2016). Increased provision of udeskole in Danish schools: An updated national population survey. *Urban Forestry and Urban Greening, 20*, 277–281. https://doi.org/10.1016/j.ufug.2016.09.012. Retrieved August 17, 2021.

Barfod, K., Mads, B., Mygind, L., Elsborg, P., Ejbye-ernst, N., & Bentsen, P. (2021). Reaping fruits of labour: Revisiting education outside the classroom provision in Denmark upon policy and research interventions. *Urban Forestry & Urban Greening, 60*(August 2020), 1–7. https://doi.org/10.1016/j.ufug.2021.127044. Retrieved August 17, 2021.

Becker, C., Lauterbach, G., Spengler, S., Dettweiler, U., & Mess, F. (2017). Effects of regular classes in outdoor education settings: A systematic review on students' learning, social and health dimensions. *International Journal of Environmental Research and Public Health, 14*(5), 1–20. https://doi.org/10.3390/ijerph14050485. Retrieved January 03, 2020.

Bentsen, P., Jensen, F. S., Mygind, E., & Randrup, T. B. (2010). The extent and dissemination of udeskole in Danish schools. *Urban Forestry & Urban Greening, 9*(3), 235–243. https://doi.org/10.1016/j.ufug.2010.02.001. Retrieved August 7, 2021.

Bentsen, P., Mygind, L., Nielsen, G., Mygind, E., & Elsborg, P. (2021). Education outside the classroom as upstream school health promotion: 'adding-in' physical activity into children's everyday life and settings. *Scandinavian Journal of Public Health*, 1–9. https://doi.org/10.1177/1403494821993715. Retrieved August 16, 2021.

Bjork, R.A., Dunlosky, J., & Kornell, N. (2013). Self-regulated learning: Beliefs, techniques, and illusions. *Annual Review Psychology, 64*, 417–44. https://www.annualreviews.org/doi/abs/10.1146/annurev-psych-113011-143823. Retrieved August 28, 2019.

Bølling, M., Mygind, E., Mygind, L., Bentsen, P., & Elsborg, P. (2021). The Association between Education Outside the Classroom and Physical Activity: Differences Attributable to the Type of Space? *Children, 8*(486). https://doi.org/10.3390/children8060486. Retrieved August 16, 2021.

Brown, P. C., Roediger III, H. L., & McDaniel M. A. (2014). *Make it stick. The Science of Successful Learning.* Cambridge, MA, London: The Belknap Press of Harvard University Press.

Centola, D. (2021). *Change. How to Make Big Things Happen.* London: John Murray.

CIIP (Conférence intercantonale de l'instruction publique de la Suisse romande et du Tessin) (2003). *Déclaration de la CIIP, relative aux finalités et objectifs de l'Ecole publique du 30 janvier 2003.* Neuchâtel: CIIP. https://www.ciip.ch/FileDownload/Get/148. Retrieved August 16, 2021.

Dankiw, K. A., Tsiros, M. D., Baldock, K. L., & Kumar, S. (2020). The impacts of unstructured nature play on health in early childhood development: A systematic review. *PLoS ONE, 15*(2), e0229006. https://doi.org/10.1371/journal.pone.0229006. Retrieved August 17, 2021.

Dennett, D. C. (2017). *From Bacteria to Bach and Back. The Evolution of Minds.* New York, London: W. W. Norton & Company.

Dirnagl, U., & Müller, J. (2016). *Ich glaub, mich trifft der Schlag. Warum das Gehirn tut, was es tun soll, oder manchmal auch nicht [I think I'm going to have a stroke. Why the brain does what it's supposed to do, or sometimes it doesn't]*. München: Droemer.

Dresel, M., Fasching, M., Steuer, G., Nitsche, S., & Dickhäuser, O. (2013). Relations between teachers' goal orientations, their instructional practices and students' motivation. *Psychology, 4,* 572–584. https://doi.org/10.4236/psych.2013.47083. Retrieved August 16, 2021.

Ericsson, A., & Pool, R. (2016). *PEAK. Secrets from the New Science of Expertise*. London: The Bodley Head (an imprint of Vintage).

Frith, C. (2007). Making up the Mind. How the Brain Creates our Mental World. Oxford: Oxford University Press.

Glasser, H. (2007). Minding the gap: the role of social learning in linking our stated desire for a more sustainable world to our everyday actions and policies. In: E. Arjen & J. Wals (Eds.), *Social learning: Towards a more sustainable world*, (pp. 35–61). Wageningen, The Netherlands: Wageningen Academic Publishers.

Glasser, H. (2019). Toward robust foundations for sustainable well-being societies: Learning to change by changing how we learn. In: J. W. Cook (ed.): *Sustainability, human well-being, and the future of education*, pp. 31–89. Cham: Palgrave Macmillan/Springer Nature. https://doi.org/ 10.1007/978-3-319-78580-6. Retrieved August 16, 2021.

Grundlagen für den Lehrplan 21 [Foundations for Curriculum 21]. (2010). Verabschiedet von der Plenarversammlung der deutschsprachigen EDK-Regionen am 18. März 2010. https://www.leh rplan21.ch/d7/sites/default/files/grundlagenbericht_def.pdf. Retrieved August 16, 2021.

Hasselhorn, M., & Gold, A. (2017). *Pädagogische Psychologie. Erfolgreiches Lernen und Lehren [Educational Psychology. Successful learning and teaching]* (4th ed.). Stuttgart: W. Kohlhammer.

Hattie, J. A. C. (2008). *Visible learning. A synthesis of over 800 meta-analyses relating to achievement*. London, New York: Routledge.

Hawkins, J. (2021). *A thousand brains: A new theory of intelligence*. Foreword by Richard Dawkins. New York: Basic Books.

Jucker, R., & Jakob von, A. (2019). Improving learning inside by enhancing learning outside: A powerful lever for facilitating the implementation of the UN SDGs. *Sustainability: The Journal of Record, 12*(2), 104–108 (Case Reports). https://doi.org/10.1089/sus.2019.29163. Retrieved August 16, 2021.

Jucker, R. (2020). *Can we cope with the complexity of reality? Why craving easy answers is at the root of our problems. Reflections on science, self-illusions, religion, democracy and education for a viable future*. Newcastle upon Tyne: Cambridge Scholars Publishing. https://www.cambri dgescholars.com/product/978-1-5275-4851-0. Retrieved August 16 2021.

Kahneman, D. (2012). *Thinking, fast and slow*. Penguin Books.

Kant, I. (1784). Beantwortung der Frage: Was ist Aufklärung? *Berlinische Monatsschrift*, December 1784. https://de.wikisource.org/wiki/Beantwortung_der_Frage:_Was_ist_ Aufkl%C3%A4rung%3F. Retrieved August 08, 2021.

Kuo, M., Jordan, C. (eds.) (2019). *The natural world as a resource for learning and development: From schoolyards to wilderness*. Lausanne: Frontiers Media. https://doi.org/10.3389/978-2-88963-138-4. Retrieved August 16, 2021.

Learning and Teaching Scotland. (2010). *Curriculum for excellence through outdoor learning*. Glasgow. https://education.gov.scot/Documents/cfe-through-outdoor-learning.pdf. Retrieved August 30, 2021.

Linden, D. J. (2016). *Touch. The science of the sense that makes us human*. London: Penguin Books.

Mann, J., Gray, T., Truong, S., Sahlberg, P., Bentsen, P., Passy, R., Ho, S., Ward, K., & Cowper, R. (2021). A systematic review protocol to identify the key benefits and efficacy of nature-based learning in outdoor educational settings. *International Journal of Environmental Research and Public Health, 18*(3), 1–10. https://doi.org/10.3390/ijerph18031199. Retrieved August 16, 2021.

Mautsch, F., & Metzger, J. (2019). *Gut führen! Was Führungskräfte erfolgreich macht [Lead well! What makes leaders successful]*. Stuttgart: Schäffer-Poeschel Verlag.

Meadows, D. H. (2009). *Thinking in systems. A primer*. In: D. Wright (Ed.), Sustainability institute. London, Sterling, VA: Earthscan.

Meyvis, T., Heeyoung, Y. (2021). Adding to our problems: Adding is favoured over subtracting in problem solving. *Nature, 592*(8. April), 189–190. https://doi.org/10.1038/d41586-021-00592-0. Retrieved August 17, 2021.

Mygind, L., Kjeldsted, E., Hartmeyer, R., Mygind, E., Bølling, M., & Bentsen, P. (2019). Mental, physical and social health benefits of immersive nature-experience for children and adolescents: A systematic review and quality assessment of the evidence. *Health & Place, 58*, 102136. https://doi.org/10.1016/j.healthplace.2019.05.014. Retrieved August 16, 2021.

Mygind, L., Kurtzhals, M., Nowell, C., Melby, P.S., Stevenson, M.P., Nieuwenhuijsen, M., Lum, J.A.G., Flensborg-Madsen, T., Bentsen, P., & Enticott, P.G. (2021). Landscapes of becoming social: A systematic review of evidence for associations and pathways between interactions with nature and socioemotional development in children. *Environment International, 146*, 106238. https://doi.org/10.1016/j.envint.2020.106238. Retrieved August 16, 2021.

Nielsen, G., Mygind, E., Bølling, M., Otte, C.R., Schneller, M.B., Schipperijn, J., Ejbye-Ernst, N., & Bentsen, P. (2016). A quasi-experimental cross-disciplinary evaluation of the impacts of education outside the classroom on pupils' physical activity, well-being and learning: The TEACHOUT study protocol. *BMC Public Health, 16*(1), Article No. 1117. https://doi.org/10.1186/s12889-016-3780-8. Retrieved August 16, 2021.

Obrecht, W. (2009). Die Struktur professionellen Wissens. Ein integrativer Beitrag zur Theorie der Professionalisierung. In: R. Becker-Lenz et al. (Eds.), *Professionalität in der Sozialen Arbeit. Standpunkte, Kontroversen, Perspektiven*, (pp. 47–72). Wiesbaden: VS Verlag für Sozialwissenschaften.

Oreskes, N. (2019). *Why trust science?* Princeton, NJ: Princeton University Press.

Pinker, S. (2018). *Enlightenment now: The case for reason, science, humanism, and progress*. London, New York: Viking.

Popper, K. (1999). "On Freedom." (1958/67). In Karl Popper, All Life is Problem Solving, Part II: Thoughts on History and Politics, Chapter 7, 81-92. Translated by Patrick Camiller. London: Routledge. https://books.google.ch/books?id=Pa3cZYwdq28C&pg=PA81&hl=de&source=gbs_toc_r&cad=3#v=onepage&q&f=false. Retrieved April 21, 2022.

Rippon, G. (2019). *The gendered brain. The new neuroscience that shatters the myth of the female brain*. London: The Bodley Head.

Rovelli, C. (2016). *Reality is not what it seems. The journey to quantum gravity*. Translated by Simon Carnell and Erica Segre. London: Allen Lane.

Rovelli, C. (2018). *The order of time*. Translated by Erica Segre and Simon Carnell. London: Allen Lane.

Sagan, C. (1995). Wonder and Skepticism. *Skeptical Inquirer*, Jan/Feb, *19*(1), 24–30. https://skepticalinquirer.org/1995/01/wonder_and_skepticism/. Retrieved August 16, 2021.

ShareAction. (2020). *Point of no returns: A ranking of 75 of the world's asset managers approaches to responsible investment*. 9 March 2020. https://shareaction.org/wp-content/uploads/2020/03/Point-of-no-Returns.pdf. Retrieved January 1, 2021.

Shaw, J. (2016). *The memory illusion. Remembering, forgetting, and the science of false memory*. London: Random House Books.

Sidler, C., Patrick, H. (2016). *Die Belastung von Lehrpersonen aus arbeitsmedizinischer und -psychologischer Sicht—eine deskriptive Beobachtungsstudie*. Baden: Ifa - Institut für Arbeitsmedizin. https://www.svlw.ch/images/download/ifa%20lang.pdf. Retrieved August 16, 2021.

SILVIVA (Eds.). (2018). *Draussen unterrichten. Das Handbuch für alle Fachbereiche | 1. und 2. Zyklus*. Bern: hep Verlag. (also available as editions for Germany and Austria, adapted to the relevant curricula). https://www.hep-verlag.ch/draussen-unterrichten. Retrieved August 16, 2021.

SILVIVA, (Ed.). (2019). *L'école à ciel ouvert. Le manuel scolaire complet pour enseigner dehors.* Neuchâtel: La Salamandre. https://boutique.salamandre.org/ecole-a-ciel-ouvert.pdt-962/. Retrieved April 21, 2022.

Studer, Regina, and Stéphane Quarroz. (2017). *Enquête sur la santé des enseignants romands.* Lausanne: Institut universitaire romand de Santé au Travail. https://edudoc.ch/record/127934. Retrieved August 08, 2021.

Thunberg, G. (2020). Greta Thunberg dismisses 'empty words' in new climate crisis appeal-video. *The Guardian,* 10.12.2020. https://www.theguardian.com/environment/video/2020/dec/10/greta-thunberg-dismisses-empty-words-in-new-climate-crisis-appeal-video. Retrieved August 15, 2021.

UNESCO. (2020). *Education for sustainable development. A roadmap. #ESDfor2030.* Paris: United Nations Educational, Scientific and Cultural Organization. https://unesdoc.unesco.org/ark:/48223/pf0000374802. Retrived August 26, 2021.

United Nations (n.y.). *The 17 [Sustainable Development] Goals.* https://sdgs.un.org/goals. Retrieved August 18, 2021.

Waack, S. (2019). *Visible learning: Hattie ranking: 252 influences and effect sizes related to student achievement.* https://visible-learning.org/hattie-ranking-influences-effect-sizes-learning-achievement/. Retrieved August 16, 2021.

Waite, S. (Ed.). (2017). *Children learning outside the classroom: From birth to eleven* (2nd ed.). London: SAGE.

Waite, S. (Ed.). (2019). *Outdoor learning research: Forms and functions.* London: Routledge.

Waite, S., Roberts, M., & Lambert, D. (2020). *National curriculum outdoors—A complete scheme of work.* London: Bloomsbury. https://nationalcurriculumoutdoors.com/. Retrieved August 16, 2021.

Waller, T., Ärlemalm-Hagsér, E., Sandseter, E. B. H., Lee-Hammond, L., Lekies, K., & Wyver, S. (Eds.). (2017). *The SAGE handbook of outdoor play and learning.* London: SAGE.

Weinert, F. E. (1996). 'Der gute Lehrer', 'die gute Lehrerin' im Spiegel der Wissenschaft ['the good teacher' in the light of science]. *Beiträge Zur Lehrerinnen- Und Lehrerbildung, 14*(2), 141–151.

Wikipedia—complex system (2021). https://en.wikipedia.org/wiki/Complex_system. Retrieved August 15, 2021.

Wikipedia—Electromagnetic spectrum. (2021). https://en.wikipedia.org/wiki/Electromagnetic_spectrum. Retrieved August 15, 2021.

Wikipedia—Hearing range. (2021). https://en.wikipedia.org/wiki/Hearing_range. Retrieved 15, 2021.

Zhang, J., & Deng, G. (2020). Protective effects of increased outdoor time against myopia: a review. *Journal of International Medical Research, 48*(3). https://doi.org/10.1177/0300060519893866. Retrieved August 16, 2021.

Rolf Jucker is currently Director of the Swiss Foundation for Nature-based Learning (SILVIVA) and a learning for sustainability expert, having previously served as Director of the Swiss Foundation for Environmental Education from 2008 to 2012. He gained an MSc in Education for Sustainability (EfS) and worked extensively on education for a viable future, publishing widely on the subject. He is the author of *Do We Know What We Are Doing?* (2014) and *Can We Cope with the Complexity of Reality? Why Craving Easy Answers Is at the Root of our Problems* (2020).

Jakob von Au currently works at the Englisches Institut Heidelberg as a teacher and at the University of Education Heidelberg as a lecturer in Outdoor Teaching and Education for Sustainable Development. He is the co-editor of the first substantial collection of research on outdoor-based learning in German, *"Raus aus dem Klassenzimmer": Outdoor Education als Unterrichtskonzept* (2016).

The Scientific Case for Outdoor Learning

A Coordinated Research Agenda for Nature-Based Learning

Cathy Jordan and Louise Chawla

Prior to this article and the special issue of *Frontiers in Psychology* in which it was embedded (Kuo & Jordan, 2019, now published as an ebook), the term "nature-based learning" (NBL) occurred occasionally in the general sense of learning in nature. This chapter describes a collaborative process to define this term in a specific way that brings together different branches of research: studies in environmental education that investigate learning *about* nature *in* nature; studies of informal learning through free play and discovery in nature; and studies of the benefits that people gain by being in nature, no matter what subject or skill they are acquiring there. The term highlights how being in nature or engaging with other living things or natural artifacts can benefit learning, development, and wellbeing in multiple ways. Since the publication of this chapter and the special issue in *Frontiers*, the term "nature-based learning" appears frequently in new studies' titles, keywords, abstracts, and texts. It has become an organizing term for a current literature review (Mann et al., 2021) and a research collection (Children & Nature Network, 2020). One means to

C. Jordan (✉)
1954 Buford Ave. Suite 325, St. Paul, MN 55108, USA
e-mail: jorda003@umn.edu

L. Chawla
78 Benthaven Place, Boulder, CO 80305, USA
e-mail: louise.chawla@colorado.edu

© The Author(s) 2022
R. Jucker and J. von Au (eds.), *High-Quality Outdoor Learning*,
https://doi.org/10.1007/978-3-031-04108-2_2

increase opportunities for nature-based learning—green schoolyard development—has become the focus of a research agenda of its own (Stevenson et al., 2020); and the term has already become the subject of critical analysis (Ross, 2020). Many new publications demonstrate active interest in different questions related to nature-based learning, and the fact that this term has been incorporated into a number of bachelors, masters, and doctoral level theses shows that it has caught the attention of emerging scholars.

1   Introduction

Although evidence is accumulating for the impact of nature-based learning (NBL) on children's outcomes, there is much we don't know (Kuo et al., 2019, see Kuo, Barnes and Jordan: Do Experiences with Nature Promote Learning? Converging Evidence of a Cause-And-Effect Relationship in this volume). A deeper understanding of how, why, for whom, and under what circumstances different forms of nature contact enhance learning and development is needed to guide practice and policy decision-making. This chapter presents the outcome of an initiative to define NBL and set a research agenda to advance the pace and rigor of research on its impact.

In 2015 the U.S. National Science Foundation (NSF) provided a three-year grant to the University of Minnesota, the Children & Nature Network (C&NN), the North American Association for Environmental Education (NAAEE) and the University of Illinois Urbana-Champaign to establish the Science of Nature-Based Learning Collaborative Research Network (NBLR Network). On three occasions, the NBLR Network convened two dozen academic researchers from diverse disciplines, practitioners, environmental organization representatives, and funders from across the U.S. The Network aimed to: (1) jointly develop a definition and research agenda to inform the rigorous development of the science of NBL, (2) disseminate research-based information, and (3) conduct collaborative research responsive to this agenda (Jordan et al., 2017). This chapter reports on the first aim of developing a definition and research agenda. It draws on an integrative literature review to determine and disseminate the status of our understanding of NBL impacts and explanatory mechanisms (see Kuo et al., 2019, see Kuo, Barnes and Jordan: Do Experiences with Nature Promote Learning? Converging Evidence of a Cause-And-Effect Relationship in this volume). Collaborative research that is responsive to agenda questions is currently underway.

The term "nature-based learning" was introduced in the grant application to NSF as part of an effort to coordinate research that had been scattered across multiple disciplines. NBLR Network members were sent a draft definition of this term by this chapter's authors, and they responded with suggestions and comments. Successive revisions were circulated until members of the network agreed on the following definition and scope for this field.

NBL, or learning through exposure to nature and nature-based activities, occurs in natural settings and where elements of nature have been brought into built environments, such as plants, animals and water. It encompasses the acquisition of knowledge, skills, values, attitudes and behaviors in realms including, but not limited to, academic achievement, personal development, and environmental stewardship. It includes learning about the natural world, but extends to engagement in any subject, skill or interest while in natural surroundings. NBL can occur with varying degrees of guidance or structure, across the age span, alone or with others, and in urban, suburban, rural and wilderness settings. NBL occurs in informal, nonformal and formal settings (La Belle, 1982).[1] With respect to children's NBL, it includes *informal* learning during children's free play or discovery in nature in their yards, near their homes, in green schoolyards, on the naturalized grounds of child care centers, or in any other natural area. It includes *nonformal* learning in nature during out-of-school programs, camps or family visits to parks or nature centers. And it includes *formal* learning when children have contact with nature during structured activities in schools, preschools, and child care centers, or during outdoor field trips.

The following section of this chapter reviews the methods used to develop an NBL research agenda. A subsequent section summarizes the agenda's major questions grounded in the literature and in the minds of educators, researchers and funders, as well as recommendations for methods, measures, and designs that will be complementary and rigorous. The intent of this chapter is to encourage more coordination and collaboration among researchers, to promote a focus on the most pertinent research questions and most robust methods in order to advance this field, and to make a case for the importance of NBL as a field for study as well as practice. We acknowledge the boundary that participants in this agenda-setting process were drawn from the U.S. They considered existing studies from around the world and intended their work to be useful internationally; yet different countries may have different research cultures, and this agenda might reflect different emphases if it were generated in another part of the world.

2 Methodology in Developing the Research Agenda

2.1 Assembling Diverse Perspectives on NBL

This section traces the process of setting a research agenda during the three-year period of the National Science Foundation grant that began in September 2015. The project's coordinating team from the grant's four lead institutions worked together to

---

[1] In the U.S., the National Science Foundation distinguishes *formal* and *informal* learning, putting *nonformal* and *informal* in one category. The three-part distinction among *formal*, *nonformal* and *informal*, used here, which is widely used in Europe and the work of UNESCO, better reflects the diversity of practices in the NBLR Network.

identify academic researchers, practitioners, representatives of environmental organizations, and funders from across the U.S. whose work related to NBL, with the goal of assembling a diverse membership for the NBLR Network, based on a variety of disciplines, methodological approaches, and stakeholder connections. The 23 members of the network first convened in November 2015 for a three-day retreat to build relationships, agree on a common vision and direction for work, and discuss possibilities for interdisciplinary collaboration. In January 2016, NBLR Network members were asked to share written answers to the following questions, which guided development of the research agenda.

1. What is the status of our knowledge about whether, how, why, under what circumstances and for whom nature impacts children's learning?
2. What are the strengths and limitations of the research?
3. What research questions would most effectively advance knowledge relevant to practice and policy?
4. Are there considerations about the state of the current research that suggest methodological recommendations for the field?

After members shared their written reflections, they participated in conference calls to further elaborate and interpret responses.

Several means were used to capture the ideas of funders and practitioners, beyond representatives of these groups in the NBLR Network. The May 2016 C&NN conference provided two opportunities for group discussion—the Blue Sky Funders' Forum and an open forum for conference attendees. Both provided occasions to tap non-NBLR Network thinking regarding needs for additional research. The Natural Start Alliance nature-based preschool conference in August of 2016 and the Research Symposium associated with the October 2016 NAAEE conference offered opportunities for small group discussions with other constituencies regarding research gaps and needs. Finally, a member survey administered by NAAEE highlighted the work of the NBLR Network and collected additional input. For more details about NBLR Network strategies, processes for identifying and convening network members, members' disciplines and fields of practice, and processes to gather information from other groups, see section Network Participants and Processes in http://doi.org/10.3389/fpsyg.2019.00766 and Jordan et al., (2017).

2.2 Generating a Literature Review to Guide Agenda Discussions

During the summer of 2016, three members of the network prepared a research review of nature's impact on academic functioning, personal development and environmental stewardship, as well as explanatory variables related to learners and learning contexts. This review of existing research was a necessary foundation for identifying promising directions for future research. Details about the review scope, scale and procedures, including search keywords and operational definitions of key terms, are provided in the review article by Kuo et al., (2019, see Kuo, Barnes and Jordan: Do Experiences with Nature Promote Learning? Converging Evidence of a Cause-And–Effect Relationship in this volume). The literature review consisted of three main phases, which are described here.

Phase 1. The first step was to utilize recent peer-reviewed research summaries relevant to NBL and identify major themes related to NBL at the time of their publication. Articles covered in these previous reviews were added to the review database. The purpose of this phase was to understand the previous state of the literature and the main themes in the literature at the time of past reviews' publication.

Phase 2. The second step was to collect peer reviewed journal articles that were published since the cut-off dates for previous reviews. This research was limited to articles published in English, although the research may have been conducted anywhere in the world, and it included work that addressed any aspect of learning and developmental outcomes associated with any aspect of nature, utilizing a variety of research methods. At this time, the purpose was to update and expand findings from the previous review papers, and to present the diversity of the literature as a whole.

Phase 3. The third and last step to identify relevant research was intended to extend and deepen results of the preceding steps. It included two processes. Because some topic areas yielded only a few articles during the initial searches, specific searches were conducted to determine if these were in fact little studied areas or under-sampled by the preceding searches. Additionally, foundational papers and reviews were sought that shed light on potential mechanisms that connect nature and learning, though these publications may have come from general research on topics such as learning, cognitive science, or developmental outcomes. For example, if existing studies indicated that learning in nature sparked children's curiosity, then there was a search for papers which reviewed the general role of curiosity in learning. The purpose was to create a cohesive narrative that suggested mechanisms through which nature might affect learning outcomes.

A link to a spreadsheet of the articles retrieved during these three phases of the literature review is reproduced here: https://goo.gl/FZ1CA9, as well as in the review by Kuo et al., (2019, see Kuo, Barnes and Jordan: Do Experiences with Nature Promote Learning? Converging Evidence of a Cause-And-Effect Relationship in this volume).

2.3 Identifying Directions for Future Research

A draft of the literature review was presented at the second NBLR Network retreat in November 2016. Network members considered the review, along with results of their own written reflections and the input gathered through C&NN and NAAEE. People worked in small groups to develop focal areas and questions for the research agenda. Because their goal was to advance research that can be translated into educational policy and practice, members proposed the following criteria, in addition to feasibility, as they deliberated.

Research agenda questions should do one or more of the following:

1. address major social issues in a compelling way
2. affect large populations
3. cross developmental stages
4. translate into educational policy to help teachers and school administrators enhance students' academic success
5. suggest how institutions can promote stewardship values and behaviors
6. help designers and urban planners create places where children can connect with nature in meaningful ways
7. achieve valued public goals in cost-effective ways, in some cases even saving public money.

Applying these criteria, retreat attendees voted for questions they considered most important to advance the field of NBL.

During 2017, a report on the voting results and associated discussions was distributed to network members. Drawing on this report, reports on the C&NN conference Funders' Forum and open forum, and NAAEE survey, the authors of this chapter condensed and categorized the questions generated, along with methodological recommendations, and circulated them to the NBLR Network in early 2018. Feedback was gathered through email and conference calls. Questions and recommendations developed as a result of this process, vetted by NBLR Network members, are presented in the sections below (see section Supplemental Material: Agenda Consensus and Challenges in http://doi.org/10.3389/fpsyg.2019.00766).

3   Priority Research Questions

Table 1 presents the key research areas and questions that emerged through this agenda setting process, with three areas of emphasis: Learning Outcomes and Differential Effects, Mechanisms of Influence, and Implications for Policy and Practice. Where some contributors to the agenda approached a general question from specific perspectives, these variations on the general question are bulleted. Topics that suggest the range of areas that a question might explore are indicated in italics.

As authors of this paper, we have observed that the study of NBL reflects the convergence of two research traditions: one interested in the influence of experiences in nature on learning across the curriculum, personal development, and environmental stewardship; and the other concerned with the influence of natural settings and surroundings on conditions for learning. The first tradition has a long history. Fieldwork in nature to learn subjects like biology and geology is well established in environmental education and science education, and the resurgence of school ground greening and school gardens has created conditions for "fieldwork" immediately outside school doors (for research reviews of different forms of outdoor learning, see

Becker et al., 2017; Dillon et al., 2006; Malone & Waite, 2016; Stern et al., 2014; Williams & Dixon, 2013). The use of the environment as an integrating context to engage students in math, science, social studies, language arts and other disciplines as they study the world beyond school walls, including natural areas, is the domain of place-based education (Chawla & Derr, 2012; Smith & Sobel, 2010). There is also a long history of observations of children's informal learning as they play and explore on natural school grounds and find nature in their local environment (Chawla, 2015). The questions in Table 1 indicate that many aspects of outdoor learning still need to be better understood, but work in this area has much to build on as it moves forward.

Table 1 A framework for research to advance the understanding and implementation of Nature-based Learning (NBL)

A. Learning Outcomes and Differential Effects

Learning Outcomes

How effectively do children learn content and skills through NBL compared with instruction in classrooms where nature is absent?

- How do schools or classrooms that practice NBL compare with schools or classrooms without nature with respect to academic achievement, graduation rates, and student and parental satisfaction?
- How do nature-based preschools and kindergartens compare with conventional early childhood programs that emphasize indoor learning in terms of preparing children for school readiness?
- Are there situations when NBL is more effective and when classroom-based instruction is more effective?
- How might NBL and classroom-based instruction complement each other?

What is the range of learning outcomes influenced by nature?
motivation to learn / knowledge gain / skill development / creativity / curiosity / cognitive processes such as attention, encoding, retention, recall / executive skills such as behavior regulation / social and emotional learning / reduced stress, improved mood and mental health / physical health / academic performance such as test scores and graduation rates / environmental stewardship values and behaviors*

Does NBL contribute to stewardship values or conservation behaviors?

Differential Effects Based on Age, Population Group, and Individual Differences

How do age and developmental stage influence the relationship between nature and learning?

- What are key elements of nature experiences important at different ages?
- What different forms of knowledge, skills, values, attitudes, and behaviors develop in nature at different ages?
- Are there critical windows for the development of different outcomes in nature?

To promote academic achievement, personal development and environmental stewardship, what types of nature experiences are most appropriate at different ages?

How does NBL affect special populations in terms of learning outcomes?

- How does NBL affect children from socioeconomically disadvantaged families?
- Does the impact of NBL differ based on historic relationships with nature grounded in cultural or ethnic background?
- Are there gender differences in nature's impact on children?
- How does nature exposure impact learning for children with special needs such as ADHD, autism or learning disabilities?

Are there individual differences in response to NBL? What determines why there may be different outcomes for children involved in the same experience?

(continued)

Table 1 (continued)

B. Mechanisms of Influence

What are the mechanisms that underlie the relationship between nature and learning?
more focused attention / improved behavior regulation / increased creativity / reduced stress / greater enthusiasm for and engagement in learning / increased physical activity / improved health and wellbeing / calmer, quieter learning context / more cooperative social context / opportunities for autonomous discovery and action / self-perception / self-identity / connection between content and the child's locality / enhanced sense of purpose*

- What mediator variables explain the relationship between nature and learning outcomes, and what is the influence of different variables separately and in combination?
- Is it possible to establish that nature impacts learning and development in a causal manner?
- What moderator variables influence the strength of the relationship between nature and learning outcomes?

Do mechanisms vary for different groups, in different contexts? If NBL has such differential effects, why?

What are key elements of nature experiences that affect children?
type of natural features / type of activities such as unstructured play and exploration, guided inquiry and adult-led instruction / degree of manipulation of natural elements / duration / frequency / individual or group experience / type of people with the child, such as teacher, parent, naturalist, classmates, friends / degree of teacher preparation and confidence in NBL approaches*

Does nature bring associated ingredients of learning together in a distinctive way? For example, does it bring opportunities for unstructured exploration, freedom to manipulate natural materials, creativity, and social cooperation together in a unique or synergistic way?

How do interpersonal dynamics among children, parents, friends, and teachers influence NBL?

How might power hierarchies or social stereotypes based on race, ethnicity, culture, class, gender or age influence NBL?

What does nature do to the brain?

- What are the channels of nature's effects?
  sight / sound / smell / touch / emotion / movement*
- Does the impact of nature on the brain differ based on age?
- Does nature contact influence the development of the brain in terms of structure or physiology?

What is the impact on learning when access to nature is reduced?
removing recess in spaces with nature / no green views from school windows / more screen time*

(continued)

Table 1 (continued)

C. Implications for Policy and Practice

Policy or Practice

What nature-based experiences are most appropriate for different developmental stages of childhood to achieve optimal learning outcomes?

Can NBL play a role in reducing the opportunity gap and achievement gap between children from more and less advantaged backgrounds?

How does nature compare with other programs and approaches that compete for educational funding in terms of its effectiveness in enhancing learning?

What are the effects on learning of the cheapest and easiest ways of bringing nature into schools and day care centers?

What are NBL best practices in different educational contexts?

What evidence, messages, and strategies encourage increased demand for NBL and the application of NBL practices by educators, parents and other people who have influence over opportunities for children?

What determines differences in access to nature, green school grounds, and NBL?

Is NBL a social justice issue?

Preparation and Professional Development

What are the best strategies for teachers to use to enhance student learning in nature?

What are effective practices for preparing and supporting teachers and administrators in the adoption of NBL in their classrooms and schools?

What are barriers to teachers' and administrators' adoption?

Technology Augmented Learning

How does technology augment, simulate or mediate NBL? Are there costs as well as benefits?

How does nature mediated or augmented through technology impact learning compared to experiences of real nature?

Under what conditions is technology effective in enhancing nature's impact on learning?

How can we leverage technology to present nature in new ways for learning?

How would new technologies function that do not substitute for nature, or for interaction with nature, but add additional forms of interaction?

*These lists are suggestive, based on current evidence, but not necessarily complete.

The second tradition—investigating the influence of nature on conditions for learning—has emerged recently, demonstrating that vegetation and other elements of nature in classrooms, on school grounds, and in the proximity of schools are associated with more effective cognitive functioning, decreased stress, improved health, and enhanced classroom and social learning environments—all of which can facilitate learning and higher student achievement (see reviews by Becker et al., 2017; Chawla, 2015; Gifford & Chen, 2016; Kuo et al., 2019, see Kuo, Barnes and Jordan: Do Experiences with Nature Promote Learning? Converging Evidence of a Cause-And-Effect Relationship in this volume). Many studies of this topic suggest productive directions for further investigation. Whereas the first research tradition focuses on learning in nature to enhance knowledge, skills and personal development, this second tradition involves children's basic wellbeing and capacity to learn efficiently. Recently, and partly with the assistance of the NSF grant to promote the Science of Nature-Based Learning, people from these different backgrounds have been sharing their work at conferences and other professional meetings.

The questions in Table 1 suggest an ambitious agenda for moving an understanding of NBL forward. They seek to understand how learning in nature affects what children learn, how they learn, and how it varies based on age, gender, socioeconomic status, ethnic background, special needs, and individual differences. They investigate the relative benefits of learning in nature and through conventional classroom-based instruction, and learning in settings where there is nature in and around buildings with learning in predominantly hardscaped, built surroundings. Outcomes of interest cover academic performance, practical skills, personal development, and environmental stewardship. Other questions seek to identify mechanisms of action in NBL and find causal explanations for the outcomes observed. To create effective conditions for NBL, the research agenda includes a number of practical questions about how to prepare teachers to work successfully in nature and encourage their adoption of this approach. Possibilities for using technology to augment learning in nature also merit exploration (such as approaches identified in Kahn, 2011). Not least, the research agenda asks whether learning in nature can address major societal issues by moderating the effect of socioeconomic disadvantage on children's outcomes, and how these benefits might be attained at reasonable costs. Although these questions outline an ambitious agenda for future research, promising results of past studies suggest that further investment in this field may significantly benefit children and their societies.

In drafting this research agenda, funders, researchers who focus on school-based initiatives, and practitioners emphasized the importance of systematically investigating how to most effectively disseminate results of NBL research and encourage implementation. It is important to match growing evidence of benefits of learning in nature with outreach to teachers, school administrators, schoolboards, schools of education, child care center directors and people in other institutions who have opportunities to apply nature-based approaches. Effective outreach depends on understanding barriers to the integration of NBL into teacher preparation and practice, how barriers can be lowered, and the types of data and messages that will help practitioners understand the value of NBL. Similar questions need to be asked relative to reaching the public at large, in order to build public support for NBL.

Though not comprehensive, the questions offered in the research agenda have the potential to significantly advance our knowledge and ability to inform policy and practice in an array of areas. Given the wide range of subjects covered by the questions proposed for this research agenda, it is reasonable to ask where to begin or what to prioritize. In Table 2 we offer a set of "game-changing" questions—research questions that are most likely to yield critical information for practice and policy decision-making.

Table 2 Examples of "Game-Changing" research questions and justifications

Question	Justification
Can nature reduce educational opportunity gaps and achievement gaps between children from different economic backgrounds?	Contact with nature shows an array of benefits for children across socioeconomic lines, at the same time as research shows that low-income families are more likely to live in urban neighborhoods with low levels of vegetation and smaller, less safe and less maintained parks, compared to middle- and high-income families (Chawla, 2015; Jesdale et al., 2013; Rigolon, 2017). Therefore, benefits of bringing children from disadvantaged backgrounds to nature and nature to their schools, child care centers and neighborhoods merits particular attention
If learning in nature can enhance children's achievement and wellbeing, how do its costs compare with other approaches that compete for educational funding?	Research is needed that analyzes the economic costs of NBL practices relative to other interventions that lack natural elements. Cost accounting should include the full valuation of NBL in terms of impact on academic achievement, physical health, mental health, behavioral function, engagement in learning, use of special education services, and interaction with the criminal justice system. A compelling case for NBL can be made if educational outcomes are similar to conventional approaches but produce cost-savings in additional arenas, and an even more compelling case if NBL can narrow gaps in educational outcomes compared to conventional approaches

(continued)

Table 2 (continued)

Question	Justification
What are the mechanisms that underlie the relationship between nature and learning?	Understanding how contact with nature facilitates and improves learning will permit the effective and efficient delivery of NBL experiences and the design of natural areas to best promote learning and development. For example, if research shows that nature enhances learning by reducing stress, then programs and settings should be designed to activate this pathway: and similarly with other potential pathways such as more focused attention or more cooperative and supportive social dynamics
How does nature impact the learning of children with special needs as a result of physical health, mental health, or cognitive conditions; learning differences; or educational disadvantages due to low income?	When individuals with special needs or disadvantages in the educational setting do not benefit from education as much as they could or do not find meaningful roles in society, there are high costs to those individuals, their families, school districts, and society in terms of expenses, lost potential and reduced well-being
What teacher characteristics and practices enhance the association between NBL approaches and educational outcomes? How can teachers be prepared and supported to adopt NBL practices?	The impact of NBL is partially dependent on the attitudes, skills and practices of teachers (Mcfarland et al., 2013). Understanding how teachers learn to value NBL, integrate it into their school day, and promote positive outcomes will facilitate effective teacher preparation and professional development programs. This information will suggest how programs of teacher education and school administrators can best support the adoption and effective implementation of NBL strategies, in both pre-service and in-service settings
What knowledge and experiences promote people's motivation and competence to protect the integrity of natural landscapes and ecosystems? How can these experiences be integrated into NBL practices?	Information is gathering on many sides that basic systems of the biosphere that support human health and wellbeing and the survival of other species are rapidly deteriorating (Intergovernmental Panel on Climate Change, 2014; Millenium Ecosystem Assessment, 2005). An essential dimension of NBL is learning to understand and care for the natural world
How can technology be most effectively harnessed to enhance the outcomes of NBL?	Technology is a common feature in current and future-looking educational programs; yet technology can be overused, resulting in reduced engagement in active, enriching activities (Singer et al., 2009), including those in nature, and disrupting cognitive functioning and optimal mental health (Chassiakos et al., 2016). Therefore, it is important to understand how technology can be used as a tool to enhance nature experiences or to present nature while mitigating risks of overuse

4 Recommendations for Future Research Approaches

Significant scientific advances are made not only by asking the most relevant and important questions, but by utilizing approaches that will yield the most useful, valid and reliable information. What general recommendations can be made to strengthen future research in this field?

The researchers, practitioners and funders who helped define this research agenda recommend a more coordinated approach to NBL research in the future. In part, this will require periodic syntheses of what is already known in relation to the questions in Tables 1 and 2, to guide further efforts to fill in gaps in understanding. To facilitate research syntheses, C&NN established an online Research Library that deposits, on an ongoing basis, lay summaries of new studies related to NBL as well as other aspects of children's relationship with nature (https://research.childrenandnature. org/). C&NN's monthly Research Digest has begun to curate existing research on selected themes, such as equitable access to nature's benefits (https://www. childrenandnature.org/resources/type/research-digest/). C&NN and NAAEE now provide a central location to access the combined resources of C&NN's and NAAEE's research libraries (naaee.org/eeresearch) to provide comprehensive coverage of the two traditions of investigation reflected in this research agenda.

More coordinated research will also require the consistent use of adequate descriptions of study contexts as well as consistent measures of study variables (see also Kuo et al., 2018, see Kuo, Browning and Penner: Refueling Students in Flight: Lessons in Nature May Boost Subsequent Classroom Engagement in this volume). Qualitative and quantitative researchers need to specify learning settings and activities, including elements of nature in each setting, length of children's time in nature, and how children engage with nature—whether it is a passive view or background, or they use it actively through their own autonomous exploration or encounters facilitated by teachers, peers or other people. Complete descriptions are important for understanding and applying results and identifying potential causal mechanisms that underlie learning.

Coordinated progress in quantitative research and experimental designs will be furthered by agreement on valid, reliable measures of nature exposure, mediating variables and learning outcomes. Many measures already exist, and they need to be evaluated to understand which are most effective with different age groups and in different learning contexts. A working group has completed a report for measures of nature connection (Salazar et al., 2020), but similar evaluations are needed of other key variables important for this research agenda. It would be helpful to have an online bank of NBL measures that researchers can draw from, along with examples of studies where they have been applied and recommendations for their appropriate use. This would encourage more reliable comparisons across studies.

NBL research needs to move forward through complementary methodological approaches. Different methods are required to investigate questions of different kinds, and therefore the field of NBL will be advanced most effectively by different methods and mixed-method approaches. For example, to understand how NBL and classroom-based approaches compare or complement each other, it can be helpful to begin with observations and interviews with teachers and students, in order to identify similarities and differences. Qualitative results may suggest how settings with and without nature afford different opportunities for teaching and learning, which may lead to different outcomes; and these outcomes can then be tested in more controlled ways through experimental designs. Experimental designs can also investigate the mechanisms that underlie results. As experiments and correlational studies establish with increasing confidence key variables that affect learning, the case builds for investments in longitudinal research that can track the effect of key variables over time. Some objectives, such as quantifying the effect of learning in nature preschools on performance in elementary school, can be addressed with relatively short-term studies; others, such as tracing the effect of childhood learning in nature on environmental stewardship values and behaviors in adulthood, require long-term studies.

NBL research will be advanced through collaboration between academic researchers and practitioners and through multidisciplinary and multiethnic perspectives. In participatory research, practitioners, parents and young people themselves can help at different stages of research, including defining questions, designing and implementing studies, interpreting results and disseminating outcomes. The audiences that researchers seek to reach are best qualified to identify the type of information that will catch their attention and resonate with their values and practical considerations. For example, the experiment reported by Kuo et al., (2018, see Kuo, Browning and Penner: Refueling Students in Flight: Lessons in Nature May Boost Subsequent Classroom Engagement in this volume) was designed to test the validity of teachers' common fear that if they take a class to an outdoor setting in nature, students will never settle down to concentrate on lessons after they return to the school building (finding, in contrast, that students concentrated better in their subsequent indoor class). In a similar way, researchers can identify NBL outcomes that matter most to teachers, school administrators, parents and children themselves as promising directions for research efforts.

5 Conclusion

Existing research suggests that NBL has many positive outcomes for children's learning and development. It suggests promising directions for future investigation; but to move forward, NBL research will benefit from a clear definition and a coordinated agenda. This paper has attempted to provide this framework by presenting a definition and a list of priority questions that have been drafted and reviewed by academic researchers from diverse disciplines, practitioners, environmental organization representatives, and funders.

Priority questions for future research cluster into three domains:

1.   learning outcomes, including understanding how learning in nature compares with learning in classrooms, preschools and child care centers, and how outcomes may vary by age, gender, socioeconomic background, ethnic background, individual differences, or special needs;
2.   the mechanisms that explain relationships between nature and learning; and
3.   how to most effectively apply research to policy and practice.

This Research Agenda also suggests that a few questions have the potential of uncovering relationships between nature and learning that could have "game changing" effects on the practices of policy makers, educators, school administrators, urban planners, designers, staff in nature centers and parks, parents, and other people who influence children's access to nature. With the aim of enhancing conditions for children's learning and development, this agenda seeks to accelerate progress on the science of NBL.

Recommended Further Reading

1.   Becker, C., Lauterbach, G., Spengler, S., Dettweiler, U., & Mess, F. (2017). Effects of regular classes in outdoor education settings: A systematic review on students' learning, social and health dimensions. *International Journal of Environmental Research and Public Health.* 14. https://doi.org/10.3390/ijerph14050485 (accessed 14/05/2021).
2.   Kuo, M., Barnes, M., & Jordan, C. (2019). Do experiences with nature promote learning? Converging evidence of a cause-and-effect relationship. *Frontiers in Psychology*, 10:305. https://doi.org/10.3389/fpsyg.2019.00305 (accessed 14/05/2021). see Kuo, Barnes and Jordan: Do Experiences with Nature Promote Learning? Converging Evidence of a Cause-And-Effect Relationship in this volume.
3.   Miller, N. C., Kumar, S., Pearce, K. L., Baldock, K. L., (2021). The outcomes of nature-based learning for primary school aged children: A systematic review of quantitative research. *Environmental Education Research, 27*(8), 1115–1140.

Acknowledgements The authors acknowledge funding from the National Science Foundation (NSF 1540919) for support of the Science of Nature-Based Learning Collaborative Research Network. This paper draws on a report by Cheryl Charles that summarized research questions generated by members of the Nature-Based Learning Research Network and recommended directions for future research. We thank her for her efforts. The authors express gratitude to the members of the NBLR Network for their diverse contributions of expertise, skills, resources and passion for connecting children to nature: Marc Berman, Judy Braus, Greg Cajete, Cheryl Charles, Scott Chazdon, Angie Chen, Avery Cleary, Nilda Cosco, Andrea Faber Taylor, Megan Gunnar, Erin Hashimoto-Martell, Peter Kahn, Ming Kuo, Sarah Milligan Toffler, Robin Moore, Scott Sampson, David Sobel, David Strayer, Jason Watson, Dilafruz Williams, Sheila Williams Ridge, and Tamra Willis. We thank Michael Barnes for his efforts in reviewing the NBL literature that contributed to setting this research agenda.

References

Becker, C., Lauterbach, G., Spengler, S., Dettweiler, U., & Mess, F. (2017). Effects of regular classes in outdoor education settings: A systematic review on students' learning, social and health dimensions. *International Journal of Environmental Research and Public Health, 14*, 485. https://doi.org/10.3390/ijerph14050485. Retrieved May 14, 2021.

Chassiakos, Y.R., Radesky, J., Christakis, D., Moreno, M.A., & Cross, C. (2016). Children and adolescents and digital media: technical report of the American Academy of Pediatrics. *Pediatrics, 138*(5). https://doi.org/10.1542/peds.2016-2593. Retrieved May 14, 2021.

Chawla, L. (2015). Benefits of nature contact for children. *Journal of Planning Literature, 30*(4), 433–452. https://doi.org/10.1177/0885412215595441. Retrieved May 15, 2021.

Chawla, L., & Derr, T. (2012). The development of conservation behaviors in childhood and youth. In S. Clayton (Ed.), *Oxford handbook of environmental and conservation psychology* (pp. 527–555). Oxford University Press.

Children and Nature Network. (2020). Research digest: Formal and nonformal nature-based education. Retrieved May 14, 2021, from, https://mailchi.mp/1539a8e2bef2/children-nature-network-research-digest-august-2020.

Dillon, J., Rickinson, M., Teamey, K., Morris, M., Choi, M. Y., Sanders, D. & Benefield, P. (2006). The value of outdoor learning: Evidence from research in the U.K. and elsewhere. *School Science Review, 87*(320), 107–111. Retrieved May 14, 2021, from https://www.researchgate.net/publication/287621860_The_value_of_outdoor_learning_Evidence_from_research_in_the_UK_and_elsewhere.

Gifford, R. & Chen, A. (2016). *Children and nature: What we know and what we do not know.* Toronto: The Lawson Foundation. Retrieved May 14, 2021, from https://lawson.ca/wp-content/uploads/2018/04/Children-an-Nature-What-We-Know-and-What-We-Do-Not.pdf.

Intergovernmental Panel on Climate Change. (2014). *Climate change 2014: Synthesis report summary for policymakers.* Geneva: IPCC. Retrieved May 14, 2021, from https://www.ipcc.ch/site/assets/uploads/2018/02/AR5_SYR_FINAL_SPM.pdf.

Jesdale, B. M., Morello-Frosch, R. & Cushing, L. (2013). The racial/ethnic distribution of heat risk-related land cover in relation to residential segregation. *Environmental Health Perspectives, 121*(7), 811–817. Retrieved May 14, 2021, from https://www.ncbi.nlm.nih.gov/pmc/articles/PMC3701995/.

Jordan, C., Charles, C., & Cleary, A. (2017). Enhancing the impact of research: Experimenting with network leadership strategies to grow a vibrant nature-based learning research network. *Interdisciplinary Journal of Partnership Studies, 4*(3). Special issue on partnership and environment. Retrieved May 14, 2021, from https://pubs.lib.umn.edu/index.php/ijps/article/view/175.

Kahn, P. (2011). *Technological nature.* MIT Press.

Kuo, M., Barnes, M., & Jordan, C. (2019). Do experiences with nature promote learning? Converging evidence of a cause-and-effect relationship. *Frontiers in Psychology, 10*, 305. https://doi.org/10.3389/fpsyg.2019.00305. Retrieved May 14, 2021.

Kuo, M., Browning, M. H. E. M. & Penner, M. L. (2018). Do lessons in nature boost subsequent classroom engagement? Refueling students in flight. *Frontiers in Psychology, 8*(2253). https://doi.org/10.3389/fpsyg.2017.02253. see Kuo, Browning and Penner: Refueling Students in Flight: Lessons in Nature May Boost Subsequent Classroom Engagement in this volume.

Kuo, M., & Jordan, C. (Eds.). (2019). *The natural world as a resource for learning and development: From schoolyards to wilderness.* (e-book). Lausanne: Frontiers Media. https://doi.org/10.3389/978-2-88963-138-4. Retrieved May 14, 2021.

La Belle, T. J. (1982). Formal, nonformal and informal learning: A holistic perspective on lifelong learning. *International Review of Education, 28*, 159–175. Retrieved May 15, 2021, from https://link.springer.com/article/. https://doi.org/10.1007/BF00598444.

Malone, K. & Waite, S. (2016). *Student outcomes and natural schooling. Pathways from Evidence to Impact Report 2016.* Plymouth: Plymouth University. Retrieved May 14,

2021, from https://www.plymouth.ac.uk/uploads/production/document/path/6/6811/Student_outcomes_and__natural_schooling_pathways_to_impact_2016.pdf.

Mann, J., Gray, T., Truong, S., Sahlberg, P., Bentsen, P., Passy, R., Ho, S., Ward, K., & Cowper, R. (2021). A systematic review protocol to identify the key benefits and efficacy of nature-based learning in outdoor educational settings. *International Journal of Environmental Research and Public Health.* 18, Article 1199. https://doi.org/10.3390/ijerph18031199. Retrieved May 14, 2021.

Mcfarland, A., Glover, B. J., Waliczek, T. M. & Zajicek, J. M. (2013). The effectiveness of the National Wildlife Foundation's Schoolyard Habitat Program: Fourth-grade students' standardized science test scores and science grades. *Horticulture, 23*(2), 187–193. https://doi.org/10.21273/HORTTECH.23.2.187. Retrieved May 14, 2021.

Millenium Ecosystem Assessment. (2005). *Ecosystems and human well-being: General synthesis.* Washington, DC: Island Press. Retrieved May 14, 2021, from https://www.millenniumassessment.org/documents/document.356.aspx.pdf.

Rigolon, A. (2017). Parks and young people: An environmental justice study of park proximity, acreage, and quality in Denver. *Colorado. Landscape and Urban Planning., 165*, 73–83. https://doi.org/10.1016/j.landurbplan.2017.05.007. Retrieved May 14, 2021.

Ross, N. (2020). Anthropocentric tendencies in environmental education: A critical discourse analysis of nature-based learning. *Ethics and Education, 15*(3), 355–370. https://doi.org/10.1080/17449642.2020.1780550. Retrieved May 14, 2021.

Salazar, G., Kunkle, K., & Monroe, M. C. (2020). Practitioner guide to assessing connection to nature. Washington, DC: North American Association for Environmental Education. Retrieved May 14, 2021, from https://naaee.org/eepro/publication/practitioner-guide-assessing-connection.

Singer, D. G., Singer, J. L., D'Agostino, & DeLong, R. (2009). Children's pastimes and play in sixteen nations: Is free play declining? *American Journal of Play, 1*(3), 283–312. Retrieved May 14, 2021, from https://www.journalofplay.org/sites/www.journalofplay.org/files/pdf-articles/1-3-article-childrens-pastimes-play-in-sixteen-nations.pdf.

Smith, G., & Sobel, D. (2010). *Place- and community-based education in schools.* Routledge.

Stern, M. J., Powell, R. B., & Hill, D. (2014). Environmental education program evaluation in the new millenium: What do we measure and what have we learned? *Environmental Education Research., 20*(5), 581–611. https://doi.org/10.1080/13504622.2013.838749. Retrieved May 14, 2021.

Stevenson, K. T., Moore, R., Cosco, N., Floyd, M. F., Sullivan, W., Brink, L., Gerstein, D., Jordan, C., & Zaplatosch, J. (2020). A national research agenda supporting green schoolyard development and equitable access to nature. *Elementa: Science of the Anthropocene, 8*(10), 406. https://doi.org/10.1525/elementa.406. Retrieved May 14, 2021.

Williams, D. R., & Dixon, P. S. (2013). Impact of garden-based learning on academic outcomes in schools: Synthesis of research between 1990 and 2010. *Review of Educational Research, 83*(2), 211–235. Retrieved May 14, 2021, from https://doi.org/10.3102/0034654313475824.

Cathy Jordan is professor of pediatrics and Director of Leadership & Education for the Institute on the Environment, University of Minnesota. She also serves as the Consulting Director of Research for the Children and Nature Network. In this role she aims to make research about nature's benefit to children's health, development and wellbeing accessible, understandable and usable by practitioners, advocates and the public.

Cathy Jordan served as the principal investigator of the Science of Nature-Based Learning Collaborative Research Network project. She surveyed the NBLR Network members, conducted discussion sessions at conferences, and supervised the graduate student conducting the literature review. She was involved in the generation and review of research questions, co-wrote the manuscript, and solicited input from NBLR Network.

Louise Chawla is Professor Emerita in the Environmental Design Program at the University of Colorado Boulder, and an active member of the university's Community Engagement, Design and Research Center. Her research and publications focus on children and nature, children in cities, and the development of committed action for the environment.

Louise Chawla was a member of the NBLR Network. She was involved in the generation and review of research questions and co-wrote the manuscript.

Do Experiences with Nature Promote Learning? Converging Evidence of a Cause-And-Effect Relationship

Ming Kuo, Michael Barnes, and Cathy Jordan

1 Introduction

The intuition that "nature is good for children" is widely held, and yet historically, the evidence for this intuition has been uncompelling, with a distressing number of weak studies and inflated claims. Now, however, an impressive body of work has accrued and converging lines of evidence paint a convincing picture.

This integrative mini-review summarizes what we know about the role of nature in learning and development. It draws on a wide array of peer-reviewed scientific evidence, ranging from research in the inner city, to the study of Attention Deficit/Hyperactivity Disorder, to neurocognitive and physiological explorations. Our overarching question was, "do experiences in nature promote learning and child development?"

M. Kuo (✉)
504 W Vermont Ave, Urbana, IL 61801, United States
e-mail: fekuo@illinois.edu

M. Barnes
310 Alderman Hall, 1970 Folwell Ave., St. Paul, Minnesota 55108, United States
e-mail: barne369@umn.edu

C. Jordan
1954 Buford Ave, Suite 325, St. Paul, MN 55108, United States
e-mail: jorda003@umn.edu

© The Author(s) 2022
R. Jucker and J. von Au (eds.), *High-Quality Outdoor Learning*,
https://doi.org/10.1007/978-3-031-04108-2_3

Throughout our review, we took care to distinguish between evidence for cause-and-effect relationships and evidence for associations; causal language (e.g., "affects," "boosts," "is reduced by") is used only where justified by experimental evidence. Where converging, but not experimental, evidence points to a likely cause-and-effect relationship, our language is qualified accordingly (e.g., "seems to increase"). Table 1 summarizes recent advances in this area and explains how those advances contribute to our confidence in a cause-and-effect relationship between nature and learning and development.

What emerged from this critical review was a coherent narrative (Fig. 1): experiences with nature do promote children's academic learning and seem to promote children's development as persons and as environmental stewards—and at least eight distinct pathways plausibly contribute to these outcomes. Below, we discuss the evidence for each of the eight pathways and then the evidence tying nature to learning, personal development, and the development of stewardship.

Figure 1 summarizes the state of the scientific literature on nature and learning. The items and pathways here emerged from our review as opposed to guiding our review; thus each item listed has been empirically associated with one or more other items in this Figure. Relationships for which there is cause-and-effect evidence are indicated with an asterisk; for example, "more able to concentrate" is asterisked because experimental research has demonstrated that exposure to nature boosts concentration. Similarly, "increased retention of subject matter content" is asterisked because experimental research has demonstrated that exposure to nature in the course of learning boosts retention of that material. The green box lists forms of nature exposure which have been tied with learning, whether directly (nature -> learning) or indirectly, via one or more of the mechanisms listed (nature -> mechanism -> learning). In this review, "nature" includes experiences of nature not only in wilderness but also within largely human-made contexts (e.g., a classroom view of a garden). This review encompassed experiences of nature regardless of context—whether during play, relaxation, or educational activities, and in informal, non-formal and formal settings. The blue boxes show probable mechanisms—intermediary variables which have been empirically tied to both nature and learning. For example, concentration is rejuvenated by exposure to nature and plays an important role in learning. Natural settings may affect learning both by directly fostering a learner's capacity to learn and by providing a more supportive context for learning. The purple box lists learning outcomes that have been tied to contact with nature. In this review, "learning" encompasses changes in knowledge, skills, behaviors, attitudes, and values. A database of articles found in the three phases of the review process (ending in 2018) is available at: https://goo.gl/FZ1CA9.

Table 1 Do nature experiences promote learning? Advances in methodology and evidence. In recent years, the evidence for a cause-and-effect relationship between nature experiences and learning has advanced considerably. Some advances can be traced to the adoption of more rigorous research methods in individual studies (first 4 rows), others can be traced to the maturation of the field (rows 5 & 6), and still others stem from broadening the kinds of evidence considered in reviews (last two rows)

We now know that…	How this advance came about and why it matters
Nature-based instruction (NBI) is, on average, more effective than traditional instruction (TI)	Early research often compared outcomes before and after NBI, showing that students benefited from nature-based instruction but not whether there was anything particularly helpful about NBI as compared to any other instruction. More recently, studies have begun comparing outcomes for NBI vs. TI, showing that incorporating nature adds value to instruction (e.g., Camasso & Jagannathan, 2018; Ernst & Stanek, 2006)
The advantage of NBI over TI does not simply reflect a tendency for better teachers, better schools, or better students to choose NBI	Early research often compared learning in classrooms offering NBI versus 'matched' classrooms offering TI, where the to-be-compared classrooms were selected to match in, say, grade, or class size, or other characteristics. But such matching did not address the likelihood that teachers (or schools) who choose to offer NBI may be more innovative, energetic, or well-funded than teachers (or schools) who do not, even when they serve similar students or are matched in other characteristics. Similarly, comparisons of students who choose extracurricular NBI versus students who do not will reflect pre-existing differences in the kinds of students who sign up for extra instruction. Recently, researchers have begun using "waitlist controls" – identifying teachers, schools, or students interested in NBI and then randomly assigning some of them to NBI and the rest to TI (e.g., Wells et al., 2015). Guarding against pre-existing differences between the teachers, schools, and students being compared lends greater confidence that any gains are due to the instruction itself

(continued)

Table 1 (continued)

We now know that…	How this advance came about and why it matters
The effects of NBI on academic learning are real; they do not simply reflect the rosy assessments of biased observers	Early research often relied on subjective assessments of outcomes by persons who believed in NBI. Advocates, practitioners, and parents or children who choose NBI may perceive benefits in the absence of any real effects, whether consciously or unconsciously. More recent research guards against such bias by employing objective measures or assessments made "blind to condition"—without knowing which students were in which condition (NBI or TI) (e.g.,Ernst & Stanek, 2006). In these studies, an advantage of NBI over TI cannot be attributed to wishful thinking
Nature-based learning shows a 'dose–response relationship'—as the magnitude of the treatment (the dose) increases, so does the outcome	Early research relied on binary comparison; for example, comparing learning with versus without nature, or in 'low' versus 'high nature'conditions. Binary comparisons leave more room for alternative explanations; for instance, if students learn more outdoors than indoors, the difference might be due to either differences in vegetation or other differences between the settings. More recent research has compared multiple levels of nature (e.g., schoolyards with 0–40% tree cover, Sivarajah et al., 2018) or multiple levels of NBI (Wells et al., 2015). When the response is proportional to the dose that lends greater confidence that the effect is attributable to the level of vegetation. Although a 'dose–response relationship' does not prove causality, it strengthens the case
The nature-learning connection holds up across topics, learners, instructors, pedagogies, places, and measures of learning	As researchers have continued to conduct studies, the body of studies testing the nature-learning hypothesis has grown larger and more diverse (e.g., Faber Taylor et al.,2002; Fremery & Bogner, 2015; Kuo et al.,2018a; Lekies et al., 2015; Maynard et al., 2013; McCree et al., 2018; O'Haire et al.,2013; Ruiz-Gallardo et al., 2013; Sivarajah et al., 2018; Swank et al., 2017). A robust association persisting across different contexts lends greater confidence in a cause-and-effect relationship (Hill, 1965, 8)

(continued)

Table 1 (continued)

We now know that...	How this advance came about and why it matters
The relationship between nature and learning holds up across different research designs	Over time, a greater variety of study designs have been employed, including true experiments (e.g., Wells et al., 2015), quasi-experiments (e.g., Benfield et al., 2015; Faber Taylor & Kuo, 2009), large-scale correlational studies with statistical controls (e.g., Kuo & Faber Taylor, 2004), and longitudinal studies (e.g., McCree et al, 2018). Findings persisting across diverse study designs strengthen the case for causality
NBI may be more effective than TI not just because of a focus on nature, but because of differences in setting and pedagogy	Previous reviews drew only upon studies examining the effects of nature-centered instruction on learning. In this review, we expanded our reach to include studies on the pedagogies associated with NBI—even where nature was not involved; specifically, educational psychologists working in the classroom have found that active, hands-on,student-centered, and collaborative forms of instruction outperform more traditional instructional approaches (Freeman et al., 2014; Granger et al., 2012; Kontra et al., 2015). Similarly, this review included studies examining the impacts of learning environments even when the settings were incidental to instruction; specifically, environmental psychologists have found better learning in 'greener' settings—even when the instruction does not incorporate the nature (Benfield et al., 2015; Kuo et al., 2018b). These additional bodies of evidence converge to reinforce and help explain the advantages of NBI over TI
Nature experiences may promote learning via at least eight distinct pathways	Again, previous reviews drew only upon direct tests of the nature-learning hypothesis—studies in which nature was the independent variable and learning was the dependent variable. This review examined indirect tests, as well—studies examining the relationship between nature and known precursors to learning such as the ability to pay attention (Rowe & Rowe, 1992). Evidence of mechanism lends greater plausibility to a cause-and-effect relationship between nature and learning. The multiple mechanisms identified here may also help explain the consistency of the nature-learning relationship. Robust phenomena are often multiply determined

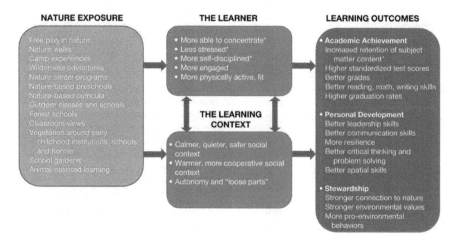

Fig. 1 Nature-based learning: Exposures, probable mechanisms, and outcomes

2 Nature May Boost Learning via Direct Effects on Learners

Five of the eight plausible pathways between nature and learning that we identified are centered in the learner. Learning is likely to improve when a learner is more attentive (Mantzicopoulos, 1995; Rowe & Rowe, 1992); less stressed (Grannis, 1992; Leppink et al., 2016); more self-disciplined (Duckworth & Seligman, 2005; Mischel et al., 1988); more engaged and interested (Taylor et al., 2014 for review); and more physically active and fit (for reviews, see Álvarez-Bueno et al., 2017; Santana et al., 2017). Evidence suggests that contact with nature contributes to each of these states or conditions in learners.

Nature has rejuvenating effects on attention. The rejuvenating effect of nature on mentally fatigued adults (e.g., Hartig et al., 1991; Kuo, 2001) and children has been demonstrated in a large body of studies, including field experiments (Faber Taylor & Kuo, 2009) and large-scale longitudinal studies (Dadvand et al., 2015). Students randomly assigned to classrooms with views of greenery perform better on concentration tests than those with views of only human-made structures (Li & Sullivan, 2016). Nature's rejuvenating effects on attention have been found in students going on field trips (van den Berg & van den Berg, 2011), Swedish preschoolers (Mårtensson et al., 2009), children in Chicago public housing (Faber Taylor et al., 2002), and 5–18-year-olds with ADHD (e.g., Kuo & Faber Taylor, 2004), using measures of attention ranging from parent and teacher ratings (O'Haire et al., 2013) to neurocognitive tests (Schutte et al., 2015).

Nature relieves stress. The stress-reducing effects of nature have been documented in adults in a large body of controlled experiments (see Kuo, 2015 Supplemental

Material for review) and the available evidence points to a similar effect in children. Nature has been related to lower levels of both self-reported and physiological measures of stress in children (Bell & Dyment, 2008; Chawla, 2015; Wiens et al., 2016). Recently, an experimental study showed that a window view of vegetation from a high school classroom yields systematic decreases in heart rate and self-reported stress, whereas unvegetated views do not (Li & Sullivan, 2016). Further, students learning in a forest setting one day a week showed healthier diurnal rhythms in cortisol in that setting than a comparison group that learned indoors—cortisol rose and then dropped over the course of the school day when lessons were held in the forest but not in the classroom—and these effects could not be attributed to the physical activity associated with learning outdoors (Dettweiler et al., 2017).

Contact with nature boosts self-discipline. In adults, the benefits of viewing scenes of nature on self-discipline have been demonstrated experimentally, using tests of impulse control (Berry et al., 2014; Chow & Lau, 2015). In children, nature contact has been tied to greater self-discipline from inner city Chicago (Faber Taylor et al., 2002) to residential Barcelona (Amoly et al., 2014); in experimental (Sahoo & Senapati, 2014), longitudinal (Ulset et al., 2017), and large-scale cross-sectional studies (Amoly et al., 2014). These benefits have been shown for neurotypical children, as well as for children with ADHD (Sahoo & Senapati, 2014) and learning difficulties (Ho et al., 2017). The types of self-discipline assessed include delay of gratification (Faber Taylor et al., 2002) and parent ratings of hyperactivity (Flouri et al., 2014). The types of "nature" include not just "greenness" but also animals, for example, contact with horses in animal-assisted learning (Ho et al., 2017). Note that impulse control effects are not always statistically significant (e.g., Amoly et al., 2014; Schutte et al., 2015). Nonetheless, in general, impulse control is better during or after children's contact with nature.

Student motivation, enjoyment, and engagement are better in natural settings, perhaps because of nature's reliably positive effects on mood (e.g., Takayama et al., 2014). In previous reviews (Becker et al., 2017; Blair, 2009) and recent studies (e.g., Alon & Tal, 2015; Lekies et al., 2015; Skinner & Chi, 2014), students and teachers report strikingly high levels of student engagement and motivation, not only for student-selected activities in nature but also for school-mandated ones. Importantly, learning in and around nature is associated with intrinsic motivation (Fägerstam & Blom, 2012; Hobbs, 2015), which, unlike extrinsic motivation, is crucial for student engagement and longevity of interest in learning. The positive effects of learning in nature seem to ripple outward to learners' engagement in subsequent, indoor lessons (Kuo et al., 2018a, see Ming, Browning & Penner: Refueling Students in Flight: Lessons in Nature May Boost Subsequent Classroom Engagement in this volume); ratings of course curriculum, materials, and resources (Benfield et al., 2015); interest in school in general (Becker et al., 2017; Blair, 2009); and lower levels of chronic absenteeism (MacNaughton et al., 2017). Encouragingly, learning in nature may improve motivation most in those students who are least motivated in traditional classrooms (Dettweiler et al., 2015).

Time outdoors is tied to higher levels of physical activity and fitness. While the evidence tying green space to physical activity is extremely mixed (see Lachowycz & Jones, 2011 for review), children's time outdoors is consistently tied to both higher levels of physical activity and physical fitness: the more time children spend outdoors, the greater their physical activity, the lesser their sedentary behavior, and the better their cardiorespiratory fitness (Gray et al., 2015). Importantly, cardiorespiratory fitness is the component of physical fitness most clearly tied to academic performance (Santana et al., 2017). Further, there is some indication greener school grounds can counter children's trend toward decreasing physical activity as they approach adolescence: in one study, girls with access to more green space and woodlands, and boys with access to ball fields, were more likely to remain physically active as they got older (Pagels et al., 2014). This pattern is echoed in later life: in older adults, physical activity declines with age—but among those living in greener neighborhoods the decline is smaller (Dalton et al., 2016).

3   Nature May Boost Learning by Providing a More Supportive Context for Learning

In addition to its effects on learners, natural settings and features may work to provide a more supportive context for learning in at least three ways. Greener environments may foster learning because they are calmer and quieter, because they foster warmer relationships, and because the combination of "loose parts" and relative autonomy elicits particularly beneficial forms of play.

Vegetated settings tend to provide calmer, quieter, safer contexts for learning. Both formal and informal learning are associated with a greater sense of calmness or peace when conducted in greener settings (Chawla et al., 2014; Maynard et al., 2013; Nedovic & Morrissey, 2013). Problematic and disruptive behaviors such as talking out of turn or pushing among children are less frequent in natural settings than in the classroom (Bassette & Taber-Doughty, 2013; Chawla et al., 2014; Nedovic & Morrissey, 2013; O'Haire et al., 2013). Further, in greener learning environments, students who previously experienced social difficulties in traditional classrooms are better able to remove themselves from conflicts and demonstrate better self-control (Maynard et al., 2013; Ruiz-Gallardo et al., 2013; Swank et al., 2017). The social environment of the classroom has long been recognized as important for learning (Rutter, 2000). Calmer environments have been tied to greater student engagement and academic success (McCormick et al, 2015; Wessler, 2003).

Natural settings seem to foster warmer, more cooperative relations. Images of nature have prosocial effects in adults (e.g., Weinstein et al., 2009), and greener settings are tied to the development of meaningful and trusting friendships between peers (Chawla et al., 2014; Warber et al., 2015; White, 2012). Maynard and colleagues (2013) theorize that natural settings provide a less restrictive context for learning than the traditional classroom, giving children more freedom to engage with one another and form ties. Indeed, learning in greener settings has been consistently tied to the bridging of both socio-cultural differences and interpersonal barriers (e.g. personality conflicts) that can interfere with group functioning in the classroom (Cooley et al., 2014; Warber et al., 2015; White, 2012). Finally, learning in nature facilitates cooperation and comfort between students and teachers, perhaps by providing a more level playing-field wherein the teacher is seen as a partner in learning (Scott & Colquhoun, 2013). More cooperative learning environments promote student engagement and academic performance (McCormick et al., 2015; Patrick et al., 2007).

Natural settings may afford "loose parts," autonomy, and distinctly beneficial forms of play. In his "theory of loose parts," Nicholson (1972) posited that the "stuff" of nature—sticks, stones, bugs, dirt, water—could promote child development by encouraging creative, self-directed play. Indeed, teachers' and principals' observations suggest children's play becomes strikingly more creative, physically active, and more social, in the presence of loose parts (e.g., Bundy et al., 2008, 2009). Interestingly, it appears that nature, loose parts, and autonomy can each independently contribute to outcomes (see Bundy et al., 2009; Niemiec & Ryan, 2009; Studente et al., 2016, respectively), raising the possibility of synergy among these factors. Although the effects of loose parts play on child development have yet to be quantitatively demonstrated (Gibson et al., 2017), the potential contributions of more creative, more social, more physically active play to cognitive, social and physical development seem clear.

4 Outcomes for Learning and Development

In school settings, **incorporating nature in instruction improves academic achievement over traditional instruction**. In a randomized controlled trial of school garden-based instruction involving over 3,000 students, students receiving garden-based instruction gained more knowledge than waitlist control peers taking traditional classes; moreover, the more garden-based instruction students received, the larger the gains (Wells et al., 2015). Further, among the over 200 other tests of nature-based instruction's academic outcomes, the vast majority of findings are positive (for reviews, see Becker et al., 2017; Williams & Dixon, 2013)—and here, too, the most impressive findings come from studies employing the largest doses of nature-based instruction (e.g., Ernst & Stanek, 2006). Findings have been consistently positive across diverse student populations, academic subjects, instructors and instructional approaches, educational settings, and research designs.

Interestingly, both the pedagogy and setting of nature-based instruction may contribute to its effects. Hands-on, student-centered, activity- and discussion-based instruction are often, although not necessarily, used in nature-based instruction— and each of these pedagogical approaches has been found to outperform traditional instruction even when conducted indoors (Freeman et al., 2014; Granger et al., 2012;

Kontra et al., 2015). And simply conducting traditional instruction in a more natural setting may boost outcomes. In multiple studies, the greener a school's surroundings, the better its standardized test performance—even after accounting for poverty and other factors (e.g., Sivarajah et al., 2018) and classrooms with green views yield similar findings (Benfield et al., 2015, although c.f. Doxey et al., 2009). The frequency of positive findings on nature-based instruction likely reflects the combination of a better pedagogy and a better educational setting.

Inside and outside the context of formal instruction, experiences of nature seem to contribute to additional outcomes. First, not only do experiences of nature enhance academic learning, but they seem to **foster personal development**—the acquisition of intrapersonal and interpersonal assets such as perseverance, critical thinking, leadership, and communication skills. While quantitative research on these outcomes is rare, the qualitative work is voluminous, striking, and near-unanimous (for reviews, see Becker et al., 2017; Cason & Gillis, 1994; Williams & Dixon, 2013). Teachers, parents, and students consistently report that wilderness and other nature experiences boost self-confidence, critical thinking, and problem-solving (e.g., Kochanowski & Carr, 2014; Troung et al., 2016) as well as leadership and communication skills such as making important decisions, listening to others, and voicing opinions in a group (e.g., Cooley et al., 2014; Jostad et al., 2012). Students emerge more resilient, with a greater capacity to meet challenges and thrive in adverse situations (Beightol et al., 2012; Cooley et al., 2014; Harun & Salamuddin, 2014; Richmond et al., 2017; Warber et al., 2015). Interestingly, greener everyday settings may also boost positive coping (Kuo, 2001) and buffer children from the impacts of stressful life events (Wells & Evans, 2003).

And second, **spending time in nature appears to grow environmental stewards.** Adults who care strongly for nature commonly attribute their caring to time, and particularly play, in nature as children—and a diverse body of studies backs them up (for review, see Chawla & Derr, 2012). Interestingly, the key ingredient in childhood nature experiences that leads to adult stewardship behavior does not seem to be conservation knowledge. Although knowledge of how and why to conserve, which could presumably be taught in a classroom setting, has typically been assumed to drive stewardship behavior, it is relatively unimportant in predicting conservation behavior (Otto & Pensini, 2017). By contrast, an emotional connection to nature, which may be more difficult to acquire in a classroom, is a powerful predictor of children's conservation behavior, explaining 69% of the variance (Otto & Pensini, 2017). Indeed, pro-environmental attitudes may foster the acquisition of environmental knowledge (Fremery & Bogner, 2014) rather than vice versa. As spending time in nature fosters an emotional connection to nature, and, in turn, conservation attitudes and behavior, direct contact with nature may be the most effective way to grow environmental stewards (Lekies et al., 2015).

5 Conclusions and Implications

Do experiences with nature really promote learning? A scientist sampling some of the studies in this area might well be dismayed initially—as we were—at the frequency of weak research designs and overly optimistic claims. But a thorough review reveals an evidence base stronger, deeper, and broader than this first impression might suggest: weak research designs are supplemented with strong ones; striking findings are replicated in multiple contexts; the research on nature and learning now includes evidence of mechanisms; and findings from entirely outside the study of nature and learning point to the same conclusions.

Robust phenomena are often robust because they are multiply determined. The eight likely pathways between exposure to nature and learning identified here may account for the consistency of the nature-learning connection. Certainly it seems likely that increasing a student's ability to concentrate, interest in the material, and self-discipline simultaneously would enhance their learning more than any of these effects alone. Moreover, in a group setting, effects on individual learners improve the learning context; when Danika fidgets less, her seatmates Jamal and JiaYing experience fewer disruptions and concentrate better; when Danika, Jamal, and JiaYing are less disruptive, the whole class learns better. These synergies—within and between students—may help explain how relatively small differences in schoolyard green cover predict significant differences in end-of-year academic achievement performance (e.g. Kuo et al., 2018b; Matsuoka, 2010).

An important question arose in the course of our review: is nature-based instruction effective for students for whom traditional instruction is ineffective? Although this review was not structured to systematically assess this question, the benefits of nature-based learning for disadvantaged students was a striking leitmotif in our reading. Not only can nature-based learning work better for disadvantaged students (McCree et al., 2018; Sivarajah et al., 2018), but it appears to boost interest in uninterested students (Dettweiler et al., 2015; Truong et al., 2016), improve some grades in low-achieving students (Camasso & Jagannathan, 2018), and reduce disruptive episodes and dropouts among 'at risk' students (Ruiz-Gallardo et al., 2013). Nature-based learning may sometimes even erase race- and income-related gaps (e.g., Taylor et al., 1998). Further, anecdotes abound in which students who ordinarily struggle in the classroom emerge as leaders in natural settings. If nature is 'equigenic'—equality-producing—then documenting this capacity is pressing, particularly in the U.S., where sixth graders in the richest school districts are four grade levels ahead of their counterparts in the poorest districts (Reardon et al., 2017).

Fully assessing and making use of the benefits of nature-based instruction can serve all children. The available evidence suggests that experiences of nature help children acquire some of the skills, attitudes, and behaviors most needed in the twenty-first century. "Noncognitive factors" such as perseverance, self-efficacy, resilience, social skills, leadership, and communication skills—so important in life beyond school (National Research Council, 2012)—are increasingly recognized by the business community and policy makers as essential in a rapidly changing world. And for generations growing up as the impacts of climate change accelerate, environmental stewardship may be as important as any academic content knowledge.

We conclude it is time to take nature seriously as a resource for learning and development. It is time to bring nature and nature-based pedagogy into formal education—to expand existing, isolated efforts into increasingly mainstream practices. Action research should assess the benefits of school gardens, green schoolyards and green walls in classrooms. Principals and school boards should support, not discourage, teachers' efforts to hold classes outdoors, take regular field trips, and partner with nearby nature centers, farms, and forest preserves. Teachers who have pioneered nature-based instruction should serve as models, helping others address its challenges and take full advantage of its benefits.

Recommended Further Reading

1. Evans, G. W., Otto, S., & Kaiser, F. G. (2018). Childhood Origins of Young Adult Environmental Behavior. *Psychological Science, 29*(5), 679–687. https://doi.org/10.1177/0956797617741894
2. Dettweiler, U., Becker, C., Auestad, B. H., Simon, P., & Kirsch, P. (2017). Stress in school. Some empirical hints on the circadian cortisol rhythm of children in outdoor and indoor classes. *International Journal of Environmental Research and Public Health, 14*, 475. https://doi.org/10.3390/ijerph14050475
3. Kuo, M. (2015). How might contact with nature promote human health? Promising mechanisms and a possible central pathway. Supplemental Material. *Frontiers in Psychology, 6*, 1093. https://doi.org/10.3389/fpsyg.2015.01093

Funding and Acknowledgments This literature review was conducted under the auspices of the Science of Nature-Based Learning Collaborative Research Network (NBLR Network) supported by the National Science Foundation under Grant No. NSF 1,540,919. Any opinions, findings, and conclusions or recommendations are those of the authors and do not necessarily reflect the views of the National Science Foundation.

We thank the members of the NBLR Network for their diverse contributions of expertise, skills, resources and passion for connecting children to nature: Marc Berman, Judy Braus, Greg Cajete, Cheryl Charles, Louise Chawla, Scott Chazdon, Angie Chen, Avery Cleary, Nilda Cosco, Andrea Faber Taylor, Megan Gunnar, Erin Hashimoto-Martell, Peter Kahn, Ming Kuo, Sarah Milligan Toffler, Robin Moore, Scott Sampson, David Sobel, David Strayer, Jason Watson, Sheila Williams Ridge, Dilafruz Williams, and Tamra Willis.

Author Contributions All three authors co-wrote and edited the manuscript. MK provided leadership for decisions of content, framing, and style and led the creation of Fig. 1 and Table 1. MB created the SoNBL literature database on which this review is based. CJ serves as the principal investigator of the Science of Nature-Based Learning Collaborative Research Network project; in addition to initiating this project and substantially shaping the Figure and Table, she solicited feedback from Network members.

References

Alon, N. L., & Tal, T. (2015). Student self-reported learning outcomes of field trips: The pedagogical impact. *International Journal of Science Education, 37*(8), 1279–1298. https://doi.org/10.1080/09500693.2015.1034797

Álvarez-Bueno, C., Pesce, C., Cavero-Redondo, I., Sánchez-López, M., Garrido-Miguel, M., & Martínez-Vizcaíno, V. (2017). Academic achievement and physical activity: A meta-analysis. *Pediatrics*, e20171498. https://doi.org/10.1542/peds.2017-1498

Amoly, E., Dadvand, P., Forns, J., López-Vicente, M., Basagaña, X., Julvez, J., et al. (2014). Green and blue spaces and behavioral development in Barcelona schoolchildren: The BREATHE project. *Environmental Health Perspectives, 122*(12), 1351–1358. https://doi.org/10.1289/ehp.1408215

Bassette, L. A., & Taber-Doughy, T. (2013). The effects of a dog reading visitation program on academic engagement behavior in three elementary students with emotional and behavioral difficulties: A single case design. *Child & Youth Care Forum, 42*(3), 239–256. https://doi.org/10.1007/s10566-013-9197-y

Becker, C., Lauterbach, G., Spengler, S., Dettweiler, U., & Mess, F. (2017). Effects of regular classes in outdoor education settings: A systematic review on students' learning, social and health dimensions. *International Journal of Environmental Research and Public Health, 14*, 485. https://doi.org/10.3390/ijerph14050485

Beightol, J., Jevertson, J., Gray, S., Carter, S., & Gass, M. A. (2012). Adventure education and resilience enhancement: A mixed methods study. *Journal of Experiential Education, 35*(2), 307–325. https://doi.org/10.1177/105382591203500203

Bell, A. C., & Dyment, J. E. (2008). Grounds for health: The intersection of school grounds and health-promoting schools. *Environmental Education Research, 14*(1), 77–90. https://doi.org/10.1080/13504620701843426

Benfield, J. A., Rainbolt, G. N., Bell, P. A., & Donovan, G. H. (2015). Classrooms with nature views: Evidence of different student perceptions and behaviors. *Environment and Behavior, 47*(2), 140–157. https://doi.org/10.1177/0013916513499583

Berry, M. S., Sweeney, M. M., Morath, J., Odum, A. L., & Jordan, K. E. (2014). The nature of impulsivity: Visual exposure to natural environments decreases impulsive decision-making in a delay discounting task. *PLoS ONE, 9*(5), e97915. https://doi.org/10.1371/journal.pone.0097915

Blair, D. (2009). The child in the garden: An evaluative review of the benefits of school gardening. *The Journal of Environmental Education, 40*(2), 15–38. https://doi.org/10.3200/JOEE.40.2.15-38

Bundy, A. C., Luckett, T., Naughton, G. A., Tranter, P. J., Wyver, S. R., Ragen, J., et al. (2008). Playful interaction: Occupational therapy for all children on the school playground. *American Journal of Occupational Therapy, 62*(5), 522–527. https://doi.org/10.5014/ajot.62.5.522

Bundy, A. C., Luckett, T., Tranter, P. J., Naughten, G. A., Wyver, S. R., Ragen, J., et al. (2009). The risk is that there is 'no risk': A simple innovative intervention to increase children's activity levels. *International Journal of Early Years Education, 17*(1), 33–45. https://doi.org/10.1080/09669760802699878

Camassao, M. J., & Jagannathan, R. (2018). Nature thru nature: Creating natural science identities in populations of disadvantaged children through community education partnership. *Journal of Environmental Education, 49*(1), 30–42.

Casey, R., Oppert, J.-M., Weber, C., Charreire, H., Salze, P., Badariotti, D., et al. (2014). Determinants of childhood obesity: What can we learn from built environment studies? *Food Quality and Preference, 31*, 164–172. https://doi.org/10.1016/j.foodqual.2011.06.003

Cason, D., & Gillis, H. L. (1994). A meta-analysis of outdoor adventure programming with adolescents. *Journal of Experiential Education, 17*(1), 40–47. https://doi.org/10.1177/105382599401700109

Chawla, L. (2015). Benefits of nature contact for children. *Journal of Planning Literature, 30*(4), 433–452. https://doi.org/10.1177/0885412215595441

Chawla, L., & Derr, V. (2012). The development of conservation behaviors in childhood and youth. In S. D. Clayton (Ed.), *The Oxford handbook of environmental and conservation psychology* (pp. 527–555). Oxford University Press.

Chawla, L., Keena, K., Pevec, I., & Stanley, E. (2014). Green schoolyards as havens from stress and resources for resilience in childhood and adolescence. *Health & Place, 28*, 1–13. https://doi.org/10.1016/j.healthplace.2014.03.001

Chow, J. T., & Lau, S. (2015). Nature gives us strength: Exposure to nature counteracts ego-depletion. *Journal of Social Psychology, 155*, 70–85. https://doi.org/10.1080/00224545.2014.972310

Cooley, S. J., Holland, M. J. G., Cumming, J., Novakovic, E. G., & Burns, V. E. (2014). Introducing the use of a semi-structured video diary room to investigate students' learning experiences during an outdoor adventure education groupwork skills course. *Higher Education, 67*, 105–121. https://doi.org/10.1007/s10734-013-9645-5

Dadvand, P., Niewenhuijsen, M. J., Esnaola, M., Forns, J., Basagaña, X., Alvarez-Pedrero, M., et al. (2015). Green spaces and cognitive development in primary schoolchildren. *Proceedings of the National Academy of Sciences, 112*(26), 7937–7942. https://doi.org/10.1073/pnas.1503402112

Dalton, A. M., Wareham, N., Griffin, S., & Jones, A. P. (2016). Neighbourhood greenspace is associated with a slower decline in physical activity in older adults: A prospective cohort study. *SSM Population Health, 2*, 683–691. https://doi.org/10.1016/j.ssmph.2016.09.006

Dettweiler, U., Becker, C., Auestad, B.H., Simon, P., & Kirsch, P. (2017). Stress in school. Some empirical hints on the circadian cortisol rhythm of children in outdoor and indoor classes. *International Journal of Environmental Research and Public Health, 14*, 475. https://doi.org/10.3390/ijerph14050475

Dettweiler, U., Ünlü, A., Lauterbach, G., Becker, C. & Gschrey, B. (2015). Investigating the motivational behavior of pupils during outdoor science teaching within self-determination theory. *Frontiers in Psychology, 6*(125). https://doi.org/10.3389/fpsyg.2015.00125

Doxey, J., Waliczek, T. M., & Zajicek, J. M. (2009). The impact of interior plants in university classrooms on student course performance and on student perceptions of the course and instructor. *Horticultural Science, 44*(2), 384–391.

Duckworth, A. L., & Seligman, M. E. P. (2005). Self-discipline outdoes IQ in predicting academic performance of adolescents. *Psychological Science, 16*(2), 939–944. https://www.sas.upenn.edu/~duckwort/images/PsychologicalScienceDec2005.pdf.

Ernst, J., & Stanek, D. (2006). The Prairie science class: A model for re-visioning environmental education within the National Wildlife Refuge System. *Human Dimensions of Wildlife, 11*, 255–265. http://www.tandfonline.com/loi/uhdw20.

Faber Taylor, A., Kuo, F., & Sullivan, W. (2002). Views of nature and self-discipline: Evidence from inner city children. *Journal of Environmental Psychology, 22*, 49–63. https://doi.org/10.1006/jevp.2001.0241

Faber Taylor, A., & Kuo, F. E. (2009). Children with attention deficits concentrate better after walk in the park. *Journal of Attention Disorders, 12*(5), 402–409. https://doi.org/10.1177/1087054708323000

Fägerstam, E., & Blom, J. (2012). Learning biology and mathematics outdoors: Effects and attitudes in a Swedish high school context. *Journal of Adventure Education & Outdoor Learning, 13*, 1–20. https://doi.org/10.1080/14729679.2011.647432

Flouri, E., Midouhas, E., & Joshi, H. (2014). The role of urban neighbourhood green space in children's emotional and behavioural resilience. *Journal of Environmental Psychology, 40*, 179–186. https://doi.org/10.1016/j.jenvp.2014.06.007

Freeman, S., Eddy, S. L., McDonough, M., Smith, M. K., Okoroafor, N., Jordt, H., et al. (2014). Active learning increases student performance in science, engineering, and mathematics. *PNAS, 111*(23), 8410–8415. https://doi.org/10.1073/pnas.1319030111

Fremery, C., & Bogner, F. X. (2014). Cognitive learning in authentic environments in relation to green attitude preferences. *Studies in Educational Evaluation, 44*, 9–15. https://doi.org/10.1016/j.stueduc.2014.11.002

Gibson, J. L., Cornell, M., & Gill, T. (2017). A systematic review of research into the impact of loose parts play on children's cognitive, social and emotional development. *School Mental Health, 9*(4), 295–309. https://doi.org/10.1007/s12310-017-9220-9

Granger, E. M., Bevis, T. H., Saka, Y., Southerland, S. A., Sampson, V., & Tate, R. L. (2012). The efficacy of student-centered instruction in supporting science learning. *Science, 338*, 105–108. https://doi.org/10.1126/science.1223709

Grannis, J. C. (1992). Students' stress, distress, and achievement in an urban intermediate school. *The Journal of Early Adolescence, 12*(1), 4–27. https://doi.org/10.1177/0272431692012001001

Gray, C., Gibbons, R., Larouche, R., Sandseter, E. B., Bienenstock, A., Brussoni, M., et al. (2015). What is the relationship between outdoor time and physical activity, sedentary behaviour, and physical fitness in children? A systematic review. *International Journal of Environmental Research in Public Health, 12*(6), 6455–6474. https://doi.org/10.3390/ijerph120606455

Hartig, T., Mang, M., & Evans, G. W. (1991). Restorative effects of natural environmental experiences. *Environment and Behavior, 23*(1), 3–26. https://doi.org/10.1177/001391659123 1001

Harun, M. T., & Salamuddin, N. (2014). Promoting social skills through outdoor education and assessing its effects. *Asian Social Science, 10*(5), 71–78. https://doi.org/10.5539/ass.v10n5p71

Hill, A. B. (1965). The environment and disease: Association or causation? *Proceedings of the Royal Society of Medicine, 58*, 295–300. https://journals.sagepub.com/doi/pdf/, https://doi.org/10.1177/003591576505800503.

Ho, N. F., Zhou, J., Fung, D. S. S., Kua, P. H. J., & Huang, Y. X. (2017). Equine-assisted learning in youths at-risk for school or social failure. *Cogent Education, 4*(1), https://doi.org/10.1080/233 1186X.2017.1334430

Hobbs, L. K. (2015). Play-based science learning activities: Engaging adults and children with informal science learning for preschoolers. *Science Communication, 37*(3), 405–414. https://doi.org/10.1177/1075547015574017

Jang, H., Reeve, J., & Deci, E. L. (2010). Engaging students in learning activities: It's not autonomy support or structure, but autonomy support and structure. *Journal of Educational Psychology, 102*, 588–600. https://doi.org/10.1037/a0019682

Jostad, J., Paisley, K., & Gookin, J. (2012). Wilderness-based semester learning: Understanding the NOLS experience. *Journal of Outdoor Recreation, Education, and Leadership, 4*, 16–26.

Kochanowski, L., & Carr, V. (2014). Nature playscapes as contexts for fostering self-determination. *Children, Youth and Environments, 24*(2), 146–167.

Kontra, C., Lyons, D. J., Fischer, S. M., & Beilock, S. L. (2015). Physical experience enhances learning. *Psychological Science, 26*(6), 737–749. https://doi.org/10.1177/0956797615569355

Kuo, F. E. (2001). Coping with poverty: Impacts of environment and attention in the inner city. *Environment & Behavior, 33*, 5–34. https://doi.org/10.1177/00139160121972846

Kuo, F. E., & Faber Taylor, A. (2004). A potential natural treatment for attention-deficit/hyperactivity disorder: Evidence from a national study. *American Journal of Public Health, 94*(9), 1580–1586.

Kuo, M. (2015). How might contact with nature promote human health? Promising mechanisms and a possible central pathway Supplemental material. *Supplemental Material. Frontiers in Psychology, 6*, 1093. https://doi.org/10.3389/fpsyg.2015.01093

Kuo, M., Browning, M. H. E. M., & Penner, M. L. (2018a). Do lessons in nature boost subsequent classroom engagement? Refueling students in flight. *Frontiers in Psychology, 8*(2253). https://doi.org/10.3389/fpsyg.2017.02253

Kuo, M., Browning, M. H. E. M., Sachdeva, S., Westphal, L., & Lee, K. (2018b). Might school performance grow on trees? Examining the link between 'greenness' and academic achievement in urban, high-poverty schools. *Frontiers in Psychology, This Issue*, 1669. https://doi.org/10.3389/fpsyg.2s018.016

Lachowitz, K., & Jones, A. P. (2011). Greenspace and obesity: A systematic review of the evidence. *Obesity Reviews, 12*(5), e183–e189. https://doi.org/10.1111/j.1467-789X.2010.00827.x

Lekies, K. S., Lost, G., & Rode, J. (2015). Urban youth's experiences of nature: Implications for outdoor adventure education. *Journal of Outdoor Recreation and Tourism, 9*, 1–10. https://doi.org/10.1016/j.jort.2015.03.002

Leppink, E. W., Odlaug, B. L., Lust, K., Christenson, G., & Grant, J. E. (2016). The young and the stressed: Stress, impulse control, and health in college students. *Journal of Nervous and Mental Disorders, 204*(12), 931–938. https://doi.org/10.1097/NMD.0000000000000586

Li, D., & Sullivan, W. C. (2016). Impact of views to school landscapes on recovery from stress and mental fatigue. *Landscape and Urban Planning, 148*, 149–158. https://doi.org/10.1016/j.landurbplan.2015.12.015

MacNaughton, P., Eitland, E., Kloog, I., Schwartz, J., & Allen, J. (2017). Impact of particulate matter exposure and surrounding 'greenness' on chronic absenteeism in Massachusetts public schools. *International Journal of Environmental Research and Public Health, 14*(2). https://doi.org/10.3390/ijerph14020207.

Mantzicopoulos, P. Y., & Morrison, D. (1995). A comparison of boys and girls with attention problems: Kindergarten through second grade. *American Journal of Orthopsychiatry, 64*(4), 522–533. https://doi.org/10.1037/h0079560

Mårtensson, F., Boldemann, C., Soderstrom, M., Blennow, M., Englund, J.-E., & Grahn, P. (2009). Outdoor environmental assessment of attention promoting settings for preschool children. *Health & Place, 15*(4), 1149–1157. https://doi.org/10.1016/j.healthplace.2009.07.002

Matsuoka, R. H. (2010). Student performance and high school landscapes: Examining the links. *Landscape and Urban Planning, 97*, 273–282. https://doi.org/10.1016/j.landurbplan.2010.06.011

Maynard, T., Waters, J., & Clement, C. (2013). Child-initiated learning, the outdoor environment and the 'underachieving' child. *Early Years, 33*(3), 212–225. https://doi.org/10.1080/09575146.2013.771152

McCormick, M. P., Cappella, E., O'Conner, E. E., & McClowry, S. G. (2015). Social-emotional learning and academic achievement: Using causal methods to explore classroom-level mechanisms. *AERA Open, 1*(3), 1–26. https://doi.org/10.1177/2332858415603959

McCree, M., Cutting, R., & Sherwin, D. (2018). The hare and the tortoise go to forest school: Taking the scenic route to academic attainment via emotional wellbeing outdoors. *Early Child Development and Care, 188*(7), 980–996. https://doi.org/10.1080/03004430.2018.1446430

Mischel, W., Shoda, Y., & Peake, P. (1988). The nature of adolescent competencies predicted by preschool delay of gratification. *Journal of Personality and Social Psychology, 54*, 687–696. https://doi.org/10.1037/0022-3514.54.4.687

National Research Council. (2012). Education for life and work: Developing transferable knowledge and skills in the 21st century. Washington, DC: The National Academies Press. https://doi.org/10.17226/13398.

Nedovic, S., & Morrissey, A. (2013). Calm, active and focused: Children's responses to an organic outdoor learning environment. *Learning Environments Research, 16*(2), 281–295. https://doi.org/10.1007/s10984-013-9127-9

Nicholson, S. (1972). The theory of loose parts, an important principle for design methodology. *Studies in Design Education Craft & Technology, 4*(2). http://jil.lboro.ac.uk/ojs/index.php/SDEC/article/view/1204.

Niemiec, C. P., & Ryan, R. M. (2009). Autonomy, competence, and relatedness in the classroom: Applying self-determination theory to educational practice. *Theory and Research in Education, 7*(2), 133–144. https://doi.org/10.1177/1477878509104318

O'Haire, M. E., Mckenzie, S. J., McCune, S., & Slaughter, V. (2013). Effects of animal-assisted activities with guinea pigs in the primary school classroom. *Anthrozoos, 26*(3), 455–458. https://doi.org/10.2752/175303713X13697429463835

Otto, S., & Pensini, P. (2017). Nature-based environmental education of children: Environmental knowledge and connectedness to nature, together, are related to ecological behaviour. *Global Environmental Change, 47*, 88–94. https://doi.org/10.1016/j.gloenvcha.2017.09.009

Pagels, P., Raustorp, A., Ponce De Leon, A., Mårtensson, F., Kylin, M., & Boldemann, C. (2014). A repeated measurement study investigating the impact of school outdoor environment upon physical activity across ages and seasons in Swedish second, fifth and eighth graders. *BioMed Central Public Health, 14*, 803. https://doi.org/10.1186/1471-2458-14-803

Patrick, H., Ryan, A. M., & Kaplan, A. (2007). Early adolescents' perceptions of the classroom social environment, motivational beliefs, and engagement. *Journal of Educational Psychology, 99*(1), 83–98. https://doi.org/10.1037/0022-0663.99.1.83

Reardon, S. F., Kalogrides, D., & Shores, K. (2017). The Geography of Racial/Ethnic Test Score Gaps (CEPA Working Paper No. 16–10). Retrieved from Stanford Center for Education Policy Analysis: http://cepa.stanford.edu/wp16-10.

Richmond, D., Sibthorp, J., Gookin, J., Annorella, S., & Ferri, S. (2017). Complementing classroom learning through outdoor adventure education: Out-of-school-time experiences that make a difference. *Journal of Adventure Education and Outdoor Learning, 18*(1), 1–17. https://doi.org/10.1080/14729679.2017.1324313

Ridgers, N. D., Knowles, Z. R., & Sayers, J. (2012). Encouraging play in the natural environment: A Child-focused case study of forest school. *Children's Geographies, 10*(1), 49–65.

Rowe, K. J., & Rowe, K. S. (1992). The relationship between inattentiveness in the classroom and reading achievement: Part B: An explanatory study. *Journal of the American Academy of Child & Adolescent Psychiatry, 31*, 357–368. https://doi.org/10.1097/00004583-199203000-00026

Ruiz-Gallardo, J., Verde, A., & Valdes, A. (2013). Garden-based learning: An experience with 'at risk' secondary education students. *The Journal of Environmental Education, 44*(4), 252–270. https://doi.org/10.1080/00958964.2013.786669

Rutter, M. (2000). School effects on pupil progress: Research findings and policy implications. In P. K. Smith & A. D. Pellegrini (Eds.), *Psychology of education: Major themes* (Vol. 1, pp. 3–150). London: Falmer Press. https://doi.org/10.2307/1129857.

Sahoo, S. K., & Senapati, A. (2014). Effect of sensory diet through outdoor play on functional behaviour in children with ADHD. *Indian Journal of Occupational Therapy, 46*(2), 49–54.

Santana, C. C. A., Azevedo, L. B., Cattuzzo, M. T., Hill, J. O., Andrade, L. P., & Prado, W. L. (2017). Physical fitness and academic performance in youth: A systematic review. *Scandinavian Journal of Medicine & Science in Sports, 27*(6), 579–603. https://doi.org/10.1111/sms.12773

Schutte, A. R., Torquati, J. C., & Beattie, H. L. (2015). Impact of urban nature on executive functioning in early and middle childhood. *Environment and Behavior, 49*(1), 3–30. https://doi.org/10.1177/0013916515603095

Scott, G., & Colquhoun, D. (2013). Changing spaces, changing relationships: The positive impact of learning out of doors. *Australian Journal of Outdoor Education, 17*(1), 47–53.

Sivarajah, S., Smith, S. M., & Thomas, S. C. (2018). Tree cover and species composition effects on academic performance of primary school students. *PLoS ONE, 13*(2), e0193254. https://doi.org/10.1371/journal.pone.0193254

Skinner, E. A., & Chi, U. (2014). Intrinsic motivation and engagement as 'active ingredients' in garden-based education: Examining models and measures derived from self-determination theory. *The Journal of Environmental Education, 43*(1), 16–36. https://doi.org/10.1080/00958964.2011.596856

Studente, S., Seppala, N., & Sadowska, N. (2016). Facilitating creative thinking in the classroom: Investigating the effects of plants and the colour green on visual and verbal creativity. *Thinking Skills and Creativity, 19*, 1–8. https://doi.org/10.1016/j.tsc.2015.09.001

Swank, J. M., Cheung, C., Prikhidko, A., & Su, Y.-W. (2017). Nature-based child-centered play therapy and behavioral concerns: A single-case design. *International Journal of Play Therapy, 26*(1), 47–57. https://doi.org/10.1037/pla0000031

Takayama, N., Korpela, K., Lee, J., Morikawa, T., Tsunetsugu, Y., Park, B. J., et al. (2014). Emotional, restorative, and vitalizing effects of forest and urban environments at four sites in Japan. *International Journal of Environmental Research and Public Health, 11*, 7207–7230. https://doi.org/10.3390/ijerph110707207

Taylor, A. F., Wiley, A., Kuo, F. E., & Sullivan, W. C. (1998). Growing up in the inner city: Green spaces as places to grow. *Environment and Behavior, 30*(1), 3–27. https://doi.org/10.1177/0013916598301001

Taylor, G., Jungert, T., Mageau, G. A., Schattke, K., Dedic, H., Rosenfield, S., et al. (2014). A self-determination theory approach to predicting school achievement over time: The unique role of intrinsic motivation. *Contemporary Educational Psychology, 39*, 342–358. https://doi.org/10.1016/j.cedpsych.2014.08.002

Truong, S., Gray, T., & Ward, K. (2016). 'Sowing and growing' life skills through garden-based learning to re-engage disengaged youth. *Learning Landscapes, 10*(1), 361–385.

Ulset, V., Vitaro, F., Brendgren, M., Bekkus, M., & Borge, A. I. H. (2017). Time spent outdoors during preschool: Links with children's cognitive and behavioral development. *Journal of Environmental Psychology, 52*, 69–80. https://doi.org/10.1016/j.jenvp.2017.05.007

van den Berg, A. E., & van den Berg, C. G. (2011). A comparison of children with ADHD in a natural and built setting. *Child Care Health and Development, 37*(3), 430–439. https://doi.org/10.1111/j.1365-2214.2010.01172.x

Warber, S. L., DeHurdy, A. A., Bialko, M. F., Marselle, M. R., & Irvine, K. N. (2015). Addressing 'nature-deficit disorder': A mixed methods pilot study of young adults attending a wilderness camp. *Evidence-Based Complementary and Alternative Medicine*. https://doi.org/10.1155/2015/651827

Weinstein, N., Przybylski, A. K., & Ryan, R. M. (2009). Can nature make us more caring? Effects of immersion in nature on intrinsic aspirations and generosity. *Personality and Social Psychology Bulletin, 35*(10), 1315–1329. https://doi.org/10.1177/0146167209341649

Wells, N. M., & Evans, G. W. (2003). Nearby nature: A buffer of life stress among rural children. *Environment and Behavior, 25*, 311. https://doi.org/10.1177/0013916503035003001

Wells, N. M., Myers, B. M., Todd, L. E., Barale, K., Gaolach, B., Ferenz, G., et al. (2015). The effects of school gardens on children's science knowledge: A randomized controlled trial of low-income elementary schools. *International Journal of Science Education, 37*(17), 2858–2878. https://doi.org/10.1080/09500693.2015.1112048

Wessler, S. L. (2003). Rebuilding classroom relationships—It's hard to learn when you're scared. *Educational Leadership, 61*(1), 40–43.

White, R. (2012). A sociocultural investigation of the efficacy of outdoor education to improve learning engagement. *Emotional and Behavioral Difficulties, 17*(1), 13–23. https://doi.org/10.1080/13632752.2012.652422

Wiens, V., Kyngäs, H., & Pölkki, T. (2016). The meaning of seasonal changes, nature, and animals for adolescent girls' wellbeing in northern Finland. A qualitative descriptive study. *International Journal of Qualitative Studies of Health and Well-being, 11*(1). https://doi.org/10.3402/qhw.v11.30160.

Williams, D. R., & Dixon, P. S. (2013). Impact of garden-based learning on academic outcomes in schools: Synthesis of research between 1990 and 2010. *Review of Educational Research, 83*(2), 211–235. https://doi.org/10.3102/0034654313475824

Ming Kuo is Associate Professor and Founder and Director of the Landscape and Human Health Lab, Department of Natural Resources & Environmental Sciences, University of Illinois at Urbana-Champaign, Urbana, IL, USA. An award-winning, internationally recognized scientist, Dr. Ming Kuo examines the role of 'everyday nature'—nature where people live, learn, work, and play—in human health and optimal functioning. Of the top 30 most read articles in her field, Dr. Kuo is an author on six.

Michael R. Barnes is currently a Postdoctoral Researcher at the University of Minnesota Twin Cities, St. Paul, MN, USA. His work specializes in utilizing interdisciplinary approaches to understand complex socio-ecological systems and sits at the intersection of psychology, sustainability, and design.

Cathy Jordan is Professor of Pediatrics and Director of Leadership & Education for the Institute on the Environment, University of Minnesota, MN, USA. She also serves as the Consulting Director of Research for the Children & Nature Network. In this role, she aims to make research about nature's benefit to children's health, development, and wellbeing accessible, understandable, and usable by practitioners, advocates and the public.

Refueling Students in Flight: Lessons in Nature May Boost Subsequent Classroom Engagement

Ming Kuo, Matthew H. E. M. Browning, and Milbert L. Penner

1 Introduction

When teachers offer lessons in relatively natural settings, students may benefit in a number of important ways. Academically, some evidence suggests students retain more after lessons in nature in biology and math (Fägerstam & Blom, 2012), language arts, social studies, and science more generally (Lieberman & Hoody, 1998) than after similar lessons indoors. Lessons in nature may also offer other benefits associated with exposure to trees, gardens, parks, and wildlife, including physical activity, stress relief, and the rejuvenation of attention (for reviews see Chawla, 2015; Kuo, 2015; see also Ming, Banres & Jordan: Do Experiences with Nature Promote Learning? Converging Evidence of a Cause-And-Effect Relationship and Chawla: Childhood Nature Connection and Constructive Hope in this volume). Furthermore, as anthropogenic climate change becomes an increasingly pressing issue, lessons in nature

M. Kuo (✉)
504 W Vermont Ave, Urbana, IL 61 801, USA
e-mail: fekuo@illinois.edu

M. H. E. M. Browning
Department of Parks, Recreation and Tourism Management, Clemson University, 263 E Lehotsky Hall, Clemson, SC 29634 0735, USA
e-mail: mhb2@clemson.edu

M. L. Penner
9317 E. 57th Place, Denver, CO 80,238, USA

© The Author(s) 2022
R. Jucker and J. von Au (eds.), *High-Quality Outdoor Learning*,
https://doi.org/10.1007/978-3-031-04108-2_4

may help build the next generation of environmental stewards; positive childhood nature experiences appear to play a key role in fostering pro-environmental behavior in adulthood (Monroe, 2003). Perhaps in response to these important potential benefits, many European countries are incorporating lessons in nature in their formal schooling (Bentsen & Jensen, 2012).

In the U.S. by contrast, there has been relatively little embrace of outdoor formal instruction beyond the preschool setting (Ernst & Tornabene, 2012). One reason lessons in nature have not caught on in the U.S. may be a concern on the part of teachers that outdoor lessons will leave students keyed up and unable to concentrate. In the pressure to meet achievement standards, instructors may view even temporary losses in classroom engagement as unacceptable. Classroom engagement—the extent to which students are on-task and paying attention to the material or activity at hand—is a major driver of learning and academic success (Godwin et al., 2016) and is easily disrupted. If lessons in nature do leave students 'keyed up' and unable to focus afterwards, then the benefits of that time might be outweighed by the costs.

Do lessons in nature impair subsequent classroom engagement? Our review of the environmental psychology literature suggests quite the opposite. Although we found no studies directly addressing this question, the indirect evidence suggests that classroom engagement will be enhanced, not impaired, immediately after lessons in nature. Specifically, spending time in relatively natural outdoor settings has a number of positive, immediate aftereffects on individuals, each of which is likely to enhance classroom engagement. Moreover, multiple studies have found that schools with greener, more vegetated surroundings perform better academically—even when socioeconomic factors are accounted for (Browning & Locke, 2020; Kuo et al., 2018, 2020). Here we review the evidence on acute doses of contact with nature and their effects on cognitive functioning, interest in learning, and stress, as well as the literature tying greener schools to greater academic achievement.

The capacity to pay attention is an important resource in student engagement (Pekrun & Linnenbrink-Garcia, 2012). Acute doses of nature, whether through a window view of a tree-lined street or a walk in a park, have positive aftereffects on attention and working memory. Attention restoration theory suggests that natural landscapes are gently engaging, inducing a state of "soft fascination" that allows the mental muscle underlying our ability to deliberately direct attention to rest. Afterwards, our capacity to direct attention is thereby refreshed (Kaplan, 1995; for reviews of empirical work on attention restoration theory, see Ohly et al., 2016; Stevenson et al., 2018). Experimental work has demonstrated these aftereffects for classroom window views of greenery vs. barren schoolyards (Li & Sullivan, 2016), and for walks in both forested (van den Berg et al., 2017) and relatively green urban settings (Faber Taylor et al., 2001) as compared to walks in less green urban settings. Thus, both a lesson in a relatively green spot in a schoolyard and the walks between that spot and the classroom might rejuvenate students' attention, enhancing their ability to concentrate on the next, indoor lesson.

Motivation is another important factor in student engagement (Deci et al., 2011), and nature-based learning has been tied to high levels of engagement and enjoyment in several studies. Although we found no studies examining aftereffects of acute doses of nature, children prefer and enjoy lessons outdoors over lessons indoors (Mygind, 2009; Wistoft, 2013), and there is some indication that outdoor nature-based learning fosters greater interest in school and learning generally (e.g., Ernst & Stanek, 2006). Importantly, these effects may be largest in precisely the students whose motivation in 'normal' classes is most lacking (Dettweiler et al., 2015). Nature-based learning appears to foster students' intrinsic motivation (Bølling et al., 2018; Fägerstam & Blom, 2012; Skinner et al., 2012). Collectively, this body of work suggests nature-based instruction makes learning more interesting and enjoyable. Might the interest and positive affect from a lesson in nature carry over to the next, indoor lesson, resulting in greater classroom engagement?

Stress is likely to be an important, negative, factor in student engagement; high levels of stress consistently predict lower levels of academic achievement (e.g., Grannis, 1992; Leppink et al., 2016). Experimental work in adults with physiological indicators shows that contact with nature offers quick and powerful reductions in stress biomarkers (e.g., Park et al., 2010; for review, see Kuo, 2015; Supplementary Materials), and this effect appears to extend to children as well. Contact with nature has been tied to lower levels of both self-reported and physiological measures of stress in multiple studies with children (Bell & Dyment, 2008; Chawla, 2015; Wiens et al., 2016). Recently an experimental study involving high school students showed that even a mere window view of vegetation from a classroom yields systematic decreases in both heart rate and self-reported stress, whereas a classroom without such views does not (Li & Sullivan, 2016). Further, students learning in a forest setting one day a week showed healthier diurnal rhythms in the stress hormone cortisol in that setting than a comparison group that did not receive outdoor learning—and these effects could not be attributed to the physical activity associated with learning outdoors (Dettweiler et al., 2017).

Not only is contact with nature tied to important factors in classroom engagement, but greener schools and classrooms have been tied to better academic achievement. Multi-year assessments of greenness around Massachusetts public schools found positive correlations between greenness and standardized test scores, even after adjusting for income and other confounding factors, although not for all seasons of the year (Wu et al., 2014). Similarly, standardized test performance of 3rd through 9th graders was higher in District of Columbia public schoolyards with higher levels of tree cover, again after adjusting for income and other factors (Kweon et al., 2017), and high school graduation rates and test scores were better for public high schools across Michigan with classroom and cafeteria views of greenspace (Matsuoka, 2010). More recently, standardized test scores have been tied to schoolyard tree cover in over 300 public schools in Chicago, again controlling for socioeconomic and other factors (Kuo et al., 2018). While these studies do not directly connect nature exposure with increased classroom engagement, they are consistent with this possibility. Indeed, it is difficult to imagine how contact with nature could boost academic achievement while reducing classroom engagement.

Thus, exposure to nature has been tied to both the antecedents and consequences of classroom engagement—the factors contributing to, and outcomes of, greater classroom engagement. Additional converging evidence comes from research in educational psychology not focused specifically on greenness. Generally speaking, time spent out of the classroom and in relatively natural outdoor settings is positive. Studies document (a) the rejuvenating effects of recess (e.g., Jarrett et al., 1998; Pellegrini & Davis, 1993; Pellegrini et al., 1995), (b) the positive impacts of students' physical activity—often in schoolyards—on on-task behavior and executive functioning in the classroom (Kvalø et al., 2017; Mahar, 2011), and (c) the motivational benefits of teacher-led education outside the classroom (EOtC)—in schoolyards, museums, and other cultural institutions (Dettweiler et al., 2015; for review see Becker et al., 2017) and of garden-based learning (Skinner et al., 2012). All these lines of investigation lend indirect support for the hypothesis that lessons in nature might enhance subsequent classroom engagement.

At the same time, it must be acknowledged that the question here differs importantly from those lines of investigation. This study differs from the research on the benefits of recess and physical activity in that the intervention involves formal instruction—teacher-led, formal lessons, delivered as part of a larger curriculum, with all the rules against student socializing and autonomous activity typical of classroom-based lessons. Similarly, unlike most education outside the classroom (EOtC) studies and the study of garden-based learning, this study holds pedagogical approach constant in comparing lessons in nature vs. in the classroom. That is, in most EOtC studies, the instruction outside the classroom is designed to take advantage of the setting; as a consequence, the experimental condition differs from the control in two ways—in setting (outside vs. in the classroom) and in pedagogical approach. In this study, pedagogical approach was held constant across conditions; the lessons inside and outside the classroom differed in setting but not instructional approach.

In sum, although it appears no study has directly examined the aftereffects of lessons in nature on classroom engagement, considerable evidence in both environmental psychology and education research points to time spent in natural outdoor settings as having positive impacts. In this study, we hypothesize that *lessons in nature have positive, immediate aftereffects on classroom engagement*—that is, we expect that when children learn outdoors, their classroom engagement after returning indoors is better than it would have been had they stayed inside the entire time. To test this hypothesis, we compared classroom engagement after a teacher gave her students a lesson in nature vs. after the same teacher gave her students a lesson on the same topic in the classroom (e.g., leaves) in the same week, replicating this comparison across 10 different topics (one topic per week), two classrooms ("classroom a," with its own teacher, students, and room; and "classroom b," with another teacher, set of students, and room), and five different measures of classroom engagement.

2 Methods

2.1 Setting and Instructors

The effects of lessons in nature on subsequent classroom engagement were examined in the context of a 300-student environmental magnet school in the Midwestern United States serving a predominantly disadvantaged population, with 87% qualifying for free or reduced lunch, 82% African American, 7% Hispanic, 5% White, and 6% Multi-racial. Written consent from parents of involved students was obtained prior to the study.

The indoor condition in this study comprised two typical classrooms (Fig. 1; although they are not shown in the photo, both classrooms had windows). The outdoor

Fig. 1 The two classrooms (**a, b**) used for indoor instruction in this study. Written permission for the publication of this figure was obtained from students' parents

condition comprised a small grassy area just outside the school (Fig. 2). This instructional area was adjacent to a stream and woodlands, neither of which were used in the lesson. While the teacher was setting up the outdoor lesson, students occasionally visited the stream bank briefly. The post-treatment (and post-control) observation period was always conducted indoors, in each class' and teacher's regular classroom.

The two teachers in this study were highly experienced and state-certified in elementary education, with Masters in Education degrees and in-service training in outdoor and environmental education. These teachers had teamed together in lesson planning over a period of 5 years prior to this study, facilitating their coordination of lessons during this study.

The students in the classrooms were in third grade. Their age range was 9–10 years old.

Fig. 2 The site of the lessons in nature (**a**) and the route students took between their classroom and the outdoor lessons (**b**). The road in the pictures was used exclusively for pedestrian traffic and (infrequently) for maintenance vehicles

2.2 Design and Procedure

At base, this study involved a mini-experiment replicated 20 times. In each mini-experiment, we examined classroom engagement after a lesson in nature vs. after a matched lesson in the classroom on the same topic, with the same teacher and students. Thus, in week 1 of our study, teacher "a" gave her students both a lesson on, say, leaf identification, outdoors, and another lesson on leaf identification in the classroom, and we compared indoor classroom engagement for that set of students after each of those two lessons. This mini-experiment was repeated across 10 different lesson topics and weeks (one topic per week), in each of the two classrooms.

Figure 3 schematically depicts a mini-experiment—the fundamental unit of comparison in this study. Both the experimental condition (the lesson in nature) and the control condition (the lesson in the classroom) were 40 min long, and the observation period for both conditions was 20 min long. Observation periods took place in the teacher's regular classroom, and included an introductory 5-min presentation by the teacher on math or language arts using a dry erase board, overhead projector, or chalkboard and 15 min of assigned individual student work completed at their desks. Before the observation period there was a water and bathroom break in both conditions.

Figure 4 shows how we replicated our fundamental unit of comparison across different instructional content, times in the school year, students, classrooms, and instructors. Each pair of lessons (one in nature, one in the classroom) was delivered in a single week. For each pair, the two teachers worked together to adapt a different theme from the Project Learning Tree (https://www.plt.org/, accessed 28/07/2021) environmental education lesson guide, with lessons on leaf, tree, and seed identification; organic matter decomposition; lifecycles; and pollution. These two instructors each delivered 10 pairs of lessons over 10 different weeks in the semester from

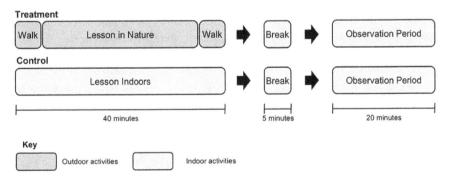

Fig. 3 Schematic diagram of a single mini-experiment. Each mini-experiment included a treatment (lesson in nature and with walks to lesson site before and after) or a control (classroom lesson indoors), followed by a 5-min indoor break and 20-min indoor observation period. Order of conditions was counterbalanced

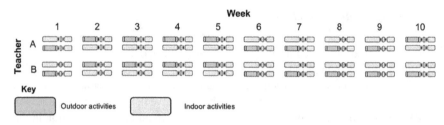

Fig. 4 Schematic diagram of all 20 mini-experiments in this study. Mini-experiments were replicated over 10 different topics and weeks, for each of two classrooms (and each of five measures). Order of conditions was counterbalanced

September–November, under a range of weather conditions.[1] Before the study began, both instructors were open-minded as to what we might find, although one tended to think the positive effects of lessons in nature might outweigh the negative, whereas the other tended to think the opposite—that lessons in nature might leave students "too wired" afterward to engage in classroom material.

Lessons were matched along the following dimensions: teacher, students and class size, topic, teaching style, week of the semester, and time of day. That is, for any given pair of lessons, both the treatment lesson (in nature) and its indoor counterpart were delivered by the same teacher to the same students, on the same topic, in the same week of the semester. Both lessons involved hands-on, experiential learning; lessons that required natural materials from the outdoor instructional site (e.g., different types of leaves) were adapted for classroom instruction by bringing these materials indoors prior to the lesson. While the pairs of lessons were offered in afternoons ($n = 12$) slightly more often than in mornings ($n = 8$), the two conditions did not differ in how often they were taught in the morning vs. the afternoon—an important consideration, given that cognitive performance generally drops over the course of the day (Sievertsen et al., 2016).

We counterbalanced the order in which conditions were delivered each week over the course of the study. It is impossible to offer both a lesson in nature and its matched classroom lesson simultaneously; thus one lesson would have to precede the other and the second lesson would always be an extension of the first. So that neither condition would have an advantage over the other, we encouraged teachers to put the lesson in nature first roughly as often as they put it second. The scheduling of lessons was constrained by the scheduling of other curriculum (e.g., physical education, art, and music) as well as weather. In the end, the lesson in nature came before its classroom counterpart four times and after it six times for each teacher.

It is important to note that there was one consistent difference between the experimental and control lessons other than setting. The 40-min lesson in nature was not purely instructional time; it required the class to walk a few minutes to and from a

---

[1] On one occasion, a planned lesson was not given as scheduled; that lesson was made up in April instead. Analyses with and without the makeup lesson and its paired classroom lesson show the same effects of lessons in nature on subsequent classroom engagement. Findings reported here were based on the full sample.

grassy area (see Setting above) to reach the instructional site—a distance of about 200 m. Thus, the lesson delivered in nature was roughly 30 min long whereas the matched indoor lesson was 40 min long.

2.3 Measures of Classroom Engagement

We developed a battery of four measures to assess classroom engagement: (1) teacher ratings; (2) student ratings; (3) 'redirects'—the number of times instructors had to interrupt instruction to redirect a student's attention to the task at-hand; and (4) independent photo ratings—ratings of classroom engagement by an independent observer based on photographs of the observation period. These four measures were then combined into a Composite Index of Classroom Engagement.

2.3.1 Teacher Ratings

At the end of each 20-min observation period, teachers rated classroom engagement on a -2 to $+2$ scale (from -2 *much worse than usual* to 2 *much better than usual*, with 0 *same as usual*). Classroom engagement was defined for teachers as students listening to instructions, looking at assigned material, and raising their hands for assistance. Teachers were asked to rate the engagement not of individual students, but of the classroom as a whole, during the observation period.

2.3.2 Student Ratings

Students also rated classroom engagement after each 20-min observation period. Unlike the teacher ratings, the student ratings consisted of three components. Each student rated their own engagement, the engagement of the students sitting close to them, and the engagement of the class as a whole on a 5-point scale indicating the period of engagement (from 1 *no time* to 5 *the whole time*).

Of the three types of engagement ratings—self, peer, and whole class—one turned out to be relatively uninformative and was not further analyzed: students consistently rated their own engagement at ceiling—5 out of 5 possible points, with little variance; perhaps as a consequence, this rating correlated relatively weakly with other measures. Students' ratings of the engagement of their seatmates and the class as a whole were somewhat informative in that they were not at ceiling and showed some variance; students' peer and whole class ratings were therefore used as another measure of classroom engagement. For each classroom after a given lesson, students' peer engagement ratings and whole class engagement ratings were averaged to produce a student-based measure of classroom engagement. This measure of classroom engagement demonstrated high internal reliability (Cronbach's alpha

$= 0.869$ for indoor lessons, 0.807 for outdoor lessons[2]); that is, different students rated engagement during a given observation period similarly.

2.3.3 'Redirects'

Each time a teacher needed to stop instruction to redirect or correct student behavior—e.g., "sit down," "you need to be working," or "I will wait"—one 'redirect' was tallied. 'Redirects' reflect the number of instances tallied for a 20-min observation period. Redirects are a concrete and important indicator of how well instruction is going. High levels of redirects indicate students are not attentive to instruction or tasks assigned. Further, redirects themselves are likely to impact learning outcomes by reducing the coherence and flow of lectures and distracting students as they work on assigned tasks.

MP, an investigator on this project and the social worker for the school where this study was conducted, was stationed at the back of the classroom during observation periods to record 'redirects.' Because MP was the school social worker, the instructors and students in this study were familiar with him and comfortable with his presence in the classroom. Pilot testing confirmed that he was able to observe the class from the back of the room without influencing class dynamics. Redirects were tallied "blind to condition"—that is, the observer assessed redirects without knowing whether the preceding lesson had been given indoors or outdoors.

2.3.4 Independent Photo Ratings

While teacher ratings and student ratings each provide a valuable window onto class engagement, both are inevitably subject to observer expectancy effects. That is, both teacher and student ratings of classroom engagement during a given observation period might be influenced by their knowledge of which condition (lesson in nature or lesson in the classroom) preceded that observation period and their expectations for the effects of lessons in nature on classroom engagement. Redirects were blind to condition, but we included a second "blind to condition" measure of classroom engagement, in which an independent observer rated photographs of each observation period without knowing what kind of lesson had preceded it.

Photographs were captured with a wide-angled camera (Nikon P90) positioned on a tripod in front of the classroom and programmed to automatically capture images of the class at even, pre-set time intervals throughout the 20-min observation period. Each observation period was represented by 10 photos; hence the complete collection of photos rated by our independent observer consisted of 400 photos, with each set of 10 photos corresponding to one of the 40 observation periods in this study (one observation period per week after the lesson in nature, another observation period

---

[2] Cronbach's alpha is a measure of scale reliability. It measures how closely related a set of items are as a group. It can take values between 0 and 1, and 0.7 or higher is considered 'acceptable'.

per week after its classroom-based counterpart, for each of two teachers, for a total of 10 weeks).

Our independent observer—an undergraduate student at the University of Illinois at Urbana-Champaign—began by acquainting herself with the entire collection of 400 photos, without knowing which observation periods belonged to which condition. This allowed her to calibrate her ratings of classroom engagement relative to both the typical levels of engagement seen in the observation periods as well as the extremes. She then rated classroom engagement for each observation period on the same −2 to +2 scale as the teachers (from −2 *much worse than usual* to 2 *much better than usual*, with 0 *same as usual*). The rater assessed classroom engagement blind to condition; that is, she made her ratings without knowing where the preceding lesson had taken place (in nature vs. the classroom).

2.3.5 Constructing a Composite Index of Classroom Engagement (CICE)

Each of the component measures in our battery is valuable in its own right. Teacher ratings and student ratings offer important lenses on classroom engagement. Redirects, as counted by an independent observer, provide external validation for teacher and student-ratings as well as a concrete measure of classroom engagement. Both redirects and the independent photo ratings provide measures of classroom engagement uncontaminated by knowledge of condition. Table 1 illustrates how each of

Table 1 Measures and criteria for assessing classroom engagement

Measure	CRITERIA FOR ASSESSING CLASSROOM ENGAGEMENT			
	Incorporates teacher perceptions	Incorporates student perceptions	Provides external validation	Is blind to condition
Teacher ratings	Yes	–	–	–
Student ratings	–	Yes	–	–
Redirects	–	–	Yes	Yes
Independent photo ratings	–	–	–	Yes
Composite index of classroom engagement	Yes	Yes	Yes	Moderately[a]

[a] *Two of four components of Index are blind to condition.*

the measures in our battery address different methodological criteria for assessing classroom engagement. Together, the measures in this battery provide a multifaceted assessment of classroom engagement, with the limitations of each measure countered by the strengths of another.

To create a single, summary measure that draws on each of these different methodological strengths, we combined the component measures into a single Composite Index of Classroom Engagement (CICE)—the average of teacher ratings, student ratings, independent photo ratings, and redirects. Because these measures are on different scales (e.g., from −2 to +2 for teacher and photo-based ratings, from 0 to 100 for student ratings), data from each measure were standardized before averaging. Thus, for example, a teacher's rating of classroom engagement for a given observation period would be expressed in terms of how that period's rating differed from the mean rating for that teacher across all observation periods, in units of standard deviations. Redirects were reverse-coded (multiplied by −1.0) so that higher values would correspond to better classroom engagement, in line with the other components of the Composite Index.

3 Results

3.1 Descriptive Statistics and Bivariate Correlations

Descriptive statistics and bivariate correlations across all observation periods (that is, regardless of whether they occurred after an indoor or outdoor lesson) are presented in Tables 2 and 3. Teacher ratings of class engagement tended toward the positive, with average ratings falling between 0 *usual* and 1 *better than usual*. Student ratings of class engagement were quite positive, averaging roughly 80% on a 0–100% scale,

Table 2   Means of classroom engagement measures by classroom

	Range	Classroom A		Classroom B	
		M	SD	M	SD
Teacher ratings (−2–+2)	−2–2	0.70	1.34	0.55	1.23
Student ratings (0–100)	62–93	81.29	8.09	79.00	7.55
Redirects (tallied)	0–8	3.70	2.62	5.10	1.86
Independent photo ratings (−2–+2)	−2–2	0.35	1.42	0.65	0.99
Composite index of classroom engagement	−1.60–1.17	0.00	0.81	0.00	0.77

Table 3 Bivariate correlations between measures of classroom engagement across 40 observation periods

	1	2	3	4	5
Teacher ratings (1)	–	0.48**	0.54**	0.87**	0.92**
Student ratings (2)		–	0.25	0.32*	0.63**
Redirect (3)			–	0.51**	0.70**
Independent photo ratings (4)				–	0.86**
Composite index of classroom engagement (5)					–

$p < 0.5$, $p < 0.01$.

with little variance. Redirects occurred with some frequency, averaging 3.7 and 5.1 in the two classrooms, respectively, in the 20-min observation window. And photo-based ratings of class engagement also tended toward the positive, with average ratings falling between 0 *usual* and 1 *better than usual*. As the CICE (Composite Index of Classroom Engagement) is based on the average of standardized scores across the four component measures for each classroom, its means for each classroom were zero by definition. In two-sided t-tests for group differences with an alpha of 0.05, the two classrooms did not significantly differ from each other on any of the measures of classroom engagement; thus data from the two classrooms were combined for further analysis except where otherwise noted.

As Table 3 shows, our measures of classroom engagement were generally highly correlated. The individual components of the CICE show high concurrent validity. Teacher ratings and independent photo-based ratings were particularly highly correlated with both each other ($r = 0.87$) and with our summary measure ($r = 0.92$). Student ratings of classroom engagement were significantly correlated with teacher ratings ($r = 0.48$) and independent photo-based ratings ($r = 0.32$), but not significantly related to the number of redirects in a given observation period.

3.2 Overall Condition Differences in Classroom Engagement

Is classroom engagement higher after a lesson in nature than after a matched lesson in the classroom? Table 4 presents the results of paired, two-tailed t-tests comparing classroom engagement after lessons in nature versus matched classroom lessons across the 10 different topics/weeks and two instructors. Lessons in nature show an advantage in subsequent classroom engagement over classroom lessons for four of the five measures. Teacher ratings of classroom engagement are roughly a standard

Table 4 Classroom engagement is better after lessons in nature than lessons in the classroom by most measures: Findings for each measure of classroom engagement

	Means		Paired differences				Effect size[a]
	Nature	Classroom	Mean	Std. dev.	t-value	df	
Teacher ratings	1.20	0.05	1.15	1.79	2.88**	19	0.74
Student ratings	81.01	79.27	1.74	6.56	1.18	19	0.60
Redirects	3.10	5.70	-2.60	2.62	4.43***	19	0.84[b]
Independent photo ratings	1.10	-0.10	1.20	1.64	3.27**	19	0.77
Composite index	0.40	-0.40	0.80	0.93	3.83***	19	0.81

[a]Common language effect size (McGraw and Wong, 1992) also known as the probability of superiority (Grissom and Kim, 2005) expresses the effect size in percentages. In this table, it reflects the probability that the score for a given classroom engagement measure will be better after a lesson in nature than after a lesson in a classroom. Controlling for differences between classrooms in classroom engagement, the likelihood that a class will score higher on teacher ratings of classroom engagement after a lesson in nature than after a lesson in a classroom is 74%.

[b]For ease of interpretation, all effect sizes reflect the likelihood of better class engagement after a lesson in nature than a matched classroom lesson; because class engagement is better when redirects are fewer, the effect size reported here reflects the likelihood that redirects are fewer after a lesson in nature. **$p < 0.01$, ***$p < 0.001$.

deviation higher, on average, after a lesson in nature than its matched, classroom-based counterpart. Consistent with this, redirects were less frequent after a lesson in nature—in fact, the number of redirects after a lesson in nature was roughly half (54%) that of redirects after a classroom lesson. If we calculate the rate of redirects by dividing the duration of our observation period (20 min) by the number of redirects, the nature condition yielded a redirect rate of roughly one redirect per 6.5 min as compared to a rate of one interruption of instruction every 3.5 min in the classroom condition. The independent, photo-based ratings of classroom engagement echo the teacher ratings. And Composite Index of Classroom Engagement scores are 4/5ths of a standard deviation higher after lessons in nature than after matched control lessons. Effect sizes for all measures except the student ratings are substantial, indicating that the magnitude of the difference between classroom-based lessons and nature-based lessons is not only statistically significant but practically meaningful.

Bayesian statistical analyses yield similar results. The Bayes factor is a ratio of the likelihood of two hypotheses being correct given a set of data. In this case, we compared the likelihood that classroom engagement was better after outdoor lessons than after indoor lessons (H_1) with the likelihood that it was not better (H_0). There was very strong evidence that the Composite Index of Classroom Engagement was better after outdoor lessons than after indoor lessons—so much so that H_1 was 33 times more likely to occur than H_0. In regard to individual measures, redirects showed extreme evidence for H_1 occurring, indicating increased classroom engagement after outdoor lessons ($BF_{01} = 0.009$, error percent $8.07e^{-7}$), while independent photo-based ratings of classroom engagement displayed strong evidence ($BF_{01} = 0.091$, error percent $= 5.12e^{-4}$) and teacher ratings of classroom engagement presented moderate evidence ($BF_{01} = 0.18$, error percent $= 0.002$) for this outdoor lesson advantage. In contrast, student ratings of classroom engagement showed no evidence of nature lessons improving classroom engagement afterward compared with indoor lessons ($BF_{01} = 2.33$, error percent $= 0.014$).

3.3 Condition Differences in Classroom Engagement for Different Classrooms, Weeks, and Measures

Our research design involved 100 paired comparisons between lessons in nature versus their matched, classroom-based counterparts across two different instructors, 10 different topics and weeks, and five different measures of classroom engagement. To give a more fine-grained view of our results, Fig. 5 schematically depicts the results for each of the 100 pairs of comparisons.

Figure 5 thus illustrates the consistency and size of the nature advantage over the entire series of mini-experiments. Of the 100 nature versus classroom comparisons, the majority of comparisons (61) show an advantage for the lesson in nature (i.e., check marks in the Figure), 25 show small or no difference (less than half a standard deviation in either direction, i.e., no symbol in the Figure), and only 14 show an

		Wk1	Wk2	Wk3	Wk4	Wk5	Wk6	Wk7	Wk8	Wk9	Wk10
Classroom a	Teacher ratings	✓✓✓	✓✓✓	✓✓			○○	✓✓			✓✓
	Student ratings	✓✓✓	✓✓	✓✓	○					○○	
	Redirects	✓	✓	✓✓✓	✓✓	✓✓✓	○○	✓✓	○	✓✓✓	✓✓
	Independent ratings	✓✓✓	✓✓✓	✓✓			○○○	✓✓		✓✓	
	Composite index	✓✓✓	✓✓	✓✓		✓	○○	✓✓		✓	✓
Classroom b	Teacher ratings	○○	✓✓✓	✓✓✓	○○	✓	✓	✓✓	✓✓	✓	✓✓✓
	Student ratings	○	✓		○○			✓			
	Redirects	○	✓✓✓		✓✓	✓✓✓		✓✓	✓✓✓	✓✓	✓✓
	Independent ratings	○	✓✓✓	✓✓✓		✓	✓✓	✓✓✓	✓✓✓	✓✓	✓✓✓
	Composite index	○	✓✓	✓✓		✓	✓	✓✓	✓✓	✓✓	✓✓

Fig. 5 Differences in classroom engagement after lessons in nature for different classrooms, weeks, and measures. Condition differences in classroom engagement are depicted with symbols. The color and shape denotes the condition which yielded better classroom engagement, for a particular measure, classroom, and week; when the lesson in nature outperformed its paired classroom lesson, there are checkmark(s); when the lesson in the classroom outperformed its paired nature lesson, there are circle(s). The number of symbols (checkmark or circle) represents the extent to which one condition outperformed the other, with one symbol corresponding to a difference between half a standard deviation and a full standard deviation (>0.5 to 1), two symbols corresponding to a difference between one and two standard deviations (>1 to 2), and three symbols corresponding to a difference of over two standard deviations. When the difference between a lesson in nature vs. the classroom did not exceed half a standard deviation, no symbols are depicted

advantage for the classroom-based lesson (circles in the Figure). Further, the size of the nature advantage is considerable: in 48 comparisons, the lesson in nature yielded classroom engagement scores a full standard deviation larger than its classroom-based counterpart; in 20 of these 48, the nature advantage was more than two standard deviations.

When we compare the results for different measures in Fig. 5, we see that four of the component classroom engagement measures—teacher ratings, redirects, and independent (photo-based) ratings—show more, and larger condition differences (more symbols), suggesting that these measures may be more sensitive to variations in classroom engagement. By contrast, student ratings appear to be a relatively insensitive measure, showing fewer and smaller condition differences than the other measures.

Similarly, visual inspection reveals no obvious trends in the size of the nature advantage over the course of the semester. Consistent with this, a *post-hoc*, two-tailed independent t-test comparing the difference between CICE scores for the first 5 weeks of the semester with CICE scores for the next 5 weeks showed no significant difference, $t_{(18)} = -0.26, p = 0.80$ ($M = 0.86, SD = 1.00$ for the first 5 weeks; $M = 0.74, SD = 0.91$ for the next 5 weeks). Interestingly, although one of the two instructors entered with some skepticism regarding the effects of lessons in nature on subsequent classroom engagement, the nature advantage is visible in both instructors' classes. Paired, two-tailed t-tests for each classroom show a significant effect of condition on classroom engagement for each instructor [$t_{(9)} = 2.27$, $p = 0.049$, for classroom a; $t_{(9)} = 3.07$, $p = 0.01$, for classroom b]. Bayesian statistical analyses confirmed there was no evidence for the first 5 weeks being different than the next 5 weeks ($BF_{01} = 2.41$, error percent $= 2.31e^{-5}$). Also, Bayes factors showed moderate evidence for classroom a ($BF_{01} = 0.20$, error percent $= 3.41e^{-4}$) and 'anecdotal' evidence for classroom b showing an outdoor lesson advantage ($BF_{01} = 0.56$, error percent $= 0.002$).

4 Discussion

What is the effect of lessons in nature on subsequent classroom engagement? Do they leave pupils too keyed up to focus—as some teachers worry—or do they enhance a class' engagement—as indirect evidence has suggested they could? In this study, classroom engagement was significantly better after lessons in nature than after matched, classroom-based lessons. This nature advantage held for four of five measures of classroom engagement: teacher ratings; redirects; independent, photo-based ratings; and our summary index of classroom engagement all showed a substantial advantage for the nature condition; student ratings did not. Further, the nature advantage held across different teachers and held equally over the initial and final 5 weeks of lessons.

The nature advantage was substantial. Common language effect size calculations (McGraw & Wong, 1992) indicate a strong advantage for lessons in nature—the likelihood that Composite Index of Classroom Engagement scores are higher after a lesson outdoors in nature than after a lesson in the classroom, in a class that receives both, is 81%. And the nature advantage is large. Out of 100 paired comparisons, classroom engagement was over a full standard deviation better in the nature condition in 48 pairs; in 20 of those 48, the nature condition bested its classroom counterpart by over two standard deviations. The rate of 'redirects,' or instances where a teacher interrupted the flow of instruction to redirect students' attention, was cut almost in half after a lesson in nature. Normally, these redirects occur roughly once every 3.5 min of instruction; after a lesson in nature, classroom engagement is such that teachers are able to teach for 6.5 min, on average, without interruption.

4.1 Accounting for the Advantage of Lessons in Nature: Alternative Explanations

To what might we attribute the advantage of the lessons in nature here? Any number of factors may affect classroom engagement: different teachers might be more skilled at eliciting student engagement; some topics are more engaging than others; hands-on lessons might be more engaging than lecture-based lessons; one set of students might be more attentive than another; a smaller class might be more engaged than one with more students; one classroom might be exposed to more distractions than another; engagement might peak at the beginning of the school year and flag as the year wears on; and students might find it easier to focus on schoolwork in the morning than the afternoon. If our nature lessons differed from our classroom lessons in any of these respects, those differences could have conceivably accounted for our findings. But because we only compared pairs of lessons *matched* on all those factors—same teacher, same topic, same instructional approach, etc.—none of those factors can account for the findings here.

Nor could positive expectations have entirely driven the nature advantage here. It is true that one of the two teachers expected the lesson in nature might have a positive effect on subsequent classroom engagement. Those positive expectations might have led her to view classroom engagement after the outdoor lesson more positively (which might have boosted teacher ratings of engagement but would not have affected our independent photo-based ratings), or might even, in a variant of the Pygmalion effect, have inspired her to teach more effectively afterwards (which would have boosted both teacher ratings and independent photo-based ratings). At the same time, the other teacher expected the opposite pattern; on the whole, she thought that the lesson in nature might leave students too keyed up to concentrate. If the nature advantage was due entirely to teacher expectations, it is not clear why both teachers showed the nature advantage.

The novelty of outdoor lessons cannot account for the nature advantage, either. If the nature advantage in subsequent classroom engagement were due to the novelty of the setting, we would expect it to decrease over the course of the semester as students habituated to having lessons outdoors. But the nature advantage was relatively stable over the course of the study.

Along similar lines, novelty of topic might theoretically account for differences in classroom engagement; each week in the study corresponded to a new topic, and if the nature lesson on a topic had generally preceded its classroom counterpart, students might have found the nature lesson more stimulating and been more engaged afterwards because of the change in topic and not because of the setting. But the order of indoor and outdoor lessons was counterbalanced such that the lesson in nature came before its classroom counterpart four times and after it six times for each teacher. Indeed, if a change in topic boosts subsequent classroom engagement, we would have expected that to result in a classroom advantage—the opposite of what we found.

In the absence of other viable explanations for the systematic pattern of superior classroom engagement after lessons in nature, it would appear that lessons in nature boost subsequent classroom engagement.

4.2 Accounting for the Advantage of Lessons in Nature: Active Ingredients

If lessons in nature boost subsequent classroom engagement, this raises another question: what *about* those lessons might account for this effect? That is, what is (or are) the active ingredient(s) in a lesson in nature? Previous research suggests a number of possibilities; each of these factors might contribute.

First, the *relatively natural setting* of the outdoor lessons may contribute to subsequent classroom engagement. Exposure to nature has immediate, beneficial aftereffects on both attention and stress, and is likely to enhance motivation as well. Further, contact with nature has also been shown to improve self-discipline and impulse control (e.g., Faber Taylor et al., 2002; van den Berg & van den Berg, 2011)—thus a lesson in nature might conceivably yield a quieter, less disruptive classroom afterwards. Note that the large effect sizes here were obtained even though both classrooms had window views; clearly, just providing visual access to the outdoors is not enough (see Faber Taylor et al., 2001, for findings showing better attention after being outdoors than after time indoors with a view).

Second, the sheer *break from classroom activity* involved in the walks to and from the classroom, and the *change in scenery* involved in the lesson in nature probably contribute to students' subsequent rejuvenation. Again, although this study involved formal instruction, not recess, Pellegrini and Davis (1993) and Pellegrini et al. (1995) found that elementary school children are progressively inattentive as a function of the amount of time since their last break. Another experimental study (Jarrett et al., 1998) found that fourth-graders were more on-task and less fidgety in the classroom on days when they had had recess, with hyperactive children among those who benefited the most. Thus, providing a lesson in nature may provide many of the same benefits normally accrued through recess.

Third, *physical activity* might also play a part: 10-min physical activity breaks during the school day have been shown to boost classroom engagement (Mahar, 2011), and the lesson in nature here included two 5 min (or less) walks between the classroom and the outdoor teaching setting, raising the possibility that the boost in classroom engagement here was due entirely to those walks. But most studies in the physical activity-classroom engagement literature have examined either brief bouts of intense physical activity (e.g., Mahar, 2011), or frequent, longer bouts of moderate physical activity—for example, one study examined the effects of adding roughly 190 min per week of moderate to vigorous physical activity—running, jump rope, hopping on one foot—over the course of 10 months (e.g., Kvalø et al., 2017). The dose of physical activity here was brief, light in intensity, and infrequent (two, 5 min walks per week) possibly too small a dose to improve classroom engagement.

Fourth and finally, another contributing factor may have been *impacts on teachers*. Teachers, just as much as students, might benefit from all these aspects of lessons in nature—perhaps teachers are able to teach in a more engaging way when their capacity to pay attention and interest are refreshed and their stress levels are lowered.

If so, simply giving teachers a break, a walk, and a dose of nature may have contributed to the boosts in classroom engagement seen here.

4.3 Generalizability

The lessons in nature here involved a particular 'dose' (duration, intensity, and frequency) of nature, administered in a particular way, to a particular population of students, by a particular set of teachers. Specifically, the lessons in nature in this study involved a 5-min walk from the classroom out to a grassy outdoor area with some nearby trees (Fig. 2) for a 30-min instructional period, followed by a walk back to the classroom, followed by a 5-min break—the classroom lesson involved no walking, and a 40-min instructional period followed by a 5-min break. Here, we consider reasons why the nature advantage might or might not generalize to other conditions, students, and teachers.

In combination with the study design, the findings here suggest the nature advantage could apply in a variety of conditions. The nature advantage persisted across 10 different topics and weeks in the school year; across different times of day; across two different teachers, including one who was predisposed to expect the opposite; and across two different groups of students, each with their own dynamics.

The levels of vegetation here (Fig. 2) do not seem entirely out of keeping with other schools; schools with grassy areas within walking distance might reasonably expect similar effects to those here. In schools with considerably greener surroundings, lessons in nature might have even larger impacts on classroom engagement; in one of the few studies including a wide variety of levels of nearby nature, the more natural a students' dormitory view, the better their cognitive performance (Tennessen & Cimprich, 1995). But many urban schools might have more barren schoolyards and surroundings—in those schools, we might expect outdoor lessons to have smaller impacts. Note, however, that we might still expect an advantage—some evidence suggests children's attention is better after time outdoors than indoors, even when the outdoor setting lacks vegetations (Kuo & Faber Taylor, 2004).

The students in this study were predominantly low-income, students of color; might lessons in nature boost subsequent classroom engagement in more well-off, predominantly White populations? Previous evidence in more privileged populations suggests they could: for example, greener school surroundings are tied to higher standardized test scores in predominantly White, relatively well-off areas, even after accounting for income (e.g., Matsuoka, 2010; Wu et al., 2014).

The teachers in the study were both highly experienced, had in-service training in outdoor and environmental education, and were open-minded as to what the study might reveal. Their relevant in-service training is likely to have given them more confidence in offering lessons in nature—and, as highly experienced instructors, they may have been more adept at recognizing the need for adjustments and making them. It seems plausible that teachers without such training, and teachers adamantly opposed to lessons in nature, might show smaller effects or even none at all.

4.4   Contributions to the Science of Nature-Based Learning

The findings here fill a gap in the previous literature on the impacts of nature on human functioning. Previous experimental work has shown immediate aftereffects of contact with nature on a variety of factors in classroom engagement—the ability to pay attention, intrinsic interest in learning, impulse control, and stress. Simultaneously, large-scale correlational work has tied greener near-school landscapes with better school-level performance on standardized academic achievement tests—even after controlling for socioeconomic and other factors. These two lines of investigation examine different kinds of functioning, scales of analysis, and units of time. The work here bridges the two lines of investigation, pointing to a potential pathway between the two.

Boosts in classroom engagement might be a steppingstone by which nature's immediate effects on an individual student might ultimately translate into long-term improvements in academic outcomes at the school level. Boosting attention, intrinsic motivation, and discipline in a student while simultaneously reducing their stress seems likely to have synergistic effects on their engagement in the classroom. Similarly, boosting engagement in multiple students in the same class is likely to result in synergies; when many of the students in a class are quieter, more focused and less disruptive, overall classroom engagement is likely to be much fuller and more sustained. These two synergies—between different psychological processes within individual students, and between students within a class—may explain the size of the nature advantage seen here at the classroom level. Furthermore, because classroom engagement is an important contributor to long-term academic achievement (Godwin et al., 2016; Skinner & Belmont, 1993), small but consistent improvements in classroom engagement over the course of a school year might have a surprisingly large cumulative effect on learning. Theoretically, this may help explain how relatively small differences in near-school green cover have been tied to significant differences in end-of-year standardized test performance (e.g., Matsuoka, 2010; Kweon et al., 2017; Sivarajah et al., 2018; Hodson & Sander, 2021; Kuo et al., 2018, 2020).

4.5   Implications for Educational Practice

The findings here provide some support and guidance for including more lessons in nature in formal education. For teachers who have been intrigued by the potential of lessons in nature but have been concerned about negative aftereffects on classroom engagement, the findings here directly address that concern. For environmental educators who have been shunted aside in favor of spending instructional time on drill and practice for standardized achievement tests, the findings here may offer a valuable argument for outdoor environmental lessons. The findings here also offer some encouragement for teachers interested in trying to adopt experiential approaches to education, which are particularly well-suited for lessons in nature.

Such approaches allow students to actively use the outdoors to apply theoretical knowledge 'in the field' and undertake problem-solving and decision-making in real world scenarios. These processes may be more effective at instilling and scaffolding long-term knowledge acquisition than other instructional strategies (Ballantyne & Packer, 2002). Curriculum that could benefit from learning styles beyond auditory and visual are also particularly well-suited for lessons in nature because the diversity of topography and vegetation in natural landscapes also provide unique kinesthetic learning opportunities (Auer, 2008; Fjørtoft & Sageie, 2000).

In students facing challenges associated with poverty, minority status, or both, academic achievement is a pressing concern. In a comparison of rich and poor school districts, sixth graders in the richest school districts were four grade levels ahead of children in the poorest districts (Reardon et al., 2016). In this population, then, the finding of an inexpensive educational practice with a consistent, large, positive effect on classroom engagement raises exciting possibilities.

While we do not know to what situations and populations the effects here will generalize, the consistency and size of the effects suggest that lessons in nature are worth trying in a broad range of settings. It is worth noting that the nature advantage, while consistent, did not occur in every pair of lessons; notably, for one teacher the first classroom lesson outperformed its outdoor counterpart. Thus, we encourage teachers to try at least two or three lessons in nature before assessing their value.

More broadly, the findings here underscore the growing view that classroom engagement is at least as limited and valuable a resource as instructional time. With the advent of No Child Left Behind legislation, the vast majority of U.S. school administrators reduced or completely cut recess time and other breaks during the school day, with the primary motivation of providing more instructional time for standardized test preparation (Robert Wood Johnson Foundation, 2010). Instructional time has been viewed by many administrators as the key, limited resource for improving academic achievement; consequently, the de facto approach to increasing student learning has been to free up instructional time by cutting school activities seen to be unhelpful to standardized test preparation—recess, physical education, art, music, theater, etc. Yet increasing the number of hours in the classroom does not translate to increasing the number of hours of student are attentively learning (Gettinger & Seibert, 2002). Estimates suggest students spend 10–50% of their time at school *unengaged and off-task* (Hollowood et al., 1994). Like pouring tea into an already full teapot, giving teachers more time to deliver standardized test content is of little value if the vessels are unable to receive. Thus, classroom engagement may in fact be the key, limited resource in academic achievement.

5   Conclusion

This study is the first to our knowledge to directly examine the effects of lessons in nature on subsequent classroom engagement. We found higher levels of classroom engagement after lessons in nature than after carefully matched classroom-based counterparts; these differences could not be explained by differences in teacher, instructional approach, class (students, classroom, and class size), time of year, or time of day, nor the order of the indoor and outdoor lessons on a given topic. It would seem that lessons in nature boost subsequent classroom engagement, and boost it a great deal; after a lesson in nature, teachers were able to teach for almost twice as long without having to interrupt instruction to redirect students' attention. This nature advantage persisted across 10 different weeks and lesson topics, and held not only for a teacher with positive expectations for nature-based lessons but also for a teacher who anticipated negative effects of such lessons. The findings here suggest that lessons in nature allow students to simultaneously learn classroom curriculum while rejuvenating their capacity for learning, "refueling them in flight." Because providing children with more contact with nature in the course of the school day is likely to yield a whole host of additional dividends as well, including improved physical and mental health (see Chawla, 2015 for review), the findings here argue for including more lessons in nature in formal education.

Recommended Further Reading

1. Kuo, M., and Jordan, C. (eds.) (2019). *The Natural World as a Resource for Learning and Development: From Schoolyards to Wilderness.* Lausanne: Frontiers. https://doi.org/10.3389/978-2-88963-138-4
2. Children and Nature Network resources for schools: https://www.childrenand nature.org/schools/
3. Miller, N. C., Kumar, S., Pearce, K. L. & Baldock, K. L. (2021). The outcomes of nature-based learning for primary school aged children: a systematic review of quantitative research. *Environmental Education Research*, 1–26. https://doi. org/10.1080/13504622.2021.1921117

Funding and Acknowledgments Funds for undergraduate coders who assisted in photo-based ratings and retrieving articles for this study were provided by a grant from the US Department of Agriculture National Institute of Food and Agriculture to Frances (Ming) Kuo on "Impacts of Schoolyard Nature on Children's Learning," Project ILLU-875–933.

We appreciate the staff at Cold Spring Environmental Studies Magnet School for allowing us to conduct this study with their students on their campus. This study would not have been possible without Ms. Howard's and Mrs. Carder's work in devising, coordinating, and conducting the lessons examined in this study, as well as collecting classroom engagement; we are deeply grateful for their leadership.

Author Contributions MK was involved in study design, the development of measures, data acquisition, data analysis, and manuscript writing. MB was involved in data analysis and manuscript writing. MP was involved in the study design, the development of measures, data acquisition, and data analysis, and commented on the manuscript.

References

Auer, M. R. (2008). Sensory perception, rationalism and outdoor environmental education. *International Research in Geographical and Environmental Education, 17*, 6–12. https://doi.org/10.2167/irgee225.0

Ballantyne, R., & Packer, J. (2002). Nature-based excursions: School students' perceptions of learning in natural environments. *International Research in Geographical and Environmental Education, 11*, 218–236. https://doi.org/10.1080/10382040208667488

Becker, C., Lauterbach, G., Spengler, S., Dettweiler, U., & Mess, F. (2017). Effects of regular classes in outdoor education settings: A systematic review on students' learning, social, and health dimensions. *International Journal of Environmental Research and Public Health, 14*, 485. https://doi.org/10.3390/ijerph14050485

Bell, A., & Dyment, J. E. (2008). Grounds for health: The intersection of green school grounds and health-promoting schools. *Environmental Education Research, 14*, 77–90. https://doi.org/10.1080/13504620701843426

Bentsen, P., & Jensen, F. S. (2012). The nature of udeskole: Outdoor learning theory and practice in Danish schools. *Journal of Adventure Education and Outdoor Leadership, 12*(3), 199–219. https://doi.org/10.1080/14729679.2012.699806.

Bølling, M., Otte, C. R., Elsborg, P., Nielsen, G., & Bentsen, P. (2018). The association between education outside the class-room and students' school motivation: Results from a one-school-year quasi-experiment. *International Journal of Educational Research, 89*(April), 22–35. https://doi.org/10.1016/j.ijer.2018.03.004

Browning, M. & Locke, D. H. (2020). The greenspace-academic performance link varies by remote sensing measure and urbanicity around Maryland Public Schools. *Landscape and Urban Planning, 19*, 103706. https://doi.org/10.1016/j.landurbplan.2019.103706

Chawla, L. (2015). Benefits of nature contact for children. *Journal of Planning Literature, 30*, 433–452. https://doi.org/10.1177/0885412215595441

Deci, E. L., Vallerand, R. J., Pelletier, L. G., & Ryan, R. M. (2011). Motivation and Education: The self-determination perspective. *Educational Psychology, 26*, 325–346. https://doi.org/10.1080/00461520.1991.9653137

Dettweiler, U., Becker, C., Auestad, B. H., Simon, P., & Kirsch, P. (2017). Stress in school. Some empirical hints on the circadian cortisol rhythm of children in outdoor and indoor classes. *International Journal of Environmental Research and Public Health, 14*, 475. https://doi.org/10.3390/ijerph14050475

Dettweiler, U., Ünlü, A., Lauterbach, G., Becker, C., & Gschrey, B. (2015). Investigating the motivational behavior of pupils during outdoor science teaching within self-determination theory. *Frontiers in Psychology, 6*, 125. https://doi.org/10.3389/fpsyg.2015.00125

Ernst, J., & Stanek, D. (2006). The prairie science class: A model for re-visioning environmental education within the national wildlife refuge system. *Human Dimensions of Wildlife, 11*, 255–265. https://doi.org/10.1080/10871200600803010

Ernst, J., & Tornabene, L. (2012). Preservice early childhood educators' perceptions of outdoor settings as learning environments. *Environmental Education Research, 18*, 643–664. https://doi.org/10.1080/13504622.2011.640749

Faber Taylor, A., Kuo, F. E., & Sullivan, W. (2001). Coping with ADD: The surprising connection to green play settings. *Environment and Behavior, 33*, 54–77. https://doi.org/10.1177/00139160121972864

Faber Taylor, A., Kuo, F. E., & Sullivan, W. C. (2002). Views of nature and self-discipline: Evidence from inner city children. *Journal of Environmental Psychology, 22*, 49–63. https://doi.org/10.1006/jevp.2001.0241

Fägerstam, E., & Blom, J. (2012). Learning biology and mathematics outdoors: Effects and attitudes in a Swedish high school context. *Journal of Adventure Education and Outdoor Leadership, 13*, 56–75. https://doi.org/10.1080/14729679.2011.647432

Fjørtoft, I., & Sageie, J. (2000). The natural environment as a playground for children: Landscape description and analyses of a natural playscape. *Landscape and Urban Planning, 48*, 83–97. https://doi.org/10.1016/S0169-2046(00)00045-1

Gettinger, M., & Seibert, J. K. (2002). Best practices in increasing academic learning time. In A. Thomas & J. Grimes (eds.), *Best Practices in School Psychology IV*, 773–787. Bethesda, MD: National Association of School Psychologists.

Godwin, K. E., Almeda, M. V., Seltman, H., Kai, S., Skerbetz, M. D., Baker, R. S., et al. (2016). Off-task behavior in elementary school children. *Learning Instruction, 44*, 128–143. https://doi.org/10.1016/j.learninstruc.2016.04.003

Grannis, J. C. (1992). Students' stress, distress, and achievement in an Urban intermediate school. *Journal of Early Adolescence, 12*, 4–27. https://doi.org/10.1177/0272431692012001001

Hodson, C. B., & Sander, H. A. (2021). Relationships between urban vegetation and academic achievement vary with social and environmental context. *Landscape and Urban Planning, 214*, 104161. https://doi.org/10.1016/j.landurbplan.2021.104161

Hollowood, T. M., Salisbury, C. L., & Rainforth, B. (1994). Use of instructional time in classrooms serving students with and without severe disabilities. *Exceptional Children, 61*, 242–252. https://doi.org/10.1177/001440299506100304

Jarrett, O. S., Maxwell, D. M., Dickerson, C., Hoge, P., Davies, G., & Yetley, A. (1998). The impact of recess on classroom behavior: Group effects and individual differences. *Journal of Education Research, 92*, 121–126. https://doi.org/10.1080/00220679809597584

Kaplan, S. (1995). The restorative benefits of nature: Toward an integrative framework. *Journal of Environmental Psychology, 15*, 169–182. https://doi.org/10.1016/0272-4944(95)90001-2

Kuo, F. E. (2015). How might contact with nature promote human health? Promising mechanisms and a possible central pathway. *Frontiers in Psychology, 6*, 1093. https://doi.org/10.3389/fpsyg.2015.01093

Kuo, F. E., & Faber Taylor, A. (2004). A potential natural treatment for Attention-Deficit/Hyperactivity Disorder: Evidence from a national study. *American Journal of Public Health, 94*, 1580–1586. https://doi.org/10.2105/AJPH.94.9.1580

Kuo, M., Browning, M. H. E. M., Sachdeva, S., Lee, K., & Westphal, L. (2018). Might school performance grow on trees? Examining the link between 'greenness' and academic achievement in urban high-poverty schools. *Frontiers in Psychology, 9*, 1669. https://doi.org/10.3389/fpsyg.2018.01669

Kuo, F., Klein, S. E., Browning, M., & Zaplatosch, J. (2020). Greening for academic achievement: Prioritizing what to plant and where. *Landscape and Urban Planning, 206*, 103962. https://doi.org/10.1016/j.landurbplan.2020.103962

Kvalø, S. E., Bru, E., Brønnick, K., & Dyrstad, S. M. (2017). Does increased physical activity in school affect children's executive function and aerobic fitness? *Scandinavian Journal of Medicine and Science in Sports, 27*, 1833–1841. https://doi.org/10.1111/sms.12856

Kweon, B.-S., Ellis, C. D., Lee, J., & Jacobs, K. (2017). The link between school environments and student academic performance. *Urban Forestry and Urban Greening, 23*, 35–43. https://doi.org/10.1016/j.ufug.2017.02.002

Leppink, E. W., Odlaug, B. L., Lust, K., Christenson, G., & Grant, J. E. (2016). The young and the stressed: Stress, impulse control, and health in college students. *The Journal of Nervous and Mental Disease, 204*, 931–938. https://doi.org/10.1097/NMD.0000000000000586

Li, D., & Sullivan, W. C. (2016). Impact of views to school landscapes on recovery from stress and mental fatigue. *Landscape and Urban Planning, 148*, 149–158. https://doi.org/10.1016/j.landurbplan.2015.12.015

Lieberman, G. A., & Hoody, L. L. (1998). Closing the achievement gap. *Educational Leadership, 58*, 1–16.

Mahar, M. T. (2011). Impact of short bouts of physical activity on attention-to-task in elementary school children. *Preventive Medicine, 52*, S60–S64. https://doi.org/10.1016/j.ypmed.2011.01.026

Matsuoka, R. H. (2010). Student performance and high school landscapes: Examining the links. *Landscape and Urban Planning, 97*, 273–282. https://doi.org/10.1016/j.landurbplan.2010.06.011

McGraw, K. O., & Wong, S. P. (1992). A common language effect size statistic. *Psychological Bulletin, 111*, 361–365. https://doi.org/10.1037/0033-2909.111.2.361

Monroe, M. C. (2003). Two avenues for encouraging conservation behaviors. *Human Ecology Review, 10*, 113–125.

Mygind, E. (2009). A comparison of children's statements about social relations and teaching in the classroom and in the outdoor environment. *Journal of Adventure Education and Outdoor Learning, 9*, 151–169. https://doi.org/10.1080/14729670902860809

Ohly, H., White, M. P., Wheeler, B. W., Bethel, A., Ukomunne, O. C., Nikolaou, V., et al. (2016). Attention restoration theory: A systematic review of the attention restoration potential of exposure to natural environments. *Journal of Toxicology & Environmental Health Part b: Critical Reviews, 19*, 305–343. https://doi.org/10.1080/10937404.2016.1196155

Park, B. J., Tsunetsugu, Y., Kasetani, T., Kagawa, T., & Miyazaki, Y. (2010). The physiological effects of Shinrin-Yoku (taking in the forest atmosphere or forest bathing): Evidence from field experiments in 24 forests across Japan. *Environmental Health and Preventive Medicine, 15*, 18–26. https://doi.org/10.1007/s12199-009-0086-9

Pekrun, R., & Linnenbrink-Garcia, L. (2012). Academic emotions and student engagement. In S. L. Christenson, A. L. Reschly, & C. Wylie (Eds.), *Handbook of research on student engagement* (pp. 259–282). Springer, US.

Pellegrini, A. D., & Davis, P. L. (1993). Relations between children's playground and classroom behaviour. *British Journal of Educational Psychology, 63*, 88–95. https://doi.org/10.1111/j.2044-8279.1993.tb01043.x

Pellegrini, A. D., Huberty, P. D., & Jones, I. (1995). The effects of recess timing on children's playground and classroom behaviors. *American Educational Research Journal, 32*, 845–864. https://doi.org/10.3102/00028312032004845

Reardon, S. F., Kalogrides, D., & Shores, K. (2016). *The Geography of Racial/Ethnic Test Score Gaps (CEPA Working Paper No. 16–10).* Stanford Center for Education Policy Analysis. http://cepa.stanford.edu/wp16-10.

Robert Wood Johnson Foundation. (2010). *The state of play: Gallup survey of principals on school recess.* Robert Wood Johnson Foundation.

Sievertsen, H. H., Gino, F., & Piovesan, M. (2016). Cognitive fatigue influences students' performance on standardized tests. *Proceedings of the National Academy of Sciences of the United States of America, 113*, 2621–2624. https://doi.org/10.1073/pnas.1516947113

Sivarajah, S., Smith, S. M., & Thomas, S. C. (2018). Tree cover and species composition effects on academic performance of primary school students. *PLoS ONE, 13*(2), e0193254-e193311. https://doi.org/10.1371/journal.pone.0193254

Skinner, E. A., & Belmont, M. J. (1993). Motivation in the classroom: Reciprocal effects of teacher behavior and student engagement across the school year. *Journal of Educational Psychology, 85*, 571–581. https://doi.org/10.1037/0022-0663.85.4.571

Skinner, E. A., Chi, U., & The Learning-Gardens Educational Assessment Group. (2012). Intrinsic motivation and engagement as "Active Ingredients" in garden-based education: Examining models and measures derived from self-determination theory. *The Journal of Environmental Education, 43*, 16–36. https://doi.org/10.1080/00958964.2011.596856

Stevenson, M. P., Schilhab, T. S. S., & Bentsen, P. (2018). Attention Restoration Theory II: A systematic review to clarify attention processes affected by exposure to natural environments. *Journal of Toxicology and Environmental Health, Part B, 21*(4), 227–268. https://doi.org/10.1080/10937404.2018.1505074

Tennessen, C. M., & Cimprich, B. (1995). Views to nature: Effects on attention. *Journal of Environmental Psychology, 15*, 77–85. https://doi.org/10.1016/0272-4944(95)90016-0

van den Berg, A. E., & van den Berg, C. G. (2011). A comparison of children with ADHD in a natural and built setting. *Child: Care, Health and Development, 37*, 430–439. https://doi.org/10.1111/j.1365-2214.2010.01172.x

van den Berg, A. E., Wesselius, J. E., Maas, J., & Tanja-Dijkstra, K. (2017). Green walls for a restorative classroom environment: A controlled evaluation study. *Environment and Behavior, 49*, 791–813. https://doi.org/10.1177/0013916516667976

Wiens, V., Kyngäs, H., & Pölkki, T. (2016). The meaning of seasonal changes, nature, and animals for adolescent girls' wellbeing in northern Finland: A qualitative descriptive study. *International Journal of Qualitative Studies on Health and Well-Being, 11*, 30160. https://doi.org/10.3402/qhw.v11.30160

Wistoft, K. (2013). The desire to learn as a kind of love: Gardening, cooking, and passion in outdoor education. *Journal of Adventure Education and Outdoor Learning, 13*, 125–141. https://doi.org/10.1080/14729679.2012.738011

Wu, C.-D., McNeely, E., Cedeño-Laurent, J. G., Pan, W.-C., Adamkiewicz, G., Dominici, F., et al. (2014). Linking student performance in Massachusetts elementary schools with the 'greenness" of school surroundings using remote sensing. *PLoS ONE, 9*, e108548. https://doi.org/10.1371/journal.pone.0108548

Ming Kuo is Associate Professor and Founder and Director of the Landscape and Human Health Lab, Department of Natural Resources & Environmental Sciences, University of Illinois at Urbana-Champaign, Urbana, IL, USA. An award-winning, internationally recognized scientist, Dr. Ming Kuo examines the role of 'everyday nature'—nature where people live, learn, work, and play—in human health and optimal functioning. Of the top 30 most read articles in her field, Dr. Kuo is an author on six.

Matthew H. E. M. Browning is a certified Environmental Educator, an environmental psychologist, and Director of the Virtual Reality & Nature Lab at Clemson University in the United States. His research uses both experimental and epidemiological approaches to study the health and cognitive performance benefits of exposure to natural environments across the lifespan.

Milbert L. Penner MSW, LCSW was a professional school social worker for forty years. His primary focus was on helping create a safe and civil learning environment for children through teaching peacemaking and social-emotional skills. His passion for outdoor education fostered his interest in assessing the connection between nature and learning in the classroom. In retirement he developed the Nature Connection which brings school kids to an outdoor learning environment in rural Nebraska.

Childhood Nature Connection and Constructive Hope

Helping Young People Connect with Nature and Cope with Environmental Loss

Louise Chawla

1   Introduction

This chapter presents an abridged version of the article in *People and Nature* that is referenced in footnote 1. Given the original article's length, this introduction summarizes its opening sections. The original article includes an overview of the topic of nature connection, details about how the paper's literature reviews were conducted, tables that describe different measures of nature connection for children aged 2–17, and fuller versions of the sections covered by this introduction. For a detailed development of these topics, see the original article. Following this summary, this chapter dives into the second half of the paper, which integrates evaluations of programs designed to connect children to nature with studies to understand and address young people's worries and alarm when they recognize the threats that the natural world currently faces from climate chaos and biodiversity loss.

The article in *People and Nature* synthesizes two research literatures. It is the first review of the topic of nature connection in children and adolescents, and it also reviews approaches to help young people cope with difficult emotions as the global environment changes. These have been independent streams of research, each developing without reference to the other. Yet as I delved into both quantitative and

---

This chapter is an abridgement of my 2020 article "Childhood Nature Connection and Constructive Hope: A Review of Research on Connecting with Nature and Coping with Environmental Loss" published in the open access journal *People and Nature*, 2, 619–642, available at http://dx.doi.org/10.1002/pan3.10128 (accessed 16/05/2021). © 2020 Louise Chawla. *People and Nature* published by John Wiley & Sons Ltd on behalf of British Ecological Society. The original article is an open access article under the terms of the Creative Commons Attribution License, which permits use, distribution and reproduction in any medium, provided the original work is properly cited.

Throughout this chapter there are references to this original article for more details and further references.

L. Chawla (✉)
Benthaven Place, Boulder, CO 80305, USA
e-mail: louise.chawla@colorado.edu

R. Jucker and J. von Au (eds.), *High-Quality Outdoor Learning*,
https://doi.org/10.1007/978-3-031-04108-2_5

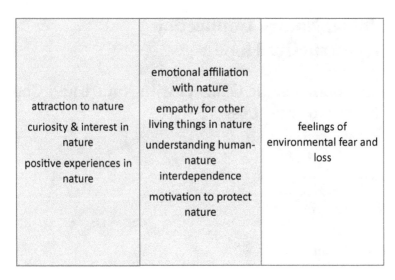

Fig. 1 Indicators of children's connection with nature (blue and green lists), children's awareness and emotions associated with environmental concern (green and yellow lists), and where these experiences overlap (green)

qualitative evaluations of young people's connection to nature, I noticed that many indicators used to define nature connection echo what young people express when they are asked about their environmental concerns and they express fears about the planet's future: feeling part of nature, empathy for other living things, understanding human reliance on nature and our capacity to harm it, and a sense of responsibility to protect the natural world. (See Fig. 1 for indicators of children's connection with nature, children's awareness and feelings associated with environmental concern, and overlapping experiences.)

I found that people studying nature connection in children and adolescents treat the understanding of human reliance on nature and feelings of belonging to nature, responsibility, and empathy for nature as if they are always positive experiences. Like enjoyment, comfort and solace in nature, surveys to assess children's levels of nature connection assume that the more children have these experiences, the better. Yet research on young people's environmental concerns and fears about the future shows that these perspectives may arouse difficult emotions. Therefore this paper explores how people who seek to connect children and teens with nature—teachers, parents, and staff at nature centers and environmental promote connection *and* constructive coping with environmental organizations—may simultaneously risks and losses.

1.1 Understanding Nature Connection in Childhood

When Ives et al. (2017) surveyed peer-reviewed articles on the human connection with nature published from 1984 through 2015, they found a steep increase from the year 2010 onward. This pattern characterizes research with children and teens as well as adults. Ives and his colleagues attributed this rise to surging evidence of health and well-being benefits when humans engage with nature, as well as concern that humans need to feel connected with nature in order to commit to its protection. This concern is related to recognition that connection commonly forms during time in nature, but an "extinction of experience" is currently underway (Pyle, 1978).

Around the world, more and more people are living in urban areas, which are becoming more densely developed, eroding opportunities for people to experience nature and feel kinship with the larger community of life. According to Soga and Gaston (2016), this sets up feedback loops that are troubling for the future of conservation. They note that as people's experience of nature declines, their interest in nature is likely to diminish. This reduces motivation to seek out natural areas. As parents, people are likely to pass their disengagement from nature to their children, and over time this can become a generational shift, with the public understanding and valuing the natural world less and feeling less investment in its protection.

Concerns about declining access to nature and children's loss of freedom outdoors have spurred efforts to define and measure nature connection in childhood, identify key experiences that contribute to its development, evaluate interventions designed to increase connection, and determine how nature connection relates to other aspects of young people's lives, such as wellbeing and care for the environment. This introduction briefly summarizes this work. It looks at nature connection through the lens of both quantitative and qualitative methods and considers evidence that connection with nature matters for children's wellbeing as well as the future of conservation. Consistent with the United Nations definition of childhood as the period from birth through age 17 (UNICEF, 1989), this chapter refers to this span of years as "childhood," populated by "children" and "young people."

1.2 Evaluating Childhood Nature Connection

The longer review for *People and Nature* discussed 10 quantitative measures of nature connection for children and adolescents that were tested for reliability and validity and published in peer-reviewed journals. Together, they cover ages 2 through 19. In developing assessment tools, researchers commonly began by reviewing and adapting measures designed for adults, with the result that characteristics of adult measures have been carried over into assessments with children. Just as there is no single consensus definition of nature connection in research with adults, a variety of definitions and terms have been used in studies with children and adolescents, including connection with nature, nature connectedness, biophilia, and emotional affinity with nature. (See original article, pp. 622–625.)

Like measures of nature connection in adults (Restall & Conrad, 2015; Tam, 2013; Zylstra et al., 2014), assessments of childhood nature connection are multidimensional. They include emotional attraction and affiliation with nature, cognitive understanding of human-nature interdependence and curiosity about natural phenomena, positive experiences in nature such as enjoyment and comfort, and motivation to protect nature. (See Fig. 1.) Enjoyment in being in nature runs across most of the childhood measures (Cheng & Monroe, 2012; Elliot, Ten Eycke, Chan & Müller, 2014; Ernst & Theimer, 2011; Giusti et al., 2014; Müller et al., 2009; Rice & Torquati, 2013; Richardson et al., 2019; Sobko et al., 2018). Some studies treat awareness of human reliance on nature and nature's vulnerability to harm as a dimension of nature connection (Ernst & Theimer, 2011; Giusti et al., 2014; Larson et al., 2011); but general knowledge about nature and environmental issues, as well as proenvironmental behavior, are treated as separate but related variables. Three studies treat empathy for nature as a dimension of connection (Cheng & Monroe, 2012; Giusti et al., 2014; Sobko et al., 2018).

1.3 Variables Associated with Nature Connection

A number of quantitative studies explore how levels of nature connection relate to access to green space, time in nature, age, gender, and family relations. A frequent finding is that young people with more access and experience in nature express higher levels of connection. Low levels of connection, in contrast, relate to more time spent inside and more hours watching television, playing digital games and following social media. The legacy of childhood time in nature reaches into adulthood. Among adults, greater connection with nature is associated with more access and interaction with nature during childhood. (See original article, pp. 624–625.)

In their assessment of biophilia, Rice and Torquati (2013) found that scores for their preschool sample of 2- to 5-year-olds increased with age. Aside from these increasing scores in very young children, a reverse pattern appears: scores for nature connection fall as young people move from early and middle childhood into adolescence. When study samples cover children, adolescents and adults, levels of nature connection are highest among 7- to 12-year-olds, falling to their lowest level in the teen years, and then gradually rising in adulthood (Hughes et al., 2019; Richardson et al., 2019).

Research related to gender differences in childhood nature connection has produced inconsistent results. The majority of studies that consider gender find that females report significantly higher levels of connection than males (see references in original article, p. 625.) Children's levels of connection are higher when parents believe it is important for their children to experience nature outdoors (Ahmetoglu, 2019) and report greater nature connection themselves (Barrable & Booth, 2020a), when children report more pro-environmental values in their family (Cheng &

Monroe, 2012), and when they talk with their parents about nature on a regular basis (Larson et al., 2011).

1.4 Qualitative Descriptions of Children's Developing Connections with Nature

The term "nature connection" rarely appears in observations of children in nature, interviews, and analyses of children's drawings and narratives about their engagement with the natural world. Nevertheless, this interdisciplinary literature that includes the fields of geography, anthropology, psychology and environmental design brings to life what dimensions of connection like enjoyment, care, curiosity, awareness of interdependence, and a sense of oneness mean in actual places. It illuminates the opportunities for action and experience that different types of natural settings afford, and it reveals omissions in quantitative assessments. (See original article, pp. 625–628.)

Descriptions of toddlers and children in nature preschools and kindergartens show their fascination with sensory details of plants, animals, and other elements of nature, as well as their empathy for other living things. These studies also show the social context of children's experience and the importance of a sense of safety: subjects on which quantitative assessments are largely silent. In her book *Children's Environmental Identity Development*, Green (2018) used the term "natural world socialization" for these dimensions of connection, when adults and peers encourage a positive connection with nature by keeping a child safe, while allowing independent exploration and appropriate risk taking, appreciating the child's accomplishments and discoveries, and promoting care for the environment (see also Chawla, 2007, 2021).

Qualitative studies show how other people serve as companions in connecting with nature, from the earliest years of childhood through adolescence. Twentieth century studies of children's use of local territories, based on observations and children's mapping and interviews, show that the middle years from about 6 through 11 were a period when parks, woods, overgrown lots and ditches, and other natural features were favorite places. Children sought out wild and semi-wild places for quiet reverie and for play with friends, constructing fort cultures, and acting out adventure stories across the landscape (Chawla, 1992; Goodenough, 2003; Hart, 1979; Moore, 1986; Sobel, 2002). As noted above, the study of children's connection with nature has been impelled partly by concern that these opportunities for adventure in nature have eroded.

In the teen years, young people value nature as a place for good times with family and friends in parks and other green gathering places, physical challenges, and quiet retreats where they can find calm and relax (Hatala, Njeze, Morton, Pear, & Bird-Naytowhow, 2020; Owens & McKinnon, 2009; Schwab et al., 2020; Ward Thompson, Travlou & Roe, 2006). Kaplan and Kaplan (2002) noted, however, that for many young people the teen years become a "time out" from nature, when they are more strongly drawn to shops and built recreational attractions like athletic fields and sports events. Social relationships and social media take center stage for many (Eames et al., 2018). These findings are consistent with quantitative studies that show a drop in nature connection in adolescence.

Also missing from quantitative assessments, but evident in qualitative research, is the value of mastering challenges in nature and the potential to bond with nature through work as well as recreation. Whether it is a toddler wading into a creek's edge, preschoolers clambering over a log, older children constructing a fort in the woods, or teenagers surfing or rock climbing, opportunities to build a sense of agency and self-confidence are an important part of natural areas' attraction (Chawla, 2021). In rural regions, children and teens often learn to know the land intimately through a combination of work and free exploration, and value it deeply as home (Gold & Gujar, 2007; MacDonald et al., 2015; Nabhan & Trimble, 1994).

1.5 Why Does Connecting with Nature Matter for Children and Nature Conservation?

Large and steadily growing bodies of research show that connecting with nature is associated with multiple benefits for young people's health and development, and that young people who express higher levels of nature connection are more likely to say that they are taking action to protect the natural world. When parents of preschoolers rated their young children's social and emotional health as well as their connection with nature, children who showed awareness and enjoyment of nature, empathy for plants and animals, and responsibility to take care of nature were also more likely to show prosocial behavior and less likely to display hyperactivity/inattention, peer problems, and emotional problems (Sobko et al., 2018). Among 11- to 14-year-olds, higher measures of nature connection were positively associated with higher self-reported levels of competence, connection with other people, confidence, caring behaviors, and character in the sense of living by positive principles and values (Bowers, Larson & Parry, 2021). These youth were also more likely to believe in a hopeful future when they expressed greater connection with nature. A number of studies show that young people in the age range from 7 to 17 are more likely to report good health and wellbeing when their nature connection scores are high. (See original article, pp. 628–629 for references.) Among teenagers, greater connection with nature is associated with more holistic and creative thinking (Leong, Fischer & McClure, 2014).

When young people connect with nature, it is beneficial for the natural world as well as their own development. Children and adolescents with higher levels of nature connection report more pro-environmental behaviors like putting food out for birds and joining a nature club, more conservation behaviors like energy saving and recycling, and more environmental citizenship behaviors like environmental volunteering and talking with others about the importance of environmental protection. They also show greater environmental knowledge and they are more likely to say that they are willing to commit to conserving nature. (See original article, p. 629 for references.)

Figure 2 provides a synthesis of the material in this introduction. Drawing on both quantitative and qualitative research, it summarizes experiences that increase or diminish nature connection, and shows that childhood experiences can influence adulthood. It itemizes benefits of connecting with nature for young people's development, as well as benefits for conservation, as young people with greater connection demonstrate greater environmental knowledge and commitment to protect the natural world.

2 Connecting to Nature in an Age of Global Environmental Change

2.1 Coping with Environmental Fears

Up to this point, this review has associated nature connection with positive experiences like free play and exploration and positive emotions like enjoyment, interest, comfort, calm, and kinship with all living things. Yet as processes of global environmental change accelerate, there is a dark side to feeling kin to creatures that are disappearing. To loving wild places that are lost. To feeling connected to a world whose life systems are unraveling. Since the 1990s, surveys and interviews that ask young people about their hopes and fears for the future reveal high levels of alarm about environmental changes (Barraza, 1999; Hicks & Holden, 2007; Hutchinson, 1997; Ojala, 2016; Strife, 2012). Some young people deny that climate change is happening or de-emphasize the seriousness of environmental problems; but many voice concern (Lawson et al., 2019; Ojala, 2012a). More often than worry about consequences for themselves, children express concern about impacts on animals (Jonsson et al., 2012; Ojala, 2016; Wilson & Snell, 2010). Although this research primarily involves young people in elementary school through high school, even children as young as 5 worry about "the Earth getting too hot" (Davis, 2010). In research with adults, painful feelings like these have been termed "ecological grief" (Cunsolo & Ellis, 2018), and when distress is due to degradation of one's own home landscape, "solastagia" (Galway, Beery, Jones-Casey & Tasala, 2019).

Research on environmental fears has not been assimilated into research on nature connection. Yet worry and fear are arguably expressions of connection. Children who voice these emotions acknowledge their interdependence with the natural world, recognize the shared vulnerability of people and nature, and feel empathy for other living things: all experiences included in assessments of nature connection (Fig. 1). This paper argues that a comprehensive view of connectedness with nature needs

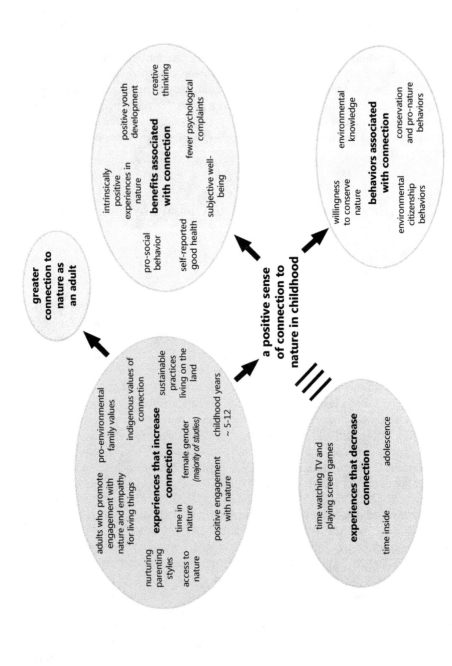

Fig. 2 Contributions to nature connection in childhood and associated benefits and behaviors

to encompass this full range of emotions. Environmental educators recommend that activities with young children should emphasize learning to love nature and feel comfort, interest and enjoyment in nature, leaving disturbing information about environmental problems for later years (Sobel, 1996; Wilson, 2018). Yet in media-soaked societies, as environments rapidly change, it is impossible to control everything that children see and hear. Therefore it is important to understand how young people cope with disturbing environmental information, and how to help them integrate positive and negative experiences.

Worry, sadness, frustration and anger about the environment are difficult emotions to carry. Working with middle school and high school students in Sweden, Ojala (2016) investigated how young people cope with feelings about climate change, biodiversity loss and other complex environmental issues—problems that cannot be solved by individual action alone. She explored how different forms of coping affect young people's willingness to acknowledge threatening information and take action to protect the environment, how their responses affect their emotional wellbeing, and how other people can help them cope in ways that are healthy for themselves and proactive for the environment. She builds on the work of Lazarus and Folkman (1984) and Folkman (2008) in health psychology, who identified three ways of coping with difficult emotions: emotion-focused, which seeks to escape painful feelings; problem-focused, which addresses problems that cause these feelings; and meaning-focused, which finds positive value in confronting problems.

Ojala (2012a) found emotion-focused coping common among young people who say they are highly worried about climate change. Most often, they tried to manage this emotion through distraction—deliberately thinking about something else, doing something else, or avoiding disturbing information. An alternative was to seek support from others like family members or friends; but Ojala (2012a, 2016) found that this was uncommon, perhaps because young people in Sweden consider it "uncool" to reveal their worries. A small group focused on feelings of hopelessness and helplessness, which she saw as a form of avoidance, because in this case they could conclude that action was pointless. Some young people deny that climate change and its consequences exist or believe that it will only affect future generations or distant places (Lawson et al., 2019; Ojala, 2012a, 2012b). All of these strategies are negatively associated with environmental action (Ojala, 2012b, 2012c, 2013; Stevenson & Peterson, 2016; Stevenson et al., 2019).

Young people who report problem-focused strategies express a sense of environmental efficacy and take action for the environment, but many also express low subjective wellbeing (Ojala, 2012b, 2013). Studies in Sweden (Ojala, 2016) and the United States (Stevenson & Peterson, 2016) found that young people almost always report individualized actions in the private sphere, such as household energy conservation, rather than collective engagement. Ojala (2016) noted that an association between individual environmental action and low subjective wellbeing among young people who worry about environmental change is consistent with general research on coping in childhood and adolescence, which shows that when a problem is more than a young person can solve alone, individual strategies can lead to feelings of futility and reduce wellbeing (Clarke, 2006).

A third form of coping is meaning-focused, and it is especially important when a problem cannot be solved quickly but requires active engagement over a long period of time (Folkman, 2008). It involves positive reappraisal, or reframing a problem to find positive meaning in the struggle to address it. For example, Ojala (2012a, 2013) found that some young people reasoned that climate change is an urgent problem, but societies know more about it now and people with influence are taking it seriously, like scientists, politicians and environmental activists. When young people use a high degree of meaning-focused coping, they are more likely to express positive feelings and life satisfaction (Ojala, 2012b, 2012c, 2013). Ojala (2016, 14) calls this ability to face environmental risks and uncertainty, believe one's own actions and the actions of others can make a difference, and find positive meaning in action, "constructive hope."

These three forms of coping can be observed in Inuit youth aged 15–25 who are already witnessing environmental changes that are disrupting their communities' traditional way of life (MacDonald et al., 2015). In interviews, they said that staying busy took their mind off these troubles (emotion-focused coping); but unlike young Swedes, they often found solace in getting out on the land, connecting with their culture and community, and seeking support from family and friends. They learned to adapt when and how they did land-based activities (problem-focused coping), and they prided themselves that adaptability to change is part of Inuit culture (meaning-focused coping).

2.2   Cultivating Hope

The study of environmental coping strategies has inspired other researchers to explore the role of hope in young people. Li and Monroe (2017) created a measure of climate change hope for adolescents, based on the psychology of hope developed by Snyder (2000), who defines a positive sense of hope as a force for action. According to Snyder, hope requires a vision of a possible future, along with awareness of pathways to reach the goal and belief in agency to achieve it. Monroe and Oxarart (2015) integrated this theory into a curriculum for high school students in the United States who studied how regional forests respond to climate change. The curriculum included activities for students to learn "things I can do" and "things we can do," as well as activities that demonstrated that "others care" and "others are doing things"—in this case scientists and landowners sharing practices to sequester carbon and promote forest resilience. Students also studied ecosystem connections that support forest resilience, and learned how decisions that people make today have the potential for positive impacts tomorrow. With this curriculum that featured possibilities for a positive future, pathways and agency, as students' knowledge increased, their hope increased (Li & Monroe, 2019; Li, Monroe & Ritchie, 2018).

Li and Monroe (2019) found that when young people feel concern about environmental problems and believe that they and others can address problems effectively, they are more likely to feel hope. Both hope and concern motivate action, whereas despair and feelings of helplessness are negatively related to action (Ojala, 2012b, 2013; Stevenson & Peterson, 2016; Stevenson et al., 2019). In reflecting on her own work and the work of others, Ojala (2017) observed that young people's responses to global environmental problems are socially embedded and social trust is vital. Young people notice how others react to these problems, and how others respond to their emotions. Ojala (2017) noted that even though the young people in her samples were much more likely to report individual rather than collective actions to address problems, they felt encouraged when they believed that others could do similar small things and together they could make a difference. In this sense, social trust gave meaning to individual actions.

Collective projects often include direct experiences of social support. Trott followed 10- to 12-year-olds in a 15-week program to study climate change and plan and implement actions at a family and community level. In focus groups, young people repeatedly expressed the value of this social dimension. As a girl noted, after her team gave a speech about local impacts of climate change to their city council and got permission to move ahead with a tree planting campaign, they felt that "you can actually do something instead of ignore the stuff around us" (2019, 53).

Reflections by researchers, environmental activists and educators produce converging lists of practices to help young people cope with difficult environmental emotions and conceive hope (Brown, 2016; Chawla, 2020; Hicks, 2014; Monroe et al., 2017; Ojala, 2017; Sobel, 2008; Trott, 2020; Winograd, 2016). A first step is discussions that allow young people to share their feelings without judgment. Adolescents are more likely to express constructive hope regarding climate change when they expect their teachers to respect their emotions and offer support, rather than being dismissive and making fun of their feelings (Ojala, 2015). They are more likely to show both problem-focused and meaning-focused coping when parents and friends respond in solution-oriented and supportive ways, rather than being dismissive or voices of doom-and-gloom (Ojala & Bengtsson, 2018). Other key steps are making information personally relevant by relating it to local issues, connecting young people with scientists and activists who can share their work and stories, supporting them in projects to care for nature in their schools and communities, and engaging them through experiential, inquiry-based, and arts-based methods (see review by Chawla, 2020). For a summary of recommended practices, see Table 1.

3   Integrating Research on Nature Connection and Coping with Environmental Change

This paper argues that distress as the natural world degrades is a dimension of connection. Working with adults in Australia, Dean et al. (2018) also suggested that future research needs to explore this complexity. They found that when relatedness with nature was measured through enjoyment and comfort in nature, it was associated with good health; but when it was measured through self-identification with nature and

Table 1 Strategies to help young people cope with environmental change

Strategy	Application of the strategy in practice
✓ Combine the science of environmental change with information about how to make a difference	Young people need to understand physical and social causes of environmental changes in order to identify effective solutions. It is equally important for them to know what they can do to address problems, what others are doing, and how decisions made today have the potential for positive impacts tomorrow
✓ Create a receptive space where young people can share emotions	Let young people know that they can safely share their feelings about the environment. Take time to listen receptively. Be supportive and solutions oriented
✓ Encourage the positive reappraisal of problems	Help young people find meaning in addressing environmental challenges and see positive possibilities in the changes societies need to make to preserve the natural world
✓ Engage in visioning	With a focus on local areas, engage young people in visioning futures they would like to see unfold and identifying realistic steps to move in the desired direction
✓ Provide young people with opportunities to experience agency	Enable young people to investigate environmental problems that concern them, determine personally meaningful actions to address the problems, and implement practical ideas that they can accomplish individually or in partnership with others
✓ Foster social trust	Bring young people together with others who are working to protect and restore the natural world, enabling them to see that they are not alone but allied with others who are working on nature's behalf
✓ Show that voluntary simplicity can be a fulfilling way of life	Introduce young people to examples of individuals and groups who find happiness in community, creativity, service and nature, instead of the accumulation of more and more material things
✓ Connect young people with nature	Give young people time in nature to become comfortable and competent in nature and feel kinship with other living things

Adapted from Chawla (2020)

interest in conserving nature, it was associated with depression, anxiety and stress. They speculated that people were reacting to environmental degradation, including recent local floods. If some experiences that define connection with nature make people vulnerable to distress, then the idea of nature connection becomes more accurately developed, theoretically, by recognizing that it includes both positive and painful facets. With a focus on young people, this section suggests that there are also practical reasons to integrate research on nature connection and coping with environmental loss.

Studies of children's connection with nature and environmental coping have the shared aims of supporting young people's wellbeing and their agency to protect the natural world. As the opening of this paper noted, interest in children's connection with nature has been spurred by concern that children are losing opportunities for free-ranging encounters with nature, with negative consequences for their health as well as their motivation to protect the environment. On the side of research into how children cope with difficult environmental information, some children respond with levels of worry that diminish their wellbeing; and when young people fall into despair and helplessness, it cripples their capacity to act. Bringing together research and practice related to both positive connection with nature and concern may create a stronger framework for fostering children's wellbeing and environmental agency.

The preceding section showed that researchers and practitioners in education and environmental protection have been exploring ways to support young people socially and emotionally as they face environmental change, by building their sense of agency, enabling them to see that they are not alone in taking action to address challenges, and encouraging hope (Table 1). The following section looks at evaluations of programs designed to increase children's connection with nature. Together, these sections open the way to ask the questions: How do strategies to support constructive coping with environmental change compare with strategies to promote nature connection? What can these two bodies of research contribute to each other? Together, what are their implications for research and practice?

3.1 Increasing Connectedness with Nature

When Britto dos Santos and Gould (2018) and Barrable and Booth (2020b) reviewed evaluations of environmental education interventions to increase young people's connection with nature, they found encouraging evidence that this is a practical goal. Based on evaluation research published since 2008 in peer-reviewed journals and environmental organizations' reports, this section covers 16 papers included in these previous reviews along with 11 additional papers, which reinforce this conclusion. Most evaluations of program outcomes use quantitative pre- and post-assessments, but some gather qualitative reflection through interviews, focus groups, journaling and open-ended narratives. Programs that successfully increase feelings of connection with nature tend to share common features.

Four quantitative studies that looked at the effect of age found better program outcomes with younger participants. Comparing younger children in the age range from 7–10 versus 11–18, Braun and Dierkes (2017), Ernst and Theimer (2011) and Liefländer et al. (2013) found larger gains in nature connection in the younger groups. When Crawford et al. (2017) evaluated the effect of nature tours on 9-to 14-year-olds, younger children had higher nature connection scores both entering and leaving activities. In the study by Liefländer et al. (2013), only 9-to 10-year-olds maintained significant gains in a four-week follow-up assessment, compared to 11-to 13-year-olds. This chapter previously cited studies that found a greater sense of nature connection in school-age children compared to adolescents (Hughes et al., 2019; Richardson et al., 2019). These evaluations of program interventions suggest that younger children may also be more receptive to initiatives designed to cultivate connection.

Most programs that produce significant quantitative gains in nature connection last several days. In different studies, extended time meant 3–5 days of immersion in residential field sites (Braun & Dierkes, 2017; Hinds & O'Malley, 2019; Liefländer et al., 2013; Mullenbach, Andrejewski & Mowen, 2019; Stern et al., 2008; Talebpour et al., 2020), 4 days to two weeks in nature-based camps or on wilderness expeditions (Barton et al., 2016; Collado et al., 2013; Ernst & Theimer, 2011; San Jose & Nelson, 2017), 4 weeks of nature play and learning in a preschool (Yilmaz, Çig & Yilmaz-Bolat, 2020), repeated field trips to natural areas (Ernst & Theimer, 2011), and school curricula that lasted several weeks and included hands-on nature experiences (Cho & Lee, 2018; Harvey et al., 2020; Sheldrake et al., 2019). But even programs that involved only a day of classroom lessons about forests combined with activities in a forest (Kossack & Bogner, 2012), a few hours of forest exploration (Dopko et al., 2019; Schneider & Schaal, 2018), or trips to natural areas or a natural history museum (Bruni et al., 2018; Crawford et al., 2017; Sheldrake et al., 2019) resulted in immediate significant gains in nature connection scores.

After a 2-h tour of local heathlands in Flanders, only students with low pre-scores expressed a greater sense of inclusion with nature (Boeve-de Pauw et al., 2019). This result is consistent with assessments by Braun and Dierkes (2017), Schneider and Schaal (2018), Bruni et al. (2018) and Harvey et al. (2020), who found that students with low initial scores made the greatest gains in nature connection. Programs to teach about climate change (Sellmann & Bogner, 2013) or surfing skills (Hignett et al., 2018) failed to increase teens' sense of inclusion with nature.

Nine of these 24 quantitative and mixed-methods studies include a follow-up assessment to determine whether young people retain their immediate gains in nature connectedness after a program ends. Retention tests show that significant gains last 3–8 weeks; but when Stern et al. (2008) conducted a three-month follow-up after residential programs in a national park, students' original gains in nature connection were lost. This result indicates the importance of long-term follow-up, and suggests that children may need repeated nature-based experiences to maintain connection.

Bruni et al. (2017) concluded that children are most likely to express connection with nature when they are encouraged to focus on nature in their own way, at their own pace. They compared three activities that, together, involved 6-to 16-year-olds. One involved an online hike through a national forest. A second sent children on an adult-led mountain hike to find metal plaques of plant and animal species and collect rubbings. A third invited children to spend time in a place of their choice outdoors in nature or in a zoo or aquarium and express their experiences through any artistic medium. Only the free choice activity resulted in significant gains in nature connection, compared to activities that directed participants to focus on metal plaques or a digital screen.

Three studies used qualitative measures to understand experiences associated with nature connection, including observation, interviews and focus groups. In an evaluation of three U.S. Fish and Wildlife programs, Theimer and Ernst (2012) found that students in a field-based middle school adjacent to prairie wetlands expressed relatedness with nature most consistently. In this program, they participated in daily natural history activities, outdoor pursuits like hiking and snowshoeing, long distance expeditions through the natural areas of the site, quiet contemplation and observation in nature, and service learning like water sampling, duck banding and prairie restoration.

Barthel et al. (2018) conducted a longitudinal evaluation of a school program that involved 10-year-olds in Stockholm in protecting salamanders during their spring migration from a local woodland to a pond near school where they laid their eggs. Students studied salamanders, searched for salamanders who needed assistance to reach the pond, and recorded numbers and species for a national monitoring program. Some described pivotal moments when they overcame fear and discomfort at touching salamanders, and most said that their understanding and empathy for these creatures increased, along with feeling more friendly to nature. Two years after participation, students still expressed these emotions, along with a sense of importance, pride and responsibility at participating in an adult conservation program.

Participants in three nature-based programs in Colorado evaluated by Colvin Williams and Chawla (2016) echoed these findings. They vividly recalled hands-on experiences outdoors, overcame fears of snakes and insects, and developed growing respect for nature. They felt empowered as they learned responsible roles like bird banding, water quality monitoring, and caring for wolves at a wolf refuge. They talked about the inspiring commitment to nature demonstrated by program staff, as well as pride and excitement at being part of a network of people who worked together across distances to study and protect the natural world.

Two mixed methods studies highlighted two factors that can affect program outcomes: group identity and weather. In another facet of the salamander program evaluation, Giusti (2019) compared results from the qualitative interviews with quantitative measures of nature connection, and found no significant change in scores before and after participation. In pretests, students in the program school expressed significantly greater empathy for salamanders than students at two control schools, even before beginning the program. The salamander program was a proud part of the school's identity, and just belonging to this school appeared to increase students' identification with salamanders. When Talebpour et al. (2020) evaluated three residential field trips in a wilderness area of California using both pre/post nature connection surveys and student journals, they found that journal entries about the weather helped explain score results. Nature connection scores fell for classes that visited the area during cold torrential rain, rose moderately during a period of mixed rain, sun and wind, and rose highest during warm sunny weather.

Successful practices described in the quantitative and qualitative evaluations are summarized in Table 2. As a whole, these studies indicate that it is possible to

Table 2 Program practices associated with gains in young people's connection with nature

- Provide time for direct engagement with nature and immersion in natural areas
- Focus on experiences that define nature connection:
  – affiliation, a sense of belonging, a sense of oneness
  – enjoyment
  – confidence in nature
  – curiosity, interest, exploration
  – challenge and achievement
  – understanding human interdependence with nature
  – empathy and concern for other living things
  – caring for wildlife and natural habitats
- Give young people time to encounter nature at their own pace, following their own interests
- Let them know that there are many ways to be a "nature person," including play and recreation in nature, working the land sustainably, gardening, studying natural history, caring for animals, making art in nature
- Make young people partners in collective efforts to study and protect the natural world
- Ground experiences in the local culture and ecology
- Share examples of people's enthusiasm and care for nature
- Make sure young people see others who look like them engaged with nature
- Enable young people to record their observations and experiences through writing, scientific record keeping, and the arts
- Start young, but provide access to nature for all ages
- Aim for extended engagement, but even short-term experiences in nature can lead to gains in nature connection
- Allow young people to overcome fears in nature or fears of particular species through gradual interactions at their level of comfort

Based on Barthel et al. (2018), Barton et al. (2016), Braun and Dierkes (2017), Bruni et al. (2017), Bruni et al. (2018), Cho and Lee (2018), Collado et al. (2013), Colvin Williams and Chawla (2015), Dopko et al. (2019), Ernst and Theimer (2011), Kossack and Bogner (2012), Liefländer et al. (2013), Sheldrake et al. (2019), Stern et al. (2008), Theimer and Ernst (2012), Yilmaz et al. (2020)

design experiences that increase a sense of connection with nature. The importance of time in nature, hands-on experiences, natural history, and service learning emerge in most studies. Qualitative evaluations also reveal feelings of pride and solidarity from working with others to protect natural habitats and wildlife: a social dimension that is missing from the quantitative measures.

3.2 Building Connection and Hope

When Table 1 on helping young people cope with environmental change and build hope is compared with Table 2 on increasing young people's connection with nature, where do effective practices overlap? Are there practices only listed for one purpose that might be useful for the other? This section compares these tables to suggest how programs for young people might simultaneously support connection with nature, action for nature, hope and wellbeing. In the process, it identifies questions for further research.

Several practices appear in both tables: providing young people with time outdoors in natural areas, enabling them to feel comfortable and competent in nature, the study of ecology and natural science, activities that enable young people to see that they can make a positive difference for the environment, and examples of other people who are making a difference. Up to this point, these practices have been recommended for one purpose or the other: to increase connection with nature, or to support hope and healthy coping with environmental change. The fact that they form a common core, recommended for both purposes, invites research to determine whether these practices can simultaneously help young people connect with nature and develop constructive responses to environmental threats. For success, are all of these program elements needed, in combination or cumulatively over time? Or are some most formative? (See Fig. 3 for a summary of experiences associated with both connecting with nature and coping with environmental change, as well as experiences primarily aligned with one outcome or the other.)

Table 1 on healthy coping includes a number of recommendations that are missing from Table 2 on promoting connection. It notes that the study of ecology and natural history needs to be combined with learning how to protect the natural world. It highlights the importance of social trust, of believing that one is not alone in taking action for nature because individual actions are amplified by the contributions of other people. It also emphasizes providing time for young people to share their emotions about environmental change and helping them find positive meaning in facing challenges. It points to the importance of developing concrete, achievable visions of a desirable future, and finding value in voluntary simplicity. Some young people in programs to increase connection with nature may struggle with fears about environmental changes, and as change accelerates, their numbers are likely to grow. Without taking time to listen, people who implement these programs will never know if young people carry these burdens. As Brown (2016) notes, silence about environmental issues communicates implicit messages. It can convey fatalism about a problem, or indifference. By including these practices, programs to connect young people with nature may support constructive coping.

Providing young people with time in nature appears in both tables, but only Table 2 identifies specific experiences associated with feelings of connection: comfort, confidence, enjoyment, exploration, challenge, achievement, freedom to follow interests at one's own pace, overcoming fears outdoors, and empathy and care for other living things. When programs want to build young people's bond with nature, they need to provide conditions for these experiences. Table 2 also includes collective activities to study nature, care for wildlife, and restore and protect natural habitats, and the importance of seeing role models who look like oneself.

Research on environmental coping and behavior shows that most young people report individual actions to address environmental problems, such as conserving energy and resources (Ojala, 2012a; Stevenson & Peterson, 2016). More research

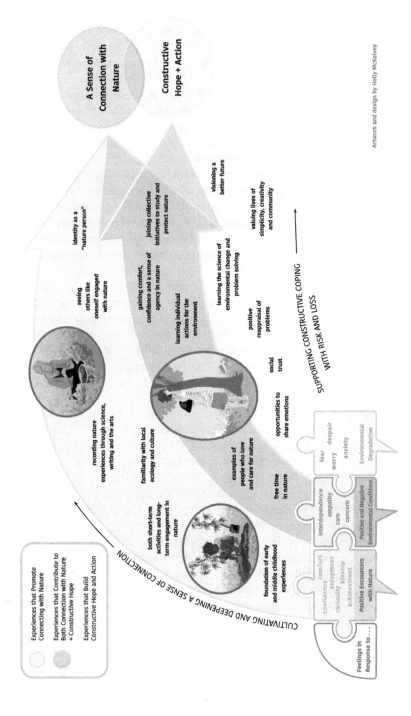

Fig. 3 Practices that help young people connect with nature and cope constructively with environmental change

is needed to understand what happens when young people have opportunities to engage in collective action. As one of the 10-to 12-year-olds who developed climate action projects for their community said, "I don't know, there's something about it .... Getting together, creating projects, knowing each other, working together" (Trott, 2019, 53). What opportunities enable young people to feel empowered rather than discouraged by the challenges they face? How does virtual organizing compare with coming together in person? Does working in alliance with nature's own powers of growth and resilience during gardening, tree planting and ecological restoration add distinctive dimensions of meaning? Table 2 also notes the importance of programs for very young children. Environmental educators emphasize positive experiences in nature for young children (Sobel, 1996; Wilson, 2018); but when young children notice upsetting environmental changes, are they better prepared to express hope if they participate with others in protecting and regenerating the natural world?

This paper's title can be revisited as a question. Can connecting with nature in childhood form a foundation for constructive hope, in the sense that it prepares children for lives of action to care for the natural world even in the face of environmental threats? As this paper has noted, adults and children who express higher levels of connection with nature are more likely to report taking action for the environment. But research has not yet tested whether this relationship between connection and action holds even when young people feel acutely threatened by environmental losses. When young people fear climate change and biodiversity loss, research shows, what matters is social trust—feeling others' support and knowing that other people are also acting to protect the natural world—and the capacity to find meaning in addressing challenges. Can connection with nature, commitment to action, and hope develop together? What experiences are necessary for this to happen? This section has proposed practices that may achieve this purpose; but there may be other approaches, waiting to be discovered through careful listening to young people and those who work beside them to engage with the challenges and possibilities of a changing planet. These are open questions that invite both qualitative and quantitative investigation.

4 Concluding Observations on Research and Practice

4.1 Developing Theory-Based Explanatory Models

In addition to the questions above, this review has raised other questions. When children are out in nature, what are the formative experiences that contribute to their sense of connection with the natural world? What are formative experiences in families? Why do levels of connection decrease in adolescence? Why does gender often make a difference? What are the developmental pathways that link child health and wellbeing to connecting with nature? What experiences simultaneously build connection and care for nature? By looking at qualitative as well as quantitative research, along with programs and practices that are intended to build connection and help young people cope constructively with a world at risk, this paper has suggested where some answers may be found. Future research needs to link children's relations with the natural world to theory grounded in basic processes of child development, and weave back and forth between qualitative and quantitative methods.

There are promising steps in this direction. For example, after creating the Connection to Nature Index, Cheng and Monroe (2012) conducted two path analyses to explain initial survey results: one showing factors that predict children's interest in participating in nature-based activities, which have been associated with health and wellbeing; and one showing factors that predict children's interest in environmentally friendly practices. Roczen et al. (2014) also built a model to explain young people's pro-environmental behavior, which is similar in key respects. In both models, connection to nature makes a strong contribution to pro-environmental practices, along with knowledge about the environment. In addition, Cheng and Monroe's model includes access to nature, experiences in nature, a sense of self-efficacy, and family values toward nature. All of these factors are evident in descriptions of developmental processes when children engage with nature (Chawla, 2021).

The research covered in this paper suggests that connecting with nature and acting to protect nature can be mutually reinforcing. Children with higher measures of nature connection report more pro-environmental behaviors of many kinds... while programs that successfully increase connection with nature often involve nature conservation activities. Future research needs to look more closely at pathways between connection and action, as well as relations between knowledge about nature and empathy for other living things. Ethnographic accounts show that when children are outdoors in nature, they are simultaneously connecting with nature and learning about the natural world; and when people around them encourage empathy and care for plants, animals and their habitats, children exhibit these emotions and behaviors (Elliot et al., 2014; Green, 2018). In the unity of children's lived experience in nature, connection, knowledge, empathy and responsible action may co-develop. More qualitative studies are needed to examine how this happens, as well as quantitative studies that measure these constructs and how they are related.

4.2   Contexts of Connection

Here and in the original article published in *People and Nature*, "nature" meant everything from a city bird or pet, to fragments of nature in dense urban districts, to wilder areas in forest schools, nature centers and large parks. In all of the studies covered, it meant nature in or near inhabited areas. Kahn and Weiss (2017) recommend experiences of "big nature" in the sense of untamed landscapes that people can trek through for weeks, but studies of nature connection have been located in neighborhoods, schools and nature programs, where most children are found. How deep wilderness experiences affect young people's connection with nature deserves a review of its own, which will need to find accounts of children who have this rare experience. Kahn and Weiss note, however, that "big nature" can be relative, and for a child in a city, it can mean a squirrel or a jump in a fountain.

What the quantitative and qualitative research covered here makes clear is the importance of direct experience as a foundation for connection, wherever children find nature. This conclusion suggests that every practice to increase children's access to nature is important, from naturalizing private yards and multifamily housing sites, to mosaics of parks and gardens, to greening the grounds of schools and child care centers, to making nature centers, camping and field trips to natural areas available for all children. Finding ways to bring nature to children, even in densely populated and low resourced parts of the world, appears essential to foster connection. Doing this can simultaneously create networks of green spaces for biodiversity and offer many opportunities for children to become involved in nature protection and restoration.

As it moves forward, research on nature connection needs to extend beyond populations in Western cultures. Only a few studies in the research covered here and in the *People and Nature article* originated in Asia, Africa, Latin America and indigenous communities. Most population growth is happening in Asia, Africa and Latin America, and these continents are where most of the world's children live (United Nations, 2018). They also contain hotspots for biodiversity protection (Myers et al., 2000). Research on young people's connection with nature, action for nature, and constructive hope needs to include diverse countries and cultures. The protection of the natural world requires committed work by people of all cultures, in agricultural and remote regions as well as cities and suburbs. Therefore it is critical to understand cultures of connection in all contexts, beginning with their development in childhood.

Recommended Further Reading

1. Chawla, Louise (2020). Helping students cope with environmental change and take constructive civic action. *Green Schools Catalyst Quarterly*, 7(1), 44–57.
2. Hicks, David (2014). *Educating for Hope in Troubled Times: Climate change and the transition to a post-carbon future*. London: Institute of Education Press.
3. Winograd, Ken (ed.). (2016). *Education in times of environmental crises: Teaching children to be agents of change*. London: Routledge.

Acknowledgements This chapter owes a great debt to Rachelle Gould and Kai Chan, editors at *People and Nature*, and Gabby Salazar, reviewer, whose supportive suggestions helped at each step in the process of bringing together the multiple literatures reviewed here. Appreciation, too, to the editors at *People and Nature* for giving me scope to develop this chapters' argument, and to Rachelle Gould and the designers Ayushi Patel and Holly McKelvey for helping me translate ideas into the graphic images in Figs. 2 and 3. Rolf Jucker provided wise advice during the process of abridging the original article to create this chapter.

References

Ahmetoglu, E. (2019). The contributions of familial and environmental factors on children's connection with nature and outdoor activities. *Early Childhood Development and Care, 189*(2), 233–243.

Barrable, A., & Booth, D. (2020a). Nature connection in early childhood: A quantitative cross-sectional study. *Sustainability*, 12, Article 375. https://doi.org/10.3390/su12010375. Retrieved May 16, 2021.

Barrable, A., & Booth, D. (2020b). Increasing nature connection in children: A mini review of interventions. *Frontiers in Psychology, 11*, Article 492. https://doi.org/10.3389/fpsyg.2020b.00492. Retrieved May 16, 2021.

Barraza, L. (1999). Children's drawings about the environment. *Environmental Education Research, 5*(1), 49–66.

Barthel, S., Belton, S., Raymond, C., & Giusti, M. (2018). Fostering children's connection to nature through authentic situations: The case of saving salamanders at school. *Frontiers in Psychology, 9.*https://doi.org/10.3389/fpsyg.2018.00928. Retrieved May 16, 2021.

Barton, J., Bragg, R., Pretty, J., Roberts, J., & Wood, C. (2016). The wilderness expedition: An effective life course intervention to improve young people's well-being and connectedness to nature. *Journal of Experiential Education, 39*(1), 59–72.

Boeve-de Pauw, J., Van Hoof, J., & Van Petegem, P. (2019). Effecive field trips in nature: The interplay between novelty and learning. *Journal of Biological Education, 53*(1), 21–33. https://doi.org/10.1080/00219266.2017.1418760. Retrieved May 16, 2021.

Bowers, E., Larson, L., & Parry, B. (2021). Nature as an ecological asset for positive youth development: Empirical evidence from rural communities. *Frontiers in Psychology, 12*, 688574. https://www.frontiersin.org/articles/10.3389/fpsyg.2021.688574/full. Retrieved May 26, 2022.

Braun, T., & Dierkes, P. (2017). Connecting students to nature—How intensity of nature experience and student age influence the success of outdoor education programs. *Environmental Education Research, 23*, 937–949.

Britto dos Santos, N. B., & Gould, R. K. (2018). Can relational values be developed and changed? Investigating relational values in the environmental education literature. *Current Opinion in Environmental Sustainability, 35*, 124–131. https://doi.org/10.1016/j.cosust.2018.10.019. Retrieved May 16, 2021.

Brown, M. Y. (2016). Supporting children emotionally in times of climate disruption: Teaching practices and strategies. In K. Winograd (Ed.), *Education in times of environmental crises* (pp. 195–209). Routledge.

Bruni, C. M., Ballew, M. T., Winter, P. L., & Omoto, A. M. (2018). Natural history museums may enhance youth's implicit connectedness with nature. *Ecopsychology, 10*, 280–288.

Bruni, C. M., Winter, P. L., Schultz, P. W., Omoto, A. M., & Tabanico, J. J. (2017). Getting to know nature: Evaluating the effects of the Get to Know Program on children's connectedness to nature. *Environmental Education Research, 23*(1), 43–62.

Chawla, L. (1992). Childhood place attachments. In I. Altman & S. Low (Eds.), *Place attachment* (pp. 63–89). Plenum Press.

Chawla, L. (2007). Childhood experiences associated with care for the natural world. *Children, Youth and Environments, 17*(4), 144–170.

Chawla, L. (2020). Helping students cope with environmental change and take constructive civic action. *Green Schools Catalyst Quarterly, 7*(1), 44–57.

Chawla, L. (2021). Knowing nature in childhood: Learning and wellbeing through engagement with the natural world. In Schutte, A., Torquati, J. & Stevens, J. (Eds.), *Nature and Psychology, Nebraska Symposium on Motivation 67* (pp. 153–193). Cham, Switzerland: Springer Nature. https://doi.org/10.1007/978-3-030-69020-5_6

Cheng, J.C.-H., & Monroe, M. C. (2012). Connection to nature: Children's affective attitude toward nature. *Environment and Behavior, 44*(1), 31–49. https://doi.org/10.1177/0013916510385082 Retrieved May 15, 2021.

Cho, Y., & Lee, D. (2018). "Love honey, hate bees": Reviving biophilia of elementary school students through environmental education program. *Environmental Education Research, 24*, 445–460.

Clarke, A. T. (2006). Coping with interpersonal stress and psychosocial health among children and adolescents: A meta-analysis. *Journal of Youth and Adolescence, 35*(1), 11–24.

Collado, S., Staats, H., & Corraliza, J. A. (2013). Experiencing nature in children's summer camps: Affective, cognitive and behavioural consequences. *Journal of Environmental Psychology, 33*, 37–44. https://doi.org/10.1016/j.jenvp.2012.08/002. Retrieved May 15, 2021.

Colvin Williams, C., & Chawla, L. (2015). Environmental identity formation in nonformal environmental education programs. *Environmental Education Research, 22*(7), 978–1001. https://doi.org/10.1080/13504622.2015.1055553

Crawford, M. R., Holder, M. D., & O'Connor, B. P. (2017). Using mobile technology to engage children with nature. *Environment and Behavior, 49*(9), 959–984. https://doi.org/10.1177/001391 6516673870

Cunsolo, A., & Ellis, N. R. (2018). Ecological grief as a mental health response to climate change-related loss. *Nature Climate Change, 8*, 275–281.

Davis, J. M. (2010). Practical possibility and pedagogical approaches for early childhood education for sustainability. In J. M. Davis (Ed.), *Young Children and the Environment* (pp. 129–131). Cambridge University Press.

Dean, J. H., Shanahan, D. F., Bush, R., Gaston, K. J., Lin, B. B., Barber, E. . . . & Fuller, R. A. (2018). Is nature relatedness associated with better mental and physical health? *International Journal of Environmental Research and Public Health, 15*(1371). https://doi.org/10.3390/ijerph 15071371

Dopko, R. L., Capaldi, C. A., & Zelenski, J. M. (2019). The psychological and social benefits of a nature experience for children. *Journal of Environmental Psychology, 63*, 134–138. https://doi.org/10.1016/j.envp.2019.05.002

Eames, C., Barker, M., & Scarff, C. (2018). Priorities, identity and the environment: Negotiating the early teenage years. *Journal of Environmental Education, 49*(3), 189–206. https://doi.org/10.1080/00958964.2017.1415195

Elliot, E., Ten Eycke, K., Chan, S., & Müller, U. (2014). Taking kindergartners outdoors: Documenting their explorations and assessing the impact on their ecological awareness. *Children, Youth and Environments, 24*(2), 102–122.

Ernst, J., & Theimer, S. (2011). Evaluating the effects of environmental education programming on connectedness to nature. *Environmental Education Research, 17*(5), 577–598. https://doi.org/10.1080/13504622.2011.565119

Folkman, S. (2008). The case for positive emotions in the stress process. *Anxiety, Stress and Coping: An International Journal, 21*(1), 3–14.

Galway, L. P., Beery, T., Jones-Casey, K., & Tasala, K. (2019). Mapping the solastalgia literature: A scoping review study. *International Journal of Environmental Research and Public Health, 16*, 2662. https://doi.org/10.3390/ijerph16152662

Giusti, M. (2019). Human-nature relationships in context. Experiential, psychological, and contextual dimensions that shape children's desire to protect nature. *PLOS One, 14*(12), e0225951. https://doi.org/10.1371/journal.pone.0225951

Giusti, M., Barthel, S., & Marcus, L. (2014). Nature routines and affinity with the biosphere: A case study of preschool children in Stockholm. *Children, Youth and Environments, 24*(3), 16–42.

Gold, A. G., & Gujar, B. R. (2007). Contentment and competence: Rajasthani children talk about work, play and school. In K. Malone (Ed.), *Child space* (pp. 193–212). Concept Publishing Company.

Goodenough, E. (Ed.). (2003). *Secret spaces of childhood*. University of Michigan Press.

Green, C. (2018). *Children's environmental identity development*. Peter Lang.

Hart, R. (1979). *Children's experience of place*. Irvington.

Harvey, D. J., Montgomery, L. N., Harvey, H., Hall, F., Gange, A. C., & Watling, D. (2020). Psychological benefits of a biodiversity-focused outdoor-learning program for primary school students. *Journal of Environmental Psychology, 67*, 101381. https://doi.org/10.1016/j.envp.2019.101381

Hatala, A. R., Njeze, C., Morton, D., Pearl, T., & Bird-Naytowhow, K. (2020). Land and nature as sources of health and resilience among Indigenous youth in an urban Canadian context: A photovoice exploration. *BMC Public Health, 20*(1), Article 538. https://doi.org/10.1186/s12889-020-08647-z

Hicks, D. (2014). *Educating for hope in troubled times*. Institute of Education Press.

Hicks, D., & Holden, C. (2007). Remembering the future: What do children think? *Environmental Education Research, 13*, 501–512. https://doi.org/10.1080/135046207015811596

Hignett, A., White, M. P., Pahl, S., Jenkin, R., & Le Froy, M. (2018). Evaluation of a surfing programme designed to increase personal well-being and connectedness to the natural environment among 'at risk' young people. *Journal of Adventure Education and Outdoor Learning, 18*(1), 53–69.

Hinds, J., & O'Malley, S. (2019). Assessing nature connection and well-being during an experiential environmental program. *Children, Youth and Environments, 29*(2), 92–107.

Hughes, J., Rogerson, M., Barton, J., & Bragg, R. (2019). Age and connection to nature: When is engagement critical? *Frontiers in Ecology and the Environment, 17*(5), 265–269. https://doi.org/10.1002/fee.2035

Hutchinson, F. (1997). Our children's futures: Are there lessons for environmental educators? *Environmental Education Research, 3*(2), 189–201.

Ives, C. D., Giusti, M., Fischer, J., Abson, D. J., Klaniecki, K., Dorninger, C., & von Wehrden, H. (2017). Human-nature connection: A multidisciplinary review. *Current Opinion in Environmental Sustainability, 26–27*, 106–113. https://doi.org/10.1016/j.cosust.2017.05.005

Jonsson, G., Sarri, C., & Alerby, E. (2012). "Too hot for the reindeer"—Voicing Sámi children's visions of the future. *International Research in Geographical and Environmental Education, 21*(2), 95–107.

Kahn, P. H., Jr., & Weiss, T. (2017). The importance of children interacting with big nature. *Children, Youth and Environments, 27*(2), 7–24.

Kaplan, R., & Kaplan, S. (2002). Adolescents and the natural environment: A time out? In P. H. Kahn & S. R. Kellert (Eds.), *Children and nature* (pp. 227–257). MIT Press.

Kossack, A., & Bogner, F. X. (2012). How does a one-day environmental education programme support individual connectedness with nature? *Journal of Biological Education (Routledge), 46*(3), 180–187. https://doi.org/10.1080/00219266.2011.634016

Larson, L. R., Green, G. T., & Castleberry, S. B. (2011). Construction and validation of an instrument to measure environmental orientations in a diverse group of children. *Environment and Behavior, 43*(1), 72–89. https://doi.org/10.1177/0013916509345212

Lawson, D. F., Stevenson, K. T., Peterson, M. N., Carrier, S. J., Seekamp, E., & Strnad, R. (2019). Evaluating climate change concern and behaviors in the family context. *Environmental Education Research, 25*(5), 678–690. https://doi.org/10.1080/13504622.2018.1564248

Lazarus, R. S., & Folkman, S. (1984). *Stress, appraisal, and coping*. Springer.

Leong, L. Y. C., Fischer, R., & McClure, J. (2014). Are nature lovers more innovative? The relationship between connectedness with nature and cognitive styles. *Journal of Environmental Psychology, 40*, 57–63. https://doi.org/10.1016/j.jenvp.2014.03.007

Li, C., & Monroe, M. C. (2017). Development and validation of the climate change hope scale for high school students. *Environment and Behavior, 50*(4), 454–479. https://doi.org/10.1177/0013916517708325

Li, C. J., & Monroe, M. C. (2019). Exploring the essential psychological factors in fostering hope concerning climate change. *Environmental Education Research, 25*(6), 936–954. https://doi.org/10.1080/13504622.2017.1367916

Li, C. J., Monroe, M. C., & Ritchie, T. (2018). Integrating social science research to advance sustainability education. In W. Leal Filho, R. W. Marans & J. Callewaert (eds.). *Handbook of sustainability and social science research* (pp. 45–61). Springer International Publishing.

Liefländer, A. K., Fröhlich, G., Bogner, F. X., & Schultz, P. W. (2013). Promoting connectedness with nature through environmental education. *Environmental Education Research, 19*(3), 370–384. https://doi.org/10.1080/13504622.2012.697545

MacDonald, J. P., Willox, A. C., Ford, J. D., Shiwak, I., Wood, M., IMHACC Team, & Rigolet Inuit Community Government. (2015). Protective factors for mental health and well-being in a changing climate: Perspectives from Inuit youth in Nunatsiavut, Labrador. *Social Science and Medicine, 141*, 133-141. https://doi.org/10.1016/j.socscimed.2015.07.017

Monroe, M. C., & Oxarart, A. (Eds.). (2015). *Southeastern forests and climate change: A Project Learning Tree secondary environmental education module* (2nd ed.). University of Florida and American Forest Foundation.

Monroe, M. C., Plate, R. R., Oxarart, A., Bowers, A., & Chaves, W. A. (2017). Identifying effective climate change education strategies: A systematic review of the research. *Environmental Education Research, 25*(6), 791–812. https://doi.org/10.1080/13504622.2017.1360842

Moore, R. C. (1986). *Childhood's domain*. Croom Helm.

Müller, M. M., Kals, E., & Pansa, R. (2009). Adolescents' emotional affinity toward nature: A cross-sectional study. *Journal of Developmental Processes, 4*(1), 59–69.

Mullenbach, L. E., Andrejewski, R. G., & Mowen, A. J. (2019). Connecting children to nature through residential outdoor environmental education. *Environmental Education Research, 25*(3), 365–374. https://doi.org/10.1080/13504622.2018.1458215

Myers, N., Mittermeier, R. A., Mittermeier, C. G., da Fonseca, G. A. B., & Kent, J. (2000). Biodiversity hotspots for conservation priorities. *Nature, 403*, 853–858.

Nabhan, G. P., & Trimble, S. (1994). *The geography of childhood*. Beacon Press.

Ojala, M. (2012a). Regulating worry, promoting hope: How do children, adolescents, and young adults cope with climate change? *International Journal of Environmental and Science Education, 7*(4), 537–561.

Ojala, M. (2012b). How do children cope with global climate change? Coping strategies, engagement, and well-being. *Journal of Environmental Psychology, 32*(3), 225–233. https://doi.org/10.1016/j.envp.2012.02.004

Ojala, M. (2012c). Hope and climate change: The importance of hope for pro-environmental engagement among young people. *Environmental Education Research, 18*(5), 625–642.

Ojala, M. (2013). Coping with climate change among adolescents: Implications for subjective well-being and environmental engagement. *Sustainability, 5*, 2191–2209. https://doi.org/10.3390/su.5052191

Ojala, M. (2015). Hope in the face of climate change: Associations with environmental engagement and student perceptions of teachers' emotion communication style and future orientation. *Journal of Environmental Education, 46*(3), 1–16.

Ojala, M. (2016). Young people and global climate change: Emotions, coping, and engagement in everyday life. In N. Ansell, N. Klocker, & T. Skelton (Eds.), *Geographies of global issues: Change and threat: Geographies of children and young people 8* (pp. 1–19). Springer Science + Business Media. https://doi.org/10.1080/00958964.2015.1021662

Ojala, M. (2017). Hope and anticipation in education for a sustainable future. *Futures, 94*, 76–84. https://doi.org/10.1016/j.futures.2016.10.004

Ojala, M., & Bengtsson, H. (2018). Young people's coping strategies concerning climate change: Relations to perceived communication with parents and friends and proenvironmental behavior. *Environment and Behavior, 51*(8), 907–935. https://doi.org/10.1177/0013916518763894

Owens, P. E., & McKinnon, I. (2009). In pursuit of nature: The role of nature in adolescents' lives. *Journal of Developmental Processes, 4*(1), 43–58.

Pyle, R. M. (1978). The extinction of experience. *Horticulture, 56*(1), 64–67.

Restall, B., & Conrad, E. (2015). A literature review of connectedness to nature and its potential for environmental management. *Journal of Environmental Management, 159*, 264–278.

Rice, C., & Torquati, J. C. (2013). Assessing connections between young children's affinity for nature and their experiences in natural settings in preschool. *Children, Youth and Environments, 23*(2), 78–102.

Richardson, M., Hunt, A., Hinds, J., Bragg, R., Fido, D., Petronzi, D., & White, M. (2019). A measure of nature connectedness for children and adults: Validation, performance, and insights. *Sustainability, 11*, 3250. https://doi.org/10.3390/su11123250

Roczen, N., Kaiser, F. G., Bogner, F. X., & Wilson, M. (2014). A competence model for environmental education. *Environment and Behavior, 46*(8), 972–992. https://doi.org/10.1177/001391 6513492416

San Jose, A., & Nelson, K. E. (2017). Increasing children's positive connection to, orientation toward, and knowledge of nature through camp experiences. *International Journal of Environmental and Science Education, 12*(5), 933–944.

Schneider, J., & Schaal, S. (2018). Location-based smartphone games in the context of environmental education and education for sustainable development: Fostering connectedness to nature with Geogames. *Environmental Education Research, 24*(11), 1597–1610. https://doi.org/10.1080/ 13504622.2017.1383360

Schwab, K., Hendricks, W. W., Greenwood, J. B., Goldenberg, M., Greenwood, B., & Higgins, L. (2020). Connecting with nature in the digital age: Intentions of adolescents in California urban areas. *Journal of Park and Recreation Administration, 38*(1), 29–49.

Sellmann, D., & Bogner, F. X. (2013). Effects of a 1-day environmental education intervention on environmental attitudes and connectedness with nature. *European Journal of Psychology of Education, 28*, 1077–1086.

Sheldrake, R., Amos, R., & Reiss, M. (2019). *Children and nature: A research evaluation for The Wildlife Trusts.* The Wildlife Trusts. https://iris.ucl.ac.uk/iris/publication/1726667/1. Retrieved May 26, 2022.

Snyder, C. R. (2000). Genesis: The birth and growth of hope. In C. R. Snyder (Ed.), *Handbook of hope* (pp. 25–38). Academic Press.

Sobel, D. (1996). *Beyond ecophobia: Reclaiming the heart in nature education.* The Orion Society.

Sobel, David. (2002). *Children's special places.* Wayne State University Press.

Sobel, David. (2008). *Childhood and nature: Design principles for educators.* Stenhouse Publishers.

Sobko, T., Jia, Z., & Brown, G. (2018). Measuring connectedness to nature in preschool children in an urban setting and its relation to psychological functioning. *PLoS ONE, 13*(11), e0207057. https://doi.org/10.1371/journal.pone.0207057

Soga, M., & Gaston, K. J. (2016). Extinction of experience: The loss of human-nature interactions. *Frontiers in Ecology and the Environment, 14*(2), 94–101. https://doi.org/10.1002/fee.1225

Stern, M. J., Powell, R. B., & Ardoin, N. M. (2008). What difference does it make? Assessing outcomes from participation in a residential environmental education program. *Journal of Environmental Education, 39*(4), 31–43.

Stevenson, K., & Peterson, N. (2016). Motivating action through fostering climate change hope and concern and avoiding despair among adolescents. *Sustainability Science, 8*(6). https://doi.org/10. 3390/su8010006

Stevenson, K. T., Peterson, M. N., & Bondell, H. D. (2019). The influence of personal beliefs, friends, and family in building climate change concern among adolescents. *Environmental Education Research, 25*(6), 832–845. https://doi.org/10.1080/13504622.2016.1177712

Strife, S. J. (2012). Children's environmental concerns: Expressing ecophobia. *Journal of Environmental Education, 43*, 37–54.

Talebpour, L. M., Busk, P. L., Heimlich, J. E., & Ardoin, N. M. (2020). Children's connection to nature as fostered through residential environmental education programs. *Environmental Education Research, 26*(1), 95–114. https://doi.org/10.1080/13504622.2019.1707778

Tam, K.-P. (2013). Concepts and measures related to connection to nature: Similarities and differences. *Journal of Environmental Psychology, 34*, 64–78. https://doi.org/10.1016/j.jenvp.2013. 01.004

Theimer, S., & Ernst, J. (2012). Fostering connectedness to nature through U.S. Fish and Wildlife Service educational and outreach programming: A qualitative evaluation. *Applied Environmental Education and Communication, 11*(2), 79–87.

Trott, C. D. (2019). Reshaping our world: Collaborating with children for community-based climate change action. *Action Research, 17*(1), 42–62. https://doi.org/10.1177/1476750319829209

Trott, C. D. (2020). Children's constructive climate change engagement: Empowering awareness, agency, and action. *Environmental Education Research, 26*(4), 532–554.

UNICEF. (1989). *Convention on the Rights of the Child*. UNICEF. www.unicef.org/child-rights-convention

United Nations. (2018). *2018 revision of world urbanization prospects, and 2017 revision of world population prospects*. United Nations, Department of Economic and Social Affairs, Population Division.

Ward Thompson, C., Travlou, P., & Roe, J. (2006). *Free-range teenagers: The role of wild adventure space in young people's lives*. OPENSpace.

Wilson, J., & Snell, C. (2010). "Bad for the penguins…because they need ice and that to live on": An exploratory study into the environmental views, concerns and knowledge of socially disadvantaged young people. *Journal of Youth Studies, 13*(2), 151–168.

Wilson, R. (2018). *Nature and young children*. Routledge.

Winograd, K. (2016). Teaching in times of environmental crises: What on earth are elementary teachers to do? In K. Winograd (Ed.), *Education in times of environmental crises* (pp. 3–13). Routledge.

Yilmaz, S., Çig, O., & Yilmaz-Bolat, E. (2020). The impact of a short-term nature-based education program on young children's biophilic tendencies. *Ilkogretim Online – Elementary Education Online, 19*(3), 1729–1739.

Zylstra, M. J., Esler, K. J., Knight, A. T., & LeGrange, L. L. (2014). Connectedness as a core conservation concern: An interdisciplinary review of theory and a call for practice. *Springer Science Reviews, 2*, 119–143.

Louise Chawla is Professor Emerita in the Environmental Design Program at the University of Colorado Boulder, and an active member of the university's Community Engagement, Design and Research Center. Her research and publications focus on children and nature, children in cities, and the development of committed action for the environment.

How to Raise the Standards of Outdoor Learning and Its Research

Summary of 'The Existing Evidence-Base About the Effectiveness of Outdoor Learning', by Fiennes et al.

Rolf Jucker

In partnership with the Institute of Outdoor Learning, the Blagrave Trust commissioned Giving Evidence and The Evidence for Policy and Practice Information and Co-ordinating Centre (EPPI-Centre) at UCL Institute of Education to produce a systematic review of the existing literature about outdoor learning (www.giving-evidence.com/outdoor-learning, accessed 12/02/2021). The Institute of Outdoor Learning (a membership body of practitioners) and the Blagrave Trust (a funder) wanted to understand the following in order to improve their co-ordination of activities and their funding in this area:

1. Categorise the various outdoor learning (OL) activities being run in the UK, in order to provide a coherent sense of the sector as a whole;
2. Identify the various outcomes which organisations running outdoor learning activities are measuring, i.e., identify the outcomes which providers seem to be seeking to achieve; and
3. Assess the designs of individual evaluations (while aware that study designs vary in their openness to bias and hence inaccuracy) and the standard of evidence generally available for different types of outdoor learning. (Fiennes et al., 2015, 5)

From 3,536 titles and abstracts found, the authors finally included 4 UK surveys, 16 systematic reviews and 57 primary UK studies in their review (ibid., 48). I am attempting here a concise summary of their review, in particular the third part which

This summary has been submitted to the authors of the original systematic review of 2015 for correctness. It has been approved on 9th February 2021. The original review can be found here: www.giving-evidence.com/outdoor-learning. We are very grateful indeed for the support of the original authors and also for granting us the copyright to reproduce 3 boxes from the original review.

R. Jucker (✉)
Stiftung SILVIVA, Jenatschstrasse 1, CH-8002 Zürich, Switzerland
e-mail: rolf.jucker@silviva.ch

© The Author(s) 2022
R. Jucker and J. von Au (eds.), *High-Quality Outdoor Learning*,
https://doi.org/10.1007/978-3-031-04108-2_6

was concerned with assessing the quality of the research designs and the available evidence.

However, the authors point out in the previous two sections that there is "no comprehensive or regular (repeated) survey of the scale of outdoor learning in the UK". Disturbingly, they cite research which shows that, at least for the 30 years up to 2010, fieldwork and residential study have declined, not risen, in the UK (ibid., 11–12), at least in Biology. The factors cited for this decline are time and cost pressure, changes in curriculum and its assessment, as well as fears around health and safety and a decline in teachers' enthusiasm and expertise (ibid., 12).

With regard to the quality of research in the field, the authors found that the then-current research base (the research was done in 2015) in the UK raised issues of research ethics, the quality of systemic reviews available, and confusion between interventions and outcomes in studies. In addition, the primary studies they found in the UK are limited by the following factors:

- The studies are thinly spread across a wide variety of populations, age groups, interventions, settings and outcomes, so "few topics have been researched more than a handful of times." (ibid., 6)
- Types of activities and participants are limited mostly to adventure or residential activity; 11–14 year olds; and the general population.
- "The outcomes measured are mainly around 'character development-type' outcomes (communication skills, teamwork, self-confidence etc.). Very few studies addressed interventions with strong links to core curriculum subjects. (…) Looking internationally, only six of the 15 systematic reviews looked at educational attainment, and only one addressed employability." (ibid.)
- "Safety is little covered in the systematic reviews and was not measured as an outcome in any of the primary studies. Safety is obviously a major issue in outdoor learning since it can be dangerous." (ibid.)
- In terms of the methodological quality of the designs of the studies, the review, using a scale developed by Project Oracle,[1] found that many UK studies did not even reach Level One of this scale. This means that they did not have an explicit theory of change ("also known as a logic model: an articulation of the inputs, the intended outcomes, how the inputs are meant to produce those outcomes, and

---

[1] The five levels are: "Project Oracle's scale 'rates' what we know about interventions on whether there are: (1) detailed project descriptions and logic models; (2) before and after studies; (3) evaluations with a control group, which one would expect for interventions beyond the pilot stage; (4) replicated evaluations of impact; and (5) multiple independent evaluations in different settings, which may imply that further evaluations are less useful." (Fiennes et al., 2015, 9) More on the Project: "Project Oracle is a children and youth evidence hub that aims to improve outcomes for young people in London. We do this by building the capacity of providers and funders to develop and commission evidence-based projects, creating an ecosystem in which evidence is widely gathered, used and shared. We also work with specific 'cohorts' or sub-sets of the sector to embed good practice, and at a national and international level to promote the wider use of evaluation and evidence. Project Oracle is funded by the Greater London Authority (GLA), the Mayor's Office for Police and Crime (MOPAC) and the Economic and Social Research Council (ESRC)." (ibid., 9, FN 2).

assumptions about context, participants or other conditions", ibid., 7). This might mean that the practitioners had a poor understanding of their intervention, and more seriously, it impedes other practitioners in assessing whether the intervention might achieve the same outcomes in their context. "No UK study, or set of studies, featured the more demanding attributes of Levels Four or Five". This means that no intervention had been replicated and studied in multiple contexts (ibid., 7).

The authors make a very effective plea for research quality (see Box 3, ibid., 28–29; reprinted as Box 1 below):

Box 1: Why we evaluate research methods

(i)   *Because different research methods give different answers*

"Two men say they're Jesus: One of them must be wrong" (Dire Straits lyric!)
    Table 1 shows the effect of a reading programme in India measured using several research methods (Innovations for Poverty Action). These methods all used the same outcome measures, but the experimental designs were different.
    The answers vary widely: some suggest that it works well, others show it to be detrimental. Clearly there can only be one correct answer! All the other answers are incorrect: and could mislead donors or practitioners to implement this programme at the expense of another which might be better.

Table 1 Different methods and impacts

Method	Impact estimate
(1) Pre-post	26.42[a]
(2) Simple difference	−5.05[a]
(3) Difference-in-difference	6.82[a]
(4) Regression	1.92
(5) Randomized experiment	5.87[a]

[a] Statistically significant at the 5% level

The answers vary because research methods vary in how open they are to biases (i.e., systematic errors). For instance, suppose that a medical trial involves giving patients a drug for two years. Suppose that that drug has horrible side-effects such that during the two years, some patients can't stand taking it so they drop out of the trial (or worse, perhaps the drug kills some of them). If the trial only collects data on patients who are still in the trial after two years, it will systematically miss the important insights about those side-effects. This 'survivor bias' will make the drug look more effective than it really is.

Somebody reading the trial results without knowing that detail wouldn't be able to distinguish the actual effect of the drug from that of this survivor bias. Similarly, if a study only looks at the outcome (in the example above, it's reading level) before the programme and then afterwards (i.e., is a pre-post study), it won't be possible to distinguish whether any improvement in reading levels was due to the programme or just to the fact that children learn over time anyway.

{As an aside, contrary to popular myth, it is not invariably the case that robust research is more expensive than unreliable research, nor that randomised controlled trials (the most reliable design for a single primary study) are invariably terribly expensive: many are cheap or free. See Appendix 12, ibid., 73}.

(ii)   *Because weaker research methods allow for more positive findings*

The UK National Audit Office searched for literally every published evaluation of a UK government programme (National Audit Office, 2013: *Evaluation in Government*). Of those, it chose a sample, and ranked on one hand, the quality of the research method ('robustness' on the x axis, i.e., how insulated the study is from bias), and on the other, the positive-ness of the programme ('claimed impact').

The trend line on the resulting graph below would slope diagonally downwards. It shows that more robust research only allows for modest impact claims whereas weak research allows much stronger claims.

Bad research can be persuaded to say almost anything, and won't allow researchers to distinguish the effects of a programme from other factors (e.g., the passage of time, the mindset of participants, other programmes) nor from chance.

Most social interventions have a small effect and a reliable research method will show what that is: bad research is likely to overstate it. The highest estimate for the reading programme above is from the pre-post study which is a weak study design (Fig. 1).

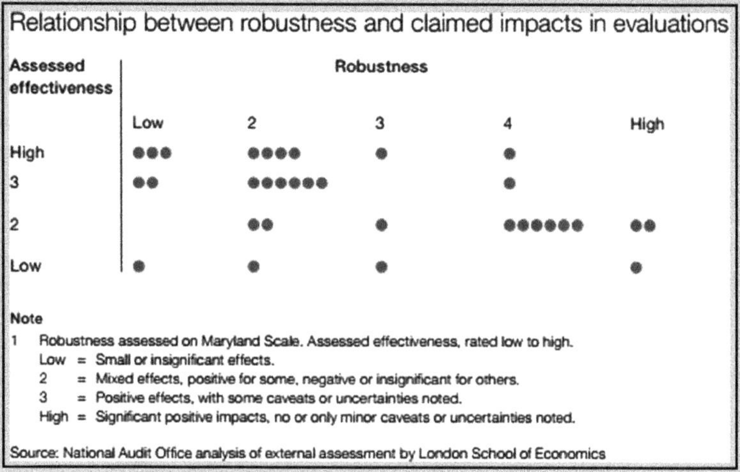

Relationship between robustness and claimed impacts in evaluations

Assessed effectiveness	Robustness				
	Low	2	3	4	High
High	●●●	●●●●	●	●	
3	●●	●●●●●●		●	
2		●●	●	●●●●●●	●●
Low	●	●	●		●

Note
1   Robustness assessed on Maryland Scale. Assessed effectiveness, rated low to high.
    Low = Small or insignificant effects.
    2   = Mixed effects, positive for some, negative or insignificant for others.
    3   = Positive effects, with some caveats or uncertainties noted.
    High = Significant positive impacts, no or only minor caveats or uncertainties noted.

Source: National Audit Office analysis of external assessment by London School of Economics

Fig. 1 Robust research allows for modest impact claims, weak research allows much stronger claims

This relationship between weak research methods and positive findings has been shown also in medical research. We found it in the studies of outdoor learning too.

It is therefore very important, and should certainly be a future aspiration both for practitioners and for researchers to adhere to robust and rigorous research designs. The authors note: "We were unable to find replicated studies that took into account differing contexts and that were sufficiently well documented for wider implementation." (Fiennes et al., 2015, 30)

Box 5 (reprinted as Box 2 below) shares guidelines for describing interventions from medical research which might help the outdoor learning sector to improve replicability of good practice (ibid., 33).

Box 2: Describing an intervention

Medical research has guidelines for describing interventions such that somebody else can replicate them accurately. They have a 12-point checklist for describing interventions, the Template for Intervention Description and Replication (TIDieR) (Hoffman et al., 2014), which is helpful and could easily be adapted for outdoor learning. It has been adapted elsewhere, e.g., by mental health charities (Kent County Council, 2014):

- The name of the intervention (brief name or phrase)
- The way it works (rationale, theory, or goal of the essential elements)
- What materials and procedures were used (physical or informational)
- What (each procedure, activity, and/or process)
- Who provided the intervention (e.g., nurse, psychologist, and give their expertise and background)
- How was it delivered (e.g., face to face, online, by phone, and whether it was provided individually or in a group)
- Where it took place
- When and how much (the number of sessions, schedule, dosage and duration)
- Tailoring (what if anything could be adapted to the individual, why and by how much)
- Modifications which happened after the study started
- How well was adherence to the plan assessed (i.e., the process for assessing adherence)
- The extent to which implementation adhered to the plan.

Given these limitations, it seems fair to suggest that the findings, implications and recommendations of the review about the effectiveness of interventions should be treated with caution. They might qualify as indications and trends, rather than established truth. The most solid findings were:

- "[The systematic reviews] almost all report that the various outdoor learning activities have positive effects on all their various outcomes, e.g., attitudes, beliefs, interpersonal and social skills, academic skills, positive behaviour, re-offending rates and self-image." (Fiennes et al., 2015, 17)
- "The effect attenuates over time: the effect as measured immediately after the intervention is stronger than in follow-up measures after a few months. This is common for social interventions. However, one meta-analysis found that effects relating to self-control were high and were normally maintained over time." (ibid.)
- "Longer programmes tend to be more effective than shorter ones. This fits with practice-based knowledge that length can allow for a more intensive and integrated experience and is obviously important given the pressure to cut length in order to reduce costs." (ibid.)
- "Strong benefits are also associated with well-designed preparatory work, and follow-up work." (ibid.)

For the following types of intervention, there was less or mixed evidence, considerable variation in effect sizes or only evidence for certain findings:

- Positive benefits on academic learning
- Creative development, emotional development and social skills. (ibid.)

For some interventions, such as mountaineering or rock climbing, evidence was weak, absent or there even was evidence of harmful impacts (ibid.).

In our context it is worth noting that the review found only "very few studies (…) of interventions with strong links to core curriculum subjects" (ibid., 21). In addition, there seemed far fewer studies looking at outdoor-based learning in a regular school day setting, compared to residential experiences (ibid., 22). In terms of age of the pupils researched, most concern 11–18 year olds.

"Strikingly few studies looked at educational attainment" (ibid., 23), whereas "non-educational outcomes", such as curiosity, relationship with nature, self-awareness, self-esteem, self-responsibility, communication or teamwork, health and well-being, healthy lifestyles, employability, youth leadership, community integration or community leadership, "have received much more research interest" (ibid., 24).[2] The authors sanguinely state: "We take no view here on whether non-educational outcomes are important, but rather notice the mismatch between research topics and the pressure schools face to achieve those educational outcomes." (ibid., 26)

Given that effect sizes of 0–0.2 are considered small, 0.5 is considered moderate, 0.8 or more is considered large, the average effect sizes in some of the systemic reviews of between 0.26 and 0.35 have to be considered small to moderate.

Recommendations

In terms of developing a coherent, robust agenda for practitioners and researchers of the outdoor-learning sector, I would translate the authors' recommendations into the following four strategies:

- On the level of practitioners of outdoor-based learning, they need to be enabled to create and use theories of change, i.e. they need to be clear about their operational models (see ibid., 32 and Box 4, reprinted as Box 3 below). Practitioner's organisations also need to have systems in place to collect relevant data but also to "support ethical practices for monitoring and research, particularly the storage and sharing of data from evaluations" (ibid., 8).
- On the level of researchers, they need to "create a system to regularly capture data on the types and volumes of activity". Only with a decent set of baseline data can the sector, funders or government agencies trace (positive or negative) developments.
- Researchers, practitioners, funders and government bodies need to reflect together on the important research topics and prioritise them deliberately. This includes

---

[2] "Other outcomes included: creativity, commitment to learning, respect for self / others, sense of social responsibility, sense of belonging, addressing fear, tenacity, confidence, social skills, motivation, concentration, physical skills, resilience, social behaviour, direction, mindset, enjoyment, inspiration, impact on schools, family and community, critical thinking, self-determination, competence, relatedness, task approach, task avoidance, ego approach, ego avoidance, Relative Autonomy Index (RAI), interest effort, value autonomy-support, metacognition, problem-solving skills, optimism, pedagogical skills." (Fiennes et al., 2015, 24).

the need for "creating a more shared language around the categories of activity" (ibid., 32).

- A new open-access culture needs to be developed which ensures that "both interventions and research are described clearly, fully and publicly" (ibid., 8).

Box 3: Theories of change

What is a theory of change?

A theory of change (or logic model: we use the terms interchangeably) is what is meant by Project Oracle's Level 1's 'we know what we want to achieve' and 'project model' (i.e., articulation of how the activities are supposed to create the intended impact). It lays out the assumptions behind an intervention, and links between activities and intended impacts (i.e., how the activities are supposed to produce those impacts, and what is assumed, e.g., parental engagement, weather…). They allow organisations to find and cite evidence suggesting that their activities are likely to produce their target outcomes.

A clear theory of change also helps other organisations considering running the intervention to see whether the assumptions are likely to hold in their contexts, i.e., whether they're likely to get similar results. It also helps other organisations make good decisions about what outcomes to try to achieve by showing what's involved in the interventions which ostensibly deliver them.

The diagram below shows the constituent pieces of a logic model (Fig. 2):

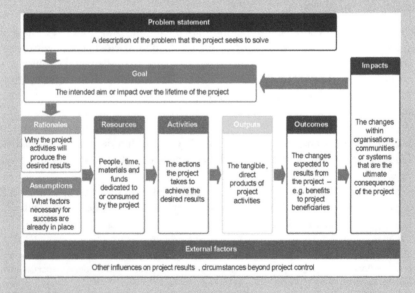

Fig. 2 Logic model

Why does having a clear logic model matter?

A clear logic model is important/essential to intelligent programme design because it enables predictions about whether a type of intervention is likely to work (for a specific population). An evaluation without a clear logic model simply shows whether a programme worked and the extent to which it worked: it gives no indication of why it worked (or not)—why it gets those results. That is, without a logic model, the intervention is like a black box: we gain no insight into whether it's likely to achieve those results again, nor elsewhere. It adds nothing to the 'science' (i.e., understanding) of these interventions. By contrast, if a provider starts with a clear logic model, they can use the existing research to see which parts are likely to be true, which are not evidenced, and therefore can:

(a) make an educated estimate of whether, when and for whom the intervention is likely to work,
(b) identify major risks and unsupported assumptions,
(c) change the design to make it more likely to succeed. It may transpire that the proposed logic model is totally fanciful and implausible, and hence this work will prevent them running a pointless intervention, or even a harmful intervention. And
(d) identify what needs testing. Maybe very little needs testing and so the practitioner is spared all the cost and hassle of evaluating.

In short, it enables practitioners to use existing research, rather than solely to produce research. Clearly this is more efficient. The focus on impact has led many organisations (particularly charities) to often produce research of bad quality, when (i) they are not set up nor incentivised to be researchers, and (ii) it might be more useful for them to leverage the (better quality) research which already exists.

Even though the review is a few years old, I think it is very useful indeed to sharpen our focus on what we need to do to improve the quality of outdoor-based learning provision as well as the quality of the research assessing its impact,[3] and thereby guiding future practice and policy development.

---

[3] Interestingly enough, this review reaches similar conclusions as the systematic review by Becker, C., Lauterbach, G., Spengler, S., Dettweiler, U., & Mess, F. (2017). Effects of regular classes in outdoor education settings: A systematic review on students' learning, social and health dimensions. *International Journal of Environmental Research and Public Health, 14*(5), 1–20. http://doi.org/10.3390/ijerph14050485).

References

Fiennes, C., Oliver, E., Dickson, K., Escobar, D., Romans, A., & Oliver, S. (2015). *The existing evidence-base about the effectiveness of outdoor learning* (pp. 1–73). www.giving-evidence. com/outdoor-learning. Accessed 12 Feb 2021. The review can also be accessed on the sites of the respective organisations: https://www.blagravetrust.org/wp-content/uploads/2015/11/The-Exi sting-Evidence-base-about-the-Effectiveness-of-Outdoor-Learning-Executive-Summary-Nov-2015.pdf. Accessed 15 Feb 2021. https://www.outdoor-learning.org/Portals/0/IOL%20Docu ments/Research/outdoor-learning-giving-evidence-revised-final-report-nov-2015-etc-v21.pdf? ver=2017-03-16-110244-937. Accessed 15 Feb 2021.

Hoffmann, T. C., Glasziou, P. P., Boutron, I., Milne, R., Perera, R., Moher, R., Altman, D. G., Barbour, V., Macdonald, H., Johnston, M., Lamb, S. E., Dixon-Wood, M., McCulloch, P., Wyatt, J. C., Chan, A.-W., & Michie, S. (2014). Better reporting of interventions: Template for intervention description and replication (TIDieR) checklist and guide. *The British Medical Journal, 348.* https://doi.org/10.1136/bmj.g1687. Accessed 19 Apr 2021.

Kent County Council. (2014). HeadStart Kent. http://www.kelsi.org.uk/__data/assets/powerp oint_doc/0010/25588/Programme-Board-Main-Presentation-19-11-14-AF-UN.pptx. Accessed 19 Apr 2021.

Rolf Jucker is currently Director of the Swiss Foundation for Nature-based Learning (SILVIVA) and a learning for sustainability expert, having previously served as Director of the Swiss Foundation for Environmental Education from 2008 to 2012. He gained an MSc in Education for Sustainability (EfS) and worked extensively on education for a viable future, publishing widely on the subject. He is the author of *Do We Know What We Are Doing?* (2014) and *Can We Cope with the Complexity of Reality? Why Craving Easy Answers Is at the Root of our Problems* (2020).

High-Quality Research—Findings from TEACHOUT

Udeskole—Pupils' Physical Activity and Gender Perspectives

Erik Mygind

1 Introduction and Background

Inactivity and obesity pose is a general and increasing health problem in many western countries. There is an ongoing debate how and with which initiatives this problematic development can be counteracted. As children aged 6–16 spend many hours a day in school, it can be argued that the school system can and should play an important role in promoting daily physical activity (PA), health and well-being (Janssen & LeBlanc, 2010). In Denmark the Ministry of Education (2014) introduced a school reform in 2013, trying to compensate for the lack of PA through a longer school day which included an additional 45 min daily PA on top of the usual few hours of physical education (PE) per week and recess—unfortunately with limited success.

Depending on the chosen teaching activities, two well organised PE lessons per week might give pupils a certain amount of moderate to vigorous activity (MVPA). There might be additional PA during the more unstructured recess school periods, which take place in a continuum from sedentary to very high activity levels. Therefore, the weekly amount of PA can be of questionable value in terms of health promotion in a school context. Some pupils are completely inactive and others very active. In general, regular PA and resulting health effects are important factors that can prevent lifestyle diseases later in adulthood, but they can also create important links between PA and learning (Sibley & Etnier, 2003; Åberg et al., 2009). The question is to what extent the school system can contribute to increase PA. A consensus conference conducted by the Arts Council in 2011 and later expanded in 2016 (Consensus, 2016) concluded an important connection between PA and learning, regardless of age. In other words, PA holds many potentials from health and learning perspectives.

A number of studies have reported that boys are generally more physically active during a day compared to girls. For example, a study across five European countries

E. Mygind (✉)
Fuglehavevej 33, 2750 Ballerup, Denmark
e-mail: emygind@ign.ku.dk

found significantly lower levels of light, moderate and high PA among 10–12 year old girls compared to boys (Verloigne et al., 2012). Similarly, reported significant differences between boys and girls (mean 52 ± 14 min/day MVPA for boys and 37 ± 14 min/day for girls). A study by Nielsen et al. (2011) showed that gender differences of daily PA were due to girls' lighter levels of PA during disorganised play in the institutional and school context. Further, it became clear that 30% of girls and 17% of boys did not achieve the recommended daily amount of PA. This emphasizes the need for initiatives that can support and increase PA. This applies in particular to girls, children from ethnic minority backgrounds, children with obesity problems and children with disadvantaged socio-economic backgrounds.

It is not on the political agenda in Denmark to increase the number of PE lessons every week and a number of teachers have difficulties to create situations during the school day where they can introduce 45 min of daily PA. This raises the question whether there are other ways to increase physical activity. In this context, *udeskole*, i.e. regular weekly curriculum-based teaching outside the classroom, might be an important tool to increase PA and at the same time create important links to learning, motivation and well-being (see Barfod & Mygind "*Udeskole*—Regular Teaching Outside the Classroom" in this volume). This teaching method offers a more varied education outside the school buildings in nature and / or cultural settings. Case studies conducted in Denmark, Norway and Germany, where objective measurement methods were used (accelerometers and heart rate monitors), have shown increased PA levels (Mygind, 2007; Grønningseter et al., 2007; Becker et al., 2017).

Very little is known concerning children's PA or mental health, but use of natural environments appears to stimulate PA (Fjørtoft, 2004; Wood et al., 2014). A systematic review by Becker et al. (2017) recommended that more quasi-experimental design and longitudinal studies with a greater number of participants are conducted, and a high methodological quality is applied to further investigate these preliminary observations. Further, there is a limited knowledge about the connection between PA and *udeskole* and to what extent this teaching method has an impact on girls' and boys' PA. The purpose of this chapter is therefore to present the results of two larger Danish *udeskole* research projects, which investigated how a weekly *udeskole* day in primary school had an impact on pupils PA compared to other school days and specific domains.

2   The Søndermark School Study in Copenhagen

The purpose of the Søndermark School study in Frederiksberg, Copenhagen, was primarily to measure PA among girls and boys in grades 3–6 during a week, comparing one *udeskole* day with (1) the average of three standard school days without PE lessons and (2) one standard school day with two PE lessons (Mygind, 2016). Further, the study aimed to compare the impact of PA when pupils are taught in nature, in a green area or in cultural institutions. An additional aim was to examine the PA levels during two PE lessons, after school time, and on weekends (for example in neighbourhoods).

The school management, teachers and parents received written and oral information about the project. Four teachers and one fourth, one fifth and two sixth grade classes accepted to participate in the study. All the data collection took place in four randomly selected weeks seven days in a row in each of the four participating classes. Each teacher and class got used to teach regularly outside the classroom for three months before data collection. The pupils completed regular self-assessment (log/diary) during the data collection period. They were instructed to record keywords and the kind of activity they have been involved in on an hourly basis. Diary notes were used in addition to the objective measurements.

Method

Students in grades 4-6 had a matchbox large accelerometer mounted in an elastic belt over the right hip (ActiGraph GT3x). The activity meter was worn for a week, but was taken off during water activities and while the student slept at night to avoid discomfort. The data collection was performed using raw acceleration with a sampling frequency of 30 Hz and data exported for 10 second epochs. At least 10 hours of recorded activity constituted a valid monitored day. A total of 96 students participated in the study. Illness and absence resulted in a reduction in the overall student population. In the end, data from 44 girls and 40 boys were accepted for comparison of different school contexts with a specific focus on days with *udeskole*, standard school days and school days with PE (Mygind, 2016).

Results

PA in different educational contexts

Results from 84 girls and boys showed that *udeskole* days (23.1%; $p < 0.001$) and school days with PE (46.1%; $p < 0.001$) had significantly higher PA levels (counts per minute) compared to standard school days without PE lessons (Mygind, 2016). These results showed that on *udeskole* days (3.4%) and days with PE lessons (4.2%) MVPA was significantly higher compared to standard school days. Expressed in another way, MVPA was 6.7 min on standard school days, 8.5 min on *udeskole* days and 11.0 min for standard the school days with PE lessons. Although the MVPA levels might seem modest, *udeskole* did contribute to raise the level of high intensity PA in a school context. However, boys seem to cause the generally higher PA levels in all settings except for standard school days with PE lessons. This issue is addressed in the following section of the TEACHOUT *udeskole* study, where data include both light PA (LPA) and MVPA (Schneller, Duncan, et al., 2017).

Gender differences

The average PA measured in counts per minute including all 84 pupils showed a significant difference between boys and girls measured in the three different educational contexts, i.e. days with *udeskole*, average of three standard school days and one standard school day with two PE lessons (Fig. 1, Mygind, 2016). *Udeskole* days had a significantly higher level of activity than standard school days without PE. Breaks and after school activity showed that the boys were significantly more physically active compared to girls except on standard school days with PE. Unorganised play, which typically took place during breaks and after school time, showed a higher level of PA for boys. Free play in connection with the breaks in *udeskole* may also explain the gender difference found in this setting, although our expectation would be that organised education outside would stimulate both sexes equally. No difference was recorded on weekends, but only a tendency that the boys were more physically active in this context too (Fig. 1).

Udeskole in green areas and cultural institutions

Each of the *udeskole* days were organised based on 'a year wheel'. The site for teaching outside the school buildings was chosen based on whether the individual teacher found it appropriate in relation to the academic content and time of the year. An interesting question, which arose, was to investigate to what degree *udeskole* days in nature /green areas or visits to culture institutions contributed to PA. A further question was which outdoor educational setting the four teachers had decided to use in the week the data collection took place.

The teachers were informed about the data collection week a few days before and at this point, the teachers had planned where to do *udeskole*; i.e. green areas or culture institutions. One teacher decided to walk and teach a class (4e) in green areas (Søndermarken/Carlsberg's garden), while the other three classes visited cultural institutions at Frederiksberg City Hall (6d), Central Station (6a) and an art gallery (5d) (Fig. 2, Mygind, 2016). The results showed no significant difference in PA (counts per minute) on *udeskole* days in the three classes visiting cultural institutions compared to standard school days without PE ($p = 0, 12$) (Fig. 2). The class being taught in green areas had significantly higher PA levels compared to standard school days ($p < 0.001$), but also compared with a standard school days with PE (25.9%, $p < 0.01$) (Fig. 2). No differences were found between the four classes in leisure time after school. However, the variation between classes was very large on *udeskole* days, standard days with PE, weekends and specific domains like recess and PE lessons (see Fig. 2). For example, the activity in PE lessons and leisure in class 6d was between 21 and 32% lower, compared to the other three classes.

Discussion

The structure of the discussion is broken down into three sections. First, a discussion of how different *udeskole* settings influence PA among the four participating classes is conducted, including differences of gender. Next, the teachers' choice of *udeskole*

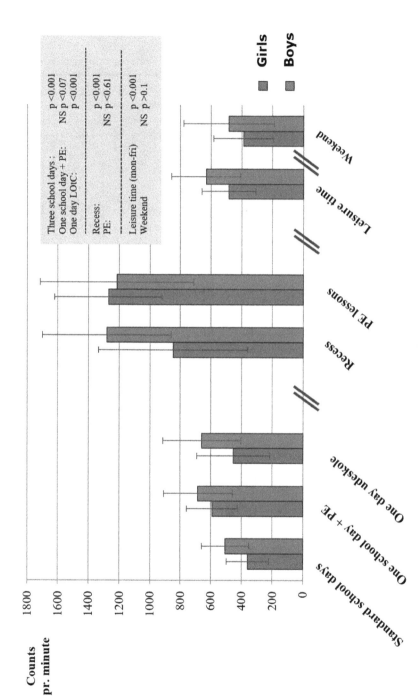

Fig. 1 Physical activity, gender, different school days and domains—Data are shown as means ± SD in counts per minute. Levels of physical activities (PA) among girls and boys are depicted from the mean of three standard school days without PE, one day with *udeskole* and one day with PE. Further, comparisons are made between recess and the two PE lessons, leisure time after five school days and weekends. Significant differences are shown in legends, $p < 0.05$ (from Mygind, 2016)

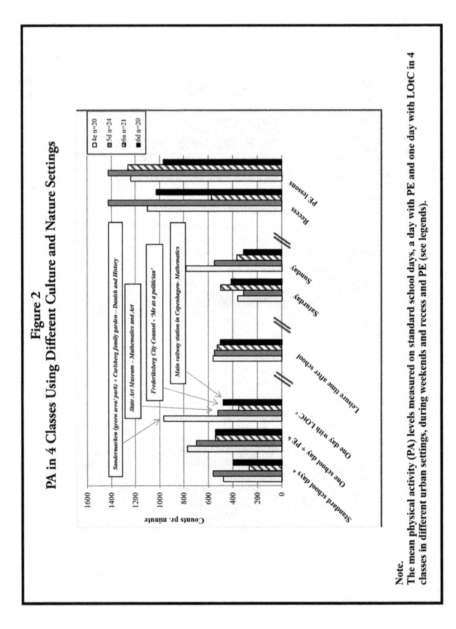

Fig. 2 PA in *udeskole* settings and gender perspectives in the Søndermark School study (from Mygind, 2016)

setting and the importance of transport to the chosen destination is considered and finally, the last section contains a summary and critical look at the study. The teachers' goals, program or choice of outdoor setting (nature / green area or cultural institution) were not known in advance. The weeks, where the measurement took place after three months preliminary *udeskole* experience in the four classes, were randomly chosen. On average, the *udeskole* days provided a significantly higher level of PA, adding 12–13 min of MVPA compared to standard school days without PE. The picture is more nuanced if one compares the three classes that were taught in urban culture institutions with the one class taught in urban green areas. The latter had a significantly higher average PA level compared to the three classes visiting cultural institutions (Frederiksberg Town Hall (6d), Central Station (6a) and the National Gallery of Art (5d) (Fig. 2). All four classes included PA through walking to and from the destination, but judging from the teachers' notes, the more modest PA during visits to cultural institutions might be due to the lower PA taking place during hours spent inside. In the three cultural institutions, there is an expectation not to run around—in fact, to keep calm and move only when necessary or instructed. A visit to nature and green areas often invite to be physical active—both through the teacher planned learning activities and not the least during breaks. Walking to and from the destinations on *udeskole* days added some PA compared to standard school days, but in particular, class 4e who visited green areas caused a significant increase of PA in the study (Fig. 2).

The very high PA activity level in this class is in line with the results of the case study with 12 girls and 7 boys from Rødkilde school project, where several accelerometer measurements in a forest summer and winter *udeskole* were compared to standard school days. Further, the level of PA corresponded to a standard school day including two lessons with PE (Mygind, 2007). This is also supported by a Norwegian *udeskole* case study with heart rate measurements in nature settings (Grønningseter et al., 2009). The mean percentage of time with heart rate >= 160 beats/minute was 5% for a standard school day and 18% for a day in the forest (p < 0.001). In other words, visiting cultural institutions does not appear conducive to PA to the same extent, as does the use of green areas.

The results showed that girls' average PA was significantly lower compared to boys in all measured school contexts, except for standard school days with PE lessons (Fig. 2). This was a bit surprising because it was expected that the teacher-managed and organised learning activities during *udeskole* days and transport to the destination would have an equal impact on girls and boys PA patterns as during PE lessons. This was not the case. One explanation might be that also in *udeskole* boys use recess and free time more to be physically active.

The importance of how unorganised and non-teacher supervised situations affect PA among girls and boys in school is underlined in a Spanish study of play in recreational areas (Martínez-Gómez et al., 2014). It was concluded that more effort should be undertaken to increase girls' activity levels. A Danish study by Nielsen et al. (2011) also showed similar gender differences. Girls were lower in everyday institutional contexts during disorganised play, school free time, and day care after school. More worryingly, about 30% of girls and 17% of boys did not live up to the recommended daily amount of PA. The results of the Søndermark School study are in line with a study by Verloigne et al. (2012), which found that objectively assessed levels of moderate and vigorous PA among 10–12 year old girls were lighter, compared to boys across five European countries. Similarly, the study by Van der Niet et al. (2015) showed significant daily differences between boys and girls (mean 52 ± 14 min MVPA for boys and 37 ± 14 min for girls).

In conclusion, schools and teachers in general should consider how to conduct organised play in recess that especially motivates girls. *Udeskole* teachers might reflect on how to combine PA and learning activities to a higher degree. *Udeskole* might be an important tool for children who do not usually participate in organised recreational activities; especially girls with ethnic minority backgrounds and children with obesity problems as well as children from disadvantaged socio-economic backgrounds. There is a need for more research to shed light on how teachers in primary schools, for example, can balance academic learning and PA through *udeskole* for the benefit of both sexes.

Udeskole—the setting and PA

The teacher's choice of place (natural or cultural) is obviously crucial for how physically active the pupils are. In organizing *udeskole* the teacher can put more or less emphasis on PA, e.g. how transport to and from the destination is organised. The weeks in which the measurements took place were randomly selected, because a structured design with equal amount of classes visiting both cultural institutions and green areas was not possible at the time being. The four teachers focused on academic learning and not specifically on integrating PA in *udeskole*, but according to their notes, they preferred to walk with their class to and from the chosen destination (Mygind, 2016).

The teachers' notes from the *udeskole* days were very important to understand the quite significant variations between classes (see Mygind, 2016). Of course, the teachers' choice of teaching methods affects the general PA level in each class, i.e. location, academic content and tasks, travel (walking, biking, taking a bus or train), distance to the destination, safety considerations, and the pupils' free time to play during the day. Cultural visits (based on the teachers notes) offer some explanations on why the fifth and two sixth classes had relatively similar levels of activity, while the fourth grade (4e) average PA level was twice as high. This class walked from school through a nature / park area (Søndermarken), visited the Carlsberg family garden and walked back again. In this way, they reached a PA amount 25, 9% higher than on a school day with PE lesson (Fig. 2). The PE activity in this specific week was high. One explanation for the very high level in 4e could be the many active hours, characterised by a lot of walking and running travelling back and forth, during teaching in the Carlsberg family garden and not least that the pupils had two periods of free play on green playgrounds. Further, it is well known that younger children are more physically active compared to older children / adolescents, and here a fourth grade class was compared to a fifth grade and the two sixth grade classes (Fig. 2).

Summary and critical remarks

The Søndermark School study provides support for other case studies, which found that combining academic learning and PA in nature and green settings yields positive results. However, it is questionable whether visits to cultural institutions contribute positively to PA, when length and type of journey to and from the destination seem to be the dominating PA factor. Unorganised leisure and recess during *udeskole* seem to benefit boys, but not to the same degree girls.

The strength of the Søndermark School study were the teachers' notes and the knowledge of how each *udeskole* day and academic program took place, making it possible to understand and explain the PA results. A weakness was the few and randomly chosen four weeks from a whole *udeskole* year, but time and financial constraints as well as limitations on additional support by the school did not allow more data collection. Only a single week was analysed in each class and a stronger picture would have appeared if, for example the four classes could have been analysed in four green as well as four cultural settings—winter and summer. Measurements carried out in other weeks may well have resulted in higher or lower PA values in the same classes depending on the *udeskole* teachers' choice of transport and academic content at the destination. Finally, a weakness is the lack of information about sedentary time and LPA. This raises an important question whether use of green areas and cultural institutions in urban settings contribute to a decrease in sedentary schoolwork and to an increase in LPA. The latter is taken into account in the TEACHOUT study, with the inclusion of significantly more classes and pupils.

3   The TEACHOUT *Udeskole* Project

The purpose of the TEACHOUT study[1] was to investigate the importance of regular weekly education outside the classroom (EOtC) or *udeskole* during a year (2014–2015) and included a high number of pupils compared to previous case studies (Nielsen et al., 2016). The study investigated how *udeskole* had an impact on PA and health, learning, motivation and well-being. *Udeskole* can be regarded as movement integration (MI) in the school context, and has shown to increase children's PA in case studies. Increased PA is a potential secondary outcome or perhaps a means to achieve the teaching aim. The TEACHOUT study design and rationale can be found in the study protocol paper (Nielsen et al., 2016). More in-depth information on *udeskole* activities in Denmark can be found in an inventory of the use of *udeskole* practice in schools across Denmark conducted in 2014–15 (Barfod et al., 2016).

---

[1] The overall aim of the Danish TEACHOUT research project was to generate knowledge about the strengths and weaknesses of practicing *udeskole* compared to mainstream education under the framework of the new school reform (2013). *Udeskole* is a broad term referring to curriculum-based teaching outside the school buildings in natural as well as cultural settings on a regular basis. TEACHOUT investigated physical activity, learning and social relations.

In Danish primary and secondary schools, teachers are allowed "freedom of methods" to achieve the curricula targets decided by the Danish Ministry of Education within each subject taught (Danish Ministry of Education, 2014). A new public school reform was implemented across Danish schools in August 2014. This reform included initiatives such as requiring school staff and children to spend 5.5 to 8.5 h more in school every week, to provide pupils with an average of 45 min of daily PA, e.g. for schools to seek more active cooperation with local sports clubs, and for teachers to empower children to more actively engage in the educational activities.

School demographics in Denmark and control classes

In Denmark, children are randomly assigned to a class within the school district where they live at enrolment in grade 0. This means that the demographic characteristics of children in two parallel classes can be expected to be comparable (Danish Ministry of Education, 2017). In the TEACHOUT study, data were collected from children who were sampled into *udeskole* intervention classes and control / parallel classes at the same school and grade level, based on the willingness of teachers to participate in the study. As such, approximately half the children from whom data were obtained attended a comparison class in which *udeskole* was not supposed to be a regular curriculum-based activity. All data from participating children were pooled and analysed as the amount of *udeskole* varied greatly between participating classes. (Schneller et al., 2017).

The present chapter focus on a subset of the TEACHOUT study, i.e. on gender perspectives and PA in standard classroom teaching, which seem to be a promising opportunity for children to increase PA. The aim was to investigate the effects of *udeskole* on children's PA by segmenting weekly activity-related behaviour into a range of day types, domains and PA levels among girls and boys analysing the extent of LPA and MVPA as indicators of the importance to health (see Schneller et al., 2017). Further, the aim was to evaluate how *udeskole* affects daily PA in a larger sample of school-aged children, including a control group (parallel class): a research approach, which has been in short supply up until now. Specifically, the proportion of time spent in different PA intensities between different day types and within certain domains specific to both school (i.e. *udeskole*, classroom activities, PE, and recess) and leisure time, i.e. after school days and weekend days, differentiated by gender.

Method

Pupils from 3rd to 6th class wore two motion meters (accelerometer model Axivity AX3) mounted on the front of the thigh and the back of the loin.

The accelerometer was worn for 9-10 days continuously. The data collection was performed using raw acceleration at a sampling rate of 50 measurements/second and translated into an estimated energy consumption second by second. To be included in the analyses, a pupil would have seven consecutive days of measurements with 24 hours of continuous recording (Schneller et al., 2017). 637 pupils wore accelerometers, but after drop-offs and absence due to sickness, holiday, etc. 346 pupils had usable measurements, which formed the basis for the comparisons at week, day and activity level. The participating classes were recruited in pairs, i.e. an *udeskole* and a control/parallel class. For day- and activity-level analyses, time periods were included in different categories based on information collected via diaries—completed by each class (for more detailed information see Schneller et al., 2017).

Results

PA over a whole week

As a basis for comparing *udeskole* and control classes, pupils from 33 classes were included. 17 classes had 4 h of *udeskole* in the measured weeks and 201 pupils' measurements of PA met the inclusion criteria (see text box). In total, 16 comparison classes attended with an average of 64 min of *udeskole* in the measured week including 160 pupils. In other words, the results reflect a comparison of classes with nearly 5 h of *udeskole* and control classes who on average did about an hour of *udeskole* instead of the expected zero hour of outdoor school. This may be because the TEACHOUT study was completed at the same time as the start of the new school reform in 2014 with a requirement for 45 min of physical student activity. Teachers in the control classes may also have been inspired by *udeskole* teachers to do some outdoor learning. The *udeskole* concept seemed to be an excellent opportunity and a practice that lay outside our control in this real life research project.

We found a significantly greater amount of weekly MVPA for boys in *udeskole* classes compared to boys in their control classes. Quite precisely, this increase was 19 min extra a day. For girls, no difference was found between *udeskole* and parallel classes seen over the week as a whole. There was no statistically significant difference in neither MVPA nor LPA between girls in *udeskole* and girls in control classes (Table 1). Another significant observation was that boys obtained 47 min more MVPA, but at the same time, 29 min less LPA per day compared to girls (see Table 1). We also saw a marked decrease in PA at increasing grade levels, corresponding to 13 min less MVPA and 18 min LPA per day per progression to a higher class grade.

PA among girls and boys by day type

Figure 3 gives an overall picture of the proportions (%) of MVPA and LPA, respectively, of all pupils divided into girls and boys and into four day types.

Table 1 Comparing groups during a week at moderate to high and light intensity PA

Groups being compared	Moderate to high intensity PA		Light intensity PA	
	Minutes/day (95% CI)	p	Minutes/day (95% CI)	p
Udeskole/EOtC versus control classes	76 (71–81) versus 68 (64–72)	**0.01**	388 (379–397) versus 389 (381–398)	0.86
Boys vs girls	95 (90–101) versus 48 (45–51)	**< 0.01**	374 (365–383) versus 403 (395–411)	**< 0.01**
Udeskole/EOtC, boys versus boys in control classes	105 (96–114) versus 86 (80–93)	**0.01**	369 (355–384) versus 378 (367–389)	1.00
Udeskole/EOtC, girls versus girls in control classes	47 (43–51) versus 49 (45–54)	1.00	408 (400–417) versus 398 (384–411)	1.00

p indicates the statistical probability that the numbers are different and the limit value is set to p < 0.05. 95% confidence intervals (CIs) indicate the values that 95% of the measurements in a group are statistically expected to be within

Boys had a significantly higher MVPA level in all four types of days, compared to girls (boys 7.8%; girls 3.8%) and standard school days without PE lessons (boys 6.7%; girls 3.8%). Both genders achieved the most MVPA intensity on days of PE (boys 8.5%; girls 4.6%) and the least on weekend days (boys 5.4%; girls 3.0%) (Fig. 3).

Girls generally had a higher proportion of LPA. The proportion was highest on *udeskole* days (girls 32.0%; boys 29.8%) and slightly lower on standard school days (girls 29.5%; boys 27.5%) and days with PE lessons (girls 29.8%; boys 27.5%). The lowest level of LPA was on weekend days (girls 23.9%; boys 22.1%). *Udeskole* days showed the highest level of LPA among both sexes compared to days with and without PE and weekends.

On school days with PE lessons, MVPA intensity was higher among girls and boys compared to *udeskole* days, standard school days without PE and weekends.

PA in six specific school contexts

Figure 4 presents an overall picture of the proportions of MVPA and LPA (%) obtained by all pupils divided into girls and boys in six specific domains.

In general, the boys in all six specific activity types had a significantly higher MVPA level compared to girls (Fig. 4—top row of bars). The boys spent a statistically significant higher proportion of *udeskole* in MVPA (14.9%) compared to teaching in the classroom (9.4%).

For girls, it was slightly different, as no statistical difference (albeit a trend) was found at MVPA intensity in *udeskole* (6.3%) compared to classroom teaching (4.4%). In general, girls had a higher LPA level in five of the six domain types (bottom bars of Fig. 4) Teaching in *udeskole* triggered a significantly higher LPA compared to classroom teaching.

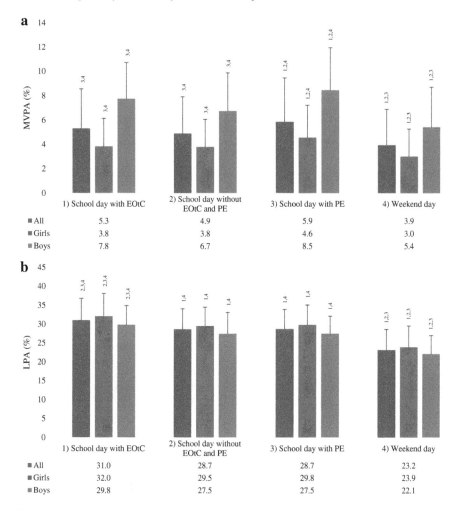

Fig. 3 Percentage of light and moderate / vigorous physical activity among girls and boys by four day types. Bars represent the differences and similarities between boys and girls and in four day types and represent the average proportion of moderate to high PA (top bars) and light PA (lower bars) measured % (± standard deviation express the spread in between measurements). There was significant difference between girls and boys within the same day type in all cases. Numbers above standard deviation bars in both **a** and **b** denote significant difference (mixed-effects regression with identity link) in the proportion of time spent in the PA intensity for the sample (all, girls or boys) (from Schneller et al., 2017)

Not surprisingly, the MVPA level was significantly higher in PE lessons and recess periods for both genders compared to the other four types of activity. Boys achieved approximately equal proportions of MVPA after school and in PE (29.9% and 31.0%, respectively). Moreover, it is worth noting, that girls had a significantly higher level of activity in PE (22.3%) compared to recess domain (13.9%). So organised and

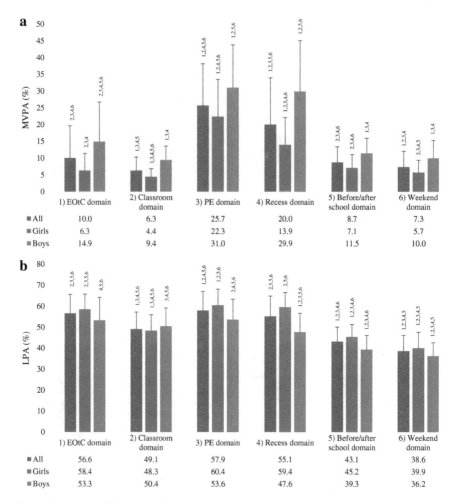

Fig. 4 Percentage of MVPA and LPA in six specific domains in the TEACHOUT study. Proportion of time spent in MVPA and LPA by domain. **a** shows mean ± sd proportion of time spent in MVPA in specific domains by sample (all, girls and boys). **b** shows mean ± sd proportion of time spent in LPA in specific domains by sample (all, girls and boys). Numbers above standard deviation bars in both **a** and **b** denote significant difference (mixed-effects regression with identity link) in the proportion of time spent in the PA intensity for the sample (all, girls or boys) in a domain compared to the other five domains (from Schneller et al., 2017)

structured teaching means a lot. Recreational activities after school and on weekends were low in terms of PA and most of all to be compared to the activity level of classroom teaching.

In summary, for all pupils *udeskole* (58.4%) triggered a higher level of LPA compared to classroom teaching (48.3%). Leisure before and after school as well as weekends showed a generally lower level of LPA compared to the more specific types of activity in school settings. A significantly higher MVPA level was found among boys having *udeskole* during a week compared to boys in their parallel control classes and girls in all day types. On the other hand, girls in *udeskole* achieved a higher LPA level compared to boys in this setting and classroom teaching situations (Fig. 4).

4   Summary Discussion and Perspectives

Gender similarities and differences in the TEACHOUT and Søndermark School studies

The TEACHOUT study and the Søndermark School study included a relatively higher number of pupils compared to previous case studies, which allow a presentation of results describing the impact of *udeskole* for both sexes. Previous case studies have not been able to comment on gender perspectives related to PA due to low number of participants. Both studies underline that boys in all day types and specific domains had significantly higher MVPA compared with girls, i.e. days with *udeskole*, days with and without PE lessons, recess domain, PE lessons and after school time and weekends. The only exception was that on days with PE girls were just as active as the boys in the Søndermark School study, whereas the TEACHOUT study showed that the boys were also the most active in this domain.

The TEACHOUT study showed that girls achieved a higher level of LPA in most types of activity compared with boys and that *udeskole* caused this increase in PA. It is characteristic that boys in recess and free time spend more time in MVPA mode, which again has an important health aspect due to the stimulation of the heart and vascular system. The increased higher LPA seen among girls in *udeskole* might have a positive impact on children with a general and very sedentary life style. In that sense, through combining academic learning and PA schools can contribute to 'kill two birds with one stone'.

The Danish studies are very much in line with the gender differences reported in European studies (Verloigne et al., 2012; Van der Niet et al., 2015; Nielsen et al., 2011). The TEACHOUT study showed that girls on *udeskole* days benefited in terms of LPA. However, it also showed that gender differences in the total amount of daily PA could be explained by girls' low level of physical activity during disorganised play in institutional and school contexts. Conditions that continue to cause concern are that approximately 1/3 of girls and almost 1/5 of boys do not reach the recommended daily amount of PA, highlighting the need for alternative approaches that can support and increase PA. This problem is particularly prominent in children with an ethnic minority background, children with obesity problems and children from disadvantaged socio-economic backgrounds. There is much to indicate that *udeskole* or regular EOtC can make a positive contribution to increasing PA.

Value of udeskole

Both Danish studies show that *udeskole* increases the weekly amount of PA for both sexes—in particular for boys. However, it is more questionable to what degree *udeskole* are beneficial for girls even if the teaching takes place in organised form. The Søndermark School project showed that the *udeskole* setting in nature surroundings did make a difference, while visits to cultural institutions did not contribute to a big change in PA as compared to a standard school day. Use of green space in *udeskole* was also analysed in TEACHOUT. Based on explorative, cross-sectional data this study showed that school days with an *udeskole* session in green space and without a PE lesson was associated with more light physical activity and less sedentary behaviour compared with school days with an *udeskole* session in cultural and societal institutions or companies and without a PE lesson. Green space seems beneficial to both girls' and boys' LPA (Bølling et al., 2021). More research is needed to assess whether nature and green spaces as well as cultural institutions are meaningful to the learning process from both academic and health perspectives.

There is still a general need for more research to shed light on how primary school teachers can balance academic learning and PA, and in particular how they can motivate girls. Finally, it should be considered how to introduce *udeskole* courses in initial and continuous teacher training and how to integrate academic learning and PA when combining in- and outdoor teaching.

Recommended Further Reading

1. Ding, D., Varela, A.R., Bauman, A.E.; Ekelund, U., Lee, I.-M., Heath, G., Katzmarzyk, P.T. Reis, R. & Pratt, M. (2020). Towards Better Evidence-Informed Global Action: Lessons Learnt from the Lancet Series and Recent Developments in Physical Activity and Public Health. *Br. J. Sports Med, 54*, 462–468
2. Inchley, J., Currie, D., Young, T., Samdal, O., Torsheim, T., Augustson, L., Mathison, F., Aleman-Diaz, A., Molcho, M., & Weber, M.; et al. (2016). *Growing up Unequal: Gender and Socioeconomic Differences in Young People's Health and Well-Being. Health Behaviour in School-Aged Children.* (HBSC) Study: International Report from the 2013/2014 Survey. Health Policy for Children and Adolescents. Copenhagen: WHO Regional Office for Europe.
3. Bentsen, P., Mygind, L., Elsborg, P., Nielsen, G., & Mygind, E. (2021). Education outside the classroom as upstream school health promo-tion: 'adding-in' physical activity into children's everyday life and set-tings. Scandinavian *Journal of Public Health*, 1–9. https://doi.org/10.1177/1403494821993715

References

Åberg, M. A., Pedersen, N. L., Torén, K., Svartengren, M., Bäckstrand, B., Johnsson, T., Cooper-Kuhn, C. M., Aberg, N. D., Nilsson, M., & Kuhn, H. G. (2009). Cardiovascular fitness is associated with cognition in young adulthood. *Proceedings of the National Academy of Sciences, 106(49)*, 20906–11. https://doi.org/10.1073/pnas.0905307106

Barfod, K., Ejbye-Ernst, N., Mygind, L., & Bentsen, P. (2016). Increased provision of udeskole in Danish schools: An updated national population survey. *Urban Forestry & Urban Greening, 20*, 277–281. https://doi.org/10.1016/j.ufug.2016.09.012

Becker, C., Lauterbach, G., Spengler, S., Dettweiler, U., & Mess, F. (2017). Effects of regular classes in outdoor education settings: A systematic review on students' learning, social and health dimensions. *International Journal of Environmental Research and Public Health, 14*, 485.

Bølling, M., Mygind, E., Mygind, L., Bentsen, P., & Elsborg, P. (2021). The association between education outside the classroom and physical activity: Differences attributable to the type of space? *Children, 8*(6), 486. https://doi.org/10.3390/children8060486

Danish Ministry of Education: Improving the Public School—Overview of reform of standards in the Danish public school (primary and lighter secondary education). (2014). http://eng.uvm.dk/primary-and-lighter-secondary-education/the-folkeskole/about-the-folkeskole. Accessed 20 Aug 2021.

Danish Ministry of Education: Classes & Class Teacher. (2017). http://eng.uvm.dk/primary-and-lighter-secondary-education/the-folkeskole/classes-and-class-teacher. Accessed 15 Feb 2021.

Fjørtoft, I., & Landscape as playscape. (2004). The effects of natural environments on children's play and motor development. *Children, Youth and Environments, 14*(2), 21–44.

Grønningsæter, I., Hallås, O., Kristiansen, T., et al. (2007). Fysisk aktivitet hos 11–12-åringar i skulen. *Tidsskrift for Den Norske Laegeforening, 127*, 2927–2929.

Janssen, I., & LeBlanc, A. G. (2010). Systematic review of the health benefits of PA and fitness in school-aged children and youth. *International Journal of Behavioral Nutrition and Physical Activity, 7*(1), 40.

Martínez-Gómez, D., Veiga, O. L., Zapatera, B., et al. (2014). Physical activity during high school recess in Spanish adolescents: The AFINOS study. *Journal of Physical Activity & Health, 11*(6), 1194–1201.

Mygind, E. (2007). A comparison between children's PA levels at school and learning in an outdoor environment. *Journal of Adventure Education and Outdoor Learning, 7*(2), 161–176.

Mygind, E. (2016). PA during learning inside and outside the classroom. *Health Behavior Policy Review, 3*(5), 455–467. 10.14485.

Mygind, E., & Schneller, M. B. (2020). Fysisk aktivitet og køn [physical activity and gender]. In Mygind, E. (eds.), *Udeskole, TEACHOUT-projektets resultater [Udeskole, results from the TEACHOUT project]* (pp. 132–150). Copenhagen, Denmark: Frydenlund.

Nielsen, G., Pfister, G., & Andersen, L. B. (2011). Gender differences in the daily physical activities of Danish school children. *European Physical Education Review., 17*(1), 69–90.

Nielsen, G., Mygind, E., Bolling, M., Otte, C. R., Schneller, M. B., Schipperijn, J., et al. (2016). A quasi-experimental cross-disciplinary evaluation of the impacts of education outside the classroom on pupils' physical activity, well-being and learning: The TEACHOUT study protocol. *BMC Public Health, 16*, 1117.

Schneller, M. B. (2017). *Effects of education outside the classroom on objectively measured physical activity: Results from the TEACHOUT study*. PhD-Thesis. The Department of Sports Science and Clinical Biomechanics, University of Southern Denmark.

Schneller, M. B., Schipperijn, J., Nielsen, G., & Bentsen, P. (2017a). Children's physical activity during a segmented school week: Results from a quasi-experimental education outside the classroom intervention. *International Journal of Behavioral Nutrition and Physical Activity, 14*, Article number: 80.

Schneller, M. B., Duncan, S., Schipperijn, J., Nielsen, G., Mygind, E., & Bentsen, P. (2017b). Are children participating in a quasi-experimental education outside the classroom intervention more physically active? *BMC Public Health, 17*. https://doi.org/10.1186/s12889-017-4430-5

Sibley, B. A., & Etnier, J. L. (2003). The relationship between physical activity and cognition in children: A meta-analysis. *Pediatric Exercise Science, 15*(3), 243–256. https://doi.org/10.1123/pes.15.3.243

van der Niet, A. G., Smith, J., Scherder, E. J. A., et al. (2015). Associations between daily physical activity and executive functioning in primary school-aged children. *Journal of Science and
Medicine in Sport 18(6)*, 673–677.

Verloigne, M., Lippevelde, W. V., Maes, L., et al. (2012). Levels of PA and sedentary time among 10-
to 12-year-old boys and girls across 5 European countries using accelerometers: An observational
study within the ENERGY-project. *International Journal of Behavioral Nutrition and Physical
Activity, 9*(1), 34.

Wood, C., Gladwell, V., & Barton, J. (2014). A repeated measures experiment of school playing
environment to increase PA and enhance self-esteem in UK schoolchildren. *PLoS ONE, 9*(9),
e108701.

Erik Mygind M.Sc. and Ph.D. (1993) in sport and exercise
science from Department of Nutrition Exercise and Sports
(NEXS), Faculty of Science, University of Copenhagen (KU)
and today associate Professor emeritus affiliated Department of
Geosciences and Nature Management (IGN), KU. Since 1982
developed and taught a number of 60 ECTS outdoor education (OE) studies, programs and courses and since 2011 Ph.D.
OE courses. Since the turn of the millennium, the research
field has focused on the interaction between nature, people and
udeskole/education outside the classroom (EOtC), with special
focus on the role of teachers and students' health, motivation
and physical activity in primary school. Erik was head of the
Danish udeskole research project 'TEACHOUT' (2014–2018)
with a total budget of 10 million DKR in partnership between
University of Copenhagen (NEXS & IGN, KU), VIA UCC
Aarhus, University of Southern Denmark and STENO Diabetes
Centre). Board member of 9th International Out-door Education
Research Conference 2022.

Pupils' Well-Being, Mental and Social Health

Erik Mygind and Mads Bølling

1   Learning and Well-Being in Schools

Udeskole is a broad term for education outside the classroom, which, on the basis of the teacher's objectives, is regularly conducted outside the school walls (see Mygind: *Udeskole*—Pupils' Physical Activity and Gender Perspectives in this volume). In research, regularity is defined as at least half a school day bi-weekly over a longer period of time. *Udeskole* provides variation to the school day and incorporates the environment outside the school buildings into the weekly or bi-weekly teaching. In some classes, pupils measure the soil temperature in science teaching and math. Others visit memorials as part of history classes, or draw inspiration in the forest for written narratives in language classes. *Udeskole* is practically oriented and concrete. Case studies indicate that most pupils welcome *udeskole* as a meaningful variation to the school day (Hartmeyer & Mygind, 2016; Mygind, 2009). This is supported by interviews with teachers, conducted as part of the TEACHOUT study (Barfod, 2017; Mygind et al., 2018, see Barfod & Mygind: *Udeskole*—Regular Teaching Outside the Classroom in this volume).

Udeskole gives rise to learning processes other than typical classroom teaching and it is expected that *udeskole* can have a bearing on pupils' interest and learning motivation (Bølling et al., 2017; Otte et al., 2019). But what about pupils' well-being?

This chapter is mainly based on perspectives, excerpts, reformulations and translations of the Ph.D. Thesis in Danish by Bølling (2018) and the chapter in Danish language 'Pupils' well-being, mental and social health' (translated title) (Bølling & Mygind, 2020). We publish this chapter with the expressed permission of the publisher Frydenlund.

E. Mygind (✉)
Fuglehavevej 33, 2750 Ballerup, Denmark
e-mail: emygind@ign.ku.dk

M. Bølling
Rygårds Alle 80, 2900 Hellerup, Denmark
e-mail: mads.boelling@regionh.dk

© The Author(s) 2022   153
R. Jucker and J. von Au (eds.), *High-Quality Outdoor Learning*,
https://doi.org/10.1007/978-3-031-04108-2_8

Although the issue is far more multifaceted than a simple separation of the learning process into learning and well-being outcomes, the question arises whether *udeskole* is a teaching method that yields benefits beyond academic learning. To what extent can we expect *udeskole* to have a positive effect on pupils' mental and social health? What are the possible causes of a possibly positive effect?

Questions about expected impact and causes are complex. *Udeskole* practices are implemented differently from teacher to teacher and pupils' prerequisites and desire to attend *udeskole* will vary. Some pupils prefer to stay at school. Others may have difficulties concentrating in a classroom—perhaps especially boys. The effect of *udeskole* on pupils' well-being should not only be seen as an occasional effect in a teaching situation. The question is whether the sum of the teaching situations during a school day which comprise *udeskole* has an impact on pupils' general well-being and health in the school context, and ultimately on their overall well-being, mental and social health (Bølling, 2018).

If a pupil enjoys teaching that is carried out as *udeskole*, it can be expected that the pupil will have a generally strengthened well-being in the school context. This context-specific well-being may entail a generally strengthened well-being that extends beyond school hours and into everyday life. If a child thrives in everyday life, this will not only have a retroactive and self-reinforcing effect on well-being in school, but also a contagious effect on well-being in other contexts, such as at home in the family and with sports. In other words, a child's well-being must not only be understood in a specific situation or context, but in relation to all the possible situations and contexts in which the child participates and the interplay between them, including the effect of social contagion on other children and teachers (see Frank, 2020).

Before we address the issue of whether *udeskole* can have a positive effect on pupils' well-being, mental and social health, we step back. Many teachers already use *udeskole* as a teaching method for subject specific learning (Barfod et al., 2016), but can *udeskole* also be justified as an initiative to promote pupils' well-being, mental and social health?

In Denmark, the core business of schools is defined by the purpose of primary and lower secondary school law to provide pupils with knowledge and skills, educational readiness and the desire to learn, and to ensure participation in the community. Much indicates that health promotion initiatives that are an integral part of the school's core business have a greater success rate and that teachers will prefer to engage in health promotion that does not compromise the core tasks and take into account a schools' uniqueness, culture and student base. In other words, an 'add-in' approach as opposed to an 'add-on' approach, where health promotion is placed on top of everyday teaching tasks, i.e. lies beyond the core tasks (Bentsen et al., 2020). However, the other side of the coin of an 'add-in' approach to health promotion in schools, is that the goals of mental and social health are moving out of focus when the schools' academic tasks are prioritized.

Udeskole is a good example of an 'add-in' approach to health promotion. It is recommended that teachers use *udeskole* when it makes sense from a professional point of view (Barfod, 2017). To teach outside the classroom, within the existing number of hours, gives teachers the opportunity to specify a subject and allow pupils to take an increased active part in their learning process, for example by collecting empirical data. A teacher's choice to use *udeskole* as a teaching method may also be rooted in the desire, for example, to 'shake the class together' and help more pupils perceive school life and school work as something positive. The goal of using *udeskole* and strengthening well-being, mental and social health in the class will probably never be isolated. In the end, a desire to promote well-being and health must be justified by the purpose of schooling and the academic goals. *Udeskole* might be a solution for promoting well-being and health within the framework of the school's core tasks.

Does *udeskole* have an effect on pupils' well-being?

Can teaching in the immediate vicinity of schools be a valuable addition to classroom teaching and contribute to pupils' academic, mental and social development? This was one of the questions raised by Professor Arne Nikolaisen Jordet in the years just before the turn of the millennium, when he attended school classes at Lutvann public primary school in Oslo (Jordet, 2008). In the classes, weekly teaching took place in the schools' local forest. Based on a large number of observations and interviews with teachers and pupils, Jordet pointed out, among other things, that *udeskole* could contribute positively to pupils' personal and social development.

A Danish research team completed the first Danish *udeskole* project in the period 2000–2003—the case study of the Rødkilde project (Mygind, 2005). At that time, few schools in Denmark were practicing *udeskole*. Two teachers from the public Rødkilde School in Copenhagen agreed to use a forest as a classroom in the subjects Danish (mother tongue teaching), mathematics, and history every Thursday for three years. Although the study involved only one class—third grade at the start of the study—the study distinguished itself by following the class's development over a number of years. One of several goals for the research team was to investigate the impact of a weekly *udeskole* day in the forest on pupils' well-being compared to classroom teaching and learning. Two almost identical questionnaires were used and adapted for either forest or classroom teaching. The questionnaires included 10 statements about social relations and 14 statements about teaching. The results showed a positive development in different social relations through the variety and combination of forest and classroom teaching tasks (Mygind, 2009). In the forest setting, pupils gained several new play relationships with other classmates. This was explained by the fact that the pupils worked together in groups in a transition from academic activities to play during breaks.

There is good reason to believe that *udeskole* has a number of positive impacts on mental and social health. With the Rødkilde project as a benchmark, a series of interviews and observational studies were initiated evaluating education outside the classroom. In UK, for example, researchers found that teachers and pupils perceived *udeskole* as a teaching method with a positive impact on schoolwork and the social climate in the classroom (Marchant et al., 2019).

In Denmark, a follow-up to the Rødkilde project showed that seven years after participating in the project, pupils and teachers highlighted that the three years of *udeskole* had a positive impact especially on the social climate in the class (Hartmeyer & Mygind, 2016). In recent years, the Danish Ministry of Education's project 'Development of *udeskole*' has documented that pupils generally perceive *udeskole* as positive, with learning and social potentials (Ejbye-Ernst & Bentsen, 2018; VIVE, 2019).

2 Mental and Social Health in the TEACHOUT Project

Across a number of Danish research institutions and in collaboration with a number of other researchers, we conducted the TEACHOUT research project in 2014–2018 including pupils from grade 3–6 and their teachers. The project constituted the most extensive study of *udeskole* to date, nationally and internationally. One of the aims of the project was to investigate whether there were positive effects on psychosocial well-being, school motivation, and social relationships in the class community after one year with *udeskole*.

Box 1

From school to school, and from teacher to teacher, it varies how much of a school year is prioritized for *udeskole*. Some schools practice *udeskole* every week the entire year, others use fall or spring and in a few cases *udeskole* is practiced at all grades. In the TEACHOUT project, the effect on well-being, mental and social health was examined in classes where *udeskole* was practised 4.7 h per week on average throughout the 2014/15 school year, equivalent to 14.2% of the standard teaching time (33 h per week). Danish, mathematics, and nature/technology were the most frequently used academic teaching subjects, with nature and green areas as the main preferred setting.

A total of 28 Danish school classes were accepted to join the TEACHOUT study and willing to teach *udeskole* one year at least 5 h per week. The 28 *udeskole* classes were compared with pupils from 20 parallel control classes, who were taught sporadically outside the classroom during the school year (in average 1.6 h per week, in 0.7 sessions). The reason why pupils in the control classes were also taught partly outside the classroom was mainly due to political demands of a revised school reform, demanding 45 min of daily physical activity and use of the surrounding society in pupils' learning process (Danish Ministry of Education, 2014).

Psychosocial well-being

The TEACHOUT project was launched in the autumn 2014. At the start of the school year and again 180 days later in spring 2015 the instrument 'Strengths and Difficulties Questionnaire' (SDQ) was used to measure 621 pupils' social strengths with a prosocial scale (Bølling et al., 2019b). In our study, social strengths were an overall expression of empathy, helpfulness and kindness. The result showed that 503 pupils in the *udeskole* group maintained the level in social strength through the school year compared to a decrease among 118 pupils in the comparison classes (Fig. 1). The decline in social strengths in the comparison classes can be interpreted as an expression of a generally reduced commitment to the social and academic school community—an expression of school fatigue (Pless, 2009). Both prosocial behaviour and intrinsic motivation for schoolwork decreased in the comparison classes. Prosocial behaviour increased slightly in the *udeskole* classes (Fig. 1). In the study of social strengths, we also measured pupils' mental and social problems (emotional symptoms, hyperactivity and attention problems, and difficulties with peers) using SDQ. After following the *udeskole* and comparison classes throughout the school year, we were unable to detect a statistically significant difference between the groups on these parameters. On the other hand, we found that there was a difference in effect between the pupils who came from resource-poor or resource-strong families, assessed based on pupils' parents' socio-economic position. We found that the pupils who came from resource-poor families had a greater reduction in hyperactivity and attention disorders, as well as a greater reduction in problems with peers. Although this result supports an assumption that *udeskole* can be particularly good for pupils from resource-poor families, the result is uncertain as the analyses included fewer than 20 pupils from resource-poor families.

Our study is not the first to examine the effect of *udeskole* on psychosocial well-being of pupils. A Swedish study using SDQ did not find that *udeskole* had a general effect on either girls or boys psychosocial well-being (Gustafsson et al., 2012). However, this study showed a distinctly positive effect for boys. Emotional and behavioural symptoms, hyperactivity and attention problems, and difficulties with peers were reduced.

The TEACHOUT and the Swedish studies are the only ones of their kind having investigated *udeskole* in a controlled experimental intervention using the SDQ questionnaire, but reach slightly different conclusions. However, it is worth noting that the TEACHOUT study was based on a high number of pupils in *udeskole* and including control classes (parallel classes) with weekly reports from teachers about where and how much *udeskole* was used. Overall, the results of TEACHOUT give quite a valid picture, but more research on psychosocial well-being and *udeskole* is needed.

Enjoyable schoolwork and intrinsic motivation

The effect of *udeskole* was also examined in relation to satisfying schoolwork, measured by intrinsic motivation for schoolwork (Bølling et al., 2018). Intrinsic motivation means that one's behaviour is self-determined by one's own interest in a

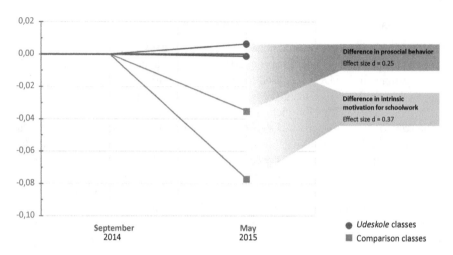

Fig. 1 Development in social strengths and intrinsic motivation for schoolwork from the start of the school year (September 2014) to the end of the school year (May 2015) for the *udeskole* and the comparison groups. Developments are measured on a scale of +1 to −1. The model indicates average values and takes into account any difference between pupils at the start of the school year, therefore the starting point is adjusted to the value 0.0

given activity, e.g. schoolwork. Intrinsic motivation is a psychological stage closely related to mental well-being (Ryan, 2009).

Box 2

From start to end of the school year 2014–15 data from 308 pupils in the *udeskole* classes had a higher level of intrinsic motivation for schoolwork compared to 77 pupils in the comparison classes. The level of intrinsic motivation for *udeskole* schoolwork was relatively stable from the start of the school year to the end, whereas we observed a decrease in intrinsic motivation for schoolwork in the comparison classes, which in practice can be interpreted as *udeskole* having a form of buffer-effect (see Fig. 1). In other words, *udeskole* seems to offset an expected decline in intrinsic motivation for schoolwork during the school year. The decline may be due to school fatigue during the school year, but may also occur during school hours (Pless, 2009).

The effect of *udeskole* on enjoyable schoolwork is one of the areas that has been the subject of research interest in recent years. Common to the studies of enjoyable schoolwork is the use of intrinsic motivation for schoolwork as a measure, but most of these studies have examined the effect of short-term school science-camps (one week) for middle-aged pupils (Dettweiler et al., 2015, 2017). Overall, these studies show that this teaching method can have a positive impact on students' intrinsic motivation.

No other studies have examined *udeskole* lasting one year, as the TEACHOUT study did. However, one Swedish study has examined *udeskole* over a 10-week duration, where two seventh grade classes moved one quarter of mathematics lessons outside the classroom (Fägerstam & Samuelsson, 2014). The two *udeskole* classes had a better intrinsic motivation for schoolwork and thus showed the same buffer effect as we found in the TEACHOUT study. Overall, these studies show evidence of a positive effect of *udeskole* for maintaining intrinsic motivation for schoolwork.

Social relationships in the class community

In TEACHOUT, we examined the extent of new friendship relationships in class communities as a measure of social relationships. 448 pupils from a total of 16 *udeskole* classes and eight comparison classes were asked which new pupils from their class they played with in the breaks. When answering the question, it was not allowed to name yourself or those with whom you were very much in contact. This question is often used to form a picture of the friendship network in classes and as a method to measure new friendship relationships among pupils. By gathering pupils' responses, we could conclude that *udeskole* had a small but positive effect on how many new relationships each pupil had on average during the school year. The number of new friendships as a result of *udeskole* showed that after one year, pupils in the *udeskole* classes on average had new friendships with 3.7% of other pupils in their class (see Box 3).

Fig. 2 New friendships after a year with *udeskole*

Box 3

In a class of 22 pupils, it is expected that on average one new friendship (exactly 0.8 pupil) will develop during a school year with *udeskole* (see Fig. 2). Our study showed that *udeskole* has a small effect on the total number of friendships. It seems that *udeskole* contributes to a modest increase in the number of new friendships. In the study on social relationships, we also examined the change in the size/number of pupils' friendship groups, but did not find a statistically significant effect of one year of *udeskole*.

The TEACHOUT study on social relationships shows that only a minimal effect of one year of *udeskole* can be expected with a view to establishing new peer relationships in the class community. This is in line with the first Danish study of *udeskole*, the Rødkilde project. In this case study 14 out of 19 new pupil relationships were formed based on one weekly *udeskole* day taking place for three years in a forest, (Mygind, 2009). Although pupils are likely to form new relationships during an *udeskole* session, these relationships do not seem to apply in general school life. Further research needs to be conducted to clarify how new friendships affects the classroom environment.

Does *udeskole* have a bearing on pupils' well-being?

Udeskole must be understood as a holistic approach in teaching that focuses not only on learning, academic benefit and education as a goal, but also on a much broader concept of well-being, including health benefits. Therefore, historically research in *udeskole* has been characterized by interdisciplinary approaches drawn on a wide range of theories (see Box 4). However, a unifying theory for *udeskole* has not been developed, which might, among other things, explain a connection between *udeskole* and pupils' well-being, mental and social health and offer arguments for teachers, school leaders and politicians whether or not *udeskole* should be an integrated part of the work of the school.

Box 4

The currently most widely used theory to explain the link between *udeskole* and pupils' well-being, mental and social health is the Self-Determination Theory (Deci & Ryan, 2000). In addition to TEACHOUT, several other studies on *udeskole* and outdoor teaching and learning have had the ambition to use the Self-Determination Theory as a theory to understand why *udeskole* can have a positive influence on pupils' well-being and health (e.g. Dettweiler et al., 2015). The theory represents a broad framework for the study of intrinsic and extrinsic sources of human motivation, devised by American psychologists Edward L. Deci and Richard M. Ryan. A crucial starting point in the Self-Determination

Theory is that humans have a fundamental need for development that can be ensured by meeting individuals' basic psychological needs, specifically the feeling of:

- Autonomy—that one's own perception is based on one's own values and interests.
- Competence—to experience that you have opportunities to be active, feel active and be able to develop one's capabilities.
- Relatedness to others—to feel closely connected to other people and communities through the care you take for each other.

In relation to strengthening well-being, mental and social health, the theory proposes that experiencing the feeling of autonomy, competence, and relatedness to others, separately and as a whole, will lead to intrinsic motivation. Well-being, understood as achieving one's full potentials, is closely related to intrinsic motivation (Ryan et al., 2006) versus psychosocial distrust, e.g., depression, anxiety, or behavioural problems (Ryan et al., 1995). The interesting thing about Self-Determination Theory is that it also has a social dimension, i.e. the need to have relationships with others, such as friendship relationships.

Udeskole is characterized by a variety of didactic approaches, for example, inductive, investigative and problem-based learning styles; tangible, concrete and practical working methods; student-centred teaching and collaboration. In light of Self-Determination Theory, it is relevant to ask how different didactic approaches, ideally, contribute to the fulfilment of the three basic psychological needs (for elaboration, see Bølling, 2018).

Does *udeskole* promote the fulfilment of the basic need of autonomy?

In *udeskole*, pupils are assigned a central role in their own learning processes. Through inductive, investigative and problem-based learning styles, pupils are invited to let their personal interests and initiatives guide the learning. Choosing a place of teaching in an *udeskole* setting can potentially have a major impact on pupils' feeling of autonomy. Places in children's everyday lives that are relevant and meaningful to them can be a source of inspiration and reinforce their interest (Bølling et al., 2017). Nature is a typically used environment in *udeskole*, such as seen in the TEACHOUT study. There are good arguments that natural environments support self-determination by stimulating investigative behaviour without expectations and pressures (Weinstein et al., 2009).

Does *udeskole* promote the fulfilment of the basic need for competence?

In *udeskole*, the work can be tangible, concrete and practical. These modes of learning are often contrasted with theoretical and academic methods used in the classroom at the school. In *udeskole*, more pupils are ideally given the opportunity to put other skills into play. There is a great social dimension to the need for competence through the feeling of being active, which in turn is linked to one's interaction with the social environment. It is essential that the need for developing competence through *udeskole* may arise when pupils are given the opportunity to contribute positively to group work and thereby show others in the class community new sides of themselves and thereby be recognized in new and different ways (Hartmeyer & Mygind, 2016).

Does *udeskole* promote the fulfilment of the basic need for relatedness?

Collaboration in groups can be a starting point for forming new relationships. Knowledge of one another, physical closeness, and similarity are three pillars in forming friendships (Bølling et al., 2019a). In small groups, pupils have physical proximity. Group work will ideally mean that pupils work towards a common goal and shared interest. As we described above, there is also the opportunity for pupils, through *udeskole*, to experience new sides of one another, to feel understood and appreciated. Through this, similarities that pupils have not been aware of before are experienced—for example, similarity in interest, values and approaches to learning.

Several studies point out that the special feature of *udeskole* in relation to social relationships is not only pupil-pupils relations, but also strengthened teacher-student relationships. In *udeskole*, the teacher can potentially experience new sides of their pupils, and vice versa. There is time and space to talk to each other. It seems that pupils will feel more closely connected to their teacher (Mygind et al., 2018). The teacher also plays a significant role in the pupil-to-pupil relationships. Teachers have the opportunity to put together groups of pupils who do not already interact. The continued group work from school day to school day allows pupils to get to know each other better, thereby creating new peer relationships.

Transportation is often a necessity for getting from school to the park, forest, or library—e.g. by bus, bike or on foot. A teacher must also consider what role transport time should play, such as group work or informal socialization on the outbound and/or the return trip? In TEACHOUT, we examined, among other things, the importance of transport time for establishing new friendship relationships. Transport was of great importance for maintaining existing friendships (Bølling et al., 2019a, b), which may be a significant contributing explanation for the fact that new friendships can be built through *udeskole*. However, informal transportation time in *udeskole* is also paradoxical. Although transport time is expected to help support a basic need for relatedness between pupils who already know each other, case studies also clarify the reverse side of transport. Transport time in *udeskole* can in the extreme case exclude pupils with weak attachment to others in class communities (Jørring et al., 2019). For pupils with a weak attachment, transportation time can mean increased social dissatisfaction because they do not necessarily socialize with others in class when on the move. Teacher should pay attention to this finding.

3   Summary of the TEACHOUT Study and a Critical Look at *udeskole*

The TEACHOUT studies have provided us with the most reliable knowledge to date about the expected effects of *udeskole* for pupils in general. The pupils who participated in the studies had, on average, a common level of mental and social health and came from families with a medium to high socio-economic background, understood as parents' position in the labour market and their level of education (Christensen et al., 2014).

Pupils have different prerequisites for participating in teaching and thus different starting points for taking advantage of *udeskole*. For example, teachers' motivation to use *udeskole* may be to give pupils from resource-poor families better opportunities to participate and learn (Fägerstam, 2014). Ideally, practical and tangible work is a special opportunity in *udeskole* (Hartmeyer & Mygind, 2016) and gives pupils—in particular boys—who may have difficulty sitting still in a classroom, a well-being boost which is also linked to more physical activity (see Mygind: *Udeskole*—Pupils' Physical Activity and Gender Perspectives in this volume; Norðdahl & Jóhannesson, 2014).

There is much evidence that *udeskole* can foster well-being and academic learning through well-designed (outdoor) teaching, a clear teaching framework, and commitment, but it does not seem that all children prefer *udeskole* as a teaching method, although the vast majority express joy at *udeskole*. There are examples that academically strong pupils prefer teaching in the school classroom, where they find it easier to concentrate (Jørring et al., 2019). In continuation of the revised Danish school reform in 2014, several follow-up evaluations were conducted including the importance of relocation teaching outside the classroom. It is clear that pupils with special needs do not always respond as well to the many shifts and instability of the school day as *udeskole* can cause. Turmoil and lack of concentration are examples of the consequences that have been highlighted (Jacobsen et al., 2017). Some of the challenges registered among pupils with special needs can also be found in pupils in general.

In the TEACHOUT study, we found that when *udeskole* is organized with few hours, it does not appear to be beneficial for reducing hyperactivity and attention. Furthermore, it seems to have a negative impact on helpfulness and empathy (Bølling et al., 2019a). Longer- duration, e.g. a whole day with *udeskole,* seem to be more beneficial for several reasons mentioned in this chapter and therefore preferred.

The socio-economic starting point for the development of pleasurable schoolwork is a well-known phenomenon in outdoor teaching and learning (Dettweiler et al., 2015). In the TEACHOUT study, we found that the effect of *udeskole* was greatest for those pupils who already had the highest degree of enjoyment and pleasure with schoolwork. Future studies of *udeskole* should have an extra focus on whether *udeskole* especially favours pupils with the highest degree of intrinsic motivation for schoolwork, but also whether *udeskole* is beneficial for pupils from more or less resourceful families. Here, the teacher's role is crucial (see Barfod & Mygind: *Udeskole*—Regular Teaching Outside the Classroom in the volume).

A small but positive effect

The TEACHOUT study of pupils' well-being, mental and social health shows that *udeskole* conducted regularly for a year reinforces pupils' desire for schoolwork. These findings are based on the fact that pupils were taught in *udeskole* equivalent to just below one sixth of the total weekly teaching time—mainly practiced in nature and green spaces and across school subjects. Social well-being, in terms of social network relationship to peers was positively affected—albeit to a modest degree— while helpfulness and empathy were strengthened.

In other words, *udeskole* emerges as a strong proposition of a teaching method that generally strengthens the well-being and health of pupils, but also that pupils with special needs are challenged when teaching is moved outside the classroom and school buildings. Some pupils are challenged by the possibility to concentrate. In order for *udeskole* to play a role in school life, it is important for teachers to become acquainted with the mental and social importance of *udeskole* in teacher education or through continuing education courses in order to experience how learning and health can be embodied in well-designed and structured regular outdoor teaching and learning sessions. In general, parents are very positive about *udeskole*. However, *udeskole* teachers point out that especially support from schools' management and colleagues is crucial to maintain commitment to weekly or bi-weekly work outside the classroom (Mygind et al., 2018).

Research of *udeskole* does not end with the results from the TEAHCOUT study. In fact, this is just the beginning of more evidence-based conclusions about *udeskole*. Based on the intervention and research design of the TEACHOUT study, the next large-scale *udeskole*-study sees the light of day. The Danish Novo Nordisk Foundation have recently granted 1 mil. EURO for the realisation of the MOVEOUT study (www.moveoutstudy.dk, accessed 31/058/2021) which includes 30 Danish schools. With an increased attention to pupils' physical activity in *udeskole*, the MOVEOUT study investigates the effect of one year of weekly use of *udeskole* on pupils' movement behaviours, academic motivation, well-being, and academic performance. In addition, it is explored which pedagogical activities cause the effects.

Recommended Further Reading

1. Becker, C., Lauterbach, G., Spengler, S., Dettweiler, U. & Mess, F. (2017). Effects of Regular Classes in Outdoor Education Settings: A Systematic Review on Students' Learning, Social and Health Dimensions. *Int. J. Environ. Res. Public Health*, 14, 485. https://doi.org/10.3390/ijerph14050485
2. Dettweiler, U., Lauterbach, G., Becker, C., Ünlü, A., Gschrey, B. (2015). Investigating the motivational behavior of pupils during outdoor science teaching within self-determination theory. *Front. Psychol.* 6, 125. https://doi.org/10.3389/fpsyg.2015.00125

3. Bentsen, P., Stevenson, M. P., Mygind, E. & Barfod, K. S. (2018). Udeskole: education outside the classroom in a Danish context. In M. T. Huang & Y. C. Jade Ho (eds.), *The Budding and Blooming of Outdoor Education in Diverse Global Contexts* (pp. 81–114). National Academy for Educational Research. Outdoor Education Research Office Book Series 3. https://www.naer.edu.tw/files/11-1000-981.php.

References

Barfod, K. (2017). Maintaining mastery but feeling professionally isolated: Experienced teachers' perceptions of teaching outside the classroom. *Journal of Adventure Education and Outdoor Learning, 18*(3), 201–213. https://doi.org/10.1080/14729679.2017.1409643

Barfod, K., Ejbye-Ernst, N., Mygind, L., & Bentsen, P. (2016). Increased provision of *udeskole* in Danish schools: An updated national population survey. *Urban Forestry & Urban Greening, 20*(Supplement C), 277–281. https://doi.org/10.1016/j.ufug.2016.09.012.

Bentsen, P., Bonde, A. H., Schneller, M. B., Danielsen, D., Bruselius-Jensen, M., & Aagaard-Hansen, J. (2020). Danish 'add-in' school-based health promotion: Integrating health in curriculum time. *Health Promotion International, 35*(1), e70–e77.

Bølling, M. (2018). *School and children's well-being. A quasi-experimental intervention study of the relationship between one year of regular exposure to udeskole and children's psychological well-being, school motivation and social relationships.* Ph.D. thesis, University of Copenhagen, Department of Nutrition, Exercise and Sports. Retrieved from https://nexs.ku.dk/arrangements/2018/phd_mads-bolling/Mads-Bolling_udeskole-phd-web.pdf.

Bølling, M., & Mygind, E. (2020). Elevers trivsel, mentale og sociale sundhed [Pupils well-being, mental and social health]. In E. Mygind (Ed.), *Udeskole, TEACHOUT-projektets resultater [Udeskole, results from the TEACHOUT project]* (pp. 154–175). Copenhagen, Denmark: Frydenlund.

Bølling, M., Hartmeyer, R., & Bentsen, P. (2017). Seven place-conscious methods to stimulate situational interest in science teaching in urban environments. *Education 3–13, 47*(2), 162–175. https://doi.org/10.1080/03004279.2017.1420096.

Bølling, M., Otte, C. R., Elsborg, P., Nielsen, G., & Bentsen, P. (2018). The association between education outside the classroom and pupils' school motivation: Results from a one-school-year quasi-experiment. *International Journal of Educational Research, 89*, 22–35. https://doi.org/10.1016/j.ijer.2018.03.004

Bølling, M., Mygind, E., Pfister, G., & Nielsen, G. (2019). Education outside the classroom and pupils' social relations? A one-year quasi-experiment. *International Journal of Educational Research, 94*(1), 29–41.

Bølling, M., Niclasen, J., Bentsen, P., & Nielsen, G. (2019). Association of education outside the classroom and pupils' psychosocial well-being: Results from a school year implementation. *Journal of School Health, 89*(3), 210–218. https://doi.org/10.1111/josh.12730

Christensen, U., Krølner, R., Nilsson, C. J., Lyngbye, P. W., Hougaard, C. Ø., Nygaard, E., … Lund, R. (2014). Addressing social inequality in aging by the danish occupational social class measurement. *Journal of Aging and Health, 26*(1), 106–127. https://doi.org/10.1177/0898264314522894.

Danish Minister of Education. (2014). https://www.uvm.dk/-/media/filer/uvm/publikationer/engelsksprogede/2014-improving-the-public-schools.pdf.

Deci, E. L., & Ryan, R. M. (2000). The 'What' and 'Why' of goal pursuits: Human needs and the self-determination of behavior. *Psychological Inquiry, 11*(4), 227–268. https://doi.org/10.1207/S15327965PLI1104_01

Dettweiler, U., Unlu, A., Lauterbach, G., Becker, C., & Gschrey, B. (2015). Investigating the motivational behavior of pupils during outdoor science teaching within self-determination theory. *Frontiers in Psychology, 6*, 125. https://doi.org/10.3389/fpsyg.2015.00125

Dettweiler, U., Lauterbach, G., Becker, C., & Simon, P. (2017). A Bayesian mixed-methods analysis of basic psychological needs satisfaction through outdoor learning and its influence on motivational behavior in science class. *Frontiers in Psychology, 8*, 2235. https://doi.org/10.3389/fpsyg.2017.02235

Ejbye-Ernst, N., & Bentsen, P., (2018). *Development of outdoor school—A three-year development and demonstration project. Results, conclusions and recommendations.* Ministry of Education, Ministry of Environment and Food, VIA University College, Steno Diabetes Center Copenhagen.

Fägerstam, E. (2014). High school teachers' experience of the educational potential of outdoor teaching and learning. *Journal of Adventure Education & Outdoor Learning, 14*(1), 56–81. https://doi.org/10.1080/14729679.2013.769887

Fägerstam, E., & Samuelsson, J. (2014). Learning arithmetic outdoors in junior high school—Influence on performance and self-regulating skills. *Education 3–13, 42*(4), 419–431. https://doi.org/10.1080/03004279.2012.713374.

Frank, R. (2020). *Under the influence: Putting peer pressure to work.* Oxford: Princeton University Press.

Gustafsson, P. E., Szczepanski, A., Nelson, N., & Gustafsson, P. A. (2012). Effects of an outdoor education intervention on the mental health of schoolchildren. *Journal of Adventure Education & Outdoor Learning, 12*(1), 63–79. https://doi.org/10.1080/14729679.2010.532994

Hartmeyer, R., & Mygind, E. (2016). A retrospective study of social relations in a Danish primary school class taught in 'outdoor school.' *Journal of Adventure Education and Outdoor Learning, 16*(1), 1–12. https://doi.org/10.1080/14729679.2015.1086659

Jacobsen, R. H., Bjørnholt, B., Krassel, K. F., Nørgaard, Jakobsen, Flarup, L. H., … Nygaard, H. (2017). *A longer and more varied school day. Implementation and impact study.* Retrieved from KORA, The National Institute for Municipalities and Regions Analysis and Research website: http://www.kora.dk/media/6661129/11013_en-laengere-og-mere-varieret-sko ledag_implementerings-og-effektundorgies.pdf.

Jordet, A. N. (2008). *Outdoor schooling in Norway—Research and experiences. Conference report: Healthier, wiser and smarter children. Outdoor school—Learning with brain, heart and body* [Report from the Conference: *Healthier, wiser and happier children. Education outside the classroom—learning with brain, heart and body*] (pp. 36–42). Retrieved from http://docplayer.dk/386 8519-Report-from-conferencen-sundere-kloere-and-gladere-boern.html.

Jørring, A. H., Bølling, M., Nielsen, G., Stevenson, M. P., & Bentsen, P. (2019). Swings and roundabouts? Pupils' experiences of social and academic well-being in education outside the classroom. *Education 3–13, 48*(4), 413–428. https://doi.org/10.1080/03004279.2019.1614643.

Marchant, E., Todd, C., Cooksey, R., Dredge, S., Jones, H., Reynolds, D., et al. (2019). Curriculum-based outdoor learning for children aged 9–11: A qualitative analysis of pupils' and teachers' views. *PLoS ONE, 14*(5), e0212242. https://doi.org/10.1371/journal.pone.0212242

Mygind, E. (2005). *Udeundervisning i folkeskolen: Et casestudie om en naturklasse på Rødkilde Skole og virkningerne af en ugentlig obligatorisk naturdag på yngste klassetrin i perioden 2000–2003 [Outdoor teaching in the public municipality school. A case study of a nature* (E. Mygind, Ed.). Copenhagen: Museum Tusculanums Forlag and Department of Exercise and Sport Sciences.

Mygind, E. (2009). A comparison of childrens' statements about social relations and teaching in the classroom and in the outdoor environment. *Journal of Adventure Education & Outdoor Learning, 9*(2), 151–169. https://doi.org/10.1080/14729670902860809

Mygind, E., Bølling, M., & Barfod, K. (2018). Primary teachers' experiences with weekly education outside the classroom during a year. *Education 3–13, 47*(5), 599–611. https://doi.org/10.1080/03004279.2018.1513544.

Norðdahl, K., & Jóhannesson, I. Á. (2014). 'Let's go outside': Icelandic teachers' views of using the outdoors. *Education 3–13, 44*(4), 391–406. https://doi.org/10.1080/03004279.2014.961946.

Otte, C. R., Bølling, M., Stevenson, M. P., Nielsen, G., Bentsen, P., & Ejbye-Ernst, N. (2019). Education outside the classroom increases children's reading competencies: Results from a one-year Danish quasi-experimental study. *Accepted in International Journal of Educational Research.* https://doi.org/10.1016/j.ijer.2019.01.009

Pless, M. (2009). *Udsatte unge på vej i uddannelsessystemet.* Retrieved from https://vbn.elsevierp ure.com/da/publications/udsatte-unge-p%C3%A5-vej-i-uddannelsessystemet.

Ryan, R. M. (2009). Self determination theory and wellbeing. *Social Psychology, 84,* 822–848.

Ryan, R. M., Deci, E. L., & Grolnick, W. S. (1995). *Autonomy, relatedness, and the self: Their relation to development and psychopathology.* Retrieved from http://psycnet.apa.org/psycinfo/ 1995-97696-020.

Ryan, R. M., Huta, V., & Deci, E. L. (2006). Living well: A self-determination theory perspective on eudaimonia. *Journal of Happiness Studies, 9*(1), 139–170.

VIVE. (2019). *Ekstern evaluering af Projekt Udvikling af udeskole.* Retrieved from https://pure. vive.dk/ws/files/2364847/11093_Ekstern_evaluering_af_Projekt_Udvikling_af_udeskole_110 119.pdf.

Weinstein, N., Przybylski, A. K., & Ryan, R. M. (2009). Can nature make us more caring? Effects of immersion in nature on intrinsic aspirations and generosity. *Personality and Social Psychology Bulletin, 35*(10), 1315–1329.

Erik Mygind, Msc. and Ph.D. (1993) in sport and exercise science from Department of Nutrition Exercise and Sports (NEXS), Faculty of Science, University of Copenhagen (KU) and today associate Professor emeritus affiliated Department of Geosciences and Nature Management (IGN), KU. Since 1982 developed and taught a number of outdoor education (OE) studies, programs and courses and since 2011 Ph.D. OE courses. Since the turn of the millennium, the research field has focused on the interaction between nature, people and udeskole / education outside the classroom (EOtC), with special focus on the role of teachers and students' health, motivation and physical activity in primary school. Erik was head of the Danish udeskole research project 'TEACHOUT' (2014–2018) with a total budget of 10 million DKR in partnership between University of Copenhagen (NEXS & IGN, KU), VIA UCC Aarhus, University of Southern Denmark and STENO Diabetes Center. Board member of 9th International Outdoor Education Research Conference 2022.

Mads Bølling is Researcher at Health Promotion Research, Steno Diabetes Center Copenhagen. He holds a MaEd in educational sociology from the Danish School of Education (DPU) at Aarhus University, and a Ph.D. in school-based health promotion from University of Copenhagen. MB's research interest has mainly focused on the influence of psychical spaces and pedagogies on aspects of children's health, wellbeing, motivation, and cognitive development. Specifically, MB is dedicated to promoting sustainable models and innovations to research-practice partnerships on development and data collection. Currently he is engaged with the MOVEOUT study, investigating one-year implementation of education outside the classroom (udeskole) as researcher and project leader—a study with the aim to replicate the Danish TEACHOUT study with an extended design and a specific focus on children's movement behaviour. Also, MB has been the frontrunner in the launch of the Danish education outside the classroom portal www.mov eoutstudy.dk.

Health and Well-Being for Pupils and Teachers

Some Impacts on Health and Wellbeing from School-Based Outdoor Learning

Sue Waite and Jennie Aronsson

1 Introduction

In this chapter, we explain some contemporary challenges to public health, focusing on the case for England and similar Western societies. We argue that school-based outdoor learning represents a medium through which health and wellbeing promoting initiatives to address these challenges can be distributed more equitably. We describe three case studies that illustrate how schools might implement and monitor such initiatives and discuss their implications for making schools a focal point for developing happier and healthier people.

2 Public Health Challenges

The health of those living in more deprived areas in England is worsening with health inequalities increasing over the last decade (Marmot et al., 2020). This is reflected in a range of health and wellbeing outcomes across the life span (Public Health England (PHE) 2019a). One of Public Health England's top priorities for 2020–2025 is to give each child the best start in life and the foundations of good health into adulthood (PHE, 2019b), yet children today increasingly face physical and mental health challenges. For example, about one quarter of children aged 4–5 are overweight or obese; by the age of 10–11, this number is a third (NHS Digital, 2019). In both age

S. Waite (✉)
Church Road, Lympstone EX8 5JT, Devon, UK
e-mail: S.J.Waite@plymouth.ac.uk

J. Aronsson
School of Nursing and Midwifery, University of Plymouth, Rolle building Level 4, Drake Circus, Plymouth 4 8AA, UK
e-mail: jennie.aronsson@plymouth.ac.uk

© The Author(s) 2022   171
R. Jucker and J. von Au (eds.), *High-Quality Outdoor Learning*,
https://doi.org/10.1007/978-3-031-04108-2_9

groups, children living in the most deprived areas are twice as likely to be obese as those living in the least deprived areas (ibid). Children and young people nowadays spend a lot of time on screens. This is associated with a higher calorific intake together with missed opportunities to be physically active, socialise and get a good night's sleep—activities that promote good health and wellbeing (Royal College of Paediatrics and Child Health, 2019). In England, one in eight children aged 5–19 suffers from at least one mental disorder; a number that has increased over the last 20 years (NHS Digital, 2018). Mental health problems have been exacerbated by the COVID-19 pandemic, particularly in children and young people from socioeconomically deprived households, with reports of sleep difficulties, feeling lonely and worrying about leaving the house (Newlove-Delgado et al., 2021). Spencer (2013) presents a range of adverse child health outcomes that would be reduced by between 18 and 59% if all children had the same outcomes as those most socially advantaged. There is an urgent need to address such health inequalities and enable all children and young people to access health and wellbeing promoting initiatives, such as spending time in greenspaces (Roberts et al., 2020).

3   What School-Based Outdoor Learning Offers in Terms of Universal Access

Unfortunately, inequalities in public health challenges are also mirrored, and indeed intensified, by uneven access to quality natural environments, which can offer so many benefits for health and wellbeing. Areas of deprivation usually have inferior quality public greenspace (Schüle et al., 2019). Inadequate access to and use of good quality greenspace exacerbates poor health outcomes for deprived communities (Allen & Balfour, 2014), yet these communities can potentially gain most from such spaces (Lovell et al., 2020). Monitoring of Engagement with the Natural Environment (MENE) surveys over a period of years have shown that infrequent users of greenspace tend to be people who are: female; older; in poor health; of lower socioeconomic status; with a physical disability; ethnic minorities; living in deprived areas; with less local access to greenspace; and living further from the coast (Boyd et al., 2018). This enormous data set has enabled analyses that show marked disparities in the amount of time families from low socioeconomic groups and ethnic minorities spend in green spaces. This may be due partly to the quality and amount of green space in local parks in areas of deprivation, problems in affording additional costs such as travel and food to go to more distant green spaces as well as cultural mismatches in current offers supporting engagement (Waite et al., 2021). However, adults spending just two hours per week in greenspace are more likely to experience better health and wellbeing than those who do not, regardless of whether they have one long, or several short visits, who they are and where they live, or what kind of natural environment they visit (White et al., 2019). The effect on their health was equivalent to improvements through living in an area of lower deprivation; being employed in a higher social grade occupation; and achieving recommended levels of physical activity (PHE, 2020).

A similar situation has been noted in the US, where access to nature is also divided along cultural and socioeconomic fault lines (Warren et al., 2014). There are attempts to redress these inequalities through community-based initiatives[1] but these approaches are frequently hampered by ongoing problems in attracting 'hard-to reach' groups (Waite et al., 2021). The fact that most children attend school irrespective of cultural or socioeconomic background presents a useful entry point for inclusive access to natural environments and healthy lifestyle programmes (Day et al., 2019). A further advantage of schools being a principal access point to nature is that they can embed outdoor learning provision *within* the curriculum (Waite et al., 2016), so that extra time and resources are not required to spend time and be active in nature.

4 Health and Wellbeing Responsibilities of Schools

Schools today are expected to provide a healthy learning environment, which promotes physical and mental health and wellbeing opportunities in addition to education. The World Health Organisation (WHO) developed the health promoting schools (HPS) concept in 1992, with a recent launch of a new initiative to make every school a health promoting school by developing and promoting global standards for HPS (WHO, 2020). In England, health and wellbeing is embedded within the Relationships Education curriculum, compulsory in primary schools since September 2020 (Department for Education, 2019). As part of this curriculum, children learn about the benefits of time spent outdoors; however, it is up to individual schools how this is implemented. Schools may choose to re-evaluate their school grounds from the perspective of providing high-quality outdoor learning environments, installing school gardens, wildlife zones and areas that can be used in all weathers with open-ended play materials, such as logs, boxes, tyres. These features can offer greater awareness of healthy eating, appreciation of and attachment to other species and enhanced physical mobility and creative play. Schools may offer lessons that enable children to learn about the natural environment and sustainability; whilst others engage pupils in curriculum learning outside the classroom across a broad range of subjects and topics.

Several countries have adopted this integrated approach to outdoor learning, for example Denmark, where *udeskole*—regular curriculum outdoor learning—is becoming more widespread supported by governmental policy (Mygind et al., 2019), or Finland, where there is a requirement to adopt experiential education in outdoor environments within the national curriculum (Sjöblom & Svens, 2019).

---

[1] WWF: People and Communities. https://www.worldwildlife.org/initiatives/people-and-commun ities; Children & Nature Network: Cities. https://www.childrenandnature.org/cities/ (both accessed 30/4/2021).

5   Combining Educational and Health Outcomes

There is growing evidence that spending time outside in natural environments, often school-based, is associated with improvements in children's skills and development (Lovell et al., 2020; PHE, 2020). Green school grounds that include natural features are associated with better behaviour and attention restoration (Fiennes et al., 2015), better learning processes and outcomes (Natural England, 2016a), and attainment of higher levels of achievement than control groups in reading, mathematics, science and social studies, physical education and drama (Browning & Rigolon, 2019). Waite et al. (2016) attribute these educational improvements to children's enjoyment of, and greater engagement with, their lessons and their experiences of success through different pedagogies and places, which together raise their self-confidence and motivation to learn. The number and breadth of research reports from multiple perspectives and disciplines have reached a critical mass, strongly indicating that positive educational and wellbeing outcomes for children derive from increased opportunities to learn in natural environments (e.g. Natural England, 2016a, b). Evidencing educational benefits is necessary to persuade school leaders to adopt such practices.

Additionally, time in nature and outdoor learning have been shown to increase physical activity levels and reduce sedentary behaviour (Calogiuri & Chroni, 2014; Aronsson et al., 2015; see Mygind: *Udeskole*—Pupils' Physical Activity and Gender Perspectives in this volume), and positive associations between access to greenspaces and mental wellbeing have been observed, including reductions in attention deficit and hyperactivity (McCormick, 2017; Tillmann et al., 2018). Vanaken and Danckaerts (2018) suggest these effects on mental health and wellbeing vary depending on children's developmental stages and types of environment. Thus, outdoor learning has demonstrable potential to combine health and wellbeing outcomes with educational aims.

In the following sections, we describe three projects that illustrate ways in which outdoor learning can make a valuable contribution to decreasing sedentary behaviour; supporting children's sense of wellbeing and enjoyment of school; and contributing to teachers' own wellbeing.

6   Case Study 1: Woodland Health for Youth (WHY): Where to Maximise Physical Activity

The first case study outlines a small-scale partnership between health, education and environmental sectors: the Woodland Health for Youth (WHY) project, undertaken in the spring of 2014 and funded by Plymouth University's Faculty of Health, Education and Society, the BIG Lottery programme *Good from Woods* and the Plymouth City Council's Green Infrastructure Team. A specialist community public health nurse/school nurse was employed as a practitioner-researcher working collaboratively with a local primary school that delivered learning outside the classroom in natural environments. This form of outdoor learning was supported through the Natural Connections Demonstration Project (Waite et al., 2016, see Passy & Blackwell: Natural Connections: Learning About Outdoor-Based Learning in this volume).

The aim of the WHY project was to evaluate the physical health benefits of outdoor learning through an action research approach. Meyer and Cooper (2015) describe action research as an approach to improve practice through a participatory research process in a real-world context. Adopting this approach, the practitioner-researcher participated in outdoor sessions at the primary school, helping the teaching staff with group management. This facilitated an understanding of the context of outdoor learning sessions and an insight into the participating children's views. Observations, discussions, thoughts and ideas were captured through a reflective log.

The school where the research took place was situated in an area of high deprivation, with many parents reliant on state support. At the time of the research, a year 2 class had weekly outdoor lessons—some within the school grounds and some in a nearby woodland. Participants were recruited from this class through information letters sent to all parents/carers of the 25 children in the class; the first ten consent forms (of equal gender distribution) returned were included in the study. Due to one girl's parent withdrawing her from the study, a boy took her place, resulting in six male and four female participants.

Quantitative data measuring children's physical activity were collected through accelerometry. An accelerometer is a device that measures acceleration of movement, which is subsequently translated into different levels of physical activity. The WHY study used wrist-worn accelerometers which had been validated on children, with cut-points developed by Phillips et al. (2011) to translate raw data into physical activity levels. For five weeks, the ten participants wore their accelerometers on the day when they had their outdoor learning session. Through statistical data analysis, activity levels during their morning indoor lessons were compared to the activity levels during their afternoon outdoor session, to test the hypothesis that children are more active when they learn outdoors.

Meyer and Cooper (2015) argue that any type of data can be collected in action research depending on the social situation and the evolving research process. The reflective evidence collated by the practitioner-researcher during outdoor learning included comments made by children:

This is fun! (girl looking for insects on a tree)

I love nature. (boy in the woodland)

I can feel the sun in my face and the fresh air. (girl in the woodland)

Correspondingly, children were observed as active during outdoor learning; when allowed, children would run instead of walk, climb on fallen trees and tree stumps, throw stones in the stream, jump between rocks, use a stick to dig in the soil and so on. The children's body language, together with their comments, reflected the joy that these activities and the outdoor environment engendered. This is likely due to a combination of well-documented mental health benefits for children that come with accessing the outdoors (McCormick, 2017) and mental health benefits related to being physically active (Department of Health and Social Care, 2019). Observational data also highlighted many other skills that developed through outdoor learning, including gross and fine motor skills; risk-taking behaviour and safe practice; curricular learning such as literacy and biology; creative activities such as art and imagination; social skills such as listening, taking turns and working together on a project; and building confidence and self-efficacy.

The main focus of the accelerometry measurements was to compare moderate-to-vigorous physical activity (MVPA) between outdoor and indoor lessons, as there is a national target in England for children aged 5–18 to spend 60 min or more a day in MVPA (Department of Health and Social Care, 2019). Additionally, the national recommendation stipulates a need to minimise sedentary behaviour, so we compared the proportion of time spent in sedentary phase during outdoor compared to indoor lessons. The results showed that children spent a significantly larger proportion of the time in MVPA during outdoor learning sessions ($17.0\% \pm 6.7$) than during indoor lessons ($6.2\% \pm 4.3$), $p < 0.001$. Since some outdoor sessions were held in the school grounds and some in the nearby woodland, a sub-analysis was performed to explore whether there was a difference in physical activity levels between the two; this showed significantly higher levels of MVPA during woodland outdoor learning ($19.0\% \pm 7.1$) than during school grounds outdoor learning ($13.7\% \pm 4.8$), $p < 0.05$. Figure 1 shows the difference between the proportion of time children spent in MVPA depending on if they were engaged in woodland outdoor learning, school grounds outdoor learning, or an indoor lesson. Furthermore, children spent a significantly smaller proportion of their time being sedentary during outdoor sessions ($44.2\% \pm 11.6$) than during indoor lessons ($60.4\% \pm 11.0$), $p < 0.001$.

The WHY project indicated through a range of data that children were more active during outdoor sessions than during indoor lessons, and that this had a positive effect on their physical health and mental wellbeing. The higher levels of physical activity

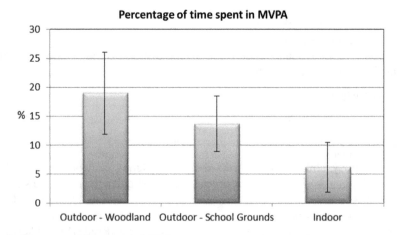

Fig. 1 Percentage of time spent in MVPA

in the woodland compared to the school grounds might be explained by the bigger and less familiar space that the woodland offered compared to the school grounds. Passy and Waite (2011) identify several benefits to woodland-based learning, including greater freedom, wilder and more natural space, child-led learning, negotiated boundaries, created activities and managed risk. Our study was undertaken in an area of high deprivation, which is a known factor in reduced access to, or use of, green spaces (Boyd et al., 2018). To expose children to natural environments as part of the curriculum removes these barriers and provides all children, regardless of their socio-economic background, the same opportunities to learn, explore, and enjoy the health and wellbeing benefits of being outdoors.

7 Case Study 2: Mapping and Measuring Healthy Outcomes: Capturing School Progress

In this next case study, we look at how schools can monitor physical activity and wellbeing to inform school development for pupils' health and wellbeing.

The Mapping and Measuring Healthy Outcomes (MMHO) research project was funded by the Naturally Healthy Devon Schools (NHDS) Project partnership of the Campaign to Protect Rural England (Devon), Natural England, Devon County Council and Plymouth University's Institute of Health and Community. The NHDS project was intended to help schools to align outdoor learning and the promotion of health and wellbeing through reducing sedentary behaviour during schooling. MMHO was small-scale research that supported the evaluation of NHDS by exploring school-friendly methods of assessing physical activity levels and wellbeing.

Accelerometers are commonly used to measure and inform health related research with both adults and children, but the cost and complicated analysis of accelerometer data are generally prohibitive for regular school-based assessments of physical activity (PA). While self-report is generally considered appropriate to measure subjective wellbeing as this concerns how an individual feels about their wellbeing, it may be biased by social desirability responses in reporting actual physical activity levels (Robson, 2011). Furthermore, Baquet et al. (2007) warn that children's PA patterns are highly variable compared to adults and that they may be less able to self-report accurately. On the other hand, the competence of children to be actively involved in research is often underestimated (Alderson, 2000), especially within medicalised literature (Montreuil & Carnevale, 2016). Our study provided an opportunity to explore whether children aged over 7 years would be capable of assessing how physically active they had been in lessons. We also considered it important to discover the extent to which less expensive technical measures, such as pedometers, might give practically valuable information for schools about pupils' levels of PA and sedentary behaviour, given schools' role in monitoring weight and reducing risks of obesity through Relationships Education responsibilities. The value of using three methods was not only that we could triangulate the results, but that children might become more aware of their PA through comparisons of their self-report and objective measures. Children's involvement in monitoring their PA would give them agency in making changes in their behaviour, whilst also offering opportunities for curricular maths, science and Relationships Education.

Over a summer term in 2015, children aged between 7 and 10 years from two primary schools in Devon, England, were given pedometers or accelerometers and questionnaires to measure sedentary behaviour and levels of PA. The two schools were purposively chosen as they were interested in finding out more about the benefits of outdoor learning. The pedometers measured the number of steps; the accelerometers measured the intensity of the activity levels; and the questionnaires were devised as a comparative tool using self-report.

For the questionnaire, children and teachers were asked to rate their perceptions of levels of activity during lessons inside or outside using a four-point scale, linked to categories of physical activity recorded by the accelerometers—sedentary, low-level, medium-level and vigorous. By comparing the quantifiable questionnaire responses from teachers and pupils with quantitative data from the measuring instruments, we intended to assess the accuracy of pupils' and teachers' perceptions of children's PA and determine whether perceptions of levels of activity correlate with actual PA.

The results were analysed using SPSS. Cross-tabulations showed that when children's responses were compared to the total counts per hour for sedentary, light to medium and moderate to vigorous activity levels, they correlated with the objective measurements to a statistically significant degree ($p < 0.05$).

The descriptions of activity level that discriminated most successfully in terms of objective measurement were "I moved and ran around most of the time" and "I mostly sat down a lot". These statements are in line with national targets for children aged 5–18 years not only to spend more time in moderate-to-vigorous physical activity but also to minimize sedentary behaviour (DHSC, 2019). Combining the intermediate categories (light and moderate physical activity levels) provided the best fit with the pedometer and accelerometer data, suggesting that children found it more difficult to distinguish finer grades of activity levels.

Figure 2 illustrates variation in individual interpretations and uptake of opportunities to be more physically active, but that on average, self-report represents PA as measured by pedometers. Similar individual variation was noted in the WHY study.

Comparisons of pupil responses with teacher reports can help to identify children who are outliers, perhaps very active in class or mostly static, even when outdoors. In the WHY project, there were marked differences between individual levels of PA in woodland, school grounds and during outdoor learning and play times. The differences between individual children's activity levels during outdoor learning were flatter compared to during free play, possibly because assigned learning tasks incorporated requirements for more PA by all children.

As Fig. 3 shows, while children and teacher assessments correspond on average, interesting anomalies may be missed. Taken together, case study 1 and 2 point to the value of outdoor learning sessions in motivating less-active children to move more, and the positive contribution that monitoring PA can have in identifying less-mobile

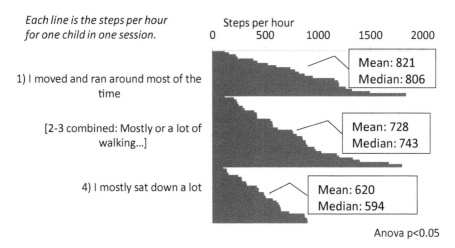

Fig. 2 Comparison of pedometer steps and self-reported activity levels

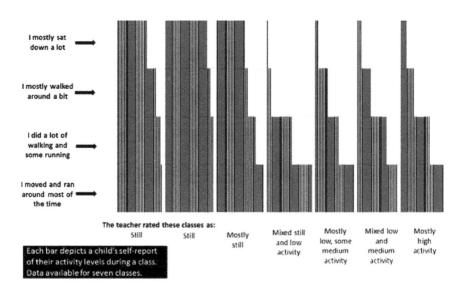

Fig. 3 Comparison of pupil and teacher perceptions of lessons

children. Greater awareness on the part of teachers and children of mismatches in their assessments, coupled with corroboration through pedometers, could help address meeting the needs of outliers in terms of appropriate physical activity levels for different lessons. The WHY project showed that outdoor learning provided a more equitable and consistent way of increasing physical activity levels for all children, compared to breaktime when greater variations were seen between individual children.

Our study also used qualitative methods that showed how lessons inside and out might be differently experienced by children. Most of the children's drawings of outdoor learning featured a social scene with two or more people, while inside activity depicted solitary children sitting still or simply the task without people included (Fig. 4), providing further evidence of the wider wellbeing benefits of outdoor learning, such as enhanced social skills.

Our trial of multiple methods of measuring activity levels suggests that schools do not need to use expensive instruments to provide evidence of reducing sedentary behaviour. Children's perceptions appear sufficiently accurate to provide indicative data and can be fruitfully compared to accepted objective measures, such as pedometers, to raise personal awareness of and engagement with healthy activity levels. The self-report questionnaire is available to show the levels of PA stimulated by different outdoor learning lessons and those delivered inside the classroom in an open access toolkit: *Creating Happy and Healthy Schools through Outdoor Learning* https://www.plymouth.ac.uk/uploads/production/document/path/10/10803/RFJ27519_Education_folder_and_amends_CORRECTProof_3A.pdf (accessed 30/4/2021).

Fig. 4 Children's depiction of outdoor and in-classroom learning

8 Case Study 3: Doing the Best for Their Pupils: Outdoor Learning and Teacher Wellbeing

In Case Study 3, we consider how outdoor learning impacts on teacher wellbeing, based upon data from the Natural Connections Demonstration project (NC) (see Passy & Blackwell: Natural Connections: Learning About Outdoor-Based Learning in this volume), and the Naturally Healthy Devon Schools project evaluation, described above.

Schools are frequently called upon to deal with many societal problems and teachers can feel overwhelmed by the number of roles they are expected to fulfil, a situation sharpened during the COVID-19 crisis and its multiple adverse effects on children and schooling. We were pleased to find that NC teachers experienced benefits for themselves as well as their pupils in adopting outdoor learning practice. For example, teachers at one primary school reported enjoying their lessons in the natural environment as much as the children. They felt staying indoors all day was oppressive and going outside was important for their mental health (case study notes, primary school, NC). Overall, in the survey data from our NC evaluation, we found that seventy-two percent of project schools reported positive impacts on participating teachers' own health and wellbeing.

Yet, in interviews with teachers, personal pleasure was less apparent. While some teachers mentioned their own experiences of childhood spent in nature and their continuing enjoyment of being outdoors, the most common route to wellbeing seemed through their professional commitment to doing the best for their pupils.

> I get a lot of personal satisfaction from it but I think that is from seeing the engagement, the enjoyment…just the joy of [children] being outside in the fresh air engaged with nature watching the seasons change... (outdoor learning lead, primary school, NC)

> ...one of the key bits of the science curriculum is the wonderment of science. I think it is hard to bring in the wonderment of science stuck in a science lab for the whole year whereas if you get outside you can give some people a real...oh my gosh! (teacher, case study, secondary school, NC)

This interpretation of an indirect route to teacher wellbeing is further supported by school survey results which showed that teachers saw positive effects on their teaching practice (79%) and their professional development (69%) which were accompanied by strong impacts on teachers' job satisfaction (69%). For some teachers, support was needed to translate their own passion and enjoyment into meaningful learning for pupils.

> I know what my childhood was like, so I knew the trees and birds and I wanted to pass that to my class [...] but since then we've been on some real good quality training (teacher, primary school, NC)

Staff also commented on improved relationships with children in an outdoor context.

> I feel I can let them go I don't have to have them within my sight every moment 'cos I think they are learning to be responsible in their own right... without an adult present (teacher, primary school, NC)

Good staff-pupil relationships are foundational to teacher wellbeing (Roffey, 2012).

Naturally Healthy Devon schools (NHDS) started from a high baseline of pupil health and wellbeing but still reported gains through curriculum outdoor learning and other health and wellbeing initiatives, including healthy eating lessons and participation in the Food for Life scheme during the project.

Positive impacts for teachers' wellbeing through outdoor teaching were also noted.

> Everyone loves teaching outside when they can, and this has been said many times across the school (survey comment, NHDS)

Teachers' enjoyment of taking their pupils outside to learn fed through to pupils' pleasure too.

> [Working outdoors] gives teachers more enjoyment and more confidence. And I think that is the number one thing that is going to help those children; the teachers, the way they are teaching (headteacher, NHDS)

However, even though this sub-project was focused on health and wellbeing,

> The health and wellbeing aspect [...] hasn't been a big part of what they are doing. (hub leader, NHDS)

A lack of emphasis on health and wellbeing may stem from recognition that the principal drivers for schools in England are standards of educational attainment, evaluated by the Office for Standards in Education (OFSTED). As in the wider NC data, teachers' source of satisfaction and wellbeing appeared to derive principally from their sense that they were improving pupils' experience of schooling.

> It has helped inspire myself, the school and our children to get out of the classroom setting. We hope that OFSTED will see the benefits that this has had on our teaching and the pupils' learning progress. (survey comment, NHDS)

In effect, teaching outside provided an antidote to the

> pressured environment for teachers where they are being told what to do and that they are not doing it very well and need to do it better. (hub leader, NC)

> [Outdoor learning] has helped staff and had a big impact, specifically it has given the staff the confidence to stand up for what they think is right and do what they think they are doing well and not go round spinning plates trying to do all these different things. (outdoor learning team, primary school, NC)

It seems that outdoor learning reconnected some teachers with their personal values and clarified their priorities (Waite, 2011). The experience may support staff and pupil wellbeing because it offers learning by the back door, reducing pressure to cram knowledge into the timetable.

> It is generally more relaxing for both staff and children. There's not that rigidity there of 'we're in this learning space to learn'—they're almost sat (sic) there learning and not realising they're doing it. (head teacher, NHDS)

Of course, some teachers were less enthusiastic about teaching outdoors for a variety of reasons, including lack of confidence or personal interest in nature. For these teachers, team teaching and practical continuing professional development through which outdoor learning was fostered in NC, coupled with witnessing the benefits for pupils first-hand as fellow teachers embraced the opportunities, provided positive experiences to build their willingness to take part. Experiencing outdoor teaching and its benefits appeared to be an effective way to influence hearts, minds and practice.

9 Discussion

The three case studies presented here all point to positive health and wellbeing impacts on children from school-based outdoor learning. Recognition of the importance of experiences in nature is not new; in 1984, Wilson formed his biophilia hypothesis, which proposes that humans have an innate love for nature, and in 2005, Louv argued that depriving children of nature experiences can lead to nature deficit disorder, with poor physical and mental health outcomes as a result. However, recent years have seen a significant increase in a robust evidence-base related to health and wellbeing benefits of being outdoors as we outlined in the introduction to the chapter.

The main finding from the WHY project (case study 1) was that children spent significantly more time in moderate-to-vigorous physical activity and less time being sedentary when learning outdoors (particularly woodlands), than in indoor lessons. This supports findings from a systematic review by Gray et al. (2015), which found positive effects of outdoor time on physical activity, sedentary behaviour, and cardiorespiratory fitness in children aged 3–12 (28 studies from nine countries; a cumulative sample of 13,798 participants). While sport is sometimes championed to address health challenges, these results indicate there are other school-based routes to reach children who are reluctant to participate in physical exercise per se.

The second case study charted the development of an evidence-based tool for schools to assess health outcomes from outdoor teaching without having to buy expensive equipment. This offers potential to increase schools' ownership of their outdoor teaching, through evaluating the outcomes of outdoor sessions, and evidencing the value that they bring. Participatory action research involving 75 teachers from five primary schools in the Netherlands identified that some of the barriers to outdoor education were related to a lack of formal status of outdoor learning, and a need for structure or a framework (van Dijk-Wesselius et al., 2020). The *Creating Happy and Healthy Schools through Outdoor Learning* toolkit provides such a framework and can support teacher confidence in adopting outdoor pedagogies. Children's involvement encourages greater responsibility for their own healthy lifestyles, whilst providing schools with data to inform effective changes to school policy and practice. In addition, empirical demonstration of these benefits at a local level should appeal to schools looking for evidence to share with staff, governors, parents and pupils that justifies the pedagogical choices they make, underpins parental and managerial understanding, and grows practitioners' confidence in taking children's learning outdoors.

The final case study allowed us to consider the impact of outdoor teaching on staff wellbeing. We found teacher wellbeing was frequently interconnected with pupil wellbeing; if teachers felt that their pupils enjoyed and benefitted from outdoor sessions, it gave them job satisfaction. Therefore, since being outdoors is good for children's wellbeing (McCormick, 2017), we can infer a knock-on effect for staff wellbeing. In a similar way, teachers' professional pride in meeting children's cognitive and affective needs through alternative teaching approaches and consequent higher levels of personal wellbeing appeared to contribute to increases in many children's enjoyment of and satisfaction with their learning experiences. Our research also suggested that for some teachers, the outdoor experience reconnected them to their own happy childhood or contemporary experiences in nature, reinforcing a sense of wellbeing. Significant life experience research suggests that adults who spent time in nature as a child have a greater possibility of working in an environmental field or, at least, have a greater environmental commitment than those who did not (Wells & Lekies, 2006). This also aligns with the biophilia hypothesis (Wilson, 1984) suggesting a need for humans to connect with nature and other living creatures, which has been reaffirmed by recent studies (Roberts et al., 2020). Positive teacher-pupil relationships fostered outdoors were also linked to teacher wellbeing (Roffey, 2012).

However, not all teachers or children will currently experience these opportunities. Through embedding school-based outdoor learning, it is possible to break cycles of disconnection from nature and create new generations that regard school time spent learning outdoors as normal and necessary.

10   Implications for Policy and Practice

A step-by-step approach is recommended for schools wishing to promote health and wellbeing outcomes through outdoor learning. First, inclusion of principles of children's voice and agency in school policy documents makes it clear to all staff, parents and governors that listening to children's opinions and providing space for them to shape how they experience school is important. Outdoor learning provides an ideal space for that to happen.

Shared steps to outdoor-based healthy outcomes

1. Form a working group with representation of managers, staff and pupils (parents and governors) for planning and progress monitoring.
2. Get children involved in design, activities, analysis and dissemination stages. Taking notice of their priorities and what they would like to include will increase their motivation.

3. Use questionnaires to find out the extent and impact on physical activity of different lessons, how children and teachers feel when learning outside, how much learning time is spent outside. Devise outdoor lesson plans that encourage movement necessary to achieve goals.
4. Use pedometers to quantify steps taken during inside and outside lessons, incentivise increased physical activity, and provide data for children to use in maths, science and PSHE lessons back inside. Monitoring personal activity levels using pedometers may encourage less-active children.
5. Use creative methods, such as writing, drama and art, to help children express what learning outside and moving more means to them.
6. Present the results to class, assembly, parent and governors' meetings, and other schools.
7. Review progress regularly.
8. Plan next actions.

Shared steps to outdoor-based wellbeing outcomes

1. Integrate children's voices into school improvement and curriculum planning to address how the outdoor learning environment (and indoor!) can be enhanced and better used for children's learning and wellbeing.
2. 'Family groups' with a teacher and children of mixed ages that report to School Council and/or the governors of the school can be effective in ensuring even the youngest children's voices are heard. It also builds a sense of community across the school.
3. Be alert to other times when children express their wishes; these often emerge during outdoor sessions where relationships between teacher and children are less formal.
4. Create action plans from these consultations that include children's active contribution. This might be through design input, fundraising, monitoring progress, for example.
5. Document and explain how children's views have shaped the curriculum and how it is delivered.
6. Remember to celebrate achievements in meeting expressed wishes, letting children have a say and role in how these are highlighted.
7. Keep the cycle going so that all children experience agency throughout their learning journey at school, and the outdoor learning environment and curriculum remain a living relevant context.
8. Check that similar respect is shown for all staff views, modelling inclusivity.

11 Conclusion

Perhaps the most compelling aspect of our case studies is linked to the stark evidence that children from lower socioeconomic backgrounds have poorer health and wellbeing outcomes (Marmot, 2020). Our case studies were conducted in areas with high levels of deprivation because we wanted to focus on those children who might benefit the most. The positive results from our studies suggest that integrating outdoor learning in the school curriculum represents an equitable and efficient way to promote positive health and wellbeing for all children attending school. Nature is a resource that can offer physical and mental space for children and young people to explore and develop; but as Maller et al. (2006) note, its potential as an upstream health promoting resource is not always realised. We hope that this chapter will provide some inspiration to maximise its rich potential.

Recommended Further Reading

1. Barton, J., Bragg, R., Wood, C. & Pretty (2016). *Green Exercise: Linking Nature, Health and Wellbeing*. London: Routledge.
2. Stevens, T. (2019). *Physical Activity and Student Learning*. Abingdon: Routledge.
3. Lambert, D., Roberts, M. & Waite, S. (2020). *The National Curriculum Outdoors: A complete scheme of work*. London: Bloomsbury Publications.

Acknowledgements We would like to thank our many funders (Natural England, Department for the Environment, Food and Rural Affairs, Historic England, Good from Woods BIG Lottery fund, the University of Plymouth School of Nursing and Midwifery Alumni fund, Campaign for the Protection of Rural England (Devon), Devon County Council, Devon Local Nature Partnership and the Institute of Health and Community, University of Plymouth), and our research collaborators: Maria Tighe-Clarke (Woodland Health for Youth); Louise Graham and Naomi Wright (Mapping and Measuring Healthy Schools); Andy Edwards-Jones, Martin Gilchrist and Rowena Passy (Natural Connections) and of course, all the children and staff who took part.

References

Alderson, P. (2000). Children as researchers: the effects of participation rights on research methodology. In P. Christensen & A. James (eds.), *Research with children: Perspectives and practices*. Falmer Press.

Allen, J., & Balfour, R. (2014). *Natural solutions for tackling health inequalities*. University College London Institute of Health Equity.

Aronsson, J., Waite, S., & Tighe-Clarke, M. (2015). Measuring the impact of outdoor learning on the physical activity of school age children: The use of accelerometry. *Education and Health*, *33*(3), 57–62. https://sheu.org.uk/sheux/EH/eh333ja.pdf. Accessed 4 Apr 2021.

Baquet, G., Stratton, Van Praagh, E., & Berthoin, S. (2007). Improving physical activity assessment in prepubertal children with high-frequency accelerometry monitoring: A methodological issue. *Preventive Medicine, 44,* 143-147.

Boyd, F., White, M. P., Bell, S. L., & Burt, J. (2018). Who doesn't visit natural environments for recreation and why: A population representative analysis of spatial, individual and temporal factors among adults in England. *Landscape and Urban Planning, 175,* 102–113.

Browning, M. H. E. M., & Rigolon, A. (2019). School green space and its impact on academic performance: A Systematic literature review. *International Journal of Environmental Research and Public Health, 16*(3), 429.

Calogiuri, G., & Chroni, S. (2014). The impact of the natural environment on the promotion of active living: An integrative systematic review. *BMC Public Health, 14*(1), 873.

Day, R. E., Sahota, P., & Christian, M. S. (2019). Effective implementation of primary school-based healthy lifestyle programmes: A qualitative study of views of school staff. *BMC Public Health, 19,* 1239.

Department for Education. (2019). Relationships Education, Relationships and Sex Education (RSE) and Health Education. https://assets.publishing.service.gov.uk/government/uploads/sys tem/uploads/attachment_data/file/908013/Relationships_Education__Relationships_and_Sex_ Education__RSE__and_Health_Education.pdf. Accessed 10 Mar 2021.

Department of Health and Social Care. (2019). UK Chief Medical Officer's physical activity guidelines. https://assets.publishing.service.gov.uk/government/uploads/system/uploads/attach ment_data/file/832868/uk-chief-medical-officers-physical-activity-guidelines.pdf. Accessed March 13, 2021.

Fiennes, C., Oliver, E., Dickson, K., Escobar, D., Romans, A., & Oliver, S. (2015). The Existing Evidence-Base about the Effectiveness of Outdoor Learning. UCL; Giving Evidence: IOL; Blagrave Trust. (See Jucker: How to Raise the Standards of Outdoor Learning and its Research in this volume).

Gray, C., Gibbons, R., Larouche, R., Sandseter, E. B. H., Bienenstock, A., Brussoni, M., Chabot, G., Herrington, S., Janssen, I., Pickett, W., Power, M., Stanger, N., Sampson, M., & Tremblay, M. S. (2015). What is the relationship between outdoor time and physical activity, sedentary behaviour, and physical fitness in children? *A Systematic Review, International Journal of Environmental Research and Public Health, 12*(6), 6455–6474.

Lovell, R., White, M. P., Wheeler, B., Taylor, T., & Elliott, L. (2020). A rapid scoping review of health and wellbeing evidence for the Green Infrastructure Standards. http://publications.natura lengland.org.uk/publication/4799558023643136. Accessed 15 Mar 2021.

Louv, R. (2005). *Last child in the woods.* Algonquin Books.

McCormick, R. (2017). Does access to green space impact the mental well-being of children: A systematic review. *Journal of Pediatric Nursing, 37,* 3–7.

Maller, C., Townsend, M., Pryor, A., Brown, P., & St Leger, L. (2006). Healthy nature healthy people: 'Contact with nature' as an upstream health promotion intervention for populations. *Health Promotion International, 21*(1), 45–54.

Marmot, M., Allen, J., Boyce, T., Goldblatt, P., & Morrison, J. (2020). *Health equity in England: The marmot review 10 years on.* Institute of Health Equity.

Meyer, J., & Cooper, J. (2015). Action research. In K. Gerrish & J. Lathlean (Eds.), *The research process in nursing* (7th ed.) Wiley.

Montreuil, M., & Carnevale, F. A. (2016). A concept analysis of children's agency within the health literature. *Journal of Child Health Care, 20*(4), 503–511.

Mygind, E., Bølling, M., & Barfod, K. S. (2019). Primary teachers' experiences with weekly education outside the classroom during a year. *Education, 3–13, 47*(5), 599–611.

Natural England. (2016a). Links between natural environments and learning: Evidence briefing (EIN017). http://publications.naturalengland.org.uk/publication/5253709953499136. Accessed 30 Apr 2021.

Natural England. (2016b). Links between natural environments and physical activity: Evidence briefing. (EIN019) http://publications.naturalengland.org.uk/publication/671981609 8906112 Accessed 30 Apr 2021.

Newlove-Delgado, T., McManus, S., Sadler, K., Thandi, S., Vizard, T., Cartwright, C., & Ford, T. (2021). Child mental health in England before and during the COVID-19 lockdown. *The Lancet Psychiatry, 8*(5), 353–354. https://doi.org/10.1016/S2215-0366(20)30570-8. Accessed 30 Apr 2021.

NHS Digital. (2018). Mental health of children and young people in England, 2017. https://digital.nhs.uk/data-and-information/publications/statistical/mental-health-of-children-and-young-people-in-england/2017/2017. Accessed 10 Mar 2021.

NHS Digital. (2019). National child measurement programme, England 2018/19 school year. https://digital.nhs.uk/data-and-information/publications/statistical/national-child-measurement-programme/2018-19-school-year. Accessed 10 Mar 2021.

NHS Digital. (2020). National child measurement programme. https://digital.nhs.uk/services/national-child-measurement-programme/. Accessed 11 Mar 2021.

Passy, R., & Waite, S. (2011). School gardens and Forest Schools. In S. Waite (Ed.), *Children learning outside the classroom from birth to eleven* (pp. 162–175). SAGE.

Phillips, L., Parfitt, G., & Rowlands, A. (2011). Calibration of the GENEA accelerometer for assessment of physical activity intensity in children. *Journal of Science and Medicine in Sports, 16*(2), 124–128.

Public Health England (PHE). (2019a). Healthy beginnings: Applying All Our Health. https://www.gov.uk/government/publications/healthy-beginnings-applying-all-our-health/healthy-beginnings-applying-all-our-health. Accessed 10 Mar 2021.

Public Health England (PHE). (2019b). PHE Strategy 2020–2025. https://assets.publishing.service.gov.uk/government/uploads/system/uploads/attachment_data/file/831562/PHE_Strategy_2020-25.pdf. Accessed 10 Mar 2021.

Public Health England (PHE). (2020). Improving access to greenspace: A new review for 2020. https://assets.publishing.service.gov.uk/government/uploads/system/uploads/attachment_data/file/904439/Improving_access_to_greenspace_2020_review.pdf. Accessed 30 Apr 2021.

Roberts, A., Hinds, J., & Camic, P. (2020). Nature activities and wellbeing in children and young people: A systematic review. *Journal of Adventure Education and Outdoor Learning, 20*(4), 298–318.

Robson, B. (2011). *Real world research.* Wiley.

Roffey, S. (2012). Pupil wellbeing-teacher wellbeing: Two sides of the same coin? *Educational and Child Psychology, 29*(4), 8–17. https://www.sueroffey.com/wp-content/uploads/import/32-Roffey%20ECP29-4.pdf. Accessed 30 Apr 2021.

Royal College of Paediatrics and Child Health. (2019). The health impacts of screen time: A guide for clinicians and parents. https://www.rcpch.ac.uk/sites/default/files/2018-12/rcpch_screen_time_guide_-_final.pdf. Accessed 13 Mar 2021.

Schüle, S. A., Hilz, L. K., Dreger, S., & Bolte, G. (2019). Social inequalities in environmental resources of green and blue spaces: A review of evidence in the WHO European region. *International Journal of Environmental Research and Public Health, 16*(7), 1216.

Sjöblom, P., & Svens, M. (2019). Learning in the finnish outdoor classroom: Pupils' views. *Journal of Adventure Education and Outdoor Learning, 19*(4), 301–314.

Spencer, N. (2013). Reducing child health inequalities: What's the problem? *Archives of Disease in Childhood, 98*, 836–837. https://doi.org/10.1136/archdischild-2013-304347. Accessed 30 Apr 2021.

Tillmann, S., Tobin, D., Avison, W., & Gilliland, J. (2018). Mental health benefits of interactions with nature in children and teenagers: A systematic review. *Journal of Epidemiology and Community Health, 72*(10), 958–966.

van Dijk-Wesselius, J. E., van den Berg, A. E., Maas, J., & Hovinga, D. (2020). Green schoolyards as outdoor learning environments: Barriers and solutions as experienced by primary school teachers. *Frontiers in Psychology, 10*, 2919–2919.

Vanaken, G. J., & Danckaerts, M. (2018). Impact of green space exposure on children's and adolescents' mental health: A systematic review. *International Journal of Environmental Research and Public Health, 15*(12).

Waite, S. (2011). Teaching and learning outside the classroom: personal values, alternative pedagogies and standards. *Education, 3–13, 39*(1), 65–82.

Waite, S., Husain, F., Scandone, B., Forsyth, E., & Piggott, H. (2021). Moving towards nature? Exploring progressive pathways to engage children and young people from disadvantaged backgrounds in nature-based activities. In M. Baker, E. Stewart & N. Carr (Eds.), *Leisure activities in the outdoors: Learning, developing and challenging,* Chapter 11, pp.130–144. Wallingford, UK: CABI (Centre for Agriculture and BioScience International.

Waite, S., Passy, R., Gilchrist, M., Hunt, A., & Blackwell, I. (2016). Natural Connections Demonstration Project 2012–2016: Final report. Natural England Commissioned report NECR215. http://publications.naturalengland.org.uk/publication/6636651036540928. Accessed 16 Sep 2020. (See Passy & Blackwell: Natural Connections: Learning about Outdoor-Based Learning in this volume).

Warren, K., Roberts, N. S., Breunig, M., & Alvarez, M. A. T. G. (2014). Social justice in outdoor experiential education: A state of knowledge review. *Journal of Experiential Education, 37*(1), 89–103.

Wells, N. M., & Lekies, K. S. (2006). Nature and the life course: Pathways from childhood nature experiences to adult environmentalism. *Children, Youth and Environments, 16*(1), 1–24.

White, M. P., Alcock, I., Grellier, J., Wheeler, B. W., Hartig, T., Warber, S. L., et al. (2019). Spending at least 120 minutes a week in nature is associated with good health and wellbeing. *Scientific Reports, 9*(1), 7730.

Wilson, E. O. (1984). *Biophilia.* Harvard University Press.

World Health Organisation. (2020). Meeting report: Global standards for health promoting schools and their implementation guidance. https://www.who.int/publications/i/item/9789240011069. Accessed 10 Mar 2021.

Sue Waite is visiting Associate Professor at Jönköping University, Sweden, and former Reader in Outdoor Learning at the University of Plymouth, UK. She has researched and published widely regarding outdoor learning and health and wellbeing benefits from nature and is a member of Natural England's Strategic Research Group on Connecting People with Nature.

Jennie Aronsson is a Lecturer in Nursing at the University of Plymouth. A specialist community public health nurse by background, she is passionate about promoting health and well-being for children and families, particularly through nature-based methods.

How Daylight Controls the Biological Clock, Organises Sleep, and Enhances Mood and Performance

Anna Wirz-Justice

1 Introduction

Outdoor-based learning: an interesting new concept for a chronobiologist. But immediately I recognised the relevance of the field of biological rhythms to the understanding of a basic factor of the outdoor environment, taken for granted yet not
completely analysed: daylight. Here a short biology lesson will show why outdoor
light can be crucial for high quality learning, via neural mechanisms that control
a broad range of behaviour, physiology and endocrine function, and support stable
mood and alertness during the day and consolidated sleep at night.

2 Daylight

Let us begin with detailing the parameter of outdoor daylight availability. Daylight
follows a predictable pattern of light intensity and spectral changes day by day
throughout the year, with twilight transitions of dawn and dusk. The daily and annual
pattern is specific for a given geographic location, and Fig. 1 shows the complexity
of daylight at a latitude of 50°N (e.g. Champagne in France).

It is extraordinary that the human eye can register this enormous range of light
intensity from a starlight minimum of 0.0003 lx to sun overhead at ca. 100,000 lx
(Fig. 2). Subjectively, we experience the brightness of skylight compressed on a log
scale, but our physiology tracks the signal in exquisite detail.

Daylight is the primary geophysical signal to which all life on earth has evolved.
Chronobiology is the science of daily (circadian), monthly, tidal, and seasonal
rhythms that are related to the regular and predictable movements of sun and moon

A. Wirz-Justice (✉)
Centre for Chronobiology, University Psychiatric Clinics, 4002 Basel, Switzerland
e-mail: anna.wirz-justice@unibas.ch

R. Jucker and J. von Au (eds.), *High-Quality Outdoor Learning*,
https://doi.org/10.1007/978-3-031-04108-2_10

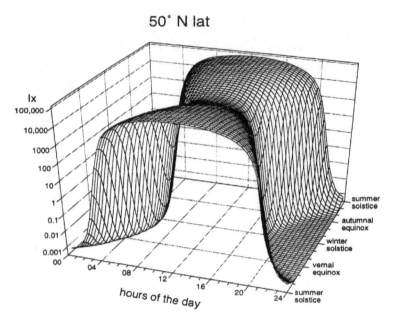

Fig. 1 A 3-D representation of daylight intensity (log lx, y-axis) across the 24-h day (x-axis) throughout the seasons of the year (z-axis) at a latitude of 50°N (M. Terman, Columbia University)

Fig. 2 Range of illumination from starlight to midday sun (log lx). Arbitrary cut-offs at approximate light intensities. Indoor room light ranges from ~10 to 300 lx. Sunrise and sunset occur around 700 lx, civil twilight ~1 lx, the full moon ~0.2 lx

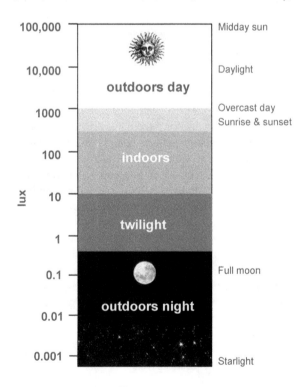

(Hastings et al., 2008). Internal temporal organisation ensures that the right function occurs at the right time (and separates incompatible functions)—within individuals, between people, and between species. The most obvious rhythms are those linked to the 24-h day-night cycle (Cajochen et al., 2010; Hastings et al., 2008). These circadian rhythms range from behavioural patterns in the general population (more accidents in the second half of the night) to the individual (the daily sleep-wake cycle and core body temperature), as well as metabolic rhythms that occur in each organ and cell. Circadian rhythms are not merely a response to the environmental time cues of light and dark, they are endogenous, that is, they are driven by molecular clock genes that tick at a frequency ~24 h (Hastings et al., 2008). Nearly all living organisms—from bacteria to plants, insects and mammals—have evolved astonishingly similar molecular timing systems (Dunlap & Loros, 2017): they guide plants to time photosynthesis, allow monarch butterflies to navigate thousands of miles, cue hamsters to hibernate, and maintain health status in humans—*as long as they live in sync with their biological clocks.*

3 The Human Circadian System

Within the biological clock, which lies in the hypothalamic suprachiasmatic nuclei (SCN), a clock gene network encodes circadian periodicity of approximately, but not exactly, 24 h (Hastings et al., 2008). The circadian system in the brain needs to receive information about the consistent external day-night cycle (Cajochen et al., 2010), and light is the major synchronising agent (or 'zeitgeber'). Photic input from the eyes to the SCN is transduced via specialised circadian photoreceptors called intrinsic photosensitive retinal ganglion cells (ipRGCs), which contain a blue-wavelength-sensitive photopigment, melanopsin (Hankins et al., 2008); these transmit the signal directly from the retina to the brain via the retinohypothalamic tract (Fig. 3).

The classical cone photoreceptors, which mediate daytime vision—color, movement, shape, and edges—and rod photoreceptors, which enable us to see in dim light and near-darkness, have secondary interactions with the non-visual ipRGC system

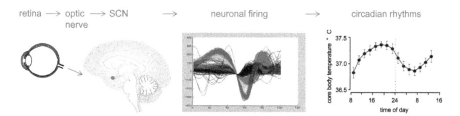

Fig. 3 The biological clock in the SCN. Light from the retinal ipRGCs (most sensitive to blue wavelengths) is transmitted to the SCN (firing patterns from a multiple unit activity record) and thereby synchronises all downstream rhythmic functions (e.g. core body temperature). Data: S. Honma, C. Cajochen

(Hankins et al., 2008). Neuronal firing patterns in the SCN convey the day-night information to many regions of the brain, driving day-night rhythms in biochemistry, physiology, and behaviour. The variety of non-visual functions directly influenced by this pathway ranges from pupil size, pineal hormone melatonin secretion, mood, vigilance, and cognitive performance, to sleep and learning.

4   Light as Zeitgeber

Of prime importance is the characteristic of light as a zeitgeber to shift circadian rhythms earlier or later depending on time of day of exposure (Minors et al., 1991; Roenneberg et al., 2013). Morning light advances the clock earlier; while evening light delays the clock (Minors et al., 1991). Additionally, regular light exposure synchronises and stabilises rhythms: all the cellular and organ clocks depend on daily zeitgeber exposure for good entrainment (Van Someren & Riemersma-Van Der Lek, 2007).

This critical role of light as zeitgeber for humans was discovered using light intensity much higher (1000 lx) than indoors (10–300 lx) (Lewy et al., 1980). In later experiments circadian responses have been observed at lower light intensities, depending on prior light exposure, duration and spectrum of the light source, and with large interindividual variability (Boivin et al., 1994; Danilenko et al., 2000; Phillips et al., 2019). In contrast, clinical applications of light use 10,000 lx (Terman & Terman, 2010), well within the range of full daylight.

Thus, there is a specific range of light intensities that affects human rhythms. In order to maintain stable entrainment—which is not only a prerequisite for good night-time sleep and daytime alertness, but also for mood state, cognition, and neurobe-havioural function—a minimum of 1000 lx for 30–60 min per day is considered adequate.

In addition to light, other zeitgebers such as physical exercise (Lewis et al., 2018), mealtimes (Lewis et al., 2020), and to a lesser extent, sleep itself (Danilenko et al., 2003), contribute to entrainment. Social signals (such jobs or school, alarm clocks, social demands) were originally considered the main zeitgebers for humans (Mistl-berger & Skene, 2004), but they are now understood to act indirectly on the SCN: they determine the timing and structure of daily habits and thus the pattern and level of exposure to outdoor and indoor light.

5   Seasonality

With the invention of artificial light, humans were able to choose their sleep-wake schedules and lifestyle. In today's 24/7 society, we no longer follow daylight duration across seasons. Rather, we have come to live under artificially designed constant day length that might be called, functionally, biological darkness. This is because we spend most of the day indoors, where room light—though adequate for vision—is insufficient to regulate our circadian rhythms.

Does seasonality still exist in humans, and if so, what would that mean? Humans do retain neurobiological responses to seasonal changes in daylength, though overt seasonal behaviour is rarely seen (Wirz-Justice, 2018). Reduced exposure to sunlight during the day with more artificial light at night leads to late circadian and sleep timing throughout the year. Natural daylight exposure (e.g. camping) in both summer and winter has been shown to rapidly entrain the biological clock to sunset and sunrise, with earlier timing compared with urban life (Stothard et al., 2017), demonstrating that we are still sensitive to these environmental cues.

Seasonal affective disorder, or winter depression, is an example of vulnerability to shorter daylength in winter. The standard application to treat winter depression is with a light box providing 10'000 lx white light for half-an-hour every morning (Terman & Terman, 2010).

6 Chronotype

Each one of us has an inborn preference to go to bed and wake up at a particular time, when we have the freedom to do so (usually only on holidays). This is called 'chronotype' (Horne & Ostberg, 1977), determined primarily by each individual's clock genes. The well-known description of extreme chronotypes are the early 'larks' and late 'owls', whereas the majority can be considered 'doves' with 'normal' sleep timing (Fig. 4).

Although our biology determines chronotype, there are shifts over the life span, probably related to hormonal changes (Roenneberg et al., 2004). Children are mostly larks until puberty, when their sleep timing shifts later and later until about the age of 20. Thereafter sleep shifts slowly earlier until older persons are larks again, with early

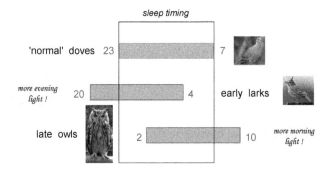

Fig. 4 Chronotypes illustrated. The grey bars represent different sleep patterns. Adolescents tend to be owls, while children and older individuals tend to be larks. The circadian system of larks can be shifted a bit later by evening light, that of owls earlier by more morning light

morning awakening. The discrepancy between internal time and social demands has been labeled 'social jet lag' (Wittmann et al., 2006).

Adolescents suffer the most. They have difficulties waking in the morning—thus the timing of classes should be later than most schools allow—and they cannot fall asleep easily (Marx et al., 2017). This leads to alarm-clock-induced shortening of sleep duration, which becomes chronic. Add to that the habit of late-night-use of iPhones and computers with bright white screens that contain a strong blue component which directly stimulates the blue-sensitive ipRGCs in the retina. Such use shifts the clock even later, thereby making falling asleep more difficult (Green et al., 2017). Morning light exposure is therefore extremely important in this age group in order to reset sleep timing earlier (a challenging exercise, but doable). Studies have looked at the effects of indoor bright light to increase students' alertness in the morning (e.g. Hansen et al., 2005), but of course the simplest solution would be to spend the first lesson of the day outdoors, where daylight provides the natural and sufficient stimulus to wake up the clock (Martinez-Nicolas et al., 2011).

7   Out of Sync

There is growing evidence for long-term health consequences of irregular, inadequate, and poorly timed light-dark cycles that disrupt sleep (Medic et al., 2017; Van Someren & Riemersma-Van Der Lek, 2007; Wirz-Justice et al., 2009). With insufficient daily light exposure—often the case if remaining indoors—our body clocks may be de-synchronised with the day-night cycle (Van Someren & Riemersma-Van Der Lek, 2007). This is most clearly experienced with shift work or transmeridian flight.

No longer being synchronised to the naturalistic dawn–dusk signal can contribute to vulnerability for mood and sleep disorders, and perpetuate or exacerbate a wide variety of clinical symptoms (Van Someren & Riemersma-Van Der Lek, 2007). For example, disrupted and poorly timed sleep has been linked to obesity and development of diabetes (Buxton et al., 2012; Potter et al., 2016). Thus students should learn how to recognise their chronotype (see automated questionnaire on https://chronotype-self-test.info, accessed 13/04/2022), be aware that social jet lag can have profound effects on emotions, performance, and alertness, and use the knowledge about daylight as a synchronising agent to improve their sleep-wake habits. Teachers also should recognise their students' chronotypes and not blame delayed sleep in adolescents on laziness or rebelliousness—it's biology! An owl will not perform well early in the day, whether training in the swimming pool or solving algebraic equations.

8 Too Much Light?

Of course, daylight has many effects beyond those related to circadian rhythms, sleep and mood (Wirz-Justice et al., 2020). It is required for Vitamin D synthesis via the skin, and for eye development in childhood (preventing myopia). In contrast, excessive ultraviolet exposure from sunlight is responsible for many skin cancers. An intelligent balance must be sought.

Blue-enhanced bright light sources in group settings such as classrooms and offices may not always be preferred given that some individuals are abnormally light sensitive, and may react with nausea, glare, and headache.

9 Light Outdoors

How then are my observations as a chronobiologist relevant to the advocacy of outdoor learning? Irregular sleep-wake cycles are associated with poorer academic performance and learning (Phillips et al., 2017; Wright et al., 2006). Regular and sufficient daylight exposure has positive effects on the quality and quantity of night-time sleep. Indoor light lacks the intensity to do this. Conversely, one has to ensure darkness in the bedroom to support stable and deep sleep.

There is some evidence that higher light exposure improves learning, but most of the data are indirect, as reflected by increased alertness, performance, faster reaction time, and memory recall (e.g. Huiberts et al., 2015; Yoshiike et al., 2019). A far larger body of evidence supports the importance of sleep for learning new skills and motor performance. The quantity and quality of sleep affect a person's memory consolidation, since sleep is a period where the brain turns recent experience into long-term memories (e.g. Ellenbogen et al., 2006; Fattinger et al., 2017; MacDonald & Cote, 2021; Walker, 2009). Finally, sleep plays an important role in brain plasticity as the young human brain develops (Dang-Vu et al., 2006; Kurth et al., 2012).

10 Conclusion

Many physiological and psychological functions are profoundly affected by daylight (and artificial indoor surrogates). All efforts to improve entrainment of rhythms with morning light will also improve alertness and performance during the day and sleep during the night. Good sleep is crucial in the educational environment since it impacts memory, motor skills, learning, mood, behaviour, immunological responses, metabolism, hormone levels, digestive processes, and more.

The growing recognition that sufficient light is important for psychological and somatic wellbeing is leading toward novel lighting solutions in architecture as well as more conscious exposure to natural daylight. In short, sufficient daily light exposure can support overall health, and the most natural and efficacious source thereof is the sun.

Recommended Further Reading

1. Center for Environmental Therapeutics www.cet.org
2. The Daylight Academy www.daylight.academy
3. Society for Light Treatment and Biological Rhythms https://sltbr.org/ (all accessed 13/04/2022)

Acknowledgements Thanks to Michael Terman, colleague and exigent editor, for much clarifying input.

References

Boivin, D. B., Duffy, J. F., Kronauer, R. E., & Czeisler, C. A. (1994). Sensitivity of the human circadian pacemaker to moderately bright light. *Journal of Biological Rhythms, 9*, 315–331.

Buxton, O. M., Cain, S. W., O'Connor, S. P., Porter, J. H., Duffy, J. F., Wang, W., Czeisler, C. A., & Shea, S. A. (2012). Adverse metabolic consequences in humans of prolonged sleep restriction combined with circadian disruption. *Science Translational Medicine, 4*, 129ra43.

Cajochen, C., Chellappa, S., & Schmidt, C. (2010). What keeps us awake?—the role of clocks and hourglasses, light, and melatonin. *International Review of Neurobiology, 93*, 57–90.

Dang-Vu, T. T., Desseilles, M., Peigneux, P., & Maquet, P. (2006). A role for sleep in brain plasticity. *Pediatric Rehabilitation, 9*, 98–118.

Danilenko, K. V., Cajochen, C., & Wirz-Justice, A. (2003). Is sleep *per se* a zeitgeber in humans? *Journal of Biological Rhythms, 18*, 170–178.

Danilenko, K. V., Wirz-Justice, A., Kräuchi, K., Weber, J. M., & Terman, M. (2000). The human circadian pacemaker can see by the dawn's early light. *Journal of Biological Rhythms, 15*, 437–446.

Dunlap, J. C., & Loros, J. J. (2017). Making time: Conservation of biological clocks from fungi to animals. *Microbiology Spectrum, 5* (3). https://doi.org/10.1128/microbiolspec.FUNK-0039-2016.

Ellenbogen, J. M., Payne, J. D., & Stickgold, R. (2006). The role of sleep in declarative memory consolidation: Passive, permissive, active or none? *Current Opinion in Neurobiology, 16*, 716–722.

Fattinger, S., de Beukelaar, T. T., Ruddy, K. L., Volk, C., Heyse, N. C., Herbst, J. A., Hahnloser, R. H. R., Wenderoth, N., & Huber, R. (2017). Deep sleep maintains learning efficiency of the human brain. *Nature Communications, 8*, 15405.

Green, A., Cohen-Zion, M., Haim, A., & Dagan, Y. (2017). Evening light exposure to computer screens disrupts human sleep, biological rhythms, and attention abilities. *Chronobiology International, 34*, 855–865.

Hankins, M. W., Peirson, S. N., & Foster, R. G. (2008). Melanopsin: An exciting photopigment. *Trends in Neurosciences, 31*, 27–36.

Hansen, M., Janssen, I., Schiff, A., Zee, P. C., & Dubocovich, M. L. (2005). The impact of school daily schedule on adolescent sleep. *Pediatrics, 115*, 1555–1561.

Hastings, M. H., Maywood, E. S., & Reddy, A. B. (2008). Two decades of circadian time. *Journal of Neuroendocrinology, 20*, 812–819.

Horne, J. A., & Ostberg, O. (1977). Individual differences in human circadian rhythms. *Biological Psychology, 5*, 179–190.

Huiberts, L. M., Smolders, K. C. H. J., & de Kort, Y. A. W. (2015). Shining light on memory: Effects of bright light on working memory performance. *Behavioural Brain Research, 294*, 234–245.

Kurth, S., Ringli, M., Lebourgeois, M. K., Geiger, A., Buchmann, A., Jenni, O. G., & Huber, R. (2012). Mapping the electrophysiological marker of sleep depth reveals skill maturation in children and adolescents. *NeuroImage, 63*, 959–965.

Lewis, P., Korf, H. W., Kuffer, L., Gross, J. V., & Erren, T. C. (2018). Exercise time cues (zeitgebers) for human circadian systems can foster health and improve performance: A systematic review. *BMJ Open Sport and Exercise Medicine, 4*, e000443.

Lewis, P., Oster, H., Korf, H. W., Foster, R. G., & Erren, T. C. (2020). Food as a circadian time cue – evidence from human studies. *Nature Reviews. Endocrinology, 16*, 213–223.

Lewy, A. J., Wehr, T. A., Goodwin, F. K., Newsome, D. A., & Markey, S. P. (1980). Light suppresses melatonin secretion in humans. *Science, 210*, 1267–1269.

MacDonald, K. J., & Cote, K. A. (2021). Contributions of post-learning REM and NREM sleep to memory retrieval. *Sleep Medicine Reviews, 59*, 101453.

Martinez-Nicolas, A., Ortiz-Tudela, E., Madrid, J. A., & Rol, M. A. (2011). Crosstalk between environmental light and internal time in humans. *Chronobiology International, 28*, 617–629.

Marx, R., Tanner-Smith, E. E., Davison, C. M., Ufholz, L. A., Freeman, J., Shankar, R., Newton, L., Brown, R. S., Parpia, A. S., Cozma, I., & Hendrikx, S. (2017). Later school start times for supporting the education, health, and well-being of high school students. *Cochrane Database of Systematic Reviews, 7*, CD009467.

Medic, G., Wille, M., & Eh Hemels, M. (2017). Short- and long-term health consequences of sleep disruption. *Nature and Science of Sleep, 9*, 151–161.

Minors, D. S., Waterhouse, J. M., & Wirz-Justice, A. (1991). A human phase-response curve to light. *Neuroscience Letters, 133*, 36–40.

Mistlberger, R. E., & Skene, D. J. (2004). Social influences on mammalian circadian rhythms: Animal and human studies. *Biological Reviews of the Cambridge Philosophical Society, 79*, 533–556.

Phillips, A. J. K., Clerx, W. M., O'Brien, C. S., Sano, A., Barger, L. K., Picard, R. W., Lockley, S. W., Klerman, E. B., & Czeisler, C. A. (2017). Irregular sleep/wake patterns are associated with poorer academic performance and delayed circadian and sleep/wake timing. *Scientific Reports, 7*, 3216.

Phillips, A. J. K., Vidafar, P., Burns, A. C., McGlashan, E. M., Anderson, C., Rajaratnam, S. M. W., Lockley, S. W., & Cain, S. W. (2019). High sensitivity and interindividual variability in the response of the human circadian system to evening light. *Proceedings of the National Academy of Sciences of the United States of America, 116*, 12019–12024.

Potter, G. D. M., Skene, D. J., Arendt, J., Cade, J. E., Grant, P. J., & Hardie, L. J. (2016). Circadian rhythm and sleep disruption: Causes, metabolic consequences and countermeasures. *Endocrine Reviews, 37*, 584–608.

Roenneberg, T., Kantermann, T., Juda, M., Vetter, C., & Allebrandt, K. V. (2013). Light and the human circadian clock. *Handbook of Experimental Pharmacology, 217*, 311–331.

Roenneberg, T., Kuehnle, T., Pramstaller, P. P., Ricken, J., Havel, M., Guth, A., & Merrow, M. (2004). A marker for the end of adolescence. *Current Biology, 14*, R1038–R1039.

Stothard, E. R., McHill, A. W., Depner, C. M., Birks, B. R., Moehlman, T. M., Ritchie, H. K., Guzzetti, J. R., Chinoy, E. D., LeBourgeois, M. K., Axelsson, J., & Wright, K. P., Jr. (2017). Circadian entrainment to the natural light-dark cycle across seasons and the weekend. *Current Biology, 27*, 508–513.

Terman, M. & Terman, J. S. (2010). Light therapy. In M. H. Kryger, T. Roth & W. C. Dement (eds.), *Principles and practice of sleep medicine* (5th ed., pp. 1682–1695). Elsevier/Saunders.

Van Someren, E. J. W., & Riemersma-Van Der Lek, R. F. (2007). Live to the rhythm, slave to the rhythm. *Sleep Medicine Reviews, 11*, 465–484.

Walker, M. P. (2009). The role of slow wave sleep in memory processing. *Journal of Clinical Sleep Medicine, 5,* S20–S26.

Wirz-Justice, A. (2018). Seasonality in affective disorders. *General and Comparative Endocrinology, 258,* 244–249.

Wirz-Justice, A., Bromundt, V., & Cajochen, C. (2009). Circadian disruption and psychiatric disorders: The importance of entrainment. *Sleep Medicine Clinics, 4,* 273–284.

Wirz-Justice, A., Skene, D. J., & Münch, M. (2020). The relevance of daylight for humans. *Biochemical Pharmacology,* 114304.

Wittmann, M., Dinich, J., Merrow, M., & Roenneberg, T. (2006). Social jetlag: Misalignment of biological and social time. *Chronobiology International, 23,* 497–509.

Wright, K. P., Jr., Hull, J. T., Hughes, R. J., Ronda, J. M., & Czeisler, C. A. (2006). Sleep and wakefulness out of phase with internal biological time impairs learning in humans. *Journal of Cognitive Neuroscience, 18,* 508–521.

Yoshiike, T., Honma, M., Ikeda, H., & Kuriyama, K. (2019). Bright light exposure advances consolidation of motor skill accuracy in humans. *Neurobiology of Learning and Memory, 166,* 107084.

Anna Wirz-Justice is Professor emeritus at the University of Basel, Switzerland, where she founded the Centre for Chronobiology and introduced light therapy for winter depression in Europe. Her research focussed on the physiological basis of circadian and seasonal rhythms, sleep, mood, and performance. She is now involved in translating biological knowledge about (day)light into architecture and healthy behaviour.

Outdoor Learning and Children's Eyesight

Richard Hobday

1 Background

In 2015, a news report entitled 'The Myopia Boom' appeared in the journal *Nature* (Dolgin, 2015). It proved highly influential, being one of the first articles to raise public awareness among a Western readership of an epidemic of myopia, or short sight, sweeping through countries in East and Southeast Asia. At the time, about 70–90% of children leaving secondary schooling in Chinese cities, and in Japan, Singapore, the Republic of Korea, Hong Kong and Taiwan, were becoming myopic. They required glasses, or other forms of correction, for clear distance viewing. Some of them—between 10 and 20%—had high levels of myopia which put them at high risk of losing their sight. A marked increase in myopia was apparent in the United States and Europe too. Around half of young adults were affected. This was double the prevalence of half a century earlier (Dolgin, 2015).

In 2016, it was estimated that if the rise of myopia was not stopped, by 2050 half the world's population, by then some 5 billion people, would be short-sighted. If so, about one billion of them will be highly myopic, and so risk losing their sight (Holden et al., 2016). High myopia is currently a major cause of blindness worldwide, especially in East Asia (Ikuno, 2017). There is growing recognition there of the huge social and economic burden the myopia epidemic will cause in the years ahead. One public health policy introduced in Taiwan, China, and other East Asian countries, is to make sure children go outside between lessons and at other times during the school day. Another is to reduce the amount of close work they undertake (Jan et al., 2020). Research is confirming what was widely believed over a century ago. Time spent outdoors in daylight prevents school myopia in children (Wu et al., 2020). Also, intensive, competitive education increases the risk of the onset and progression of the condition (Morgan et al., 2018).

R. Hobday (✉)
8 Springvale, Cwmbran NP44 5BG, UK
e-mail: rah001@tutanota.com

2   What Causes Myopia?

The great German astronomer Johannes Kepler (1571–1630) gave the first accurate explanation of myopia four hundred years ago. Kepler showed the condition is the result of abnormal lengthening of the eye. This makes light focus ahead of the retina at the back of the eye rather than onto it which results in blurred vision. Kepler also noted that short sight was more common among young people who spend a lot of time doing close work (Mark, 1971).

During the 19th century, when school attendance became compulsory in many countries, myopia became a common problem among children. However, the cause proved difficult to identify. There were many competing theories. Some eye experts argued that short sight was an entirely inherited condition. For them, there was no convincing evidence that close work, or any other aspect of school life, damaged children's eyesight. Others believed schools, and the way children were taught in them, were the cause. If so, 'school myopia' as it became known, was a preventable condition. Theirs became the dominant view; and so measures were put in place in schools to protect children's eyesight. The pioneer of this preventive approach was Professor Hermann Cohn (1838–1906), an eye specialist at Breslau University in Prussia (Hobday, 2016).

3   Daylight and Myopia in the Classroom

Prussia was among the first modern states to require its children to attend school. In 1867, Cohn published the results of a survey of Prussian children's vision. He had measured the eyesight of 10,060 children, and found four times more myopia among those in elementary schools in towns than those attending in schools in rural areas. Cohn also discovered that the longer children were in school the more likely they were to become short-sighted. Also, myopia became more common, and more severe, as educational levels increased (Cohn, 1867). In Prussia's high schools, or 'Gymnasium', the percentages of myopia went up progressively from the first year of school attendance to the sixth. More than half of the children he examined in the final year of their education in these schools were short-sighted (Cohn, 1867).

Cohn also investigated the effects of lighting on myopia. He compared daylight levels in classrooms with the number of myopic children in them. If buildings surrounding schools darkened their interiors, rates were high. Cohn paid particular attention to the height, width, number and orientation of classroom windows. Based on his findings he proposed a minimum window area for schools of one-fifth the floor area (Cohn, 1867). Cohn wrote that there could never be too much natural light in a school; as long as heat and glare from the sun were properly controlled. Based on his own research, and that of other scientists, he considered some myopia to be inherited. But, in many cases, heredity was not the cause. It was close work in bad light (Cohn, 1886).

His work proved influential. By the beginning of the last century, high levels of daylight in classrooms and play outdoors were two measures that were widely believed to prevent myopia. Cohn's ideas proved popular among British eye specialists who introduced his concept of 'ocular hygiene' into schools. Some argued that children should not be taught to read and write, or do close work at a young age; especially if they were at high risk of myopia or showed the first signs of it. Chief among them was the ophthalmologist Dr Nathaniel Bishop Harman (1869–1945). Working with Dr James Kerr (1862–1941), who was School Medical Officer for London from 1902 to 1911, Harman began setting up special 'myope classes' to try to educate very short-sighted children in a manner that protected their vision from further decline. These classes were soon taken up in a number of other countries; notably in the United States where they became known as 'sight-saving classes' (Harman, 1945).

In 1903, Kerr measured the eyesight of 20,000 children attending London schools. He found higher levels of myopia among girls than boys. His colleague, Dr Harman, later wrote that the difference may have been due to the way girls lived and were educated:

> This excessive incidence amongst the girls may in part be accounted for by the fact that the boys played about in the clean, wide streets, sharpening their wits and their physical faculties, whilst the girls were kept at home to help in domestic duties. That is part of the condition that tends to produce this difference in visual acuity. The other part is the nature of the work done in schools: girls do finer work, boys do no needlework; so that in vision-testing boys have an advantage, for their accommodation muscles are in a better state of tone on account of their outdoor life, and at the same time they are less fatigued by their school work. (Harman, 1909)

Based on these findings Harman recommended that reading and other close work in schools, especially needlework, should be reduced to a minimum. He argued that girls who excelled in fine sewing should have their vision tested in case they were myopic. Also, if girls were to protect their sight they had to be able to exercise outdoors, just like boys. At the time, parents objected to their girls playing in the streets. So Harman called for more playgrounds and open spaces in cities (Harman, 1909). Some of the ideas promoted by leading eye specialists such as Cohn, and then Harman, were adopted in the decades that followed. For example, by the 1950s, high levels of natural light had become a statutory requirement in all British schools to protect children's sight; even though daylight's impact on eyesight was still poorly understood (Hobday, 2016).

4   Changing Attitudes

In the 1960s, there was a marked reversal in medical thinking on myopia. A report published by the British Medical Research Council concluded that myopia was almost entirely inherited (Sorsby, 1962). The results of studies of twins seemed to show that the environment in which children were raised had hardly any effect on myopia. This research was later found to be deeply flawed. Nevertheless, it proved highly influential, and genetic determinism became the prevailing orthodoxy. It remained so until recently (Morgan & Rose, 2019). Consequently for more than 50 years, myopia has not been considered preventable. The idea that reading in dim light damages eyesight became a 'Medical Myth' (Vreeman & Carroll, 2007). And there was less emphasis on high daylight levels in classrooms (Hobday, 2016). Also, attitudes towards myopia changed. A century ago, all forms of myopia, whether moderate or high, were considered harmful to children by some experts, which is why measures were put in place to try and prevent it. But over time, myopia has come to be regarded by both the eye-care professions and the public as an inconvenience and not a disease. Yet myopia is not a benign condition. It can affect children's self-perception, quality of life, and choice of career. It can also cause significant psychological distress (Wang et al., 2019).

Research now shows that any level of myopia, whether it is severe or mild, significantly increases the risk of developing sight-threatening conditions such as cataract, retinal detachment, glaucoma, and macular degeneration. There is no safe threshold for myopia (Flitcroft, 2012). So the old saying 'a myopic eye is a diseased eye' has some validity (Aylesworth, 1938).

5   Myopia and the Digital Age

As the prevalence of myopia has risen around the world, the age of onset has fallen. Becoming short sighted in early childhood allows more time for the condition to progress toward high myopia (Ikuno, 2017). Unfortunately, in recent years the demands placed on children's eyesight have increased. More and more younger children are spending many hours each day indoors online using laptops, e-readers, tablets, and mobile phones. This digital lifestyle puts them at greater risk of myopia; and also of vitamin D deficiency, obesity, sleep disorders, anxiety and depression (Dresp-Langley, 2020). So, in addition to 'school myopia' there is now 'digital eyestrain' to contend with (Sheppard & Wolffsohn, 2018). The confinement of children indoors during the early months of the COVID-19 pandemic appears to have made myopia more prevalent in younger children. There is evidence of a significant increase among those aged 6–8 years (Wang et al., 2021). There are concerns that 'myopigenic' habits acquired during this formative period of their lives could become entrenched and have negative impact on their visual health in the years ahead (Wong et al., 2020).

6   Myopia and Educational Pressures

The Myopia Boom of the last three decades seems to have started among pre-school and primary school children (Lin et al., 2004). In urban China, pre-schooling is highly competitive and places great emphasis on early academic achievement. The syllabus in kindergartens and childcare centres is demanding and can include digital technologies (Pan et al., 2018). By contrast, in some rural areas of China myopia rates remain comparatively low. The findings of a study from 2018 suggest this is because children are not under the same educational pressure. Chinese children in rural schools devote less time to intensive learning and more time in outdoor play in their early years compared to their peers in cities. Nevertheless, the study found that students who had completed six years of primary school still had a much higher prevalence of myopia compared with those in the first year of attendance. One-third of the increase among the older children was attributed to a reduction in the amount of time they spent outdoors (Pan et al., 2018).

The results of other research in schools shows that an additional 1–2 h per day outdoors reduce the incidence of myopia in children by between 25 and 50%. This is most effective in children under 12 years of age (He et al., 2015; Wu et al., 2013, 2020). Also, there is evidence that time spent outdoors in daylight can slow the progression of the condition as well as prevent it (Ho et al., 2019). Taiwan and China now have national programmes which stipulate two hours per day outdoors in schools. China also has a 1–2-h daily period of outdoor time specified in its national myopia control programme (Jan et al., 2020). However, there is resistance to this from parents and teachers because of a belief that giving children more time outdoors will adversely affect their education (Jan et al., 2020). The Chinese government's plans also include a ban on written homework in the first two years of school and further limits for older children.

7 'Myope Classes'—Again?

The measures being introduced to prevent myopia in Asian countries will be familiar to readers of Dr Harman's writings on the subject from a century ago. However, Harman went much further in his approach to 'ocular hygiene' and to myopia prevention. In particular, he recognised the harm that early-onset myopia and high myopia could inflict on children and that their eyesight needed to be protected from further deterioration. So he developed a form of education for them which was largely based on oral instruction and practical work. He described this as a return to an 'almost prehistoric' approach. It was, he suggested, similar to that of a wise elder passing on the skills and traditions of a tribe to children (Harman, 1913). There was no place in Harman's syllabus for what he regarded as the modern, inferior substitute for such personalised education—the book. He did not approve of teachers relying on books to educate the young. And he was adamant that children should not learn to read before it was absolutely necessary for them to do so: "Educationally there is no gain in early reading, rather the reverse. Physically, early reading is a habit to be banned." (Harman, 1915).

In support of Harman, it is worth noting that among hunter-gatherer societies, myopia is rare. The impact of compulsory school attendance on their children's eyesight can be dramatic. Within a single generation, incidence rates for myopia can reach 60% (Morgan & Rose, 2019). Significantly, there is one country that has achieved high academic standards in its schools yet has not followed the global onward trend of myopia. In 2018, a study of 16–19-year-old Norwegians found just 13% of them were affected by myopia (Hagen et al., 2018). Why the prevalence is so much lower than in East Asia and elsewhere is unclear at the present time. However, one notable difference between Norway and other countries is that young children are outdoors for long periods. According to a survey of Norwegian Kindergartens, during the summer they spend more than two-thirds of their time outside and during winter semester it is still about a third of the time. Norway's Kindergartens are designed to facilitate this (Moser & Martinsen, 2010).

8 Outdoor Learning and Myopia

For reasons that are not understood, the Norwegian education system protects most children from myopia; even though it is not designed to do so. Norway serves as a valuable model which other countries who wish to reduce the burden of myopia could copy. Currently, there are no reports of 'myope classes' in East Asia, or elsewhere, for children who have become myopic at a young age, or those severely affected. Their education continues as normal. But if the health risks are to be mitigated, this has to be addressed.

There has been much confusion and disagreement about the cause, or causes, of myopia for decades. Thankfully, research now confirms that increasing the time school children spend outdoors in daylight can reduce the incidence of myopia by half. Outdoor activities can also slow the progression of myopia among those already affected. Given these findings, greater emphasis should be placed on outdoor learning and play in schools and rather less on intensive, competitive education at a young age. The latter clearly harms children's health and happiness and will affect their future lives adversely. The cost to society in the years ahead will be significant too.

The available evidence suggests that stopping the Myopia Boom requires a new approach both to children's education and to wider public health policy. Raising awareness of the need for this among parents, educators, government agencies—and children—is essential. Effective preventive strategies have to be devised and implemented. Outdoor education could be central to this.

Recommended Further Reading

1.   Dolgin, E. (2015). The myopia boom. *Nature, 519*(7543), 276–8.
2.   Dresp-Langley, B. (2020). Children's health in the Digital Age. *Int J Environ Res Public Health, 17*(9), 3240.
3.   Pan, C.W., Wu, R.K., Li, J. & Zhong, H. (2018). Low prevalence of myopia among school children in rural China. *BMC Ophthalmol, 18*(1), 140.

References

Aylesworth, F. A. (1938). The young myope. *Canadian Medical Association Journal, 39*(4), 374–375.

Cohn, H. (1867). *Untersuchungen der Augen von 10,060 Schulkindern nebst Vorschlagen zur Verbesserung der den Augen nachtheiligen Schuleinrichtungen. Eine atiologische Studie.* Leipzig: F. Fleischer.

Cohn, H. (1886). *Hygiene of the eye in schools.* Simpkin, Marshall and Co.

Dolgin, E. (2015). The myopia boom. *Nature, 519*(7543), 276–278.

Dresp-Langley, B. (2020). Children's health in the digital age. *International Journal of Environmental Research and Public Health, 17*(9), 3240.

Flitcroft, D. I. (2012). The complex interactions of retinal, optical and environmental factors in myopia aetiology. *Progress in Retinal and Eye Research, 31*(6), 622–660.

Hagen, L. A., Gjelle, J. V. B., Arnegard, S., Pedersen, H. R., Gilson, S. J., & Baraas, R. C. (2018). Prevalence and possible factors of myopia in Norwegian adolescents. *Science and Reports, 8*(1), 13479.

Harman, N. B. (1909). The effects of school life upon the vision of the child. *Proceedings of the Royal Society of Medicine, 2* (Sect Study Dis Child), 206–16, 209.

Harman, N. B. (1913). The education of high myopes. *Proceedings of the Royal Society of Medicine, 6* (Sect Ophthalmol), 146–63, 148.

Harman, N. B. (1915). The education of children with defective vision. *Proceedings of the Royal Society of Medicine, 8* (Sect Ophthalmol), 107–22, 111.

Harman, N. B. (1945). Sight-saving classes. *BMJ, 1*(4384), 53–54.

He, M., Xiang, F., Zeng, Y., Mai, J., Chen, Q., Zhang, J., et al. (2015). Effect of time spent outdoors at school on the development of myopia among children in China: A randomized clinical trial. *JAMA, 314*(11), 1142–1148.

Ho, C. L., Wu, W. F., & Liou, Y. M. (2019). Dose-response relationship of outdoor exposure and myopia indicators: A systematic review and meta-analysis of various research methods. *International Journal of Environmental Research and Public Health, 16*(14), 2595.

Hobday, R. (2016). Myopia and daylight in schools: A neglected aspect of public health? *Perspectives in Public Health, 136*, 50–55.

Holden, B. A., Fricke, T. R., Wilson, D. A., Jong, M., Naidoo, K. S., Sankaridurg, P., Wong, T. Y., Naduvilath, T. J., & Resnikoff, S. (2016). Global prevalence of myopia and high myopia and temporal trends from 2000 through 2050. *Ophthalmology, 123*, 1036–1042.

Ikuno, Y. (2017). Overview of the complications of high myopia. *Retina, 37*(12), 2347–2351.

Jan, C., Li, L., Keay, L., Stafford, R. S., Congdon, N., & Morgan, I. (2020). Prevention of myopia, China. *Bulletin of the World Health Organization, 98*(6), 435–437.

Lin, L. L., Shih, Y. F., Hsiao, C. K., & Chen, C. J. (2004). Prevalence of myopia in Taiwanese schoolchildren: 1983 to 2000. *Annals of the Academy of Medicine, Singapore, 33*(1), 27–33.

Mark, H. H. (1971). Johannes Kepler on the eye and vision. *American Journal of Ophthalmology, 72*(5), 869–878.

Morgan, I. G., & Rose, K. A. (2019). Myopia: Is the nature-nurture debate finally over? *Clinical and Experimental Optometry, 102*(1), 3–17.

Morgan, I. G., French, A. N., & Rose, K. A. (2018). Intense schooling linked to myopia. *BMJ, 6* Jun, 361.

Moser, T., & Martinsen, M. T. (2010). The outdoor environment in Norwegian kindergartens as pedagogical space for toddlers' play, learning and development. *EECERJ, 18*(4), 457–471.

Pan, C. W., Wu, R. K., Li, J., & Zhong, H. (2018). Low prevalence of myopia among school children in rural China. *BMC Ophthalmology, 18*(1), 140.

Sheppard, A. L., & Wolffsohn, J. S. (2018). Digital eye strain: Prevalence, measurement and amelioration. *BMJ Open Ophthalmology, 3*(1), e000146.

Sorsby, A. (1962). *Refraction and its components in twins. Privy Council. Medical Research Council Special Report no. 303.* London: HMSO.

Vreeman, R. C., & Carroll, A. E. (2007). Medical myths. *BMJ, 335*(7633), 1288–1289.

Wang, D., Yang, J., Xian, Y. J., Wu, P. P., & Lin, S. L. (2019). [Current status of social anxiety among primary school students with myopia in Urumqi, China and risk factors for myopia]. *Zhongguo Dang Dai Er Ke Za Zhi*, 21 Feb, (2), 184–188. Chinese.

Wang, J., Li, Y., Musch, D. C., Wei, N., Qi, X., Ding, G., Li, X., Li, J., Song, L., Zhang, Y., Ning, Y., Zeng, X., Hua, N., Li, S., & Qian, X. (2021). Progression of myopia in school-aged children after COVID-19 home confinement. *JAMA Ophthalmology*, e206239. https://doi.org/10.1001/jamaop hthalmol.2020.6239. Epub ahead of print.

Wong, C. W., Tsai, A., Jonas, J. B., Ohno-Matsui, K., Chen, J., Ang, M., & Ting, D. S. W. (2020). Digital screen time during the COVID-19 pandemic: Risk for a further myopia boom? *American Journal of Ophthalmology, 223*, 333–337.

Wu, P. C., Chen, C. T., Chang, L. C., Niu, Y. Z., Chen, M. L., Liao, L. L., Rose, K., & Morgan, I. G. (2020). Increased time outdoors is followed by reversal of the long-term trend to reduced visual acuity in Taiwan primary school students. *Ophthalmology, 127*(11), 1462–1469.

Wu, P. C., Tsai, C. L., Wu, H. L., Yang, Y. H., & Kuo, H. K. (2013). Outdoor activity during class recess reduces myopia onset and progression in school children. *Ophthalmology, 120*(5), 1080–1085.

Richard Hobday is an independent researcher and author. He has a Ph.D in engineering from Cranfield University, where he designed solar collectors for buildings, and for spacecraft. While working on passive solar architecture projects he became aware of a 'lost' tradition of designing sunlit hospitals to prevent the spread of infections and promote well-being. He is now an internationally recognised authority on health in the built environment. Dr. Hobday's recent research focus has been global health threats.

Outdoor Learning Fosters Twenty-First Century Competencies

Rediscovering the Potential of Outdoor Learning for Developing 21st Century Competencies

Jeff Mann, Tonia Gray, and Son Truong

1 What Are 21st Century Competencies and Why Are They Important Now?

Global changes in technology and demographics are influencing the competencies people need to thrive in their work and community settings in the 21st century. New problems and opportunities are emerging from accelerated developments in: climate change, automation, globalisation, brain and genomic research, mass migration and mental health issues (Lambert, 2017). We can add to this list the widespread economic and social ripples emanating from the global COVID-19 pandemic, which are yet to be fully realised at the time of writing. Technical expertise is becoming progressively more specific as knowledge and technology advances, requiring collaborative skills for different experts to work together to creatively solve new and complex problems (Geisinger, 2016).

Most education jurisdictions around the world recognise that schooling outcomes need to be much broader than subject knowledge, and should also include higher-order thinking skills, attitudinal skills and socio-emotional skills (Lamb et al., 2017). As well as foundational literacy and numeracy skills and job-specific skills, the

J. Mann (✉)
Doctoral Student, School of Education, Western Sydney University, Locked Bag 1797, Penrith, NSW 2751, Australia
e-mail: j3ffmann1@gmail.com

T. Gray
Senior Researcher Centre for Educational Research, School of Education, Western Sydney University, Locked Bag 1797, Penrith, NSW 2751, Australia
e-mail: t.gray@westernsydney.edu.au

S. Truong
Adjunct Faculty Member School of Education, Western Sydney University, Locked Bag 1797, Penrith, NSW 2751, Australia
e-mail: Son.Truong@dal.ca

© The Author(s) 2022
R. Jucker and J. von Au (eds.), *High-Quality Outdoor Learning*,
https://doi.org/10.1007/978-3-031-04108-2_12

Organisation for Economic Cooperation and Development (OECD) Skills Strategy identified that individuals need meta-cognitive and social-emotional skills in order to be competent workers and engaged citizens (OECD, 2019).

Many definitions of 21st century competencies have been proposed, each with their own list of competencies and frameworks. Some examples include:

- Creativity and innovation, critical thinking and problem solving, communication and collaboration (Trilling, 2009);
- Character education, citizenship, communication, critical thinking and problem solving, collaboration, creativity and imagination (Fullan & Langworthy, 2013);
- Creativity, critical thinking/problem solving, communication, collaboration (World Economic Forum, 2015);
- Creativity, critical thinking, communication, collaboration (Fadel, 2016); and
- Creativity, critical thinking, complex problem solving, learning to learn, self-regulation, conscientiousness, responsibility, empathy, self-efficacy, collaboration (OECD, 2019).

These competencies form a dense conceptual web with potential overlaps and complex interactions, and research is yet to confirm whether they are domain-specific or transferable across learning areas (Lamb et al., 2017). Despite these definitional issues, there are four common factors across the various lists of 21st century competencies: the individual cognitive skills of *creativity* and *critical thinking*, and the social skills of *communication* and *collaboration*, i.e. what is often referred to as the 4Cs.

These skills are not new to the 21st century, but rather are newly important (Silva, 2009). In fact, personal and social skills have always been important to flourishing in the workplace and community. However, as the rate of societal change has accelerated this century and artificial intelligence allows the automation of more mechanistic tasks, the need for uniquely human competencies has gained prominence in educational planning (Vincent-Lancrin et al., 2019). Traditional didactic classroom learning is not well suited to develop 21st century competencies, and so new learning contexts need to be explored.

2   Why Learn Outdoors?

Outside learning environments, and the learner-centred pedagogical approaches they allow, provide a rich platform for developing interpersonal and intrapersonal competencies. Whilst outdoor learning can include built-environment locations (such as museums), it is mostly conducted in natural settings. 'Outdoors' has been conceived in concentric circles radiating out from school grounds to the local neighbourhood, and further afield on day trips through to multi-day residentials and expeditions (Beames et al., 2012). The drivers for taking learning outside include: enjoyment and engagement of learning, health and wellbeing, and connection to nature (Passy et al., 2019). These benefits have seen outdoor learning grow from 'grass roots' movements to widespread practice in a number of countries (Quay, 2005).

There are many terms and definitions around outdoor learning (Becker et al., 2017), and different forms are often grouped together without appreciation of their distinctive characteristics (Bentsen et al., 2017). Two traditions are described in this chapter: outdoor adventure education (OAE), and learning outside the classroom (LOTC). OAE has typically been distinct from academic learning, and uses challenging experiences to facilitate personal and social development. These often occur in the context of multi-day programs, which could be a series of discrete adventurous activities based at a 'hard top' residential centre or a 'soft top' tent-based expedition through a natural environment (Beames et al., 2012). LOTC is defined as the teacher-facilitated learning of traditional academic subjects in a natural outdoor setting, during the normal school day (Bentsen et al., 2021). Having made this distinction, there is some overlap between the two traditions. For example, outdoor adventure programs may include a field studies curricular component (Lugg & Quay, 2020; McLeod & Allen-Craig, 2007; Nicol & Waite, 2020), and LOTC is sometimes achieved through a multi-day 'residential' experiences (Gray, 1997; Kendall et al., 2015).

3 Theoretical Underpinnings of Experiential Learning

Outdoor learning relies on students actively learning through direct experience, rather than a passive model of absorbing knowledge imparted by teachers. It is certainly slower to facilitate learning through experience when compared to direct instruction, and the specific learning outcomes are less predictable—so why would teachers choose this learning approach either inside or outside the classroom?

Learning through experience is a rich personal and relational undertaking. John Dewey, one of the early theorists of modern education, argued that learners need direct interaction with the world in order to understand it, and that knowledge is more easily memorised when it is linked to a related sensory experience (Dewey, 1938). Subsequent theory explains that all learning is based on sensory inputs, however when various sensory sources do not match each other the quality of learning is shallow and is more likely to be filtered out before it penetrates to long term memory, compared to when sensory inputs complement and reinforce each other (Thorburn & Marshall, 2014). Experiential learning allows students to actively grapple with new concepts by encountering them in lived experience, rather than by passively listening to their teacher explaining a concept as an abstract principle (Quay, 2005).

High quality experiential learning is founded on 'real-world' experiences which are relevant to students' lives outside school (Breunig et al., 2015), and incorporate relational and affective elements (Gray, 2018). Learning experiences which are inherently interesting and relevant to curriculum goals, allow students to understand and internalise their own sense of agency in the learning process (Sibthorp et al., 2015). A novel experience challenges habitual ways of thinking and acting, and this cognitive dissonance affords the learner an opportunity to consider how they can incorporate new behaviours and attitudes into their normal context (Nicol & Waite, 2020). Learning through experience can be achieved on school grounds, and even within the classroom, however outdoor natural environments provide many of these foundational elements for deeper learning to occur. As with any pedagogy, experiential learning does not produce deep learning without being well designed and facilitated, and students quickly forget irrelevant (indoor or outdoor) learning experiences (Rickinson et al., 2004).

The process of experiential learning is as diverse as the teachers who design and deliver it, but there are some common elements. Kolb's (1984) Experiential Learning Cycle describes an ongoing process of a concrete experience, reflective observation, abstract conceptualisation and active experimentation. Others have since visualised the experiential learning process in three dimensions, as a rising spiral of successive learning cycles (Schenck & Cruickshank, 2015). We all go through experiences of some sort each day, however intentional reflection on the meaning and implications of an experience is pivotal to its learning impact (Nicol & Waite, 2020). Early forms of OAE simply provided an opportunity for personal reflection without guidance, but progressively more sophisticated models of facilitation include: speaking for the experience, debriefing or funnelling, frontloading the experience, isomorphic framing of the experience, and indirect framing (Priest & Gass, 2005).

4   The Value of Connecting with Natural Environments

As well as being a rich platform for experiential learning, outdoor learning results in direct benefits from exposure to natural environments. The link between our connection to nature and human flourishing can be traced in literature, science, poetry, philosophy and indigenous wisdom through the ages (Braus & Milligan-Toffler, 2018). The benefit of contact with nature is not limited to children or education. A review of empirical studies on contact with natural settings indicated improved attention, reduced stress, mental restoration, decreased attention deficit, enhanced self-perceived health and increased longevity (Grinde & Patil, 2009). Even surgical patients who merely have a view of green space from their bed recover faster than those facing a brick wall (Ulrich, 1984).

Richard Louv's lighthouse publication *The Last Child in the Woods* (Louv, 2005) warned of the myriad of risks to a generation of children who rarely explore natural environments, and coined the term 'nature deficit disorder'. A systematic review of academic research confirmed that spending time in natural settings promotes children's healthy development and wellbeing (Gill, 2014). Having trees and natural spaces in the community is not only important for children's health, but also encourages creative play (Chawla, 2015). For example, a study of two Australian early-childhood centres compared natural outdoor play spaces with an indoor simulated natural space, and found that the outdoor setting resulted in more imaginative play and improved peer relationships (Dowdell et al., 2011). Immersing children in nature has a number of benefits, including: reduced stress, increased social and emotional skills, higher civic engagement (Hartig et al., 2014), attention restoration, reduced ADHD symptoms and behaviours, and even higher academic performance (McCormick, 2017). Pertinent to the focus of this chapter on 21st century competencies, a systematic review of young people engaging regularly in natural settings indicated that these experiences develop critical and creative thinking skills (Adams & Savahl, 2017), and lack of exposure to natural environments is suggested to be detrimental to creativity and innovation (Malone & Waite, 2016). Another recent review showed that time spent in nature positively influences: perseverance, resilience, critical thinking, problem solving, leadership and teamwork (Kuo et al., 2019, see Kuo, Barnes and Jordan: Do Experiences with Nature Promote Learning? Converging Evidence of a Cause-And-Effect Relationship in this volume).

5   Outdoor Adventure Education (OAE)—An Established Platform for Developing Personal Competencies

Adventure has been an intrinsic element of human experience since our prehistoric ancestors, with an innate desire to 'journey into the unknown'. The origin of structured OAE is linked to educationalist Kurt Hahn, who started an experientially-based model of schooling in the early 20th century in the belief that young men needed to develop a sense of adventure in their schooling (Hahn, 1959). Hahn, along with his less acknowledged co-founder Marina Ewald (Gray et al., 2017; Mitten et al., 2018), went on to found the Outward Bound organisation. Both Hahn and Ewald saw the merit of incorporating challenging outdoor activities to facilitate experiences of self-discovery, triumph and defeat, self-effacement in the common cause, periods of silence for reflection, and training of the imagination (Hahn, 1930). By 1994, 40,000 students participated in Outward Bound programs alone (Hattie et al., 1997), not counting many other school-based and independent OAE providers.

OAE can take many forms, but is characterised by an intentionally challenging outdoor experience followed by reflection on personal learning. Traditional OAE programs comprised an extended expedition (Martin & Legg, 2002) through a natural environment, but OAE can also focus on a single activity such as a high ropes challenge course (Gillis & Speelman, 2008). Appropriately managed risk is essential to the paradigm of OAE (Gray & Bailey, 2022), and careful programming aims for the actual risk to be lower than the subjective risk as perceived by the participants (Priest & Gass, 2005). This leads to a peak adventure experience without being overwhelming, and the ensuing cognitive dissonance is a catalyst for new ways of thinking, acting or relating (Cooley et al., 2015).

Anecdotal evidence indicates that proponents of OAE support its effectiveness for personal growth, however by the end of the 20th century a significant meta-analysis of 96 extended adventure education programs (2–4 weeks), showed a moderate effect size on forty outcomes, such as locus of control, self-concept, and leadership (Hattie et al., 1997). Critical thinking competencies were shown in decision making and problem solving outcomes, which both developed even further in follow-up measurements. Other OAE outcomes aligned to 21st century competencies were communication and cooperation/relating skills (collaboration), which had small to moderate effect sizes immediately after the program and modest additional growth at a six month follow up. Two other meta-analyses (Cason & Gillis, 1994; Hans, 2000) similarly concluded that OAE programs have a small to medium effect on outcomes like self-concept, self-confidence and locus of control.

OAE research continued to demonstrate developmental outcomes such as character development, personal growth, enhanced interpersonal skills, and leadership development (Ewert & Garvey, 2007). A meta-analysis of 44 studies (Gillis & Speelman, 2008) focusing only on challenge ropes courses (i.e. navigating through an obstacle course of ropes/cables at height) reported a medium effect size on self-concept, personality factors and group dynamics (including 21st century collaborative categories of interpersonal skills, group cohesion and group effectiveness), when compared with groups on a wait list or experiencing alternate programming. A final meta-analysis of 11 studies examined the benefits of OAE on group work skills, specifically in higher education students, showing that transferable 21st century competencies (specifically communication, cooperation, team cohesion, role allocation, working well with others) are developed during OAE programs and retained on their return to the higher education environment (Cooley et al., 2015). OAE research has also shown outcomes in emotional intelligence (Opper et al., 2014) and life-effectiveness skills, which relate to the 21st century competencies of collaboration (social competence) and creativity (intellectual flexibility) (Gray, 1997; McLeod & Allen-Craig, 2007). UK residential adventure programs have reported benefits a year onwards in self-confidence, independence and 21st century competencies of communication and collaboration (cooperation and teamwork) (Prince, 2020). These meta-analyses and other research studies broadly demonstrate that OAE is effective, but are not fine grained enough to look into the black box of *how* these outcomes are achieved. Key process factors still need to be identified, which could include: participant age and background, voluntary or compulsory participation, length of program, type of activities, intensity of subjective challenge, quality of facilitation, frontloading before the program and guided reflection afterward.

Extended OAE programs understandably achieve the most significant outcomes, however many young people's experience of OAE is through attending shorter annual school camps where they participate in a range of bite-sized outdoor activities (Lugg & Quay, 2020). For example, an Australian survey of outdoor youth programs indicated a typical OEP experience comprised a group of 40 students aged 10–16 years attending a 3–5 day camp (Williams & Allen, 2012). Over 80% of outdoor youth program providers in this survey believed that their participants gained personal and social skills, however most relied on informal and anecdotal evidence and less than 7% conducted robust research. On the other hand, there has been criticism of the learning value of short packaged adventure experiences (Brown & Beames, 2017). Summer camps are an established part of American youth culture, although have explicitly recreational aims rather than an educational focus. Notwithstanding this recreational emphasis, a study of over 3,000 children and their parents across 80 US summer camps showed significant perceived increases in positive identity, social skills, physical and thinking skills and positive identity, both immediately after camp and 6 months later (Thurber et al., 2007).

In conclusion, there is an established base of evidence for the small to moderate efficacy of OAE to develop a range of interpersonal and intrapersonal competencies. These could be described as life-effectiveness skills, incorporating personal attitudes and abilities (for instance self-confidence, perseverance, emotional intelligence, self-regulation) and interpersonal 21st century competencies of communication and collaboration. Evidence for creative and critical thinking competencies in OAE is minimal, however most research studies have not been focused on these specific outcomes. While most educators would endorse the value of developing these 'non-academic' competencies in their students, OAE has only been able to gain compulsory inclusion in the national curricula of a few countries like Singapore (Passy et al., 2019), and a marginal place in others such as the UK (Brown et al., 2016) and Australia (Passy et al., 2019).

6 Learning Outside the Classroom (LOtC)—Emerging Pedagogies for Holistic Learning

Outdoor 'in-situ' learning was the norm for human cultures through most of history (Nicol & Waite, 2020), and on-the-job learning through trade apprenticeships occurred commonly in European countries and their colonies from at least the 13th century (Perrot et al., 2014). It wasn't until the advent of mass-schooling in the 19th century that the place of learning was moved inside to a schoolroom (Joyce, 2012). In recent decades, however, curriculum-based learning in settings other than the classroom have received more interest in many industrialised countries (Barfod & Bentsen, 2018).

LOTC can be broadly described as taking curriculum learning outdoors, and making academic learning experiential and practical. Whilst LOTC can be conducted in indoor (e.g. a museum) or built (e.g. a city streetscape) environments, most proponents place value on learning in natural outdoor settings (Waite, 2020; see Waite: International Views on School-based Outdoor Learning in this volume). Locations for LOTC can be described in terms of their radiating proximity and time away from the classroom: an outdoor lesson within the school grounds, a short trip into the local neighbourhood, day excursions into natural spaces, and overnight/residential expeditions into wilderness areas (Beames et al., 2012; Lloyd et al., 2018a).

Scandinavian countries are considered by many to be leaders in LOTC (Barfod & Bentsen, 2018; Gray, 2018). The educational philosophy of 'udeskole' (outdoor school) fits well with the broader Scandanavian culture of 'friluftsliv' (outdoor living), where enjoying natural environments is encouraged irrespective of the weather (Bentsen et al., 2009). Denmark's TEACHOUT research project of LOTC has shown benefits for primary student physical activity (Schneller et al., 2017, see also Mygind: *Udeskole*—Pupils' Physical Activity and Gender Perspectives in this volume), wellbeing (Bølling et al., 2019, see Mygind & Bølling: Pupils' Well-Being, Mental and Social Health in this volume), and school engagement (Bølling et al., 2018), however 21st century competencies were not assessed (see also Dettweiler, Lauterbach, Mall & Kermish-Allen: Fostering 21st Century Skills through Autonomy Supportive Science Education Outside the Classroom in this volume). Danish teachers have a large degree of autonomy in both curriculum content and pedagogical approach, however 'udeskole' has been encouraged through government funding and mandated daily physical activity (Passy et al., 2019). Despite this 'grass roots' momentum towards LOTC and supportive government policies, only one fifth of Danish schools actually choose to implement regular sessions of LOTC (Barfod & Bentsen, 2018; Bentsen et al., 2010).

The UK Forest School movement has also been influential in advocating the value of learning outside and connecting with nature, and traces its roots to Scandinavian practice (Kemp, 2019). Forest schools prioritise regular sessions of child-centred learning in natural woodland settings, and have been run mainly for early childhood and primary aged children (Harris, 2015). As well as the UK, forest schools (or their cousins beach and bush schools) have been founded in the US, Germany, Switzerland, Asian countries, Australia and New Zealand (Blackwell, 2019). Forest School practitioners tend to focus on social and emotional learning outcomes, such as intrapersonal and interpersonal relationships, risk taking and connection with nature. Student growth specifically in the 21st century competencies of communication and collaboration (cooperation and teamwork) has been observed in Forest School programs (Harris, 2015). In contrast, 'udeskole' is seen by Danish teachers as an alternate pedagogical setting from which they can deliver the academic curriculum (Waite et al., 2016a).

Also in the UK, the Natural Connections Demonstration Project (Waite, 2016b; see Passy & Blackwell: Natural Connections: Learning About Outdoor-Based Learning in this volume) aimed to stimulate demand for curriculum-based LOTC, and recruited 125 English schools involving over 40,000 students. As well as an enjoyment and connection to nature, LOTC improved students' social skills (including communication and teamwork), engagement with lessons, positive behaviour, opportunity to be physically active, and space to reflect. Teachers reported benefits to their teaching practice, health and wellbeing, and professional development; however LOTC competes with many other priorities in a crowded and highly regulated UK curriculum (Christie et al., 2016; Passy et al., 2019).

LOTC was recently recognised in the Australian national curriculum from 2017, albeit only as one of six 'curriculum connections' which can be utilised by teachers to trace conceptual themes across the curriculum (Gray, 2018). There is a wide variety in the level of implementation of outdoor learning between Australian states, which each have their own distinct curricula and pre-service teacher training priorities (Passy et al., 2019). As examples, urban NSW primary schools have seen positive socio-emotional (including collaboration, communication and critical thinking) and academic impacts from pilot studies of LOTC (Lloyd et al., 2018b; Tracey et al.,

2018; Truong et al., 2016), but this occurs at the discretion of individual schools and teachers (Gray & Pigott, 2018).

An audit of LOTC and OAE research in 15 systematic reviews looked at the range of outcomes being measured, and reported 13 of 57 unique studies in the UK included teamwork (collaboration) or communication in their outcomes (Fiennes et al., 2015, see Jucker "How to Raise the Standards of Outdoor Learning and Its Research" in this volume). Other studies assessed outcomes related to 21st century competencies (such as creativity, social skills, critical thinking, and problem solving), however the number of studies covering each outcome was not detailed. The authors were critical of methodological quality across the entire audit, yet nevertheless concluded that almost all outdoor learning activities have some positive effect on the outcomes they are trying to achieve, that overnight programs are more effective than shorter ones, but that effects tend to diminish 6 months after the intervention. A more tightly defined systematic review of 13 curriculum-based LOTC studies, involving at least 4 h per week for 2 months or more, indicated benefits to self-confidence, sense of belonging, self-esteem and social relations (including cooperation, teamwork and communication) in eight studies (Becker et al., 2017). A review of 61 studies on forest schools found improvements in self-confidence, social skills and communication (Gill, 2011). The Learning Away program focused on the residential component of LOTC in 60 primary and secondary schools across the UK, and benefits were reported to peer and staff-student relationships, self-confidence, engagement with learning (especially for secondary students) and the 21st century competency of creativity (Kendall et al., 2015). An earlier study of sixth grade Californian students attending a week-long outdoor science school in one of three locations, found significantly higher levels of cooperation and conflict resolution collaborative competencies 6–10 weeks later than a waitlist comparison group. Teacher ratings of each student similarly showed significantly higher gains in self-esteem, peer relationships, conflict resolution, problem solving, motivation to learn and positive behaviour, compared to the waitlist group (Parrish et al., 2005).

Are the personal and social benefits of LOTC at the expense of academic progress? Nature-based instruction has been shown in some instances to actually outperform traditional classroom learning, in terms of boosting foundational academic learning skills, such as improved attention, self-discipline and enjoyment of learning (Kuo et al., 2019, see Kuo, Barnes and Jordan: Do Experiences with Nature Promote Learning? Converging Evidence of a Cause-And-Effect Relationship in this volume). Participation in environmental education programs in California resulted in higher scores on standardised state tests in motivation and the 21st century competency of critical thinking (Athman & Monroe, 2004). A systematic review of 42 studies investigating exposure to natural environments found improvements in cognitive abilities like working memory, cognitive flexibility and attentional control, which are underlying skills for academic learning (Stevenson et al., 2018).

There is also some evidence that LOTC can directly benefit academic performance. For example, middle school students in Washington who attended an environmental education program out-performed their peers in standardised maths, reading and writing tests (Bartosh et al., 2009). It should be noted that the quality of environmental education research has not always been high. A review of 100 studies identified only eight which provided strong evidence of a correlation with academic achievement (Norman et al., 2006). A small but significant effect of regular LOTC on reading performance was established in 500 Danish primary students across 15 schools (Otte et al., 2019). Quantitative data gathered from UK residential programs support that students achieved higher than their predicted grade on matriculation tests, and some studies showed statistically higher academic achievement than comparison groups (Kendall et al., 2015). Week long 'outdoor science school' programs for at-risk primary students in California improved their science scores and they maintained this increase for months (Parrish et al., 2005). Finally, in a rigorous systematic review of curriculum-based outdoor learning, seven of thirteen studies reported learning impacts of LOTC, including improved academic performance across several subjects, and improved ability to apply knowledge to real-world situations (Becker et al., 2017).

The capacity of LOTC for developing personal competencies, whilst maintaining or even boosting academic performance, reflects a broader philosophy of education as a process for holistic development of young people to flourish as future citizens (Mann, 2018), rather than a narrow economistic view of education as a means of assessing competitiveness in national and international employment markets (Passy et al., 2019). Not all LOTC programs effectively realise these outcomes, however. The quality of LOTC is undergirded by participant, program, and place factors (Rickinson et al., 2004). For example, LOTC programs need to avoid a formulaic 'drag and drop' approach to new locations (Lloyd et al., 2018a), but instead should be tailored to the local environment and the unique learning opportunities it provides (Nicol & Waite, 2020).

To conclude, LOTC describes a burgeoning movement of learning approaches centred around using natural environments as a learning platform. LOTC is effective in engaging students, improving health and wellbeing, and developing personal competencies, all without compromising academic performance (or even enhancing it in some cases). The evidence-base for LOTC promoting socially oriented 21st century competencies of communication and collaboration is much stronger than for the cognitive competencies of creativity and critical thinking, however there are some examples of the latter outcomes. Despite this evidence of effectiveness across a range of outcomes, however, LOTC still seems to occur only at the discretion of individual teachers, rather than being supported and resourced at a state or national level.

7 Challenges for Bringing Outdoor Learning into Schools

The evidence base presented in this chapter demonstrates that outdoor learning (OAE and LOTC) engages students and facilitates their holistic growth, so one may question why it is not standard practice in schools across the globe? There are a range of barriers which have limited the integration of learning outdoors.

Access for all students to outdoor learning is the clearest challenge, particularly for OAE (Ewert & Garvey, 2007). Increased safety standards require more highly trained staff at larger ratios, which, along with the need for 24-h supervision for multi-day programs, results in high program costs. Every educational program has a cost, so the question is not whether OAE is too expensive, but rather if the required financial investment is cost-effective for achieving evidence-based outcomes that are deemed important. The UK-based Education Endowment Fund attempts to do just this for various initiatives, and rates OAE as having a moderate effect of 4 months of additional academic progress, for a moderate cost (Education Endowment Foundation, 2018). LOTC is more accessible for most schools as it does not require specialist facilities and equipment or large blocks of time, however the time and cost to travel to green spaces can still be prohibitive in some schools (Waite et al., 2016). Planning an outdoor lesson also involves an additional administrative burden for teachers, similarly to organising any other off-campus excursion (Passy et al., 2019; Waite, 2020).

Aversion to risk can be a cultural barrier to outdoor learning. A general societal trend away from risk-taking over the last few decades (Dillon et al., 2006; Rickinson et al., 2004), has resulted in a 'cotton wool culture' (Hyndman & Telford, 2015) where risk is to be minimised wherever possible. Parents who would like their children to be fearless can themselves be fearful about exposing their children to risky play, and thereby inhibit opportunities for them to develop resilience and courage (Niehues et al., 2013). Schools and youth organisations have also become more risk-averse (Harper, 2017), which has resulted in an increased administrative burden of risk management for teachers planning outdoor learning experiences for their students.

A significant barrier for student participation in both OAE and LOTC is their inclusion in an often-crowded state or national curriculum. While adventurous 'school camp' experiences are permitted or recommended in some national curriculums (Lugg & Quay, 2020), it is rare that OAE is systematically integrated into the mandated curricular offering for all students. There has been some confusion of identity even within the outdoor education community, as to whether it should be a stand-alone subject with discrete content, or an effective method to achieve other academic or socio-emotional curricular objectives (Quay, 2016). Crowded curriculum is similarly a challenge for teachers wanting to utilise LOTC (Passy et al., 2019). LOTC is typically scheduled within regular school hours, however fitting extended lessons into a busy school timetable can be difficult (Barfod & Bentsen, 2018). Scandinavian countries with a broadly defined curriculum allow more autonomy for teachers to adopt LOTC (Bentsen et al., 2009), however the curriculum is tightly defined in many countries which leaves teachers feeling that they have no time for creative pedagogies like LOTC (Becker et al., 2017; Waite et al., 2016).

The skillset for effective outdoor learning combines familiarity with the academic curriculum and facilitating experiential learning in natural settings, and OAE and LOTC educators are often confident in only one of these domains (Nicol & Waite, 2020). Pre-service teachers need to be trained in student-centred pedagogies and how to link the curriculum with outdoor learning experiences, and these courses also need to be available for in-service teachers across all subjects (Barfod & Bentsen, 2018).

Individual student factors are not necessarily barriers, but need to be taken into account when designing LOTC experiences. These factors include age (younger students tend to be more enthusiastic about being outdoors), prior experiences with LOTC, phobias around dangerous fauna or simply being away from built environments, preference for didactic rather than student-led learning styles, physical and learning disabilities, and ethnic and cultural identity (Dillon et al., 2006).

8 Conclusion and Recommendations

Learning in the outdoors has great potential for developing personal and social competencies, which are increasingly recognised in the 21st century as being critical skills across most areas of professional and community life. Communication and collaboration outcomes have seen much more research focus to date than creative and critical thinking, and future research needs to investigate the effect of outdoor learning on the latter intrapersonal competencies. Recent reviews of outdoor learning research have been critical of methodological quality, and recommend repeated findings, quasi-experimental study design, randomised controlled trials and longitudinal studies (Becker et al., 2017; Fiennes et al., 2015). Whilst the effective practice of OAE and LOTC can be seen in many countries, it is rare that they are part of the normal educational experience of most students. Numerous challenges to the widespread implementation of learning in natural settings include: financial cost, a crowded curriculum, cultural bias towards risk aversion, and the lack of teacher training in student-centred pedagogies and utilising outdoor environments for learning.

The lynchpin for the mainstream adoption of outdoor learning is the formal inclusion of socio-emotional competencies in the curriculum. Most teachers recognise the importance of developing personal competencies, however academic performance metrics, by which both students and teachers are currently assessed, inhibit prioritisation of these broader educational goals. If state and national curriculum structures are expanded to include socio-emotional development, then OAE and LOTC would be core pedagogical platforms to achieve formal curricular outcomes. This top-down catalyst of curricular change would influence educational budgeting for outdoor learning opportunities, and cascade to bottom-up initiatives in teacher pre-service training and in-service upskilling in outdoor pedagogies.

Research to date has provided a general evidence base of OAE and LOTC programs promoting the growth of 21st century competencies, and future research can build on this foundation by finessing the conditions under which outdoor learning is most effective for achieving these outcomes (Mann et al., 2021). The following specific questions are worthy of further exploration:

- What are the political and cultural drivers which would motivate a jurisdiction to de-clutter its educational curriculum in order to integrate outdoor learning?

- How can 21st century competencies be rigorously and pragmatically assessed in (indoor and outdoor) school settings?
- What elements (e.g. participant factors, facilitation style and quality, program duration and frequency) of outdoor learning programs are necessary to achieve significant gains in 21st century competencies?
- Under what conditions does outdoor learning enhance academic learning?
- What are the elements of effective pre-service and in-service teacher training which would result in teachers feeling confident to design and facilitate learning in natural spaces?

Converging evidence has provided a clear picture of the benefits of outdoor learning for the development of 21st century competencies. As Kuo and colleagues conclude, "it is time to take nature seriously as a resource for learning and development—to expand existing, isolated efforts into mainstream practices" (Kuo et al., 2019, 6; see Kuo, Barnes and Jordan: Do Experiences with Nature Promote Learning? Converging Evidence of a Cause-And-Effect Relationship in this volume). OAE and LOTC have an integral part to play in equipping young people to flourish in a world where critical and complex thinking and effective communication and collaboration are essential.

Recommended Further Reading

1. OECD. (2019). *OECD Skills Strategy 2019: Skills to Shape a Better Future.*; OECD Publishing: Paris. https://www.oecd.org/skills/oecd-skills-strategy-2019-9789264313835-en.htm
2. Kuo, M., Barnes, M., Jordan, C. (2019). Do Experiences With Nature Promote Learning? Converging Evidence of a Cause-and-Effect Relationship. *Frontiers in Psychology, 10,* 305–305. https://doi.org/10.3389/fpsyg.2019.00305 (reprinted as Kuo, Barnes and Jordan: Do Experiences with Nature Promote Learning? Converging Evidence of a Cause-And-Effect Relationship in this volume).
3. Beames, S., Higgins, P., Nicol, R. (2012). *Learning Outside the Classroom: Theory and Guidelines for Practice.* London: Routledge.

References

Adams, S., & Savahl, S. (2017). Nature as children's space: A systematic review. *The Journal of Environmental Education, 48*(5), 291–321. https://doi.org/10.1080/00958964.2017.1366160.

Athman, J., & Monroe, M. C. (2004). The effects of environment-based education on students' achievement motivation. *Journal of Interpretation Research, 9*(1), 9–25.

Barfod, K., & Bentsen, P. (2018). Don't ask how outdoor education can be integrated into the school curriculum; ask how the school curriculum can be taught outside the classroom. *Curriculum Perspectives, 38*(2), 151–156. https://doi.org/10.1007/s41297-018-0055-9.

Bartosh, O., Ferguson, L., Tudor, M., & Taylor, C. (2009). Impact of environment-based teaching on student achievement: A study of Washington State Middle Schools. *Middle Grades Research Journal, 4*(4).

Beames, S., Higgins, P., & Nicol, R. (2012). *Learning Outside the Classroom: Theory and Guidelines for Practice.* Routledge.

Becker, C., Lauterbach, G., Spengler, S., Dettweiler, U., & Mess, F. (2017). Effects of regular classes in outdoor education settings: A systematic review on students' learning, social and health dimensions. *International Journal of Environmental Research and Public Health, 14*(5), 485. https://doi.org/10.3390/ijerph14050485.

Bentsen, P., Ho, S., Gray, T., & Waite, S. (2017). A global view of learning outside the classroom. In *Children Learning Outside the Classroom from Birth to Eleven* (pp. 53–66). Sage.

Bentsen, P., Mygind, E., & Randrup, T. B. (2009). Towards an understanding of udeskole: Education outside the classroom in a Danish context. *Education, 3–13, 37*(1), 29–44. https://doi.org/10.1080/03004270802291780.

Bentsen, P., Mygind, L., Elsborg, P., Nielsen, G., & Mygind, E. (2021). Education outside the classroom as upstream school health promotion: 'Adding-in' physical activity into children's everyday life and settings. *Scandinavian Journal of Public Health.* https://doi.org/10.1177/1403494821993715.

Bentsen, P., Søndergaard Jensen, F., Mygind, E., & Barfoed Randrup, T. (2010). The extent and dissemination of udeskole in Danish schools. *Urban Forestry and Urban Greening, 9*(3), 235–243. https://doi.org/10.1016/j.ufug.2010.02.001.

Blackwell, S. (2019). *About Forest Schools Education.* Forest Schools Association. https://www.forestschools.com/pages/about. Accessed January 21, 2021.

Braus, J., & Milligan-Toffler, S. (2018). The children and nature connection: Why it matters. *Ecopsychology, 10*(4), 193–194.

Breunig, M., Murtell, J., & Russell, C. (2015). Students' experiences with/in integrated environmental studies programs in Ontario. *Journal of Adventure Education and Outdoor Learning, 15*(4), 267–283. https://doi.org/10.1080/14729679.2014.955354.

Brown, H., Harris, I., & Porter, S. (2016). Professional accreditation in the UK outdoor sector. In B. Humberstone, H. Prince & K. Henderson (Eds.), *Routledge International Handbook of Outdoor Studies* (1st ed., pp. 178–188). Routledge. https://doi.org/10.4324/9781315768465-21.

Brown, M., & Beames, S. (2017). Adventure education: Redux. *Journal of Adventure Education and Outdoor Learning, 17*(4), 294–306. https://doi.org/10.1080/14729679.2016.1246257.

Bølling, M., Niclasen, J., Bentsen, P., & Nielsen, G. (2019). Association of education outside the classroom and pupils' psychosocial well-being: Results from a school year implementation. *The Journal of School Health, 89*(3), 210–218. https://doi.org/10.1111/josh.12730.

Bølling, M., Otte, C. R., Elsborg, P., Nielsen, G., & Bentsen, P. (2018). The association between education outside the classroom and students' school motivation: Results from a one-school-year quasi-experiment. *International Journal of Educational Research, 89*, 22–35. https://doi.org/10.1016/j.ijer.2018.03.004.

Cason, D., & Gillis, H. L. (1994). A meta-analysis of outdoor adventure programming with adolescents. *Journal of Experiential Education, 17*(1), 40–47.

Chawla, L. (2015). Benefits of nature contact for children. *Journal of Planning Literature, 30*(4), 433–452. https://doi.org/10.1177/0885412215595441.

Christie, B., Beames, S., & Higgins, P. (2016). Context, culture and critical thinking: Scottish secondary school teachers' and pupils' experiences of outdoor learning. *British Educational Research Journal, 42*(3), 417–437. https://doi.org/10.1002/berj.3213.

Cooley, S. J., Burns, V. E., & Cumming, J. (2015). The role of outdoor adventure education in facilitating groupwork in higher education. *Higher Education, 69*(4), 567–582. https://doi.org/10.1007/s10734-014-9791-4.

Dewey, J. (1938). *Experience and education.* The Macmillan Company.

Dillon, J., Rickinson, M., Teamey, K., Morris, M., Choi, M. Y., Sanders, D., & Benefield, P. (2006). The value of outdoor learning: Evidence from research in the UK and elsewhere. *School Science Review, 87*(320), 107.

Dowdell, K., Gray, T., & Malone, K. (2011). Nature and its influence on children's outdoor play. *Journal of Outdoor and Environmental Education, 15*(2), 24–35. https://link.springer.com/article/https://doi.org/10.1007/BF03400925.

Education Endowment Foundation. (2018). Outdoor adventure learning. *Teaching and learning toolkit.* https://educationendowmentfoundation.org.uk/evidence-summaries/teaching-learning-toolkit/outdoor-adventure-learning/. Accessed February 24, 2021.

Ewert, A., & Garvey, D. (2007). Philosophy and theory of adventure education. *Adventure education: Theory and Applications, 19*–32.

Fadel, C. (2016). Redesigning the curriculum for a 21st century education. https://curriculumredesign.org/wp-content/uploads/CCR-FoundationalPaper-Updated-Jan2016.pdf. Accessed January 24, 2021.

Fiennes, C., Oliver, E., Dickson, K., Escobar, D., Romans, A., & Oliver, S. (2015). *The existing evidence-base about the effectiveness of outdoor learning.* Institute of Outdoor Learning. London, UK.

Fullan, M., & Langworthy, M. (2013). *Towards a new end: New pedagogies for deep learning.* C. Impact. https://michaelfullan.ca/wp-content/uploads/2013/08/New-Pedagogies-for-Deep-Learning-An-Invitation-to-Partner-2013-6-201.pdf. Accessed 24 February, 2021.

Geisinger, K. F. (2016). 21st century skills: What are they and how do we assess them? *Applied Measurement in Education, 29*(4), 245–249. https://doi.org/10.1080/08957347.2016.1209207.

Gill, T. (2011). *Children and nature: A quasi-systematic review of the empirical evidence.* London Sustainable Development Commission.

Gill, T. (2014). The benefits of children's engagement with nature: A systematic literature review. *Children, Youth and Environments, 24*(2), 10–34. https://doi.org/10.7721/chilyoutenvi.24.2.0010.

Gillis, H. L., & Speelman, E. (2008). Are challenge (ropes) courses an effective tool? A meta-analysis. *Journal of Experiential Education, 31*, 111–135. https://doi.org/10.5193/JEE.31.2.111.

Gray, T. (1997). *The impact of an extended stay outdoor education school program upon adolescent participants.* University of Wollongong. http://ro.uow.edu.au/theses/1799.

Gray, T. (2018). Outdoor learning: Not new, just newly important. *Curriculum Perspectives, 38*(2), 145–149. https://doi.org/10.1007/s41297-018-0054-x.

Gray, T., & Bailey, P. (2022). Gone Rogue: Re-wilding education in alternative outdoor learning environments. In R. Cutting & R. Passy (Eds.), *Contemporary Approaches to Outdoor Learning: Animals, the Environment and New Methods.* Palgrave Macmillan.

Gray, T., Mitten, D., Loeffler, T., Allen-Craig, S., & Carpenter, C. (2017). Defining moments: An examination of the gender divide in women's contribution to outdoor education. *Research in Outdoor Education, 15*, 47–71.

Gray, T., & Pigott, F. (2018). Lasting lessons in outdoor learning: A facilitation model emerging from 30 Years of reflective practice. *Ecopsychology, 10*(4), 195–204.

Grinde, B., & Patil, G. G. (2009). Biophilia: Does visual contact with nature impact on health and well-being? *International Journal of Environmental Research and Public Health, 6*(9), 2332–2343.

Hahn, K. (1930). *The seven laws of Salem.* In Schule Schloss Salem.

Hahn, K. (1959). Dr. Kurt Hahn at the forty-eighth annual dinner of old centralians. *The Central: The Journal of Old Centralians,* (119), 3–8.

Hans, T. A. (2000). A meta-analysis of the effects of adventure programming on locus of control. *Journal of Contemporary Psychotherapy, 30*(1), 33–60.

Harper, N. J. (2017). Outdoor risky play and healthy child development in the shadow of the "risk society": A forest and nature school perspective. *Child and Youth Services, 38*(4), 318–334. https://doi.org/10.1080/0145935X.2017.1412825.

Harris, F. (2015). The nature of learning at forest school: Practitioners' perspectives. *Education 3–13, 45*(2), 272–291. https://doi.org/10.1080/03004279.2015.1078833.

Hartig, T., Mitchell, R., De Vries, S., & Frumkin, H. (2014). Nature and health. *Annual Review of Public Health, 35*, 207–228.

Hattie, J., Marsh, H. W., Neill, J. T., & Richards, G. E. (1997). Adventure education and outward bound: Out-of-class experiences that make a lasting difference. *Review of Educational Research, 67*(1), 43–87. https://doi.org/10.2307/1170619.

Hyndman, B. P., & Telford, A. (2015). Should educators be 'wrapping school playgrounds in cotton wool' to encourage physical activity? Exploring primary and secondary students' voices from the school playground. *Australian Journal of Teacher Education, 40*(6), 4.

Joyce, R. (2012). *Outdoor Learning: Past and Present*. Open University Press.

Kemp, N. (2019). Views from the staffroom: Forest school in English primary schools. *Journal of Adventure Education and Outdoor Learning, 20*(4), 1–12. https://doi.org/10.1080/14729679.2019.1697712.

Kendall, S., Rodger, J., & Laxton, C. (2015). *Evaluation of Learning Away: Final Report*. York Consulting.

Kolb, D. A. (1984). *Experiential Learning: Experience as the Source of Learning and Development*. Prentice-Hall.

Kuo, M., Barnes, M., & Jordan, C. (2019). Do experiences with nature promote learning? Converging evidence of a cause-and-effect relationship. *Frontiers in Psychology, 10*, 305–305. https://doi.org/10.3389/fpsyg.2019.00305.

Lamb, S., Maire, Q., & Doecke, E. (2017). *Key Skills for the 21st Century: An Evidence-based Review*. https://vuir.vu.edu.au/35865/1/Key-Skills-for-the-21st-Century-Analytical-Report.pdf. Accessed May 13, 2021.

Lambert, P. (2017). *Hard Focus on "Soft" Skills*. https://cica.org.au/wp-content/uploads/Hard_focus_on_soft_skills_Dr_Phil_Lambert.pdf. Accessed May 13, 2021.

Lloyd, A., Truong, S., & Gray, T. (2018a). Place-based outdoor learning: More than a drag and drop approach. *Journal of Outdoor and Environmental Education, 21*(1), 45–60. https://doi.org/10.1007/s42322-017-0002-5.

Lloyd, A., Truong, S., & Gray, T. (2018b). Take the class outside! A call for place-based outdoor learning in the Australian primary school curriculum. *Curriculum Perspectives, 38*(2), 163–167. https://doi.org/10.1007/s41297-018-0050-1.

Louv, R. (2005). *Last Child in the Woods: Saving our Children from Nature-Deficit Disorder* (Updated and expanded. ed.). Algonquin Books of Chapel Hill.

Lugg, A., & Quay, J. (2020). Curriculum in outdoor and environmental education. In M. Peters (Ed.), *Encyclopedia of Teacher Education*. Springer.

Malone, K., & Waite, S. (2016). Student outcomes and natural schooling: Pathways From Evidence to Impact Report 2016.

Mann, J. (2018). Is school working for teenage boys? Outdoor learning and real-life skills could be the keys to re-engagement. *Curriculum Perspectives, 38*(2), 169–174.

Martin, A., & Legg, S. (2002). Investigating the inward sounds of outward bound. *Journal of Outdoor and Environmental Education, 6*(2), 27–36. https://doi.org/10.1007/BF03400753.

McCormick, R. (2017). Does access to green space impact the mental well-being of children: A systematic review. *Journal of Pediatric Nursing, 37*, 3–7. https://doi.org/10.1016/j.pedn.2017.08.027.

McLeod, B., & Allen-Craig, S. (2007). What outcomes are we trying to achieve in our outdoor education programs? *Australian Journal of Outdoor Education, 11*(2), 41–49.

Mann, J., Gray, T., Truong, S., Sahlberg, P., Bentsen, P., Passy, R., Ho, S., Ward, K., & Cowper, R. (2021). A Systematic Review Protocol to Identify the Key Benefits and Efficacy of Nature-Based Learning in Outdoor Educational Settings. *International Journal of Environmental Research and Public Health, 18*(2).

Mitten, D., Gray, T., Allen-Craig, S., Loeffler, T. A., & Carpenter, C. (2018). The invisibility cloak: Women's contributions to outdoor and environmental education. *The Journal of Environmental Education, 49*(4), 318–327. https://doi.org/10.1080/00958964.2017.1366890.

Nicol, R., & Waite, S. (2020). Outdoor Learning. In M. A. Peters (Ed.), *Encyclopedia of Teacher Education* (pp. 1–6). Springer. https://doi.org/10.1007/978-981-13-1179-6_354-1.

Niehues, A. N., Bundy, A., Broom, A., Tranter, P., Ragen, J., & Engelen, L. (2013). Everyday uncertainties: Reframing perceptions of risk in outdoor free play. *Journal of Adventure Education and Outdoor Learning, 13*(3), 223–237. https://doi.org/10.1080/14729679.2013.798588.

Norman, N., Jennings, A., & Wahl, L. (2006). *The impact of environmentally-related education on academic achievement: A literature survey.* http://citeseerx.ist.psu.edu/viewdoc/download?doi=10.1.1.508.1028&rep=rep1&type=pdf. Accessed 24 February, 2021.

OECD. (2019). *OECD Skills Strategy 2019: Skills to Shape a Better Future.* OECD Publishing. https://doi.org/10.1787/9789264313835-en.

Opper, B., Maree, J. G., Fletcher, L., & Sommerville, J. (2014). Efficacy of outdoor adventure education in developing emotional intelligence during adolescence. *Journal of Psychology in Africa, 24*(2), 193–196. https://doi.org/10.1080/14330237.2014.903076.

Otte, C. R., Bølling, M., Stevenson, M. P., Ejbye-Ernst, N., Nielsen, G., & Bentsen, P. (2019). Education outside the classroom increases children's reading performance: Results from a one-year quasi-experimental study. *International Journal of Educational Research, 94*, 42–51. https://doi.org/10.1016/j.ijer.2019.01.009.

Parrish, D., Phillips, G., Levine, R., Hikawa, H., Gaertner, M., Agosta, N., & Doyal, D. (2005). *Effects of Outdoor Education Programs for Children in California.* American Institutes for Research.

Passy, R., Bentsen, P., Gray, T., & Ho, S. (2019). Integrating outdoor learning into the curriculum: An exploration in four nations. *Curriculum Perspectives, 39*(1), 73–78. https://doi.org/10.1007/s41297-019-00070-8.

Perrot, S., Bauer, T. N., Abonneau, D., Campoy, E., Erdogan, B., & Liden, R. C. (2014). Organizational socialization tactics and newcomer adjustment: The moderating role of perceived organizational support. *Group and Organization Management, 39*(3), 247–273. https://doi.org/10.1177/1059601114535469.

Priest, S., & Gass, M. (2005). *Effective Leadership in Adventure Programming* (2nd ed.). Human Kinetics.

Prince, H. E. (2020). The lasting impacts of outdoor adventure residential experiences on young people. *Journal of Adventure Education and Outdoor Learning,* 1–16. https://doi.org/10.1080/14729679.2020.1784764.

Quay, J. (2005). Connecting social and environmental education through the practice of outdoor education. In T. Dickson, T. Gray & B. Hayllar (Eds.), *Outdoor and Experiential Learning in Australia and New Zealand: Views From the Top* (pp. 82–94). Otago University Print.

Quay, J. (2016). Outdoor education and school curriculum distinctiveness: More than content, more than process. *Journal of Outdoor and Environmental Education, 19*(2), 42–50. https://doi.org/10.1007/bf03400993.

Rickinson, M., Dillon, J., Teamey, K., Morris, M., Choi, M. Y., Sanders, D., & Benefield, P. (2004). *A Review of Research on Outdoor Learning.* National Foundation for Educational Research and King's College London (1851538933).

Schenck, J., & Cruickshank, J. (2015). Evolving Kolb: Experiential education in the age of neuroscience. *Journal of Experiential Education, 38*(1), 73–95. https://doi.org/10.1177/1053825914547153.

Schneller, M. B., Duncan, S., Schipperijn, J., Nielsen, G., Mygind, E., & Bentsen, P. (2017). Are children participating in a quasi-experimental education outside the classroom intervention more physically active? *BMC Public Health, 17*(1), 523. https://doi.org/10.1186/s12889-017-4430-5.

Sibthorp, J., Collins, R., Rathunde, K., Paisley, K., Schumann, S., Pohja, M., Gookin, J., & Baynes, S. (2015). Fostering experiential self-regulation through outdoor adventure education. *The Journal of Experiential Education, 38*(1), 26–40. https://doi.org/10.1177/1053825913516735.

Silva, E. (2009). Measuring skills for 21st-century learning. *Phi Delta Kappan, 90*(9), 630–634. https://doi.org/10.1177/003172170909000905.

Stevenson, M. P., Schilhab, T., & Bentsen, P. (2018). Attention restoration theory II: A systematic review to clarify attention processes affected by exposure to natural environments. *Journal of*

Toxicology and Environmental Health. Part B, Critical reviews, 21(4), 227–268. https://doi.org/10.1080/10937404.2018.1505571.

Thorburn, M., & Marshall, A. (2014). Cultivating lived-body consciousness: Enhancing cognition and emotion through outdoor learning. *Journal of Pedagogy, 5*(1), 115–132. https://doi.org/10.2478/jped-2014-0006.

Thurber, C. A., Scanlin, M. M., Scheuler, L., & Henderson, K. A. (2007). Youth development outcomes of the camp experience: Evidence for multidimensional growth. *Journal of Youth and Adolescence, 36*(3), 241–254.

Tracey, D., Gray, T., Truong, S., & Ward, K. (2018). Combining acceptance and commitment therapy with adventure therapy to promote psychological wellbeing for children at-risk. *Frontiers in Psychology, 9*(1565). https://doi.org/10.3389/fpsyg.2018.01565.

Trilling, B. (2009). *21st Century Skills: Learning for Life in our Times* (1st ed.). Jossey-Bass.

Truong, S., Gray, T., & Ward, K. (2016). "Sowing and growing" life skills through garden-based learning to reengage disengaged youth. *LEARNing landscapes, 10*(1), 361–385. https://doi.org/10.36510/learnland.v10i1.738.

Ulrich, R. S. (1984). View through a window may influence recovery from surgery. *Science, 224*(4647), 420–421.

Vincent-Lancrin, S., González-Sancho, C., Bouckaert, M., Luca, F. d., Fernández-Barrerra, M., Jacotin, G., Urgel, J., & Vidal, Q. (2019). *Fostering Students' Creativity and Critical Thinking*. https://doi.org/10.1787/62212c37-en.

Waite, S. (2020). Where are we going? International views on purposes, practices and barriers in school-based outdoor learning. *Education Sciences, 10*(11), 311.

Waite, S., Bølling, M., & Bentsen, P. (2016a). Comparing apples and pears?: A conceptual framework for understanding forms of outdoor learning through comparison of English Forest Schools and Danish udeskole. *Environmental Education Research, 22*(6), 868–892. https://doi.org/10.1080/13504622.2015.1075193.

Waite, S., Passy, R., Gilchrist, M., Hunt, A., & Blackwell, I. (2016b). Natural Connections Demonstration Project, 2012–2016: Final Report. *Natural England Commissioned Reports*. http://publications.naturalengland.org.uk/publication/6636651036540928. Accessed on 24 February, 2021.

Williams, I., & Allen, N. (2012). *National Survey of Australian Outdoor Youth Programs: Summary Report of the Outdoor Youth Programs Research Alliance*. Murdoch Children's Research Institute. https://oypra.org.au/our-research/national-survey/.

World Economic Forum. (2015). *New Vision for Education: Unlocking the Potential of Technology*. http://www3.weforum.org/docs/WEFUSA_NewVisionforEducation_Report2015.pdf.

Jeff Mann Jeff is a Doctoral Student at the School of Education, Western Sydney University, Penrith, Australia. He has a background of fifteen years in the outdoor education sector, and has worked in the school education contexts for the last five years. Having worked in a number of boys schools, Jeff's initial research interest was in the intersection of classroom and outdoor pedagogies for boys. This developed into his doctoral project on outdoor learning models to engage teenage boys and girls in school, and their potential for developing important 21st century skills.

Tonia Gray is a Senior Researcher in the Centre for Educational Research at Western Sydney University. With a Masters in Community Health and a PhD in Education, Tonia's transdisciplinary research explores the intersection of experiential education, human-nature relationships, and health/wellbeing. Her twinned passions for teaching and research have earned Tonia several major awards such as the 2019 International Association of Experiential Education Distinguished Researcher of the Year and the prestigious 2014 Australian Award for University Teaching.

Son Truong is an Associate Professor in the School of Health and Human Performance at Dalhousie University. He is also currently an Adjunct Fellow in the School of Education at Western Sydney University. He has extensive experience working in diverse community settings, including in the education sector, environmental education, and mental health, in both minority and majority world contexts. His interdisciplinary and community-based research focuses on wellbeing, play, outdoor learning, and nature-based programming, particularly with underserved and vulnerable communities.

Fostering 21st Century Skills Through Autonomy Supportive Science Education Outside the Classroom

Ulrich Dettweiler, Gabriele Lauterbach, Christoph Mall, and Ruth Kermish-Allen

1 Introduction

1.1 21st Century Skills

In the face of economic, environmental, and social challenges, education, or more specifically science education, is even more important today than in the past (National Research Council, 2012), and concepts for the convergence between environmental and science education still need to be implemented (Wals et al., 2014). Public education should provide young people with the knowledge and experiences to become responsible citizens, decision-makers, and problem solvers, capable of addressing serious economic, environmental and social issues. These types of aptitudes and knowledge are termed 21st century skills and have been promoted in several different frameworks by governmental organizations, such as the European Union (2006) and the Organisation for Economic Co-operation and Development (OECD) (2005), as well as (semi-)commercial organizations including Partnership for 21st century skills (P21) (2015), ATC21S™ (Griffin et al., 2012) and EnGauge (Burkhardt et al., 2003). In their meta-review, Voogt and Roblin (2012) have pointed out that all of

U. Dettweiler (✉) · G. Lauterbach
Faculty of Arts and Education, University of Stavanger, 4021 Stavanger, Norway
e-mail: ulrich.dettweiler@uis.no

G. Lauterbach
e-mail: gabriele.lauterbach@uis.no

C. Mall
Department of Sport and Health Sciences, Technical University of Munich, Georg-Brauchle-Ring 62, 80992 Munich, Germany
e-mail: christoph.mall@tum.de

R. Kermish-Allen
Maine Mathematics and Science Alliance (MMSA), Augusta, ME 04,330, USA
e-mail: rkermishallen@mmsa.org

© The Author(s) 2022
R. Jucker and J. von Au (eds.), *High-Quality Outdoor Learning*,
https://doi.org/10.1007/978-3-031-04108-2_13

231

the above-mentioned concepts include information- and communication technology (ICT) related competences, collaboration, communication, as well as social and cultural competences. In addition, some of the frameworks encompass outcomes that represent self-regulatory competences with autonomous decision making in real-life scenario learning. All those features are described as enriching classical classroom settings.

It has been argued by a number of authors that societies require citizens, who can independently analyse problems, make choices (even when the choice challenges social norms), and work collaboratively to find solutions (cf. the anthology by Krasny & Dillon, 2012). Therefore, effective education should cultivate autonomous decision-making as well as collective problem solving (Chawla & Derr, 2012). Our children need to become "resilient learners" (Sterling, 2010), capable of collaborating across boundaries, working towards solutions, and thinking critically from multiple perspectives.

In order to address this call to action, science education in the USA, for example, has been undergoing a period of transition from a disconnected fact-based system to a more holistic approach. Scientific practices that span across the scientific disciplines are integrated into real-world scenarios. This transformative vision has been laid out in detail by the National Academy of Sciences in both the Framework for K-12 Science Education (National Research Council, 2012) and the Next Generation Science Standards (NGSS Lead States, 2013). The NGSS challenges educators to do the work of scientists in real-world contexts and paves the way for crafting experiential educational experiences that relate specifically to learners' interests, lives, and issues they care about. Even if this is not systematically integrated in national curricula, school curricula and classroom activities, many of those 21st century skills are implicitly enacted in teachers' current conceptions in science class (van de Oudeweetering & Voogt, 2018).

1.2   Education Outside the Classroom (EOtC) and 21st Century Skills

In northern European countries, such 21st century skills are often (implicitly) addressed with educational concepts outside the classroom.[1] To our knowledge, there exist only a few explicit school policies in this respect. In Scotland, we can find governmental support for the role of outdoor education in the delivery of curricular and non-curricular educational themes, such as personal, social, environmental and health education (Nicol et al., 2012). In Norway, formalized and regular EOtC concepts emerged in the 1990es (Jordet, 1998). They are deeply rooted in the Nordic

---

[1] Originally, the term "Education Outside the Classroom (EOtC)" was coined by Bentsen et al. (2009) in order to refer to the Danish concept of *udeskole*, regular and compulsory outdoor teaching over the whole school year with a frequency of at least three hours at least every two weeks. We will use this term also for short-term curriculum-based science teaching interventions.

version of outdoor sports of the 1920s and many teachers still design EOtC with a physical activity (PA) focus (Helle, 2017). With respect to 21st century skills, the 'Sustainable Backpack' project is a national program using EOtC, which was initiated by the Ministry of Education and Research and the Ministry of Climate and Environment to support Norwegian schools to implement education for sustainable development. To date, more than 550 schools had been enrolled since 2009 (Scheie, 2017). In Sweden, EOtC is seen as an integral part of school culture, however, no reliable data on the prevalence of outdoor teaching is available today (Skoven i Skolen, 2021). In Finland, outdoor teaching is predominantly found in short term residential programs at specific centres, however, as in Sweden, there exists no systematic overview. In Denmark, on the contrary, the extent and dissemination of EOtC is very well documented. Three major surveys from 2007 (Bentsen et al., 2010; Barfod et al., 2016; Barfod et al., 2021) show that at least 19.5% of Danish general schools and 34.0% of Danish special-needs schools practised one or more classes of regular EOtC in 2019. Although the extent of the provision among general schools has been stable since 2014, the number of classes providing regular EOtC in general public schools has increased by 31.8%.

The focus of EOtC research in Denmark lies on pupils' PA, well-being and learning (Nielsen et al., 2016), and very little is known on the use of EOtC for the development of 21st century skills. However, a conceptual paper exploring the similarities and differences between English Forest Schools and Danish *udeskole* ("outdoor school"), found that despite different national educational and cultural contexts, the two concepts share several commonalities within a naturalistic/progressive pedagogical tradition. Differences appear mainly in the degree of integration within national educational systems. Furthermore, global calls for increased connection to nature and recent alignment of results-driven school systems in both countries influence their foundational principles, perhaps leading to greater convergence in the future (Waite et al., 2015). Especially the TEACHOUT research project from 2013 to 2018 on health-related, social, motivational, and academic effects of EOtC has generated evidence based on reasonably large samples in Denmark (Bentsen et al., 2021). With respect to PA and thus health prevention, particularly boys seem to benefit from regular EOtC (Schneller et al., 2017; Schneller et al., 2017). Children's academic achievements in reading skills seem to improve in EOtC compared to normal schooling irrespective of gender (Otte, 2018) and their overall motivation for school seems to increase through regular EOtC (Bølling et al., 2018).

1.3 Autonomous Learning and Practical Relevance Through EOtC in the 21st Century Skills Framework

There is a wealth of empirical studies that have shown the potential benefits of motivation interventions to enhance educational outcomes (Lazowski & Hulleman, 2016). In their meta-analysis, the authors conclude that more intervention research is needed to inform practice and policy about educational settings for the students' benefit. Within self-determination theory (SDT), students' motivation and interest for curriculum related contents are key determinants for their learning and academic success. The more one's behaviour is self-determined, the more it shifts from external to intrinsic motivation (Deci & Ryan, 2000, 2002). Especially intrinsic motivation is of great importance in educational settings. If a student is intrinsically motivated to learn specific contents, she or he is more likely to achieve better academic outcomes (Taylor et al., 2014).

According to self-determination theory, intrinsic motivation is achieved by the satisfaction of basic psychological needs (BPN). Those are autonomy and competence support, as well as experiences of relatedness (Deci & Vansteenkiste, 2004). The more the school environment enables the students' autonomy, their experience of competence, and social relatedness, the more likely they develop intrinsic motivation and become increasingly engaged in school (Reeve et al., 2004). However, teachers tend to apply more controlling instead of autonomy supportive teaching styles (Reeve, 2009). Whereas the importance of BPN-satisfaction for educational success has been widely discussed in the educational literature (Niemiec & Ryan, 2009; Vansteenkiste et al., 2006), only a few studies focus on the perceived relevance of content (Vansteenkiste et al., 2006). Assor et al. (2002) have shown that the main autonomy-enhancing behaviour of teachers in different subjects, e.g. fostering relevance, was positively associated with behavioural and cognitive engagement and positive feelings. Rakoczy et al. (2008) were able to connect the students' perceived relevance of content with self-determined learning in mathematics.

In their multiple-methods survey on learning environments for 21st century students, Lemley et al. (2014) identified the students' autonomy support and perceived relevance of material, presentation, and teacher competence as critical for the students' motivation and learning attitude. The authors connect 21st century skills explicitly to self-determination theory, and define the 21st century classroom as a flexible learning space with multimedia materials, and opportunities for networking and collaboration. Darner (2009) proposes three educational means to effectively create a 21st century classroom. Firstly, one needs to support the students' need for autonomy, for example via curricular activities that include sufficient opportunities for students to actively engage in solving environmental problems of their choosing. This will secondly foster the students' scientific understanding which will satisfy their need for competence. Thirdly, students should get a chance to experience the practical relevance of the teaching content, for example by getting exposed to real-world problems and meeting people in their communities who deal with those problems.

1.4 Research Rationale

Inspired by the above-mentioned research, we wanted to find out how accurately we can estimate the perceived relevance of content (PRC) in science classes from the relative importance of the four basic psychological needs (BPN), autonomy support (A), competence support (C), student-teacher relations (RT), and student-student-relations (RS) in normal and EOtC-learning environments. Our hypothesis is that BPN-satisfaction is a good predictor for perceived practical relevance of content (PRC) in any teaching context.

To address our research question, we combined data from two different EOtC interventions. Study A presents results from a within-subjects design study with n = 281 students studying BPN-satisfaction and PRC in normal science classes and a one-week residential science 'research week' (Dettweiler et al., 2017a, b). We conducted a secondary analysis of this data with a new focus. Study B offers insights into a between-subjects design study in science teaching, using the same instruments as in study A. An intervention group (IG) was taught science classes outdoors one day per week over a school year. The IG was compared to a control group (CG) with normal schooling. Data on students' PA and biological stress responses from study B have been published elsewhere (Dettweiler et al., 2017a, b).

2 Materials and Methods

2.1 Study Design and Intervention

2.1.1 Study A: A Within-Subjects Design Intervention Study

Data was collected from students in relation to learning in two distinct educational settings: (i) the regular science classroom context, and (ii) a curriculum-based residential outdoor science learning course—referred to as 'research week' (Dettweiler et al., 2015).

During the research weeks, specific topics from the curriculum in biology, geography, and mathematics were both taught in the laboratory and during a two-day research expedition into the Berchtesgaden National Park Area for data collection, with an overnight-stay in a secluded mountain hut (cf. Table 1).

The study was conducted from 2012 to 2016 during the months of May to September at the Student Research Centre near Berchtesgaden, Germany. The Student Research Centre is run by the Technical University of Munich. Feasibility of the program was tested in 2012 and program content standardized thereafter (Becker, 2012). Data from 2013 were used as a pilot study (Dettweiler et al., 2015) and to test and validate the measures applied (Dettweiler & Ünlü, 2015). Data from 2014 to 2016 provide the basis of the current study.

The study group consisted of a convenience sample of n = 281 students (168 female: mean age = 12.48 years, SD = 1.76; 113 male: mean age = 12.49 years, SD = 1.71) from ten classes and five different schools, with a bias in the proportion of girls to boys of 3:2. All students attended lower secondary schools in Germany. The socio-cultural backgrounds were considered to be similar; and grades in mathematics

Table 1 Teaching schedules in the two studies

Study A (within-subject design)

Schedule	EOtC[a]
Sunday	Arrival at the Student Research Centre. Welcome and introductory class, repeating curriculum from science class
Monday	Introduction to the laboratory work in small groups, identifying and defining research topics, preparing for the expedition
Tuesday	First day of the expedition. Collecting data along a transect of 1000 m elevation in the individual groups of 3–4, each accompanied by either a teacher, pre-service teacher student, or staff from the Student Research Centre
Wednesday	Second day of the expedition. Continuing with data collection on the way down in the individual groups
Thursday	Data analysis in the individual groups, then re-grouping (group puzzle) and cross-group (disciplinary) discussion and documentation of the findings. Poster session Issuing of the questionnaire
Friday	Meeting with researchers from the National Park Service and presentation and discussion of the findings. Departure

Study B (between-subject design)

Schedule	EOtC	Normal
07.55–08.40	Meeting at 8.00 and short mini-bus transfer to outdoor 'classroom'; preparing for the day	Regular class according to curriculum
08.45–09.30	Forest class according to curriculum	Regular class according to curriculum
09.30–09.45	Break	Break
09.45–10.30	Continued forest class according to curriculum	Regular class according to curriculum
10.35–11.20	Continued forest class according to curriculum	Regular class according to curriculum
11.20–11.35	Break Issuing of the questionnaire	Break Issuing of the questionnaire
11.35–12.20	Continued forest class according to curriculum	Regular class according to curriculum
12.25–01.05	Continued forest class according to curriculum	Regular class according to curriculum

[a]The normal teaching schedules in biology, geography and mathematics in study A follow the ordinary individual plans in the respective schools, with normally two hours biology, two hours geography, and four-five hours mathematics lessons per week. The questionnaire was issued during one of the science classes about six weeks prior to the research week by a trained researcher

and German suggested a normal distribution of overall academic achievement in our study group.

Data collection was administered during the week of learning in each educational setting, with the regular classroom context occurring about six weeks prior to the EOtC week. The self-reported questionnaires contained socio-demographic data and two validated constructs. The explanatory variables were comprised of an adapted version of the Basic Psychological Need Satisfaction Scale (BPNS) (Deci & Ryan, 2000). The BPNS consists of four scales, i.e. "autonomy support (A)", "competence support (C)", "student-teacher relatedness (RT)", and "student-student relatedness (RS)". The A-scale consists of eleven items and is divided in three sub-scales, asking for "ascertained respect", "possibilities of choice" and "comprehended reasons". The scale showed excellent internal consistency (Cronbach's alpha = 0.88).[2] The C-scale consists of eight items in two subscales, "perceived support", and "perceived structure" (Cronbach's alpha = 0.78). Each of the relatedness-scales (RT, RS) consists of four items, asking for the quality of social interactions, with good reliability measures of Cronbach's alpha = 0.84 for RS and Cronbach's alpha = 0.87 for RT. As the pedagogical/didactical response variable we chose to operationalize the German construct developed for measuring PRC in mathematics in our target age-group (Rakoczy et al., 2008), since this construct has specifically been developed within self-determination theory (SDT) and the concept of BPN-satisfaction. This scale consists of five items checking on the students' experiences with examples, transfer of knowledge, and practical applications of the learned contents during science class. Cronbach's alpha for the PRC-scale is 0.76.

2.1.2 Study B: A Longitudinal Between-Subjects Design Intervention Study

Study B is a longitudinal control group design using a convenience sample at a private secondary school in Heidelberg, one of the few schools in Germany practicing regular and compulsory outdoor schooling. The compulsory element was important to keep the motivational attitude as constant as possible in the intervention (EOtC) and control (Normal) groups.

Since basic psychological needs (BPNs) are rather constant traits (Deci & Vansteenkiste, 2004), we considered three measurements during the school year sufficient. The first measurement was scheduled four weeks after schools had started (fall), in order to allow the students enough experiences to make their judgements, the second at mid-term (spring), and the third shortly before the summer holidays (summer).

The intervention consisted of one school-day per week in the forest, with 5 × 45 min "science classes" and 1 × 45 min "physical education" (PE) allocated over the school day as specified in Table 1. Looking at the respective schedules, two major

---

[2] Cronbach's alpha is a measure of scale reliability. It measures how closely related a set of items are as a group. It can take values between 0 and 1, and 0.7 or higher is considered "acceptable".

differences can be seen: (1) the curriculum in EOtC is taught in cross-disciplinary units on the forest days, whereas it is taught in segments, subject by subject, in normal class; and (2) the pedagogical approach of the outdoor-learning program includes opportunities to autonomously use the space in which the teaching is going on, including physical activation such as walks (the rather informal PE part in the intervention design) to reach specific places in the forest. In contrast, the frame for science lessons within the Normal group is connected to traditional indoor teaching concepts with less opportunities and variability with respect to space. With respect to the cognitive load and academic demand, we consider both teaching contexts to be equivalent since the curriculum is not different from the control classes in the EOtC setting.

Participants were recruited from 5 and 6th grades from the above mentioned secondary school in Heidelberg, Germany.

We were able to include 48 students into the study, 37 in the EOtC group, and 11 in normal class. This imbalance was a consequence of last-minute changes to the design after the school had decided to accommodate parents' demands for a third EOtC class rather than sticking to the plan with two. As we will describe in the methods section, this has been accounted for in the statistical analysis. As of normal occurrence, some students were absent from school during data collection, which accordingly lead to missing data. Table 2 summarizes the enrolment data, and we can see a bias in the proportion of girls to boys of 4:6. The socio-economic status can be considered similar. Data were collected at the end of each of the three school days using a paper-based composite questionnaire, containing socio-demographic data and the same constructs as in Study A, the Basic Psychological Need Satisfaction Scale and the Perceived Relevance of Contents Scale. The reliability measures showed

Table 2 Enrolment data for the two studies

Sample Study A (within-subjects, missing cases deleted)			
	Normal	**EOtC**	**Statistics**
	281 total	281 total	
Gender	113 (40%) male	113 (40%) male	$BF_{01} = 0.0$
	168 (60%) female	168 (60%) female	
Age in summer	12.5 years		

Sample Study B (between-subjects, missing cases treated as "missing" in the models)				
	Participants Recruited	**Fall**	**Spring**	**Summer**
Total	48	46	45	46
EOtC	37	35	35	35
Normal	11	11	10	11
	Normal (CG)	**EOtC (IG)**		**Statistics**
Gender	7 (64%) male 4 (36%) female	23 (62%) male 14 (38%) female		$BF_{01} = 0.0$
Age in summer	12.5 years	12.0 years		–

again acceptable values, Cronbach's alpha = 0.89 for autonomy support, 0.84 for competence support, 0.87 for student-teacher relatedness and 0.86 for student-student relatedness. Cronbach's alpha for the PRC-scale was 0.79.

2.2 Data Analysis

Due to the clustered and unbalanced design as well as the theoretical and statistical non-independence of the four BPN variables, the data structure is rather complex. Thus, Bayesian modelling has been applied which is particularly able to handle those problems. The Bayesian approach, named after the rev. Thomas Bayes (1702–1761), has a number of advantages over classical ('frequentist') statistical null-hypothesis testing, which we can use to address our problem. First of all, Bayesian statistics tests the probability of a hypothesis directly on the data, rather than testing the probability of the data given a null-hypothesis which is never true, as in the classical approach. Moreover, Bayes theorem takes into account prior beliefs which are specified as distribution functions for all parameters that are estimated in a given statistical model. This is a critical step in the analysis: Technically, the defining of so-called "*prior* probability functions" (i.e. our beliefs with regard to the outcomes, based on our experience and previous research, expressed in mathematical form) makes it possible to directly quantify the probability distribution of the estimates (the so-called *posterior* distribution function), and the more realistically this distribution is defined, the more accurate are the posterior estimates. In classical statistical analysis, the same probability is assigned over the infinite range of possible values, which does not really make sense and leads to overestimation. Prudently chosen prior distribution functions (or short: "priors") mitigate overfitting (i.e. an overestimation of the results). Another important feature of Bayesian statistics is that the posterior estimates are derived from *simulations* of generated data, based on the distribution parameters of the *observed* data. Those simulations are run several times with a huge number of iterations, often more than 20.000, and the results of the simulations are then cross-validated with the observed data. If the deviation between the two sets of estimates, the observed and the simulated, is small, we have good reason to trust the simulation and the parameter estimates derived and can directly inspect the uncertainty attached to each estimate. Thus, if (a) the simulation worked (which is not a given since misspecified models often collapse) and if (b) the uncertainty associated with an estimate is low, i.e. the posterior distribution function has a low standard deviation and the credibility interval does not include zero), the sign of the parameter estimates indicating a positive or negative effect from unbalanced groups can be trusted.

In study A, data have been treated on class-level, accounting for the different settings of those ten courses that have been run over three summers. In study B,

Table 3 Descriptive results summary table for outcome variable PRC in the two models

Gender	Context	Enquiry	Mean	SD	N[a]
PRC Study A (within-subjects design)					
Female	Normal	–	3.222	0.792	164
	EOtC	–	4.019	0.647	167
Male	Normal	–	3.163	0.832	107
	EOtC	–	4.045	0.592	112
PRC Study B (between-subjects design)					
Female	Normal	Fall	3.050	1.237	4
		Spring	2.850	0.915	4
		Summer	2.700	0.503	4
	EOtC	Fall	4.042	0.517	12
		Spring	4.135	0.786	10
		Summer	3.923	0.815	13
Male	Normal	Fall	3.093	0.563	7
		Spring	3.700	0.533	6
		Summer	3.240	1.135	5
	EOtC	Fall	3.755	0.582	22
		Spring	4.168	0.616	19
		Summer	3.741	0.696	17

[a] In study A, two cases needed to be deleted for incomplete data for the calculation of the centred predictor variables

data have been modelled on the individual subject level, i.e. taking the individual children's learning experiences into consideration.[3]

3 Results

3.1 Descriptive Results and Correlation Analysis

Table 3 summarizes the descriptive results for the outcome variable PRC, factored on gender, group and enquiry in the respective studies.

It can be seen that in both studies (the within-subjects design A and the between-subjects design B) the relevance of the teaching content was perceived higher in the EOtC context. In study B, the effect is constant over the school year, with a moderate

---

[3] A more detailed description of the analytical approach and technical information for the model can be obtained from the corresponding author.

Table 4 Pearson correlation matrix of the four compositional explanatory variables A, C, RT, RS for the two models

Study A, within-subject design, n = 281

		A		C		RT		RS
A	Pearson's r	–	–	–	–	–	–	–
	$\log(BF_{10})$	–	–	–	–	–	–	–
C	Pearson's r	0.749	***	–	–	–	–	–
	$\log(BF_{10})$	221.19	–	–	–	–	–	–
RT	Pearson's r	0.693	***	0.595	***	–	–	–
	$\log(BF_{10})$	175.51	–	115.545	–	–	–	–
RS	Pearson's r	0.217	***	0.168	***	0.242	***	–
	$\log(BF_{10})$	10.18	–	4.872	–	13.57	–	–

Study B, between-subject design, n = 48

		A		C		RT		RS
A	Pearson's r	–	–	–	–	–	–	–
	$\log(BF_{10})$	–	–	–	–	–	–	–
C	Pearson's r	0.729	***	–	–	–	–	–
	$\log(BF_{10})$	137.73	–	–	–	–	–	–
RT	Pearson's r	0.596	***	0.576	***	–	–	–
	$\log(BF_{10})$	78.95	–	71.867	–	–	–	–
RS	Pearson's r	0.323	***	0.232	***	0.248	***	–
	$\log(BF_{10})$	17.7	–	7.383	–	9.075	–	–

* $\log(BF_{10}) > \log(10)$, ** $\log(BF_{10}) > \log(30)$, *** $\log(BF_{10}) > \log(100)$. The Bayes Factor ($BF_{10}$) quantifies the amount by which we should prefer the hypothesis that there is a correlation (H_1) over the Null-Hypothesis (that there is no correlation) H_0 (thus the direction 1–0 in the subscript). We log-transformed the values just for cosmetic reasons to avoid huge numbers. The cut-off points marked with the asterisk can be interpreted analogously to the classical p-value in the Pearson correlation matrix despite its different meaning

peak at mid-term (spring) and a slight decline towards the end of the school year for the boys in the Normal group.

Table 4 displays the correlation matrix of the four explanatory BPN-variables. It can be seen that the Pearson's r is rather constant across the two studies.

3.2 Main Effects

The simulation worked just fine for all parameters in both studies. Figure 1 displays the 95% credible intervals for the respective parameters in the above specified models.

In study A, of the main effects "gender" and "context", only "context" is credible. The students' estimated score for the EOtC is about 0.3 units higher on the 5-point

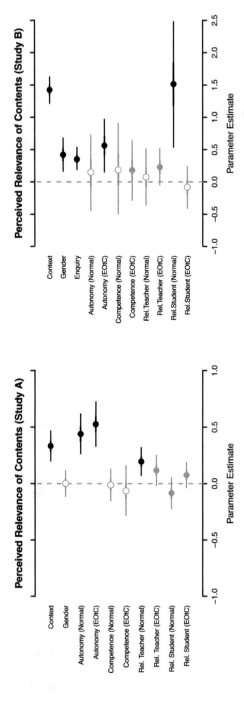

Fig. 1 The two panels display the highest probability densities for main effects context, gender and time-point of enquiry (study B only), and interaction effects of the four explanatory basic psychological needs variables with context (Normal/EOtC) in the two studies. Shading, whether 50% of credible interval (CRI; grey with open circle), 95% CRI (grey with closed circle), or neither (black) do overlap 0. Black dots indicate of a strong association between the outcome and explanatory variable

PRC Likert scale than in the normal school setting, adding statistical credibility to the above-mentioned descriptive results. The relative effect size (for an explanation cf. footnote [†] in Table 5) of 4.9 is medium, and there is no risk of a wrong sign (type-S error, Gelman & Carlin, 2014). In study B, the students in the EOtC group have on average 1.4 higher unit values on the five unit PRC-scale than their peers in the normal school setting, with a particularly high relative effect size of 13.7, with virtually zero probability of a type S error. Different from the short-term within-subject design, a relatively moderate gender effect (3.2) can be determined in the between-subject study B, with boys benefiting on average 0.4 units more from the EOtC setting. Moreover, the time point of enquiry seems to be of some importance. As Table 3 indicates, the midterm measures in spring for PRC tend to be higher compared to the baseline in fall and the measure at the end of the school year in summer, with one exception: the girls' values in the control group seem to decline in PRC from fall to spring.

3.3 Interaction Effects

The interaction effects for group differences with respect to the four basic psychological needs values (autonomy and competence support, relatedness with respect to peers and teachers) are interesting: In both studies, autonomy support has by far the greatest relative importance on perceived practical relevance of the content PRC.

In study A, autonomy support shows moderate relative importance on how relevant the students perceive the taught content, which holds true in both teaching settings, however on a slightly higher level in the EOtC group. In study B, autonomy support shows a moderate effect on PRC in the EOtC group (rel. effect size 2.7, type-S error 0.4%). Most interestingly, the relative importance of perceived competence support does not show any effect on PRC in neither study.

In study A, the students' relatedness with the teachers (RT) seem to matter in the normal school setting but not in EOtC. We can deem a moderate relative effect (3.1) with essentially no risk of type-S error for the within-subjects study. In study B, no effect can be attributed to RT in neither context.

The reverse seems to hold true for relatedness with peers (RS). In Study A, RS appears to have no relative importance in neither teaching context. However, in study B, a moderate relative effect (3.1) can be observed for the students in the normal classes.

Table 5 Parameter estimates of main and interaction effects

Parameter	d	s	2.5%	97.5%	Type S error (%)[a]	Rel. effect size[b] $\left\|\frac{d}{s}\right\|$
Study A, within-subject design, n = 281, Bayesian $P = 0.52$						
Main effects:						
Gender	0.002	0.058	−0.112	0.116	49.2	0.0
Context	**0.332**	**0.068**	**0.198**	**0.466**	**0.0**	**4.9**
Interaction effects:						
Autonomy (Normal)	**0.438**	**0.09**	**0.263**	**0.615**	**0.0**	**4.9**
Autonomy (EOtC)	**0.525**	**0.1**	**0.328**	**0.723**	**0.0**	**5.2**
Competence (Normal)	−0.013	0.071	−0.153	0.127	42.6	-0.2
Competence (EOtC)	−0.064	0.113	−0.287	0.157	28.4	-0.6
Rel. teacher (Normal)	**0.194**	**0.063**	**0.071**	**0.317**	**0.1**	**3.1**
Rel. teacher (EOtC)	0.116	0.067	−0.016	0.25	4.1	1.7
Rel. student (Normal)	−0.085	0.07	−0.222	0.052	11.3	-1.2
Rel. student (EOtC)	0.075	0.056	−0.035	0.185	8.9	1.3
Random effects:						
mu_alpha	0.144	0.349	−0.545	0.829	–	–
Residuals						
sigma_alpha	3.206	0.774	2.094	5.066	–	–
sigma	0.599	0.019	0.564	0.638	–	–
Study B, between-subject design, n = 48, Bayesian $P = 0.62$						
Main effects:						
Gender	**0.421**	**0.132**	**0.164**	**0.68**	**0.1**	**3.2**
Context	**1.422**	**0.104**	**1.215**	**1.623**	**0.0**	**13.7**
Enquiry	**0.355**	**0.088**	**0.191**	**0.532**	**0.0**	**4.0**
Interaction effects:						
Autonomy (Normal)	0.144	0.299	−0.443	0.725	31.3	0.5
Autonomy (EOtC)	**0.563**	**0.209**	**0.153**	**0.967**	**0.4**	**2.7**

(continued)

Table 5 (continued)

Parameter	d	s	2.5%	97.5%	Type S error (%)[a]	Rel. effect size[b] $\left\|\frac{d}{s}\right\|$
Competence (Normal)	0.192	0.355	−0.499	0.905	29.5	0.5
Competence (EOtC)	0.18	0.236	−0.285	0.639	22.1	0.8
Rel. teacher (Normal)	0.075	0.221	−0.357	0.512	36.7	0.3
Rel. teacher (EOtC)	0.232	0.142	−0.044	0.514	4.8	1.6
Rel. student (Normal)	**1.512**	**0.494**	**0.538**	**2.481**	**0.1**	**3.1**
Rel. student (EOtC)	−0.081	0.165	−0.41	0.239	31.1	-0.5
Random effects:						
mu_alpha	0.341	0.357	−0.353	1.049	–	–
Residuals:						
sigma_alpha	0.416	0.14	0.078	0.684	–	–
sigma	0.61	0.078	0.475	0.775	–	–

[a] The probability that the estimate has the incorrect sign

[b] A ratio of $\left|\frac{d}{s}\right| > 2$ is considered a noteworthy relative and thus context-specific statistical effect and displayed in bold letters (Gelman & Carlin, 2014). A ratio > 4 indicates very trustworthy and big effects

4   Discussion

4.1   Practical Relevance of Science Teaching and Basic Psychological Needs Satisfaction

The considerably strong main effect of teaching context in favour of EOtC in both, the within-subject design and the between-subject design on the PRC adds another consistent piece to the puzzle of positive effects of EOtC compared to 'normal' schooling reported in a review by Becker et al. (2017), and empirical results published since (Barfod & Bentsen, 2018; Bølling et al., 2018; Kuo et al., 2018a, b; Schneller et al., 2017; Schneller et al., 2017). In line with the above referenced studies, we did not find any sizeable gender effects with respect to how relevant the students did perceive the teaching in science class in the within-subjects design. However, gender matters in study B, as does the time-point of enquiry due to the nature of the longitudinal design in study B. To our knowledge, the gender effect with boys benefiting more than girls in the longitudinal design but not in the short-term intervention, cannot be sensibly explained with reference to existing research from a theoretical perspective. But given the unbalanced data and the small number of observations in the gender-split groups in study B (4 girls and 7 boys in the control group), the main effect for gender cannot be deemed practically significant despite the stable statistical effect.

The analysis of the relative importance of the basic psychological needs-satisfaction variables ("autonomy support (A)", "competence support (C)", "student-teacher relatedness (RT)", and "student-student relatedness (RS)") in each respective context in the two studies yields interesting results: Here, we can see consistent patterns across the studies.

Most obviously, competence support does not seem to substantially contribute to how relevant the students perceived the teaching, in neither study. This is surprising, since perceived competence support and perceived autonomy support are highly correlated (cf. Table 3), and it could well be argued that the perceived support for the mastery of a taught subject (competence) should make it appear more practically relevant. Yet, the results show that the teacher-centred competence-approach is not the driving force for perceived practical relevance of the teaching contents, and the data suggest furthermore, that teacher-student relations do not substantially contribute to the perceived relevance of the teaching contents, and if so, then only in the normal school setting in the within-subjects design.

It is, however, more in line with our expectations that peer relations (RS) have little influence on how relevant students perceive the teaching in science classes, and if so, then only in the normal school context. There, RS can be deemed more important than in the EOtC context, where the educational setting is enriched with other values. In her analysis of 334 EOtC settings in England, Waite (2011) associates personal values with the outdoors including "freedom and fun; ownership and autonomy; authenticity; love of rich sensory environment and physicality in pedagogical practice". Those personal values make outdoor learning less dependent on social relations, be it with peers, or with teachers.

What is driving basic psychological needs for perceived practical relevance of content overall is clearly perceived autonomy support. Our data strongly suggest that the level of perceived A support can explain the practical relevance of the teaching especially in the EOtC context, in both the within-subjects design and the between-subjects design. The fact that this effect does not show in the between-subjects design in study B might again be partially explained by the nature of the research design rather than by a substantial or theoretical difference between within- or between-subjects design or the type of intervention, i.e. short term (within) or long-term (between). A qualitative analysis of the perceived science teaching in study A shows that the students' positive experiences in the 'normal' science classes can be attributed to teaching forms that use experiential, hands-on learning methods, often in the near outdoor environments of the schools (Dettweiler et al., 2017a, b). This additionally hints at a potential selection bias in the data of study A: the teachers, who are willing to go the extra mile to enrol their students in this program, are certainly more likely to apply alternative teaching methods, i.e. deliver science classes in more enriched classroom settings than the average teacher is prone to. This can be shown in the piloting of study A with a sample of n = 84, where we focused on the analysis of the motivational behaviour of students enrolled in the intervention. The students' self-determination index (Müller et al., 2007) in normal science classes with enriched classroom settings was considerably higher than the empirical baseline of the validation study (Dettweiler et al., 2015). The normal group in study B did not experience such enriched classroom settings, which might explain the missing effect of perceived A support in the normal school setting in the between-subjects design.

We can conclude that this is the first study in EOtC that applies the same BPN-measures in a cross-sectional short-term within-subjects intervention and a longitudinal between-subject intervention. That the relative importance of BPN-satisfaction for the PRC is virtually identical in both studies, i.e. cross-sectional and longitudinal, is an important finding for EOtC practice and research and adds to closing a gap in conceptual understanding of short-term and long-term EOtC interventions.

4.2 EOtC and 21st Century Skills

Our data confirm findings by Lemley et al. (2014), who identified the students' autonomy support and perceived relevance of material as critical for the students' motivation and learning attitude in 21st century classrooms. The criteria that create such enriched classrooms, i.e. offering the students a flexible learning space with multimedia materials, and opportunities for networking and collaboration, can also be identified in the two EOtC contexts described above (cf. Table 1). We might thus conclude that EOtC can well be understood within the theoretical frame of 21st century skills and that future research and practice should in fact extend the scope and explicitly include the outdoors as a viable teaching arena in the transformation of K-12 science education.

It appears that teaching science outdoors is less dependent on the students' perceived competence support, i.e. naturally less teacher-centred, and less vulnerable to the students' distraction through (bad) peer relations. The flexibility—and maybe also the complexity—of the outdoor learning space certainly adds into the equation that lets science education in EOtC appear to be of more practical relevant to the students. They are learning in the real world with obviously real examples.

4.3 Limitations

There are a number of limitations to the results of this study.

On the design-level, both studies rely on an imbalanced sample with respect to gender, and a too small sample in study B to meaningfully interpret gender effects. Moreover, study B has an overall too small sample with yet another imbalance in the control- and intervention-groups. The particularly high relative context-effect reported above should thus be seen critically.

Due to different hierarchical data- and time-structures in the two studies, we were not able to directly test the effect of the design itself—within-subjects or between-subjects—as a factor in one model. This might have been beneficial for the subsequent research question if there is a substantial difference between the two designs, i.e. ways to approach EOtC in practice.

With respect to the statistical analyses, a hierarchical/multilevel Bayesian structural equations model (SEM) would have been favourable to account for the latent variable structures in the psychological constructs and the hierarchical clusters. However, this was not possible because of high correlations and non-independence of the explanatory variables, since the demand for independence of the predictors in SEM would have been violated. But more importantly, the rather sparse data in study B did not allow SEM.

Next steps are clearly to collect balanced data for comparison of within-subject and between-subject designs for normal and EOtC science teaching, to perform follow-up design studies for measuring the 'sustainability' of EOtC over time, compared to other 21st century classroom settings, and to include controlled academic achievement measures in the design.

5 Conclusion

We can conclude that the practical relevance of science teaching in EOtC contexts is perceived higher than in normal classroom settings, both in the short-term, cross-sectional within-subjects design as well as in the long-term, longitudinal between-subjects design. This can be best explained by the degree of the students perceived autonomy support. Thus, science teaching in EOtC fosters 21st century skills through less teacher-centration and more flexible and collaborative settings.

Recommended Further Reading

1. Beames, S., & Brown, M. (2016). *Adventurous learning: a pedagogy for a changing world*. London; New York: Routledge.
2. Brymer, E., Rogerson, M. & Barton. J. (2021): *Nature and Health. Physical Activity in Nature*, London; New York: Routledge.
3. Humberstone, B., Prince, H., & Henderson, K. (2016). *Routledge International Handbook of Outdoor Studies*. London; New York: Routledge.

Acknowledgements UD conceived and planned studies A and B, was the principal investigator and raised the funds for study A. He also analysed the data in both studies and wrote most of the manuscript. GL and CM conceived and optimized the intervention of study A, RKA contributed with respect to its theoretical frame. CM collected data in both studies, GL collected the data in study A. All authors interpreted the results. All authors contributed to the writing of different sections of the manuscript and approved its final version.

References

Assor, A., Kaplan, H., & Roth, G. (2002). Choice is good, but relevance is excellent: Autonomy-enhancing and suppressing teacher behaviours predicting students' engagement in schoolwork. *British Journal of Educational Psychology, 72*(2), 261–278. https://doi.org/10.1348/000709902 158883.

Barfod, K., & Bentsen, P. (2018). Don't ask how outdoor education can be integrated into the school curriculum; ask how the school curriculum can be taught outside the classroom. *Curriculum Perspectives, 38*(2), 151–156. https://doi.org/10.1007/s41297-018-0055-9.

Barfod, K., Bølling, M., Mygind, L., Elsborg, P., Ejbye-Ernst, N., & Bentsen, P. (2021). Reaping fruits of labour: Revisiting Education Outside the Classroom provision in Denmark upon policy and research interventions. *Urban Forestry and Urban Greening, 60*, 127044. https://doi.org/10.1016/j.ufug.2021.127044.

Barfod, K., Ejbye-Ernst, N., Mygind, L., & Bentsen, P. (2016). Increased provision of udeskole in Danish schools: An updated national population survey. *Urban Forestry and Urban Greening, 20*, 277–281. https://doi.org/10.1016/j.ufug.2016.09.012.

Becker, C. (2012). *MINT in Bewegung: Eine Fallstudie zur möglichen Integrierung von Expeditionary Learning Alpine (ELPIN) in den fächerübergreifenden gymnasialen Unterricht unter besonderer Berücksichtigung lernmotivationler und gesund-heitsrelevanter Parameter für das Fach Natur und Technik.* (Diploma), Technische Universität München, München.

Becker, C., Lauterbach, G., Spengler, S., Dettweiler, U., & Mess, F. (2017). Effects of regular classes in outdoor education settings: A systematic review on students' learning, social and health dimensions. *International Journal of Environmental Research and Public Health, 14*(5), 485. https://doi.org/10.3390/ijerph14050485.

Bentsen, P., Jensen, F. S., Mygind, E., & Randrup, T. B. (2010). The extent and dissemination of udeskole in Danish schools. *Urban Forestry and Urban Greening, 9*(3), 235–243. https://doi.org/10.1016/j.ufug.2010.02.001.

Bentsen, P., Mygind, L., Elsborg, P., Nielsen, G., & Mygind, E. (2021). Education outside the classroom as upstream school health promotion: 'Adding-in' physical activity into children's everyday life and settings. *Scandinavian Journal of Public Health*. https://doi.org/10.1177/140 3494821993715.

Bentsen, P., Mygind, E., & Randrup, T. B. (2009). Towards an understanding of udeskole: Education outside the classroom in a Danish context. *Education 3–13, 3*(37), 29–44.

Burkhardt, G., Monsour, M., Valdez, G., Gunn, C., Dawson, M., Lemke, C., Martin, C. (2003). *Literacy in the digital age: EnGauge 21st century skills for 21st century learners report.* Naperville, IL: North Central Regional Educational Laboratory (NCREL) and the Metiri Group https://firstnationspedagogy.com/engauge21st.pdf.

Bølling, M., Otte, C. R., Elsborg, P., Nielsen, G., & Bentsen, P. (2018). The association between education outside the classroom and students' school motivation: Results from a one-school-year quasi-experiment. *International Journal of Educational Research, 89*, 22–35. https://doi.org/10.1016/j.ijer.2018.03.004.

Chawla, L., & Derr, V. (2012). The development of conservation behaviors in childhood and youth. In S. D. Clayton (Ed.), *The Oxford handbook of environmental and conservation psychology* (pp. 527–555). Oxford University Press.

Darner, R. (2009). Self-determination theory as a guide to fostering environmental motivation. *Journal of Environmental Education, 40*(2), 39–49.

Deci, E. L., & Ryan, R. M. (2000). The 'what' and 'why' of goal pursuits: Human needs and the self-determination of behavior. *Psychological Inquiry, 11*, 227–268.

Deci, E. L., & Ryan, R. M. (2002). Overview of self-determination theory: An organismic dialectical perspective. In E. L. Deci & R. M. Ryan (Eds.), *Handbook of self-determination research* (pp. 3–33). University of Rochester Press.

Deci, E. L., & Vansteenkiste, M. (2004). Self-determination theory and basic need satisfaction: Understanding human development in positive psychology. *Ricerche Di Psichologia, 27*, 17–34.

Dettweiler, U., Becker, C., Auestad, B. H., Simon, P., & Kirsch, P. (2017a). Stress in school. Some Empirical hints on the circadian cortisol rhythm of children in outdoor and indoor classes. *International Journal of Environmental Research and Public Health, 14*(5), 475. https://doi.org/10.3390/ijerph14050475.

Dettweiler, U., Lauterbach, G., Becker, C., & Simon, P. (2017b). A bayesian mixed-methods analysis of basic psychological needs satisfaction through outdoor learning and its influence on motivational behavior in science class. *Frontiers in Psychology, 8*(2235). https://doi.org/10.3389/fpsyg.2017.02235.

Dettweiler, U., & Ünlü, A. (2015). *Testing the reliability and validity of a reduced Academic Self-Regulation Questionnaire (SRQ-A) in a mixed-methods approach.* Paper presented at the eighth SELF Biennial international conference, Kiel.

Dettweiler, U., Ünlü, A., Lauterbach, G., Becker, C., & Gschrey, B. (2015). Investigating the motivational behaviour of pupils during outdoor science teaching within self-determination theory. *Frontiers in Psychology, 6*(125). https://doi.org/10.3389/fpsyg.2015.00125.

European Union (EU). (2006). *Recommendations of the European Parliament and of the Council of 18 December 2006 on key competences for lifelong learning (2006/962/EC).* Brussels. http://eur-lex.europa.eu/legal-content/EN/TXT/?uri=celex%3A32006H0962.

Gelman, A., & Carlin, J. (2014). Beyond power calculations. Assessing Type S (Sign) and Type M (Magnitude) errors. *Perspectives on Psychological Science, 9*(6), 641–651. https://doi.org/10.1177/1745691614551642.

Griffin, P., McGaw, B., & Care, E. (2012). *Assessment and teaching of 21st century skills.* Springer.

Helle, M. K. (2017). *Friluftsliv i skolen. En kvalitativ studie av elevers erfaringer med friluftsliv på idrettslinjen.* (Master Thesis), Universitetet i Tromsø. http://hdl.handle.net/10037/11928.

Jordet, A. N. (1998). *Nærmiljøet som klasserom. Uteskole i teori og praksis [The local neighbourhood as classroom. 'Uteskole' in theory and praxis].* Oslo: Cappelen Akademisk Forlag.

Krasny, M. E., & Dillon, J. (2012). *Trading zones in environmental education: Creating transdisciplinary dialogue.* Peter Lang.

Kuo, M., Browning, M., Sachdeva, S., Lee, K., & Westphal, L. (2018a). Might school performance grow on trees? Examining the link between 'greenness' and academic achievement in urban high-poverty schools. *Frontiers in Psychology, 9*, 1669. https://doi.org/10.3389/fpsyg.2018.01669.

Kuo, M., Browning, M. H. E. M., & Penner, M. L. (2018b). Do lessons in nature boost subsequent classroom engagement? Refueling students in flight. *Frontiers in Psychology, 8*. https://doi.org/10.3389/fpsyg.2017.02253.

Lazowski, R. A., & Hulleman, C. S. (2016). Motivation interventions in education: A meta-analytic review. *Review of Educational Research, 86*(2), 602–640. https://doi.org/10.3102/0034654315617832.

Lemley, J. B., Schumacher, G., & Vesey, W. (2014). What learning environments best address 21st-century students' perceived needs at the secondary level of instruction? *NASSP Bulletin, 98*(2), 101–125. https://doi.org/10.1177/0192636514528748.

Müller, F., Hanfstingl, B., & Andreitz, I. (2007). *Skalen zur motivationalen Regulation beim Lernen von Schülerinnen und Schülern. Adaptierte und ergänzte Version des Academic Self-Regulation Questionnaire (SRQ-A) nach Ryan & Connell [Scales of motivational learning regulation of pupils. Adapted and extended version of the Academic Self-Regulation Questionnarie (SRQ-A) of Ryan & Connell].* Klagenfurt. http://ius.uni-klu.ac.at/inhalte/publikationen/486_IUS_Forschungsbericht_1_Motivationsskalen.pdf.

National Research Council. (2012). *Education for life and work: Developing transferable knowledge and skills in the 21st century.* The National Academies Press.

NGSS Lead States. (2013). *Next generation science standards: For states, by states.* The National Academies Press.

Nicol, R., Higgins, P., Rossi, H., & Mannion, G. (2012). *Outdoor education in Scotland: A summary of recent research*. Edinburgh. http://www.education.ed.ac.uk/outdoored/research/nicol_et_al_oe_scotland_research.pdf.

Nielsen, G., Mygind, E., Bølling, M., Otte, C. R., Schneller, M. B., Schipperijn, J., Ejbye-Ernst, N. & Bentsen, P. (2016). A quasi-experimental cross-disciplinary evaluation of the impacts of education outside the classroom on pupils' physical activity, well-being and learning: the TEACHOUT study protocol. *BMC Public Health, 16*(1), 1117. https://doi.org/10.1186/s12889-016-3780-8.

Niemiec, C. P., & Ryan, R. M. (2009). Autonomy, competence, and relatedness in the classroom. *School Field, 7*(2), 133–144. https://doi.org/10.1177/1477878509104318.

OECD. (2005). *The definition and selection of key competencies. [Executive summary]*. https://www.oecd.org/pisa/35070367.pdf.

Otte, C. R. (2018). *Perspektiver på udeskole i relation til læsning, matematik og motivation for læring*. (Ph.D), University of Copenhagen, Copenhagen.

Partnership for 21st century skills (P21). (2015). *Framework for 21st century learning*. http://www.p21.org/storage/documents/P21_framework_0515.pdf.

Rakoczy, K., Klieme, E., & Pauli, C. (2008). Die Bedeutung der wahrgenommenen Unterstützung motivationsrelevanter Bedürfnisse und des Alltagsbezugs im Mathematikunterricht für die selbstbestimmte Motivation [The meaning of perceived support for motivational needs and the practice orientation in maths teaching for self-determined motivation]. *Zeitschrift Für Pädagogische Psychologie, 22*(1), 25–35.

Reeve, J. (2009). Why teachers adopt a controlling motivating style toward students and how they can become more autonomy supportive. *Educational Psychologist, 44*(3), 159–175. https://doi.org/10.1080/00461520903028990.

Reeve, J., Jang, H., Carrell, D., Jeon, S., & Barch, J. (2004). Enhancing students' engagement by increasing teachers' autonomy support. *Motivation and Emotion, 28*(2), 147–169. https://doi.org/10.1023/B:MOEM.0000032312.95499.6f.

Scheie, E. (2017). *Den naturlige skolesekken, Årsrapport*. Oslo: natursekken. https://www.natursekken.no/c1187995/binfil/download2.php?tid=2192651.

Schneller, M. B., Bentsen, P., Nielsen, G., Brønd, J. C., Ried-Larsen, M., Mygind, E., & Schipperijn, J. (2017a). Measuring Children's Physical Activity: Compliance Using Skin-Taped Accelerometers. *Medicine and Science in Sports and Exercise, 49*(6), 1261–1269. https://doi.org/10.1249/mss.0000000000001222.

Schneller, M. B., Duncan, S., Schipperijn, J., Nielsen, G., Mygind, E., & Bentsen, P. (2017). Are children participating in a quasi-experimental education outside the classroom intervention more physically active? *BMC Public Health, 17*(1), 523. https://doi.org/10.1186/s12889-017-4430-5.

Skoven i Skolen. (2021). Udeskole i Norden. http://www.skoven-i-skolen.dk/internationalt.

Sterling, S. (2010). Learning for resilience, or the resilient learner? Towards a necessary reconciliation in a paradigm of sustainable education. *Environmental Education Research, 16*(5–6), 511–528. https://doi.org/10.1080/13504622.2010.505427.

Taylor, G., Jungert, T., Mageau, G. A., Schattke, K., Dedic, H., Rosenfield, S., & Koestner, R. (2014). A self-determination theory approach to predicting school achievement over time: the unique role of intrinsic motivation. *Contemporary Educational Psychology, 39*(4), 342–358. https://doi.org/10.1016/j.cedpsych.2014.08.002.

van de Oudeweetering, K., & Voogt, J. (2018). Teachers' conceptualization and enactment of twenty-first century competences: Exploring dimensions for new curricula. *The Curriculum Journal, 29*(1), 116–133. https://doi.org/10.1080/09585176.2017.1369136.

Vansteenkiste, M., Lens, W., & Deci, E. L. (2006). Intrinsic versus extrinsic goal contents in self-determination theory: Another look at the quality of academic motivation. *Educational Psychologist, 41*(1), 19–31. https://doi.org/10.1207/s15326985ep4101_4.

Voogt, J., & Roblin, N. P. (2012). A comparative analysis of international frameworks for 21st century competences: Implications for national curriculum policies. *Journal of Curriculum Studies*, 44, 299–321. https://doi.org/10.1080/00220272.2012.668938.

Waite, S. (2011). Teaching and learning outside the classroom: personal values, alternative pedagogies and standards. *Education 3–13, 39*(1), 65–82. https://doi.org/10.1080/030042709032
06141.
Waite, S., Bølling, M., & Bentsen, P. (2015). Comparing apples and pears?: A conceptual framework
for understanding forms of outdoor learning through comparison of English Forest Schools and
Danish udeskole. *Environmental Education Research,* 1–25. https://doi.org/10.1080/13504622.
2015.1075193.
Wals, A. E., Brody, M., Dillon, J., & Stevenson, R. B. (2014). Convergence between science and
environmental education. *Science, 344*(6184), 583–584.

Ulrich Dettweiler is professor of pedagogy at the University of
Stavanger, Norway. His research focuses on the effects of Education Outside the Classroom on children's learning and he is
especially interested in the psychological and bio-physiological
mechanisms associated with learning processes in nature.

Gabriele Lauterbach holds a PhD-stipend in Educational
Science at the University of Stavanger, Norway. In her project,
she tries to map *uteskole* in Norway, both with respect to its
dissemination and its pedagogy, and is especially interested in
the inclusive potential of Education Outside the Classroom.

Christoph Mall has a doctoral degree in sports science and works as a lecturer at the Technical University in Munich. He is doing research on physical activity, health and learning motivation with a special focus on students' physical activity levels, their stress response and learning motivation during Education Outside the Classroom.

Ruth Kermish-Allen began her career as a forest ecologist and serves now as Executive Director at the Maine Mathematics and Science Alliance. She has extensive experience in STEM education research, project development, implementation, and evaluation.

Teacher Competencies in Focus

Research and Documentation of Outdoor-Based Teaching in Teacher Education—The EOT Project

Christina Wolf, Patrick Kunz, and Nicolas Robin

1 The Perspective of Outdoor Teaching

During the last two decades, a great number of studies showed that outdoor education programs could positively affect pupils' and teachers' attitudes, motivation and self-efficacy (see Clusters I–IV above). However, significantly fewer articles were published in this context on pre-service teachers and even fewer on teacher educators. Yet, this scarcity of research is surprising, given the twin facts that "learning is particularly successful if it is situated" (Karst & Dickhäuser, 2021, 23) and the empirical evidence that "greater expertise is favourable for the quality of teaching if the depth of processing and the degree of interconnectedness of the professional knowledge are high" (Wilhelm, 2021, 28). Given the potential positive impact of outdoor learning on pupils, teachers and teacher educators, exploring outdoor learning and teaching in teacher training seems very important.

The scientific literature on the subject gives us a more complex picture. On the one side, in-service teachers describe how outdoor learning with their classes contributes to their own sense of personal wellbeing and rejuvenate their sense of professional identity (Cosgriff, 2017; Marchant et al., 2019; see Barfod & Mygind: *Udeskole*—Regular Teaching Outside the Classroom in this volume). Marchant et al. (2019) concluded that taking pupils outdoors on a weekly basis increased teachers' job satisfaction. On the other side, literature shows us the challenges or barriers encountered by educators in the implementation of outdoor school-based activities. Besides the consideration of practical aspects regarding resources, planning

C. Wolf (✉) · P. Kunz · N. Robin
Pädagogische Hochschule St.Gallen, Notkerstrasse 27, 9000 St. Gallen, Switzerland
e-mail: Christina.Wolf@phsg.ch

P. Kunz
e-mail: patrick.kunz@phsg.ch

N. Robin
e-mail: Nicolas.Robin@phsg.ch

© The Author(s) 2022
R. Jucker and J. von Au (eds.), *High-Quality Outdoor Learning*,
https://doi.org/10.1007/978-3-031-04108-2_14

and risk assessment (school culture), teachers' main barrier seems to be their confidence to teach outdoors (Scott et al., 2015). According to experiences and knowledge, teachers wish to have more method-related information to integrate outdoor activities (Torkos, 2018). Researchers examining outdoor teaching in teacher training have concluded that "teacher training should include outdoor learning and teaching". Researchers stress the importance of including outdoor learning and teaching into initial teacher training and to facilitate interdisciplinarity, use of local resources and outdoor learning environments for teacher training (Feille, 2017; Hursen & Islek, 2017; Kubat, 2017; Tuuling et al., 2019). So far, however, there is no record of the status quo of outdoor teaching in teacher training.

2   The Potential of Outdoor Teaching and Learning

Authors and researchers have pointed out the importance of outdoor education for the personal development of present and future generations, especially in terms of attitude and behaviour in their environment and community (Louv, 2005; Rickinson et al., 2004). However, training of teachers and pre-service teachers seems not to include the transfer from research into teaching practice. More precisely, teachers and teacher educators still discuss (a) the value of using the natural and cultural environment as a context for learning in all disciplines and (b) the integration of outdoor education into the curriculum for developing environmental consciousness and maintaining motivation and well-being in the educational environment (Torkos, 2018, 211).

Centuries ago, children grew up in and learned about the natural (real) world by studying their natural environment directly. Children who got educated by teachers learned to name the things around them and to understand its roles and functions in the world with all senses stimulated.

However, today children grow up and learn in two worlds, the real and the digital world and they can choose how much time of the day they like to spend in one world or the other. Children and adults connect to the real world through multiple and diverse experiences. However, what if only experiences in and knowledge about the real nature would enable us to move more confidently in the natural world? What does reducing the duration and intensity of natural primary experiences in the outdoors mean for children's personal development and self-confidence to act and interact in the real world?

Louv concluded in his book *Last child in the woods* (2005) that less time in nature increases the likelihood of developing what he called 'nature deficit disorder', which is associated with various mental and/or physical illnesses (Donovan et al., 2019; Yang et al., 2019). Research showed that children (0–8 years-olds) (Rideout, 2017; Rideout & Robb, 2020) and adolescents (Rideout et al., 2010) spend an increasing amount of time with screens and/or media use. This reduces the time they can spend building social, emotional, physical and mental health foundations (OECD, 2019, 46–57). Researchers correlated daily media use with increasing risks of poorer health conditions (Mathers et al., 2009), poorer sleep efficiency (Fobian et al., 2016) or metabolic and cardiovascular diseases (Hardy et al., 2010; Martinez-Gomez et al., 2009, 2011). Those studies clearly suggest a reduction in screen time and online consumption as well as in sedentary behaviour for a large part of the day.

However, learning in the outdoors, with and about the outdoor environment can improve schoolchildren's social and health foundations and their environmental attitude and behaviour through outdoor learning (Becker et al., 2017). When, if not now, should we be thinking about how to connect schoolchildren with both the real natural world and the digital worlds?

Although there is quite a debate about how and when to introduce children and students to the digital world, we may be missing the opportunity to *first connect* children with the natural environment. The natural and cultural environment, including community and society, provides the adequate context for intra- and interdisciplinary learning. Children can build a connection to the environment and link their knowledge and curiosity to think about present and future problems as well as to imagine possible solutions. Without being connected to their natural and cultural enviroment, children might be unable to understand the complexity of the world and (self-) confidently act in it.

This is the great potential of outdoor learning and teaching. It supports students, especially young students, to connect to their natural learning environment through primary learning experiences with all senses. In the students' educational journey, these multi-sensory learning experiences form the basic framework for knowledge about their environment. These educational journeys are supported by teachers who can move flexibly and confidently within and between the natural and the digital worlds, and so provide opportunities for students to learn this flexibility and self-confidence themselves (Fig. 1).

Teacher education needs to provide pre-service teachers with knowledge and opportunities to practice outdoor teaching in different disciplines and on an interdisciplinary level. Regarding outdoor teaching, teachers themselves need to make their own outdoor learning experiences, if not during their own time at school as pupils, then at the latest during their teacher training.

3 Research and Development Project 'Enabling Outdoor-Based Teaching' (EOT) in Teacher Education in Switzerland

Why is it important to integrate and develop outdoor teaching in teacher education? For many years, educational research has provided us with numerous empirical data regarding the positive effects of teaching and learning in nature. But, do pre-service teachers acquire the necessary skills for interdisciplinary teaching in nature during their teacher training? The Institute for Science Teacher Education at St. Gallen University of Teacher Education is establishing a new research area on this topic.

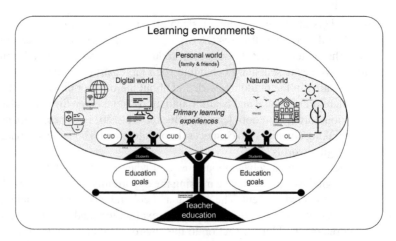

Fig. 1 The potential of outdoor learning and teaching. Regarding education, young students grow up with natural and digital world experiences. Outdoor leaning (OL) supports students to connect to the natural world, especially through primary learning experiences with all senses. The confident use of digitalization (CUD) supports students to learn how to work in the digital world. The natural, the digital and the personal world, including family and friends, form learning environments. Outdoor learning and a confident use of digitalization are essential foundations for students' personal and academic development. The teacher has to find the right balance between the education goals for the natural and the digital learning environments. The professional skills of the teacher influence the natural and digital learning environments of students. Teacher education provides the foundation for developing teachers' professional skills in the digital *and* in the natural world. Icons are free downloads from https://thenounproject.com

In this context, we stress the importance to re-emphasise interdisciplinary teaching outside the classroom as one central aspect of teaching practice, and not to neglect it alongside the implementation of the new curricula and the initiatives on digitalisation. One would think that the training of future teachers in teaching outside the classroom and especially in nature would be self-evident, at least in cycles 1 and 2 (Kindergarten to 6th grade). Unfortunately, this is not the case. Together with the foundations Mercator Schweiz, Salvia and SILVIVA, the new research project enables us to investigate how pre-service teachers are trained to implement school-based outdoor learning and teaching.

The project 'Enabling outdoor-based teaching' (EOT) follows three main goals:

1. To document the current state of teaching practice on 'outdoor teaching' in teacher education at nursery and primary level (cycle 1 and 2, Kindergarten to 6th grade) in Switzerland
2. To transfer current didactical research findings into teacher education and
3. To support a community of teacher educators who share knowledge and experience about methods, skills, and issues that arise on the topic.

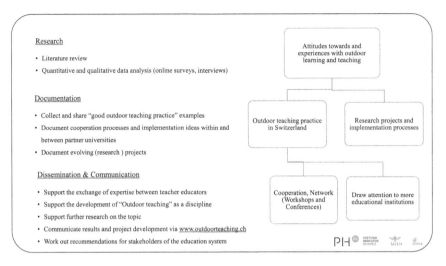

Fig. 2 The figure shows the main objectives of the EOT project (white squares) within their operational levels (research, documentation, dissemination and communication)

Started in November 2019, the project team strives to implement those three goals within five years. The EOT project operates on four levels: Research, Documentation, Dissemination and Communication (overview of the EOT project, see Fig. 2).

Research:

As a basis, a literature review shall reveal what we know from research about outdoor teaching in teacher education in general (see Wolf et al., submitted).

We examine attitudes about and experiences with outdoor teaching among pre-service teachers and teacher educators in Switzerland. We are interested in possible differences between the start and end of pre-service teachers' training. What is common and what is different about outdoor teaching in different disciplines? How do we support interdisciplinary outdoor teaching within teacher training? We tackle these questions with surveys and interviews with pre-service teachers and teacher educators from the participating Universities of Teacher Education.

Data is collected from a representative number of Universities of Teacher Education, from the German, French and Italian speaking part of Switzerland (see Fig. 3).

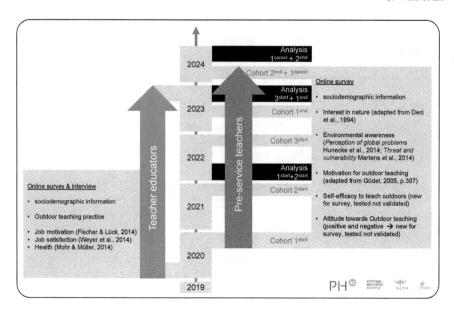

Fig. 3 Research design of the EOT project, which started in November 2019 and ends October 2024. We collect quantitative and qualitative data (online survey and interview) from volunteer teacher educators between 2020 and 2023. We survey attitudes and experiences from volunteer pre-service teachers at the start (cohorts 1, 2, 3) and end of their three-year training (cohorts 1, 2) and if possible at the start of their teaching career (cohort 1) (longitudinal study design).

Documentation:

Our research is part of a process, in which the critical and fruitful exchange of the participants' experiences and thoughts leads to new ideas and suggestions for implementation and further research on outdoor learning and teaching, which gives the project a clear developmental character.

We document the teaching practice of participating teacher educators to put together a collection of 'Good outdoor teaching practice' examples, which can support the access and distribution of outdoor teaching in the several teacher education curricula in Switzerland (at cycle 1 and 2, Kindergarten to 6th grade). We further want to document as many collaboration processes as possible to develop a recommendation for a fundamental and holistic integration of outdoor teaching into teacher education.

The documentation process also reveals questions about the relevance of outdoor-based teaching as a discipline in teacher education.

Dissemination:

Teacher educators from partner universities can participate in workshops and conferences, which support and facilitate exchange of expertise and questioning on theory and practice. This way, we try to support a sustainable integration of outdoor teaching into teacher education.

We support the establishment of a teacher educator community that shares outdoor learning and teaching ideas and material and creates collaborations between experts from different disciplines and between partner universities.

Communication

Examining the attitudes and experiences of pre-service teachers and teacher educators in the EOT project provides a basis for educational research to go deeper into the pedagogical and didactical, holistic method of outdoor teaching.

In the EOT project, we want to collect and document the know-how of experts and make it accessible to more teacher educators and thus also to more pre-service teachers. With that, we hope to encourage the distribution of available expertise.

One aim of the EOT project is to provide recommendations for the teacher education curriculum based on the results of the surveys and the collection of 'good outdoor teaching practice' examples. The EOT project draws attention to the *know-how* and *know-why* of outdoor learning and teaching and can inform stakeholders of the education system, especially school headmasters, Cantonal offices of education and Directorates of Education. With that, the EOT project supports the efforts and goals of SILVIVA, the national competence centre for nature-based learning, who is a core partner of the project.

Recommended Further Readings

1. Wolf, Ch., Kunz, P. & Robin, N. (forthcoming). Outdoor teaching in teacher education—A literature review. (submitted to the *Journal of Environmental Education*).
2. Barnes & Shirley (2007) Strangely familiar: cross-curricular and creative thinking in teacher education. *Improving Schools, 10*(2), 162–179. https://doi. org/10.1177/1365480207078580.
3. Thomas & Munge (2017) Innovative outdoor fieldwork pedagogies in the higher education sector: Optimising the use of technology. *Journal of Outdoor and Environmental Education, 20*, 7–13. https://doi.org/10.1007/BF03400998

Acknowledgements We like to thank the project partners for their participation and support and we thank our institute team for the creative discussions.

References

Becker, C., Lauterbach, G., Spengler, S., Dettweiler, U., & Mess, F. (2017). Effects of regular classes in outdoor education settings: A systematic review on students' learning, social and health dimensions. *International Journal of Environmental Research and Public Health, 14*(5), 485. PubMed. https://doi.org/10.3390/ijerph14050485.

Cosgriff, M. (2017). The rewards of professional change: Two primary school teachers' experiences of transforming outdoor education. *Teachers and Curriculum, 17*(1), 23–29. https://doi.org/10.15663/tandc.v17i1.172.

Donovan, G. H., Michael, Y. L., Gatziolis, D., Mannetje, A. 't, & Douwes, J. (2019). Association between exposure to the natural environment, rurality, and attention-deficit hyperactivity disorder in children in New Zealand: A linkage study. *The Lancet Planetary Health, 3*(5), e226–e234. https://doi.org/10.1016/S2542-5196(19)30070-1.

Feille, K. (2017). Teaching in the field: What teacher professional life histories tell about how they learn to teach in the outdoor learning environment. *Research in Science Education, 47*(3), 603–620. https://doi.org/10.1007/s11165-016-9519-9.

Fischer, L., & Lück, H. E. (2014). Allgemeine Arbeitszufriedenheit. *Zusammenstellung Sozialwissenschaftlicher Items Und Skalen (ZIS).* https://doi.org/10.6102/zis1.

Fobian, A. D., Avis, K., & Schwebel, D. C. (2016). Impact of media use on adolescent sleep efficiency. *Journal of Developmental and Behavioral Pediatrics : JDBP, 37*(1), 9–14. PubMed. https://doi.org/10.1097/DBP.0000000000000239.

Hardy, L. L., Denney-Wilson, E., Thrift, A. P., Okely, A. D., & Baur, L. A. (2010). Screen time and metabolic risk factors among adolescents. *Archives of Pediatrics and Adolescent Medicine, 164*(7), 643–649. https://doi.org/10.1001/archpediatrics.2010.88.

Hunecke, M., Blöbaum, A., Matthies, E., & Höger, R. (2014). Problemwahrnehmung global. *Zusammenstellung Sozialwissenschaftlicher Items Und Skalen (ZIS).* https://doi.org/10.6102/zis176.

Hursen, C., & Islek, D. (2017). The effect of a school-based outdoor education program on visual arts teachers' success and self-efficacy beliefs. *South African Journal of Education, 37*(3), 1–17. ehh.

Karst, K., & Dickhäuser, O. (2021). Die Perspektive der Pädagogischen Psychologie auf die Gestaltung qualitätsvollen Unterrichts [The perspective of educational psychology on the design of quality teaching]. In V. Reinhardt, M. Rehm & M. Wilhelm (Eds.), *Wirksamer Fachunterricht. Eine metaanalytische Betrachtung von Expertisen aus 17 Schulfächern [Effective Teaching of Subjects. A meta-analytical consideration of expert reports from 17 school subjects],* 17–25. Schneider Verlag Hohengehren.

Kubat, U. (2017). Determination of science teachers' opinions about outdoor education. *Online Submission, 3*(12), 344–354.

Louv, R. (2005). *The last child in the woods: Saving our children from nature-deficit disorder* (pp. 336). Algonquin Books. ISBN 1565123913.

Marchant, E., Todd, C., Cooksey, R., Dredge, S., Jones, H., Reynolds, D., Stratton, G., Dwyer, R., Lyons, R., & Brophy, S. (2019). Curriculum-based outdoor learning for children aged 9–11: A qualitative analysis of pupils' and teachers' views. *PLoS ONE, 14*(5). APA PsycInfo. https://doi.org/10.1371/journal.pone.0212242.

Martens, T., Rost, J., & Gresele, C. (2014). Bedrohung und Vulnerabilität. *Zusammenstellung Sozialwissenschaftlicher Items Und Skalen (ZIS).* https://doi.org/10.6102/zis179.

Martinez-Gomez, D., Ortega, F. B., Ruiz, J. R., Vicente-Rodriguez, G., Veiga, O. L., Widhalm, K., Manios, Y., Béghin, L., Valtueña, J., Kafatos, A., Molnar, D., Moreno, L. A., Marcos, A., Castillo, M. J., Sjöström, M., & on behalf of the HELENA study group. (2011). Excessive sedentary time and low cardiorespiratory fitness in European adolescents: The HELENA study. *Archives of Disease in Childhood, 96*(3), 240. https://doi.org/10.1136/adc.2010.187161.

Martinez-Gomez, D., Tucker, J., Heelan, K. A., Welk, G. J., & Eisenmann, J. C. (2009). Associations between sedentary behavior and blood pressure in young children. *Archives of Pediatrics & Adolescent Medicine, 163*(8), 724–730. https://doi.org/10.1001/archpediatrics.2009.90.

Mathers, M., Canterford, L., Olds, T., Hesketh, K., Ridley, K., & Wake, M. (2009). Electronic media use and adolescent health and well-being: Cross-sectional community study. *Academic Pediatrics, 9*(5), 307–314. https://doi.org/10.1016/j.acap.2009.04.003.

Mohr, G., & Müller, A. (2014). Psychosomatische Beschwerden im nichtklinischen Kontext. *Zusammenstellung Sozialwissenschaftlicher Items Und Skalen (ZIS).* https://doi.org/10.6102/zis78.

OECD. (2019). *OECD Future of Education and Skills 2030: OECD Learning Compass 2030. A Series of Concept Notes* (pp. 46–57). https://www.oecd.org/education/2030-project/teaching-and-learning/learning/learning-compass-2030/OECD_Learning_Compass_2030_Concept_Note_Series.pdf.

Rickinson, M., Dillon, J., Teamey, K., Morris, M., Choi, M. Y., Sanders, D., & Benefield, P. (2004). *A review of research on outdoor learning.* London: National Foundation for Educational Research and King's College London. https://www.yumpu.com/en/document/read/44220526/a-review-of-research-on-outdoor-learning-field-studies-council.

Rideout, V., Foehr, U., & Roberts, D. (2010*). Generation M²: Media in the Lives of 8- to 18-Year-Olds.* Henry J. Kaiser Family Foundation. https://www.kff.org/wp-content/uploads/2013/01/8010.pdf.

Rideout, V. (2017). *The common sense census : Media use by kids age zero to eight.* https://www.commonsensemedia.org/sites/default/files/uploads/research/csm_zerotoeight_fullreport_release_2.pdf.

Rideout, V., & Robb, M. B. (2020). *The common sense census: Media use by kids age zero to eight.* https://www.commonsensemedia.org/sites/default/files/uploads/research/2020_zero_to_eight_census_final_web.pdf.

Scott, G. W., Boyd, M., Scott, L., & Colquhoun, D. (2015). Barriers to biological fieldwork: What really prevents teaching out of doors? *Journal of Biological Education, 49*(2), 165–178. https://doi.org/10.1080/00219266.2014.914556.

Torkos, H. (2018). Introducing new education types: Teachers' opinions on outdoor education. *Journal plus Education/Educatia plus, 20*(2), 198–212.

Tuuling, L., Õun, T., & Ugaste, A. (2019). Teachers' opinions on utilizing outdoor learning in the preschools of Estonia. *Journal of Adventure Education and Outdoor Learning, 19*(4), 358–370. https://doi.org/10.1080/14729679.2018.1553722.

Weyer, G., Hodapp, V., & Neuhäuser, S. (2014). Subjektive Zufriedenheit und Belastung von Arbeit und Beruf. *Zusammenstellung Sozialwissenschaftlicher Items Und Skalen (ZIS).* https://doi.org/10.6102/zis3.

Wilhelm, M. (2021). Wie lässt sich das vielleicht bedeutendste Emergenzphänomen, das Leben verstehen? Zur Wirksamkeit von Biologieunterricht [How can we understand perhaps the most significant emergent phenomenon, life? On the effectiveness of biology teaching]. In V. Reinhardt, M. Rehm, & M. Wilhelm (Eds.), *Wirksamer Fachunterricht. Eine metaanalytische Betrachtung von Expertisen aus 17 Schulfächern [Effective Teaching of Subjects. A meta-analytical consideration of expert reports from 17 school subjects]* (pp. 26–55). Schneider Verlag Hohengehren.

Wolf, Ch., Kunz, P., & Robin, N. (forthcoming). Outdoor teaching in teacher education—A literature review. (submitted to the *Journal of Environmental Education*).

Yang, B., Zeng, X.-W., Markevych, I., Bloom, M., Knibbs, L., Dharmage, S., Lin, S., Jalava, P., Guo, Y., Jalaludin, B., Morawska, L., Zhou, Y., Hu, L.-W., Yu, H.-Y., Yu, Y., & Dong, G.-H. (2019). Association between greenness surrounding schools and kindergartens and attention-deficit/hyperactivity disorder in children in China. *JAMA the Journal of the American Medical Association, 2*, e1917862. https://doi.org/10.1001/jamanetworkopen.2019.17862.

Christina Wolf is currently working as senior researcher at St. Gallen University of Teacher Education (Switzerland). She is the scientific leader of the project 'Enabling outdoor-based teaching' (EOT). Christina graduated in Biology (Germany, Switzerland) and animal nutrition (PhD, ETH Zurich, Switzerland). She worked in a national environmental education program with primary and secondary school students on biodiversity and climate change (GLOBE Swiss). She was an assistant lecturer for 'Animal Sciences in the World Food System' at ETH Zurich. Her current research interests are theory, practice and implementations of outdoor teaching in teacher education, education for sustainable development, and outdoor education.

Patrick Kunz is currently working as professor, developer and researcher for Science Education at the St. Gallen University of Teacher Education (Switzerland). He works as an expert for the open access journal *Progress in Science Education* (PriSE) and is member of several national professional associations for education. His current research interests and projects include, among others, STEM education, education for sustainable development, and outdoor education.

Nicolas Robin is currently working as Professor of Science Education and director of the Research Institute for Science Teacher Education at the St. Gallen University of Teacher Education (Switzerland). His current research interests and projects include, among others, STEM education, environmental education, and the history and culture of natural sciences.

Bonding with the World: A Pedagogical Approach

Nadia Lausselet and Ismaël Zosso

1 Introduction

The relationship that humans maintain with their environment is an old question that has become pressing in recent years: it is presenting itself with force and translates into various expressions in public and political spaces. Never in teachers' memory had students gone on strike for the environment. The current pandemic, which disrupts the rhythms of our lives, also raises serious questions about the way we relate with the world. The question is so acute that many political bodies are obliged to push sustainability to the top of their priority lists and turn it into a key concept in their legislative agendas.

Various levels of the education system have committed to these emerging issues for quite a few years already, in the hope that schools will empower children and young people to relate to the world in a different way than in the recent past. This is a well-established process of handing over responsibility: The school is vested with an ambitious political function (see e.g. Künzli David & Bertschy, 2018). Transversal approaches such as peace and human rights education, health or global citizenship education and education for sustainable development (ESD) have thus arisen in the educational discourse. However, they scarcely make their way into official curricula and translate even less consistently into teaching practices (see e.g. Curnier, 2017). A consensual version of ESD is a noteworthy exception. In some respects, it is a success today, as it is embedded in curricula and is gradually becoming established in classroom teaching and learning practices as well as in institutional development plans. This is the result of a very long process based on sustainability as an emerging

N. Lausselet (✉) · I. Zosso
HEP Vaud, Av. de Cour 39, 1014 Lausanne, Switzerland
e-mail: nadia.lausselet@hepl.ch

I. Zosso
e-mail: ismael.zosso@hepl.ch

© The Author(s) 2022
R. Jucker and J. von Au (eds.), *High-Quality Outdoor Learning*,
https://doi.org/10.1007/978-3-031-04108-2_15

autonomous scientific field, and supported by a progressively clear political will in the field of education.

At the same time, there is an increasing enthusiasm for teaching outside the classroom. Inspired by practices made in neighbouring countries, especially Nordic ones, and reinforced by the pandemic, experiments are recently flourishing in French-speaking Swiss schools. The press has seized on the subject by relaying the hope that outdoor education can strengthen pupils' relationship with 'nature' or improve children's physical and mental health in our digital societies. The link to ESD is sometimes made, expressing the will to relate with the world beyond textbooks. To live up to these expectations, it is essential not to limit outdoor education to a series of activities outside the classroom, a fad or a counterweight to current socio-environmental problems. Rather, it should be seen as a pedagogical approach that aims to build an environmental literacy and agency, leading to schools that act tangibly in and on their surroundings. This implies developing teaching rooted in places and lived experiences within these places, thus questioning targeted outcomes and the link to prescribed curricula on the one hand, and teachers' professional posture and practice on the other hand. However, the current flurry around outdoor education in French-speaking Switzerland mostly enjoys neither a conceptual framework nor an institutional structure to link current practices to a coherent outdoor curriculum. It is therefore difficult to turn the ongoing various experiments into real education processes—for both teachers and students—with an added value that goes beyond punctual experiences for a person or a classroom. Outdoor education practices are thus currently based mainly on the use of specifically dedicated places (e.g. *canapé forestier,* or forest couch) and on the will of individuals or specialised organisations, sometimes gathering in networks (e.g. outdoor teacher association *en dehors,* NGO-led "enseignerdehors.ch" network).

An outdoor competence centre has been created at a swiss teacher training university, the *Haute Ecole Pédagogique Vaud* (HEPVD), in order to promote a quality outdoor education in its training offer. The overall aim is to contribute to ongoing efforts, in Switzerland and abroad, to offer a more systematic and solid professional approach to outdoor education, and to frame it within the challenges of the Anthropocene. The approach worked on in this competence centre is based on a theoretical framework referring to place-based education and ESD on the one hand, and on empirical work done over years with both pupils and future teachers on the other. The latter has shown the necessity to articulate outdoor education along competences that are to be tackled progressively over the years, and are situated explicitly within the context of sustainability (see Lausselet & Zosso, 2022). Outdoor education is thus considered as a set of practices as well as creative and thinking tools that progressively enable an environmental literacy and that foster a proactive relationship with the world—or in other words, an agency—while taking the paradigm shift imposed by the current socio-environmental challenges seriously. Its integration within curricula, from early age to post-compulsory higher secondary, should develop and gain strength over the school years. Indeed, it is through regular practice in different settings that the effects of quality outdoor education are likely to unfold and that learners will progress in mastering the competencies[1] necessary to build their environmental literacy and agency. In other words, the approach presented here hopes to contribute to the ongoing discourse by looking at a way to operationalise outdoor education within a learning progression aiming at and framed within sustainability. Establishing a theoretical framework that allows for this construction of a curricular progression is thus essential to move towards a concept both coherent with prescribed curricula and a citizenship relevant within the Anthropocene. In line with the idea of a learning progression for pupils, it is necessary to consider teacher education over time, with a progression in their outdoor teaching competencies.[2] Questions arise both at the epistemological level—the relevance of the taught academic (inter)disciplinary knowledge and possible ways to combine it with critical and community knowledge (Gutstein, 2007)—and at the level of modalities, places and actors of learning, all of which put present educational paradigms under new perspectives. Our approach is thus part of a wider reflection on the role of school in a society in transition, a school in which outdoor education takes a prominent place (Curnier, 2017; Higgins & Kirk, 2006; Lugg, 2007; Orr, 2004).

This chapter will present this pedagogical and didactic approach to outdoor education, both at a conceptual level and at the level of its operationalization. The first part will thus focus on the theoretical framework, while the second part presents a curricular learning progression for pupils and (student) teachers. We will address some related institutional issues before concluding.

2   Transformative Outdoor Education

The theoretical framework we work with is based on three pillars: active outdoor learning, place-based education, and citizenship education in a transformative ESD perspective. This approach has emerged from our specific educational and institutional context, and is summarised in Lausselet & Zosso (2022). It echoes a more general evolution within outdoor education studies looking at the nexus between transformative, outdoor and sustainability education as mentioned by Hill and Brown (2014).

2.1   Space, Places and Education

It is not surprising that geography provides the initial impetus to go out. Space is its central concept and it seems meaningful to explore it through outdoor work. Indeed,

---

[1] We understand competencies as defined by Weinert (2001): the ability and motivation to mobilise content-knowledge, skills and attitude in order to solve a problem.

[2] This also applies to other outdoor educators (from NGO, natural parks,…), but we will not delve further into this aspect.

the 'field' (in the sense of fieldwork) has been a key concept in geography since its early days, with investigation and data collection at its core (Morgan, 2013). This is reflected in school geography and related official documents, for which field work is as specific to the discipline as working with maps (IGU-CGE, 2016). Kinder (2013, 181) even believes that working outdoors in geography provides an opportunity to "rediscover the spirit of exploration that helped create the discipline". The approach we present in this article takes on this idea of exploring places not initially designed for teaching (Dickel, 2006),[3] with various possible purposes (e.g. to problematise, to discover, to observe, etc.) and various shapes.

We can further break down field work in terms of the autonomy afforded to students in their exploration of a place. Ohl and Neeb (2012), for example, have developed a categorisation ranging from a survey field trip—in which place-related knowledge is delivered to passive pupils—to a working field trip promoting autonomy in the pupils' exploration of the place. For example, geographic inquiry, built around a question identified either by the teacher or the pupils, is a type of working field trip. Pupils can also be allowed to explore the place freely, in a less pre-set form as proposed by Job et al. (1999), the teacher then making use of what arises. In our approach, we adhere to this perspective of a working field trip which favours an active encounter, as autonomous as possible, between place and pupil.

The third distinction is between rather cognitive and rather experiential approaches. The first one essentially focuses on observation or data collection, thus tending towards a scientific method. It contrasts with approaches mobilising senses and affect, more experiential in nature (Briand, 2015; Golubchikov, 2015; Preston, 2016). In the first case, the place remains an external object of study, in the other it becomes a subject, interacting with the pupil. Job et al. spoke as early as 1999 of "sensory fieldwork" enabling pupils to develop new sensitivities and perceptions of place, and thus a new way of relating with, and caring for it. Our approach lies in a dialogue between these cognitive and experiential dimensions, with care as its ultimate goal (see further down).

In brief, we set our approach in the context of exploratory outdoor work which favours an active encounter between pupil and place in a dialectic between sensory, affective and cognitive experience. This approach is rooted in the framework for outdoor education proposed by Simon Priest (1986, 13–14), which has the following characteristics: outdoor education builds on the heritage of experiential pedagogy; outdoor activities are vital for learning; learning is achieved through the mobilisation of cognitive, affective and motor skills; outdoor activities are part of an interdisciplinary curriculum (but can relate to disciplines and articulate them); and finally outdoor education develops relational skills.

Three issues we will look at more closely arise from our approach: the relation of sensory and place-based education with learning, the need for competent outdoor

---

[3] In German-speaking countries, learning outside the classroom, or *Ausserschulisches Lernen*, also includes didactic devices provided by third parties in indoor scientific or cultural venues (museums, laboratories, …), a dimension which we will not address.

teaching, and the relevance of a transformative sustainability education as framing for outdoor education in the Anthropocene.

2.2 Sensory and Place-Based Education

Preston points out that, in discourses about outdoor education, practices increasingly pretend to centre on learners and mobilise a sensory and affective dimension. She then demonstrates, through an analysis of a body of field trips carried out in Australia where outdoor work forms an inherent part of the curriculum, that they still remain strongly teacher-led with relatively little autonomy for pupils, and that they almost never focus consciously on the sensory and affective dimensions. Thus the "opportunities for a more critical, embodied, and socially engaged interaction with places are reduced" (Preston, 2016, 9). The author also points out that when these dimensions do appear, they concentrate on visual perceptions (e.g. through landscape sketch or photographs), with the other senses too little used for knowledge construction. She therefore shows that there is a gap between the discourse on practices or relative intentions, and the actual practices. Our analysis of practices and texts in scientific and professional literature seem to confirm this gap, which is widening as pupils progress through the education system.

We seek to reduce this gap by focusing on the idea of transforming a place into a place of learning, and by favouring, as mentioned above, a dialectic between cognitive and experiential dimensions. We explicitly seek the mobilisation of the senses and affect, while fostering a dialogue with the cognitive. We thus align with Golubchikov, who speaks of "feel trip" to designate an "explicitly-more-than-cognitive" approach "creating more stimulating learning conditions with lasting effects on the students' imaginaries and thinking" (2015, 144). For him, outdoor education has the unique potential to go beyond the "stylised knowledge of the classroom and explore the complexities, messiness and imperfections of the real world, while constructing important imaginary tools and skills for seeking social and spatial justice" (ibid.). In order to promote in-depth learning, we must therefore not ignore the cognitive dimension, but link it with an experiential and affective dimension, avoiding what Nairn describes as "disembodied fieldwork" (1996, 89) where pupils do not really come into contact with a place (e.g. when observing a landscape from a hill). The author also advocates integrating a critical perspective to contribute to an education based on the idea of social and spatial justice. In the broad field of outdoor education, this approach relates to what is defined as "place-based education" (e.g. Wattchow & Brown, 2011), implying that we benefit from the specific characteristics of a place when imagining a related outdoor activity. It is this kind of experiential place-based education that we work with in our teacher training activities.

2.3   Competent Outdoor Teaching: A Dialogue with Places

To take these elements into account, Golubchikov insists on the importance of a high level of professionalism including careful preparation both in terms of the choice of place and activity, and support for the pupils' reflective process. In Switzerland, Adamina (2010) also argues for the need to design activities that encourage autonomous exploration of places and make it possible to keep records of the work carried out outdoors. This allows to better entrench the outdoor activity in regular teaching, in line with the idea that "field trips only reach (...) their full educational potential if they contribute to a didactic sequence favouring reflection, problematisation and learning, in a dialectic between concrete and abstract, experimentation and conceptualisation" (Kent et al., 1997; Schroeder, 1998; Mérenne-Schoumaker, 2005, in Curnier, 2017, 184). In this context, the teacher plays both a central and peripheral role: central because, although place is at the heart of the approach, the role of the teacher remains essential in setting up the didactic device and moderating the process allowing these dialectics; peripheral because it means adopting a non-transmissive posture leaving room for a genuine encounter between pupil and place. In other words, transforming a place into a place of learning is not self-evident and must be learned and trained. For this we have found using what we term the 'trilogy of outdoor activity' to be useful for (student)-teachers:

- to actually use the place: the activity must not be feasible in the classroom, nor in other places except if they share similar features;
- to allow a lively encounter between pupil and place: the activity must allow a sensory, physical and emotional experience and offer a degree of autonomy to pupils;
- to contribute to learning outcomes: the link between the place-based experience and learning has to be reflected and made explicit, be it in relation to content-knowledge, skills or ways to connect to the world.

In order to take this trilogy seriously, we must go beyond expectations expressed by teachers who are interested in initial and in-service training courses and mostly wish to learn the logistics of organizing a field trip and managing a class outdoors on the one hand, and to have access to ready-made activities on the other. According to our observations, trainees do also need help to learn to mobilise this trilogy of outdoor activity, to link it with the prescribed curriculum and classroom work, and to go beyond isolated field trips in order to consider their outdoor work over time (Lausselet & Zosso, 2018). This approach thus seeks "through exploratory and prospective work" to push "the limits of what exists", to leave "established routines, traditions and customs" (Lange, 2017, 355), and contribute to the evolution of today's school. It is in order to address this need for competent outdoor teachers and quality outdoor education that the outdoor learning progression presented at the end has been conceptualised.

2.4   Environmental Resonance and Agency

While remaining within this general framework, our approach has progressively integrated a political dimension in the broad sense (Lugg, 1999), and thinking tools important to the humanities and social sciences such as notions of interdependencies, scales (spatial or temporal), actors, or emergence. In line with the societal issues mentioned in the introduction, we have gradually connected our approach to a transformative sustainability education. For many years Lugg (2007) has linked ESD with outdoor education, stimulated by the integration of ESD in Scottish schools through strong support at policy level. Indeed, outdoor education is mentioned as a possible approach to promote environmental awareness, active citizenship and interdisciplinarity. Higgins and Kirk (2006, in Lugg, 2007) sought on this basis to promote trans- and interdisciplinary approaches by emphasising the need to train teachers in these approaches. They echoed Orr (2004) for whom interdisciplinary outdoor learning is fundamental, as there is a direct correlation between disciplinary learning in the classroom and the overuse of nature. Orr believes that disciplinary learning in a classroom prevents a systemic vision on the one hand, and cuts us off from the affective dimension that links us to nature on the other, leading to a double disconnect. Even before Higgins & Kirk, Brookes (1998, in Lugg, 2007, 107) distinguished between a "reconciling" approach, in which teaching adapts to the potentialities of the place, and a "colonising" approach, in which teaching imposes on the place, perpetuating the existing power relation between humans and their environment. Our approach fits into this discussion with a key concept developed by Rosa (2018): resonance. Rosa defines it as follows:

> Resonance is a cognitive, affective and physical relationship to the world in which the subject, on the one hand, is touched [...] by a fragment of the world, and where, on the other hand, he or she 'responds' to the world by acting concretely on it, thus experiencing her or his own efficacy. (2018, 187).

Furthermore, with Wallenhorst and Pierron (2019) we contrast this strongly individual concept with the idea of resistance, more politicised and collective. Indeed, some places and contexts are so degraded or under so much pressure that they call for resistance, which implies a political dimension, rather than resonance. The actions undertaken by Galician classes during the Prestige oil spill are a good illustration of this idea of collective resistance (Jimenez-Aleixandre, 2003, 2006). Eventually, in order to avoid the previously mentioned 'colonising' approach and to strengthen an ethical base, we have taken up the idea of 'care', as already mentioned. Initially coming from the field of bio-ethics, authors such as Chwala (2017) have associated it with learning processes in the field of environmental education. We thus consider 'care' as a central element to build a positive resonant relationship with the world, and to enter into a constructive resistance leading to action.

In ESD discourse, and less specifically relating to outdoor pedagogy, Lotz-Sisitka et al. (2015) echoes this by insisting on the importance of implementing a transformative pedagogy to face current challenges, i.e. a pedagogy that teaches to transform society, and does so while teaching it. They argue for a tertiary education that questions educational norms and speaks of "transformative and transgressive social learning". Curnier (2017) indirectly relates to this by conducting an in-depth reflection on the role of school in a society in transition, and stresses the importance of transforming our relationship:

- to the world, by giving humanity a more humble position and questioning our anthropocentric perspective;
- to the human being, by placing her or him in a wider context and by (re)learning to articulate her or his individual well-being with the common good on the one hand, and the respect of the intrinsic value of the biosphere and its limits on the other;
- to knowledge(s), by perceiving learning as "a system composed of activities mobilising cognition, emotions and experience" (Curnier, 2017, 194), with learning taking place not only in interaction with others but also in interaction with the environment and therefore place.

In this context, the author assigns a particular importance to outdoor education, quoting Freire: "no one educates others, no one educates himself alone, humans educate each other, through the world" (1970/2001, 62, quoted in Curnier, 2017, 226). Curnier mentions in particular the multiplicity of knowledges (including content-knowledge, skills and attitudes) that can be worked on, the opportunity of tackling the link between knowledge, action and impact in a concrete way, or that of re-establishing a connection with our environment, and particularly the natural one.

Barthes et al. also articulate outdoor work and ESD around territorial foresight as a "tool (…) to analyse spaces and related social phenomena" (2019, 1). As previously mentioned authors, they claim the need for new relationships to knowledge, the world and alterity. They explicitly add the need for a critical perspective on power issues and related institutions and their impact on space, thus integrating the political and social dimension specific to place-based education. According to them, "territorial foresight includes issues of collective participation in the evolution of a place" (ibid.), based on local, even micro-local dynamics. They formalise the idea of citizens' knowledge production as well as the necessity of reconnecting with collective imaginations in a transformative perspective.

We believe that outdoor pedagogy understood in this way, through its entrenchment in experience, its intrinsically interdisciplinary dimension, its conception of knowledge and of the world as a construct, and its progressively political and transformative dimension, can respond to the societal issues mentioned in the introduction. Upon this theoretical basis we have developed a proposal for an outdoor curricular learning progression for pupils which should then enable us to structure a coherent training offer for teachers.

3   A Learning Progression for Outdoor Education: A Curricular Proposal

When journalists ask outdoor teachers why they practice outdoor education, the most common answer is to create or recreate a link to the environment (or to nature). This formulation is very convenient and, perhaps for that reason, frequently used. It nevertheless raises several questions if we want this link to become effective and not to remain at the level of wishful thinking. The first question is of a pedagogical and didactic nature. What type of link can reasonably be worked on at each educational stage in order to foster a strong bonding with the world? And, consequently, what competencies are needed by teachers to achieve this objective? In other words, is it possible to implement this concept of bonding and make it part of a curricular progression? This idea of progression is particularly critical to us because, in the perspective of integrating outdoor education into regular teaching practices, it is important that pupils progress in mastering competencies specific to working and learning outdoors, with and within the world. Furthermore, since we are working within a paradigm of a transformative pedagogy, we must acknowledge that this paradigm cannot be achieved by an accumulation of isolated activities raising environmental awareness but must be part of a long-term educational project with an emancipatory aim.

3.1   Bonding with the World: A Curricular Progression

French-speaking Switzerland is part of the HarmoS concordat, a national contract between the Confederation and the federal states or *cantons*. This does not allow the legal and regulatory framework to be modified to make outdoor education compulsory within the prescribed curricula. We are therefore far from certain Anglo-Saxon or Nordic situations, where there are official incentives for outdoor education. Thus, the aim of a curricular perspective as presented hereafter can only be to help integrate outdoor education within the prescribed curricula in a coherent manner, avoiding an additional layer of prescription or a normative will in a field of school practices which still remain relatively unregulated. It is to support this coherent integration that teacher training institutions such as the HEPVD need to formalise a framework to develop meaningful practices and set milestones for a progression: the aim is to progressively train competencies necessary to build an environmental literacy and agency while contributing to quality outdoor education. The challenge is to give outdoor education a recognised status that goes beyond the categorisation of this practice as a 'personal choice' for some convinced teachers. This status should also allow for the perpetuation of collective projects that are institutionally entrenched and have an impact in and on the world. In other words, it has to be acknowledged that outdoor education is not a practice that depends solely on an individual environmental sensitivity—a personal attitude—but rather is an established and necessary pedagogy—a crucial part of our education system—in which educators can be trained and in which they must progress to achieve professional expertise. More broadly, with a curricular and transformative approach we can move beyond perspectives considering outdoor education superficially, or in a manner that is not thought for a school context, as mentioned at the beginning. We have therefore attempted to build an outdoor education learning progression in order to provide a framework than opens up perspectives for progress, for pupils as well as teachers, in their environmental literacy and agency, and related didactics for the latter. This learning progression can also be viewed as a tool to place outdoor education within practices contributing to a transformative pedagogy. We will now look at this double curricular learning progression, one for pupils and the other for (future) teachers.

3.2   A Progression for Pupils

As the aim is to work on the pupils' bond to the world through outdoor education, we must define this bond and structure it in a progression tending towards a resonant and socially relevant link. Based on the clusters of disciplinary and cross-curricular objectives of the prescribed curricula, in our case the French-speaking *Plan d'Etude Romand* (PER) in Switzerland, we propose a priority learning objective for each level (in French *cycle*) of compulsory education, as well as for post-compulsory education (higher-secondary), bearing in mind that the boundaries between these levels must remain porous (Table 1):

Table 1 Training pupils and young people through outdoor education

Early childhood (4–8 year-olds)	Primary (8–12 year-olds)	Secondary (12–15 year-olds)	Higher secondary (over 15 years old)
Sense of belonging	Exploration (guided)	Exploration (autonomous)	Reflexivity
Feeling safe within the environment	Adaptation (place <-> self)	Adaptation (place <-> self) and commitment	Commitment
Sense of well-being in the environment	Sense of well-being in the environment	Thinking the environment and myself in it	Communication to and with others about environment
Awakening to the complexity and richness of the environment	Caring for the environment	Caring for the environment	Networking with societal actors for the environment
Curiosity (about the living world)	Curiosity (about biodiversity) and understanding	Prospective curiosity (about possible transformations of the environment)	Action and agency
Inclusive bond	**Adaptive bond**	**Transformative bond**	**Performative bond**

- The objective for early childhood education (cycle 1: 4 to 8 year-olds) would be to build an inclusive bond with the environment: pupils learn to include the environment in the construction of their reality, their identity and their relationships and therefore also to include themselves in it by grasping the idea of interdependence. From the outset, we consider the environment not as a resource to be taken advantage of, but as a constitutive element of personal and collective identities as well as a referent of social practices.
- The objective for primary education (cycle 2: 8 to 12 year-olds) would be to work on an adaptive bond. This means giving pupils the opportunity, through activities and projects, to experience places in different ways. The aim is to acquire the capacity to understand the environment in order to be able to adapt to it, and adapt it in an adequate manner for one's needs (e.g. by building a small shelter with branches and leaves). In other words, pupils, individually and collectively, should be able to create a dialogic relationship with places, to get to know them and feel them better, and thus adapt to them and regulate their impact in a caring way.
- Once they have gone through these two stages, inclusion and adaptation, we think that secondary pupils (cycle 3: 12 to 15 year-olds) will be able to think how to transform places in the sense of prospective thinking, which would be a prospective bond. This implies transforming one's perception of a place, seeing its potential, and imagine what transformations would be needed in order to allow this potential to flourish. Activities and projects that consistently include reflecting (the pupils are outside and think outside) and conceptualising (the pupils do land art not just for the aesthetic but to work on an idea of nature, planetary limits, etc., and are aware of this) dimensions. Based on this, it becomes possible to start thinking about the potentials of a place, and possible ways towards it, in a prospective perspective.
- Finally, higher secondary pupils will work on a performative bond that makes them act. At this stage, the pupils are able to go beyond the class and rely on the bond they have built in order to mobilise their environmental literacy and use it for an environmental agency within society.

3.3   A Progression for (Future) Teachers

In order to implement the curricular learning progression presented here, we need to train educational actors in this direction. In the same way, we need to think about training in outdoor education in a progressive manner, be it to distinguish between approaches at primary and secondary level, or between beginners and experienced professionals. Many quality training courses exist on the Swiss market, but as a higher education institution, our task was to define a coherent theoretical framework allowing for consistency, and, based on this, define and implement relevant learning progression for teachers. Three levels of expertise, co-existing in this vast field of outdoor education, have been defined:

- Implementing outdoor activities: at this first level, the emphasis is on doing. It means carrying out and facilitating established activities outside the classroom to transmit or work on subject-knowledge and possibly raise awareness. The visit to the sewage treatment plant or a forester's activity on the importance of forest insects fall into this category. Popular, high-quality books provide numerous suggestions for such activities outside the classroom.
- Teaching outside: at this second level, the emphasis is on instruction. Curricular contents are transposed into a different spatial context to make them more real. We go to the forest to see the trees in real life and study them, we study the industrial revolution by doing an inquiry in a wasteland or in urban remains of industrialisation. Subject-specific didactics apply to this type of thematic outdoor work, with no specific, transversal outdoor education methodology.
- Outdoor education: at this third level, the emphasis is on education. In other words, this approach integrates questions of values and systems, works on the bond between pupil and place, and thus contributes to the construction of an environmental literacy and agency. It therefore requires using a pedagogy of bonding with the world practised over time. It also implies questioning our view and our educational practices in, on, with and for our environment. The goal is to build a reflective and critical professional attitude, informed by research and practice, contributing to a quality education that reflects contemporary issues.

As seen, we do not mean to limit ourselves to giving examples of good outdoor education practices or to list themes for integrating the outdoors into the prescribed curriculum. We need to make intellectual, didactic and curricular tools available. These allow teachers and trainers to consider bonding with the world from a truly holistic, reflective and critical perspective. We locate the HEPVD's training architecture at this level, useful for both training and research. More concretely, this translates into the division of training in two blocks, one part in initial teacher training which moves rapidly from implementing to teaching, thus from facilitation to the design of disciplinary and interdisciplinary or a-disciplinary (if the focus is, for example, on cross-curricular skills) activities, to their integration into broader sequences. The initial training also aims to delve into environmental literacy by addressing some of the possibilities to start working on it with pupils. We leave mastering the systematic integration of outdoor sequences in pupils' curricula to in-service teacher training as it requires a broader vision of school calendars and tasks. In-service training also aims to better understand and deepen the possibilities of working on environmental literacy with pupils, before addressing environmental agency. In both blocks, we stress didactic tools allowing the transposition between place and knowledge, a transposition specific to outdoor education (OE for short in Table 2).

Table 2 Training teachers to outdoor education

Discover OE principles and practices	Create OE activities/sequences	Carry out OE activities/sequences	Plan OE activities/sequences and integrate them into the curriculum	Question OE
Discover pluralistic OE types and approaches	Create disciplinary, inter-disciplinary and a-disciplinary activities rooted in place	Implement activities and regulate learning situations outside the classroom	Master the link between outdoor activities and learning outcomes over the school years	Differentiate activities for pupils with specific needs
Discover concepts of environmental literacy	Integrate concepts of environmental literacy	Act safely on, with and for the environment; discover concepts of environmental agency	Integrate concepts of environmental agency	Reflect the impact of OE on the environment
Understand themes of environmental literacy	Mobilise themes of environmental literacy	Communicate and link with school and environmental actors	Handle disciplinary, cross-curricular and life skills	Look at research practices Get into networking
Initial teacher training			**In-service teacher training**	

4   A Need for Institutional Change: A Competence Centre for Outdoor Education

To pilot these two learning progressions, but also to develop research and training in outdoor education more widely, the HEPVD has created a specific competence centre in 2020. This project has proved necessary to meet the ever-increasing demand for training, but also to develop course content, meeting the theoretical and curricular goals presented here. Moreover, the existing institutional structures, divided into disciplines and transversal approaches, did not allow for the trans- and inter-disciplinary perspective at the core of outdoor education. Nor did they allow for the overall vision and the flexibility necessary to coordinate between—and work with—the wide range of other actors implicated in formal outdoor education. This autonomous centre, albeit affiliated to the institution, can be more responsive, operates in a decentralised manner with this large number of actors, and offers freedom of thought and action to examine and improve what exists, both in terms of training and research. This competence centre is based on three pillars: training (both initial and in-service), research and community service (e.g., collaborating with nature parks). It also contributes to coordinating efforts and political lobbying within and for the field. Materialising outdoor education through this new structure and linking it to ongoing sustainability education processes helps supporting the high expectations of outdoor education mindful of current socio-environmental issues and striving towards higher-quality education.

Our goal is that outdoor education becomes a relatively autonomous pedagogical field in French-speaking Switzerland. For that, we must meet three main conditions. First, we need to define boundaries for our field, both practically and conceptually, so as to interact with other fields and be recognised by them. Second, we must produce a discourse from our field and not only about our field. Therefore, we not only need to develop tools to analyse and criticise our practices and theories, but we also need to think about the school from the perspective of our practices and our theoretical framework. Thus, we need to develop discourses rooted in outdoor education on sustainable development and ESD, on digital learning, on inclusive (or exclusive) education, on gender issues or on assessment. Finally, we aim to create a teaching and training community that goes beyond our state institution to operate on a regional scale. In this way, differences in perspective between institutions can be mutually enriching and strengthen the legitimacy of outdoor education. No single project and no single disciplinary-focused structure can meet these conditions. The establishment of a specific outdoor competence centre aims at making a decisive contribution to this project of epistemic, didactic, pedagogical and institutional empowerment.

5   Conclusion: Achieving Hope, Daring Utopia

The recent and brutal emergence in the public arena of civilisational, even eschatological, anxieties induces, whether we like it or not, an extensive redrafting of our relationship to our environment, to society, to nature, to the wild, to our habitat, and to politics as well. Not that these reflections were previously absent, as scientists had brought up the topic long ago, but there was no socially imposed urgency. We must take up part of the challenge which the socio-environmental situation imposes on the whole of human society: that of education. Although it cannot and should not be the role solely of education to change the world, we believe that schools must be consistent with current issues, and can contribute to establishing an environmental literacy and agency that allows us both to maintain hope in the face of crises and to bring about new perspectives among young people. They will thus be able to think, invent and experiment new forms of resonances with the environment. Outdoor education is one of the tools that should enable this environmental literacy and agency. But given its complexity, its innovative character within the Swiss education system, and the high expectations placed on it, we must emphasise quality of teaching and therefore of training. Only in this way can outdoor education contribute to quality education. The present uncertainty keeps us on the move and encourages us to collectively map out alternative paths in order to explore our present and re-imagine this world of finite resources with infinite possibilities. Outdoor education as presented here aims to contribute to this.

Recommended Further Reading

1. Lugg, A. (2007). Developing sustainability-literate citizens through outdoor learning: possibilities for outdoor education in Higher Education. *Journal of Adventure Education & Outdoor Learning, 7*(2): 97–112.
2. Rosa, H. (2018). *Resonance: A Sociology of Our Relationship to the World.* London: Polity Press.
3. Golubchikov, O. (2015). Negotiating critical geographies through a "feel-trip": Experiential, affective and critical learning in engaged fieldwork. *Journal of Geography in Higher Education*, n°39, 143–157.

References

Adamina, M. (2010). *Ausserschulische Lernorte (ASLO).* . Retrieved April 24, 2019, from http://docplayer.org/38514377-Ausserschulische-lernorte-aslo-1.html.

Barthes, A., Blanc-Maximin, S., & Dorier-Appril, E. (2019). Quelles balises curriculaires en éducation à la prospective territoriale durable ? Valeurs d'émancipation et finalités d'implications politiques des jeunes dans les études de cas en géographie. *Éducation et socialisation, 51.* Retrieved April 25, 2019, from https://journals.openedition.org/edso/5755.

Briand, M. (2015). La géographie scolaire au prisme des sorties : Pour une approche sensible à l'école élémentaire. *ESO Travaux & Documents CNRS, 38*, 75–83.

Brookes, A. (1998). Place and experience in Australian outdoor education and nature tourism. In Outdoor recreation – Practice and ideology from an international comparative perspective, Umea, Sweden.

Chwala, L. (2017). Le soin de la nature chez les enfants et les adolescents : expériences marquantes pour le développement du sens de la connexion. In C.Fleury & A-C. Prévot (Eds.), *Le souci de la nature : apprendre, inventer, gouverner* (pp.191–206). Paris: CNRS.

Curnier, D. (2017). *Quel rôle pour l'école dans la transition écologique ? Esquisse d'une sociologie politique, environnementale et prospective du curriculum prescrit.* Lausanne: Université de Lausanne.

Dickel, M. (2006). Zur Philosophie von Exkursionen. In: W. Hennings, D. Kanwischer, & T. Rhode - Jüchtern (Eds.), *Exkursionsdidaktik innovativ? Geographiedidaktische Forschungen* (Bd. 35, pp. 31–49). Weingarten, Selbstverlag.

Freire, P. (1970/2001). Pédagogie des opprimés. Paris: La Découverte.

Golubchikov, O. (2015). Negotiating critical geographies through a "feel-trip": Experiential, affective and critical learning in engaged fieldwork. *Journal of Geography in Higher Education, No, 39*, 143–157.

Gutstein, E. (2007). Connecting community, critical and classical knowledge in teaching mathematics for social justice. In: The Montana Mathematics Enthusiast, Monograph 1 (pp.109–118). Retrieved February 04, 2021, from http://radicalmath.org/docs/Gutstein.pdf.

Higgins, P., & Kirk, G. (2006). Sustainability education in Scotland: The impact of national and international initiatives on teacher education and outdoor education. *Journal of Geography in Higher Education, 30*(2), 313–326.

Hill, A., & Brown, M. (2014). Intersections between place, sustainability and transformative outdoor experiences. *Journal of Adventure Education & Outdoor Learning, 14*(3), 217–232.

IGU-CGE. (2016). International Charter on Geographical Education. [En ligne]. http://www.igu-cge.org/Charters-pdf/2016/IGU_2016_def.pdf (consulté le 12.03.2019).

Jimenez-Aleixandre, M-P. (2003). Educación en un contexto social: la marea negra en los centros escolares gallegos. Aula. 122/2003.

Jimenez-Aleixandre, M-P. (2006). Les personnes peuvent-elles agir sur la réalité ? La théorie critique et la marée noire du prestige. In A. Legardez, L. Simmoneaux (Eds.), L'école à L'épreuve de l'actualité. Issy-les-Moulineaux: ESF.

Job, D., Day, C., & Smyth, T. (1999). Beyond the bikesheds: Fresh approaches to fieldwork in the school locality. Sheffield: Geographical Association.

Kent, M., Gilbertson, D., & Hunt, C. (1997). Fieldwork in geography teaching. A critical review of the literature and approaches. *Journal of Geography in Higher Education, 21*(3), 313–332.

Kinder, A. (2013). What is the contribution of fieldwork to school geography? In D. Lambert & M. Jones (Eds.), *Debates in geography education* (pp. 180–192). Abingdon: Routledge.

Künzli David, C., & Bertschy, F. (2018). Bildung als Reparaturwerkstatt der Gesellschaft? – Die zu unterscheidenden Facetten von Bildung im Kontext einer Nachhaltigen Entwicklung. In S. Meisch, U.Jäger, & T. Nielebock (Hrsg.). Erziehung zur Friedensliebe: Annäherungen an ein Ziel aus der Landesverfassung Baden-Württemberg (pp. 289–304). Baden-Baden: Nomos.

Lange, J-M. (2017). Curriculum. In : A. Barthes, J-M. Lange, & N. Tutiaux-Guillon (Eds.), Dictionnaire critique des enjeux et concepts des "éducations à" (pp.351–359) Paris: L'Harmattan.

Lausselet, N., & Zosso, I. (2018). Projektarbeit an ausserschulischen Lernorten - ein Beitrag zur Bildung für Nachhaltige Entwicklung? In: P. Gautschi, A. Rempfler, B. Sommer, & M. Wilhelm (Eds.), *Aneignungspraktiken an ausserschulischen Lernorten: Tagungsband zur 5. Tagung Ausserschulische Lernorte der PH Luzern vom 9. und 10. Juni 2017*, Zürich, LIT Verlag (pp. 173–181).

Lausselet, N., & Zosso, I. (2022). Outdoor and sustainability education: How to link and implement them in teacher education? An empirical perspective. In P. Vare, N. Lausselet, & M. Rieckmann, (Eds). *Competences in education for sustainable development: Critical perspectives.* New York: Springer (pp.167–174).

Lotz-Sisitka, H., Wals, A., Kronlid, D., & McGarry, D. (2015). Transformative, transgressive social learning : Rethinking higher education pedagogy in times of systemic global dysfunction. *Current Opinion in Environmental Sustainability, 16*, 73–80.

Loynes, C. (2002). The generative paradigm. *Journal of Adventure Education & Outdoor Learning, 2*(2), 113–125.

Lugg, A. (1999). Directions in outdoor education curriculum. *Australian Journal of Outdoor Education, 4*(1), 25–32.

Lugg, A. (2007). Developing sustainability-literate citizens through outdoor learning: Possibilities for outdoor education in Higher Education. *Journal of Adventure Education & Outdoor Learning, 7*(2), 97–112.

Merenne-Schoumaker, B. (2005). *Didactique de la géographie. Organiser les apprentissages.* Bruxelles: De Boeck.

Morgan, J. (2013). What do we mean by thinking geographically? In D. Lambert & M. Jones (Eds.), *Debates in geography education* (pp. 273–281). Abingdon: Routledge.

Nairn, K. (1996). Parties on geography field trips: embodied fieldwork? *New Zealand Women's Studies Journal, 12*(Special Issue: Educating Sexuality), 86–97.

Ohl, U., & Neeb, K. (2012). Exkursionsdidaktik. Methodenvielfalt im Spektrum von Kognitivismus und Konstruktivismus. In: J.-B. Haversath (Ed.) Geographiedidaktik. Theorie - Themen – Forschung, Braunschweig, Das Geographische Seminar (pp. 259–288).

Orr, D. W. (2004) *Earth in mind: On education, environment, and the human prospect* (rev. ed., 221p.). Washington: Island Press.

Preston, L. (2016). Field 'Work' vs 'Feel' trip: Approaches to Out-of-Class experiences in geography education. *Geographical Education, 29*, 9–22.

Priest, S. (1986). Redefining outdoor education: A matter of many relationship. *Journal of Environmental Education, 17*(3), 13–15.

Rosa, H. (2018). *Résonance: une sociologie de la relation au monde.* Paris: Editions La Découverte.

Schroeder, J. (1998). La leçon de géographie: une relecture d'auteurs anciens. In J.-L. Klein & S. Laurin (Eds.), *L'éducation géographique formation du citoyen et conscience territoriale* (pp. 159–182). Sainte-Foy: Presses de l'Université du Québec.

Wattchow, B., & Brown, M. (2011). *A pedagogy of place : Outdoor education for a changing World* (244p.). Clayton: Monsah University publishing.

Wallenhorst, N., & Pierron, J.-P. (2019). *Éduquer en anthropocène.* Lormont: Le bord de l'eau.

Weinert, F. E. (2001). A concept of competence: A conceptual clarification. In: D. S. Rychen, & L. H. Salganik (Eds), *Defining and selecting key competencies* (pp. 45–65). Seattle: Hogrefe & Huber.

Nadia Lausselet has been working for more than 15 years in the field of sustainability education, as a teacher, member of an NGO and teacher trainer. Her research interests focus on teacher competencies for sustainability education, outdoor education and intercultural perspectives on sustainability education. She has contributed to launch and now leads the implemen-tation of sustainability education in her teacher training institution.

Ismaël Zosso has been working for more than 20 years in the field of outdoor education, as a teacher and a teacher trainer. His research interests focus on outdoor and place-based education. He has implemented and is now leading the outdoor competence centre mentioned in this article, and is turning his dream of a place for outdoor education in the Alps into a reality.

Udeskole—Regular Teaching Outside the Classroom

Karen Barfod and Erik Mygind

1 Introduction

When teachers choose to teach outdoors,[1] they want to achieve something tangible based on their teaching convictions and set of values.[2] There is an intentional choice behind overcoming the challenges of *udeskole* and actually going out with the pupils. This choice is justified by the teachers partly through learning theory, but also from an educational viewpoint of *Bildung*, where the pupils' independent work, thinking skills and ability to approach tasks in several ways are of great value. The didactic field of *udeskole* has been analysed through observational studies in theory and practice (Jordet, 2010). One of the elements defining the uniqueness of *udeskole* are studies indicating that the teacher often use hands on and inquiry-based approaches in their teaching (Barfod & Daugbjerg, 2018).

---

[1] *Udeskole* is among Danish *udeskole* researchers defined as curriculum-based teaching and learning outside the classroom and school buildings in natural as well as cultural settings one day or two half days a week or every fortnight on a regular basis, e.g. lasting months or years.

[2] The overall aim of the Danish TEACHOUT research project was to generate knowledge about the strengths and weaknesses of practicing *udeskole* compared to mainstream education under the framework of the new school reform. TEACHOUT investigated physical activity, learning and social relations.

This chapter is mainly based on perspectives, excerpts, reformulations and translations of the Ph.D. Thesis by Barfod (2018), Mygind et al. (2018) and the chapter in Danish language 'Udeskole— Regular teaching outside the classroom' (translated title) (Barfod et al., 2020). We publish this chapter with the expressed permission of the publisher Frydenlund.

K. Barfod (✉)
VIA University College, Svinget 5, 7620 Lemvig, DK, Denmark
e-mail: ksba@via.dk

E. Mygind
Fuglehavevej 33, 2750 Ballerup, DK, Denmark
e-mail: emygind@ign.ku.dk

© The Author(s) 2022
R. Jucker and J. von Au (eds.), *High-Quality Outdoor Learning*,
https://doi.org/10.1007/978-3-031-04108-2_16

2 How Are Teachers Motivated to Teach Outdoors?

Teachers express a wide range of positive elements connected to their experience of regular teaching outdoors. The motivational elements can be divided into pupils' learning and development, social relations and the experience of professional fulfilment (Barfod, 2017).

Pupils learning and development

Teachers experience how *udeskole* gives pupils the opportunity to deal with topics and subjects in the surrounding community. *Udeskole* is an opening to the world outside the school buildings, and teachers experience how abstract concepts become concrete to pupils. The process of learning becomes, according to the teachers, more meaningful for the pupils.

In addition, teachers experience that there are far fewer conflicts between the pupils than inside. The social structures in the class are softened in a positive way. It can be other pupils who perform outdoors than indoors in a classroom setting, thus playing a positive role in terms of pupils' interaction and recognition of each other. This has a positive influence on the classroom environment and affects the learning processes taking place. Teachers find that many pupils benefit in many different ways by being taught outdoors, both socially and cognitive (e.g. Fägerstam, 2014).

Social relations

We found that teachers mention more positive relationships between pupils when they experience each other in different situations outside as compared to inside teaching (Mygind et al., 2018). Some pupils who need more space and to 'let off steam' do not seem so disruptive outdoors. This in turn means that other pupils perceive them as less annoying and deal with them more openly.

Another important element for teachers is their own increased positive relationships with pupils. In the motivation theory called self-determination theory (Deci & Ryan, 2014), the opportunities to exercise competence, work autonomously, and establish positive relationships are fundamental to employees being highly motivated in the workplace. In our studies, teachers express how they feel that practicing *udeskole* supports good teacher-student relationships (Mygind et al., 2018). During the outdoor lessons, there is time during transportation to the outdoor place to make a non-committal conversation about, for example, changes at home or personal stuff. A difficult conversation about divorce, new siblings, or general well-being is easier to have while walking, digging, or otherwise doing something together.

Experiences of common challenges are also seen as something that can connect teachers and pupils more closely. The teacher–pupil relationship can become more balanced when both experience the same, thus creating a 'common third'. A sudden shower also makes the teacher wet. When the bus does not arrive, the teacher also has to wait. When there is a long way to go, the teacher must also go a long way. A teacher even calls his/her relationship with the pupils "brothers-in-arms" as they try to solve tasks together, and show loyalty, responsibility and trust in each other (Mygind et al., 2018, 604).

The main thing (in *udeskole*) is, that there is something external, a problem, a question, a common concern and a goal, both parts aim to solve. The philosopher Michael Husen (1996) introduced a concept describing unusual situations named 'the common third'. The expression was used when teacher and pupils carry out a task together, towards a mutual goal (e.g. make a fire, explain marks from animals, make a shelter from rain, etc.). The common third expresses the sharing of a task, collaboratively formulated by teacher and pupils in an attempt to solve the task, share an experience not previously experienced. The experiences with 'common third' situations support development of an enriched teacher–pupil relationship. It could be argued that this is an important pedagogical outcome from *udeskole* that seems to provide learning opportunities with mutual benefits to the indoor teaching as well (Mygind et al., 2018, 606).

Teachers reinforce their professionalism through working with *udeskole*

In our studies, the experienced teachers perceive that the teaching culture has developed in 'neo-liberal' directions, reducing their tasks. They feel that they are checking whether students are doing well in tests, thus measuring only a fraction of the knowledge, skills and attitudes students acquire through (school) life. Often, teachers are not given the opportunity to make use of all their professionalism and professional identity in the classroom. Emphasis on narrow learning goals, testable skills and marks tighten the open space for the art of teaching and professional judgement. Choosing outdoor teaching helps them to maintain or even regain their sense of professional mastery (Barfod, 2017). When teachers choose to teach outdoors, they step out of the classroom with books series and national tests, and into a space of unpredictable challenges and opportunities. Teachers say they are set free to think about the purpose of the lessons themselves and the means to achieve these aims. The self-selected frameworks for teaching are perceived by teachers as setting them free to practice teaching that is not limited by books or online portals in advance. The teacher turns, once again, into the professional who makes choices, acts, plans, implements, and evaluates teaching. At the same time, teaching outdoors is also consistent with teachers' own preferences and values. According to the teachers, school education should be more than grades and test results, and many teachers relate how their educational goals of teaching are supported by *udeskole* (Mygind et al., 2018). According to the teachers, *Udeskole* supports a holistic development of pupils, through activities involving bodies and senses, to a greater extent than the classroom does. Both novel and experienced *udeskole* teachers who participated in our research are people with a positive attitude to nature, and with experiences from scouting, outdoor sports or other outdoor activities. Some teachers describe how the concept of *udeskole* legitimized an educational practice they already knew worked. Teachers often have experiences of thriving outdoor themselves, and transfer these experiences to their professional lives. However, when teachers' understanding is experience-based and positive, a critical attention to and look at the practice may be lacking. A dilemma may arise between the fiery-soul-driven teaching, and the lack of professional reflective criticism of one's own outdoor practice (Ejbye-Ernst & Bentsen, 2017).

3   What Challenges Do the Outdoor Teachers Face?

Teachers meet several barriers to outdoor teaching, both structural and in relation to content. On the one hand they meet barriers associated with the structure of the school day being divided up into time-limited classes and related teacher coverage, on the other hand barriers associated with time and resources for planning and implementing well-designed and professionally sound teaching.

School structures

Traditionally, the school has been designed for classroom teaching, in terms of both physical design and other structures such as subjects, teacher coverage and times for the school bell. When the whole class goes out and away from the school grounds, it often takes more time than a set schedule at school allows. If the individual teacher has to switch lessons with colleagues by themselves every time, and has to apply for and find an accompanying adult, it can become a major administrative task. Therefore, the backing by management and colleagues, or at least acceptance, for flexible timetabling is important for organizing outdoor teaching. At the same time, a regular *udeskole* day, e.g. every second Thursday, can make it easier for parents to remember a little extra in the lunch box and appropriate clothing. Structures and frameworks can be developed and supported for *udeskole*, but this support from management does not apply in all places.

Preparing for teaching outdoors is perceived as a big job

When the teacher is teaching outside, it is often with less use of already made resources and pre-printed materials. Teachers feel that when their professionalism comes more into play, it is both challenging and exciting, but also exhausting. Preparation time and the other resources provided for teaching today, rarely cover the effort required for the teacher to implement good teaching outdoors. Over time, pupils and teachers establish routines, and the teacher builds up a 'bank' of materials that can be used outdoors. There are freely accessible public websites with ideas and materials (skoven-i-skolen.dk; udeskole.nu; draussenunterrichten.ch) but even experienced teachers still concede that elaborate preparation is needed for *udeskole*.

The teacher can feel unnoticed

In many schools, there is only one teacher who teaches outdoors, although the recent development in Denmark shows how more and more teachers at the schools with at least one *udeskole*-class start up (Barfod et al., 2020). It can be tough in several ways being the only one: The teacher him/herself has to invent or adapt many teaching materials. There might be a lack of cooperation and support from colleagues, and in addition, some teachers may feel a bit isolated in the staff room (Barfod, 2017). Stereotyped notions that *udeskole*, outdoor and adventure education are the same, or attitudes about how learning is best promoted inside the classroom can make outdoor teachers feeling alone at their school.

Another barrier to practicing *udeskole* is the uncertainty about pupils' learning. Both novel and experienced teachers now and then feel uncertain whether the teaching and learning is truly educational enough in terms of the acquisition of testable skills, although research has shown that pupils learn just as much of what is tested when they learn outdoors (Otte et al., 2019). Learning is still commonly tested with ordinary test-tools in primary school.

Uncertainty and unpredictability

An interesting dilemma, or ambiguous concept in working outdoor, is uncertainty (Barfod, 2017; Beames & Brown, 2016). There are a large number of 'uncertainties' associated with *udeskole*, in terms of content, meaning and process. Leaving the classroom is also leaving the predictable framework, which adds to the uncertainty of teaching. Although the teacher has carefully planned the day, it is always unpredictable how the weather will be, whether a large dog will pass the campsite or if there is major contractor work in progress in the parking lot where the pupils should gather. But at the same time, there is also the possibility of something unplanned happening that increases learning outcomes, strengthens curiosity or provides new perspectives on the subject of teaching. Thus, there is increased *uncertainty* about the outcome of teaching and also unpredictability about the process of teaching (Beames & Brown, 2016). The rational, effective and controllable process of education gives way to what American educational philosopher John Dewey called "indefinite situations without obvious answers" (quoted in Beames & Brown, 2016, 76) outdoors. Uncertainty can be accentuated as a major positive factor in teaching, as proposed by the Dutch educational researcher Biesta (2010). Biesta argues that teaching loses its original purpose when it becomes "strong, safe, predictable and risk-free". In contrast to this predictability, educationally desirable teaching creates an opportunity for something new to be brought into the world. Biesta even believes that teaching should be an open system without unambiguous cause-effect relationships. Many studies show that habits, routines, discipline and clear goals help make pupils feel safe and ensure good results outdoors (Glackin, 2018). *Udeskole* regularity itself is part of this establishment of routines, and popular *udeskole* booklets also cite habits and routines as essential elements of outdoor school (see, e.g. Bendix & Barfod, 2012). The question therefore seems to be whether there is a contradiction between school discipline in the form of habits and routines, and subject oriented, open, inquiry-based education, enhanced by the curiosity induced through unpredictability.

Pedagogy

Pedagogical approaches to *udeskole* are primarily described in Nordic literature, as literature with Anglo-Saxon backgrounds often is based on a more adventure-oriented practice than the *udeskole* concept of Danish primary school. One of the things that is special about Nordic *udeskole* is that it is often the teacher him/herself who is responsible for the teaching, and they only sometimes draw on external providers when it makes sense. In many other countries and cultures, outdoor education is left to experts, such as rangers, nature guides, and museum tour guides, and the potential to link experiences and teaching within the classroom with the outdoor days can be limited. Therefore, it is especially important that it is the teacher who plans the subject and overall content of the teaching and ties learning from the different arenas together. However, the teacher can easily hire nature guides or others who supplement the subject matter the class is working on if the teacher has an overall plan for the aims. *Udeskole* is a part of the total teaching provision in primary school. The teaching should be seen as a unified whole, with strong links between what goes on outside the classroom and what goes on inside the classroom. *Udeskole* is not an 'add on' of extracurricular activities, but an 'add in' of varied work methods taught in each subject (Bentsen et al., 2018). When the teacher chooses to relocate parts of the teaching outside the classroom, it often has consequences in relation to the teaching and working methods that come into play. The objectives of education are aimed at a balanced and holistic formation of the student's head, hand and heart— or in other words, the student's cognitive development, the student's skills and the student's attitudes and feelings (Jordet, 2010).

What does it take for outdoor education to become motivating and educational? The question 'What is good schooling?' is inextricably linked to the question 'What is good teaching?'. *Udeskole* is per definition a part of the overall teaching of the school, and thus works within the school's main aims and goals. *Udeskole* provides variety in teaching and opens up to different forms of teaching.

Inquiry-based teaching in *udeskole*

Teaching methods that "strengthen relevance, meaning and application orientation in a differentiated teaching" have received increased attention, especially in the field of science (Albrechtsen & Qvortrup, 2017, 25). The prevalence and peculiarity of inquiry-based teaching has been intensely discussed and investigated, but very different practices have been called inquiry-based. Pupils do not necessarily have freedom to make choices during the teaching, even if it is called inquiry-based, as these methods can include very closed 'cookbook' experiments where a particular procedure must be followed closely. Notions such as problem-based teaching and problem-solving activities can be linked to the study concept (Artigue & Blomhøj, 2013). Skovsmose (2003) introduces the concept of 'study landscapes', in which mathematics education can invite pupils into exploration and to work problem-oriented. It has been emphasized in reports on Danish mathematics teaching that teaching is less problem-oriented and mainly consists of more closed training tasks (Bundsgaard & Hansen, 2016) as opposed to tasks that allow pupils to make conscious and meaningful choices while solving them (Katz & Assor, 2007; Skovsmose, 2003). In more experimental and inquiry-based teaching, pupils make a choice of method based on a reflection on the consequences and, during the work, ask themselves the question: "What if …" (Blomhøj & Skånstrøm, 2016). Thus, the tasks include elements of openness. The term 'inquiry-based' is here applied to teaching situations where pupils are challenged by working with something unknown using something already known, where 'study landscapes' are organized so pupils can choose methods or find solutions to mathematical problems. In *udeskole*, the concept 'inquiry-based' is thus connected both to situations where pupils, through experiences and reflection, inductively examine relevant elements (e.g. by studying details in nature through a magnifying glass), and those situations where pupils work with the scientific method as long as these are not fully teacher-controlled.

Using this understanding of inquiry-based teaching, half of the tasks presented in Danish *udeskole* are inquiry-based (Barfod & Daugbjerg, 2018). Thus, compared to a very low proportion of inquiry-based teaching in classroom teaching (Bundsgaard & Hansen, 2016), *udeskole* has a great potential to increase the proportion of inquiry-based teaching in everyday education.

Good teaching outdoors from a teacher perspective

To start with, 'good' is a normative and difficult concept in teaching. The term 'good' must be seen in relation to the goals set by teachers for teaching, and can therefore not be considered in absolute terms. Furthermore, experienced teachers regard *udeskole* as a *both-and*-practice that can accommodate several goals, goals that aim to both improve pupils' achievement in academic national tests and holistic developmental goals. Teachers consider *udeskole* as 'good':

- when pupils can see the meaning and coherence in teaching,
- when they work problem-solving, are engaged and get 'their brains turned on',
- when they are cognitively active, and use their senses and their body,
- when pupils share experiences with teachers and peers,
- when out-of-school teaching contains both academic and educational content,
- and when *udeskole* opens the opportunity for the teacher to 'seize the day' and take advantage of the unpredictability of the surroundings. (Barfod & Stelter, 2019)

In addition, experienced teachers perceive *udeskole* as good when there is time for both planned and unpredictable experiences with students and teachers (Barfod & Stelter, 2019). In the teachers' view, *udeskole* is good when it includes tasks with pupil-activating work methods that challenge pupils' ability to think for themselves and solve problems, and when pupils experience connections in and meaning through teaching.

4 Discussion

Is school simply getting 'better' by going outdoors, no matter what is going on out there? First, it depends on what is meant by 'better'—and in relation to what. Positive outcomes in terms of better grades? Better performance, or healthier and happier lives? It is a normative discussion when we talk about 'a better school'. Among outdoor educators, there has been a lack of self-criticism, and a trend toward 'outdoor is better'. Recently, there is an incipient self-critical movement, discussing the implicit positive self-understanding and promotion of the outdoors as 'better' (Bentsen & Jensen, 2012; Ejbye-Ernst & Bentsen, 2017). This can be called 'the second wave of teaching outdoors', signifying that outdoor educators also are aware of the limitations and pitfalls.

Turning to the analysis of the positive outcomes, we also wander into the unknown. Is it nature in itself, or the organization of teaching, that contributes to the positive meaning of *udeskole* for pupils, or is it a combination? Beames and Brown (2016) emphasize that it is essential that pupils learn through unpredictable situations where there are no clear solutions, and that general principles of good teaching thus become more easily accessible in teaching if it is moved outside. About half of the teaching events we have studied outdoors are inquiry-based (Barfod & Daugbjerg, 2018). But it is not a given that inquiry-based teaching is good teaching, or better than anything else. Essential to good teaching is method diversity and variation in teaching to meet students' different learning needs. With its particularly large proportion of inquiry-based teaching, outdoor school can contribute to this variation.

Both-and-goals

Kruse (2005) argues that the effectiveness of *udeskole* should be measured in relation to pupils' realized learning, and that "outdoor education increases school well-being but creates problems in meeting clear measurable requirements" (Kruse, 2005, 88). But at the same time, Kruse emphasizes that outdoor education should be assessed on whether it improves (or exacerbates) the students' overall journey through life, which is a rather unattainable goal.

Udeskole has been used as a tool to reach subject-related aims, but the influence on the pupils' overall development should also be emphasized. It is generally considered to weaken and limit the teacher's ability to exert their teacher professionalism if the overall aim is restricted to academic goals.

Teachers are educated to teach subjects, but also to engage in pedagogical reflexivity. We must stand by our courage and let teachers use their professional mastery. Teaching outdoors can be one way to encourage this. Both the novel and experienced *udeskole*-teachers we have interviewed and worked with are convinced that teaching should be based on experiences, holistic and student-activating learning, and they use *udeskole* to teach in accordance with their conviction and values.

Recommended further reading

1. Barfod, K., & Bentsen, P. (2018). Don't ask how outdoor education can be integrated into the school curriculum; ask how the school curriculum can be taught outside the classroom. *Curriculum Perspectives, 38*(2), 1–51,156. https://doi.org/10.1007/s41297-018-0055-9.
2. Bentsen, P., Nielsen, G., Bølling, M., Mygind, L., Stevenson, M & Mygind, E. (2019). Book: *Physical Activity in Natural Settings.* Chapter: *Greening Education. Education outside the classroom in natural settings as a school-based health promotion approach for child and youth populations.* 1st Edition. Routledge. eBook ISBN 9781315180144.
3. Hartmeyer, R. & Mygind, E. (2016). A retrospective study of socialrelations in a Danish primary school class taught in 'udeskole', *Journal of Adventure Educationand Outdoor Learning, 16*(1), 78–89. https://doi.org/10.1080/14729679.2015.1086659.

References

Artigue, M., & Blomhøj, M. (2013). Conceptualizing Inquiry-Based Education in Mathematics. *ZDM Mathematics Education, 45*(6), 797–810. https://doi.org/10.1007/s11858-013-0506-6

Barfod, K. S. (2017). Maintaining mastery but feeling professionally isolated: Experienced teachers' perceptions of teaching outside the classroom. *Journal of Adventure Education and Outdoor Learning, 18*, 1–13. https://doi.org/10.1080/14729679.2017.1409643

Barfod, K. S. (2018). *At undervise i udeskole. Perspektiver på didaktik og lærerens arbejde. [To teach in udeskole. Perspectives on didactics and the teacher's work].* Ph.D. thesis. Department of Nutrition, Exercise and Sports, University of Copenhagen Barfod.

Barfod, K. S., & Daugbjerg, P. (2018). Potentials in Udeskole: Inquiry-based teaching outside the classroom. *Frontiers in Education, 3.*https://doi.org/10.3389/feduc.2018.00034.

Barfod, K. S., & Stelter, R. (2019). *God udeskole fra et lærerperspektiv.* Acceptet til Nordisk tidsskrift for Allmendidaktik.

Barfod, K., Mygind, E., & Hartmeyer, R. (2020). Undervisning, didaktik og evaluering [teaching, didactics and evaluation]. In E. Mygind (Ed.), *Udeskole, TEACHOUT- projektets resultater [Udeskole, results from the TEACHOUT project]* (78–100pp.). Copenhagen, Denmark: Frydenlund.

Barfod, K., Bølling, M., Mygind, L., Elsborg, P., Ejbye, N., & Bentsen, P. (2021). Reaping fruits of labour: Revisiting Education Outside the Classroom provision in Denmark upon policy and research interventions. *Urban Forestry & Urban Greening, 60*, 127044. https://doi.org/10.1016/j.ufug.2021.127044

Beames, S., & Brown, M. (2016). *Adventurous learning: A pedagogy for a changing world.* Routledge.

Bendix, M., & Barfod, K. (2012). *Udeskole – viden i virkeligheden: en kort vejledning om udeskolens praksis og didaktik.* Frederiksberg: Skoven i Skolen, Udeskole.dk & VIA University College. http://www.skoven-i-skolen.dk/sites/skoven-i-skolen.dk/files/filer/PDF-filer/udeskole_printnet_final.pdf.

Bentsen, P., & Jensen, F. S. (2012). The nature of udeskole: outdoor learning theory and practice in Danish schools. *Journal of Adventure Education and Outdoor Learning*, 12(3), 199–219. https://doi.org/10.1080/14729679.2012.699806.

Bentsen, P., Bonde, A. H., Schneller, M. B., Danielsen, D., Bruselius, M., & Aagaard, J. (2018). Danish 'add-in' school-based health promotion: Integrating health in curriculum time. *Health Promotion International*. https://doi.org/10.1093/heapro/day095

Biesta, G. J. J. (2010). Why "What Works" still won't work: From evidence-based education to value-based education. *Studies in Philosophy and Education, 29*(5), 491–503. https://doi.org/10.1007/s11217-010-9191-x

Blomhøj, M., & Skånstrøm, M. (2016). Det kommer an på. In H. Alrø & T. E. Rangnes (red.), *Matematikklæring for framtida*. Norge: Caspar Forlag.

Bundsgaard, J., & Hansen, T. I. (2016). *Blik på undervisning. Rapport over observationsstudier af undervisning gennemført i demonstrationsskoleforsøgene*. Tilgået 21.11.2017 på https://pure.au.dk/ws/files/95991875/Bundsgaard_Hansen_2016._Blik_p_undervisning._Rapport_om_observationsstudier_af_undervisning_gennemf_rt_i_demonstrationsskolefors_gene.pdf.

Deci, E. L., & Ryan, R. M. (2014). The Importance of Universal Psychological Needs for Understanding Motivation in the workplace. In M. Gagné (red.), *The Oxford handbook of work engagement, motivation, and self-determination theory*. USA: Oxford University Press.

Ejbye-Ernst, N., & Bentsen, P. (2017). Fem idéer om udeskole – kritik af slogans. In N. Ejbye-Ernst, K. Barfod, & P. Bentsen (Ed.), *Udeskoledidaktik*. København: Hans Reitzel.

Fägerstam, E. (2014). High school teachers' experience of the educational potential of outdoor teaching and learning. *Journal of Adventure Education and Outdoor Learning, 14*(1), 56–81. https://doi.org/10.1080/14729679.2013.769887

Glackin, M. (2018). 'Control must be maintained': Exploring teachers' pedagogical practice outside the classroom. *British Journal of Sociology of Education, 39*(1), 61–76. https://doi.org/10.1080/01425692.2017.1304204

Jordet, A. N. (2010). *Klasserommet utenfor. tilpasset oplæring i et utvidet læringsrom*. Oslo: Cappelen akademisk forlag [på Norsk].

Katz, I., & Assor, A. (2007). When choice motivates and when it does not. *Educational Psychology Review, 19*(4), 429–442. https://doi.org/10.1007/s10648-006-9027-y

Kruse, S. (2005). En udeundervisningens didaktik. In Mygind (red.), *Udeundervisning i folkeskolen*. København: Museum Tusculanum.

Mygind, E., Bølling, M., & Barfod, K. (2018). Primary teachers' experiences with weekly education outside the classroom during a year. *Education, 3–13*, 1–13. https://doi.org/10.1080/03004279.2018.1513544

Otte, C., Bølling, M., Stevenson, M., Ejbye, N., Nielsen, G., & Bentsen, P. (2019). Education outside the classroom increases children's reading performance: Results from a one-year quasi-experimental study. *International Journal of Educational Research, 94*(2019), 42–51. https://doi.org/10.1016/j.ijer.2019.01.009

Skovsmose, O. (2003). Undersøgelseslandskaber. In O. Skovsmose & M. Blomhøj (red.), *Kan det virkelig passe?* København: L&R uddannelse.

Karen Barfod is a research leader in Outdoor studies at the Research Centre for Pedagogy and Education, University College VIA, Denmark. She holds a MA in biology and physical education, and a PhD in educational science. She has been head of the Board of the national Network UdeskoleNet, gathering all professionals with interest in Education Outside the Classroom, since 2007. Apart from training teachers at the Institute at VIA, she is a well-known researcher and speaker in the field, being involved at many levels of udeskole practice, development and research. In 2014, Karen Barfod received the national Udeskole Award, Udeskoleprisen, for her continuous work for and with udeskole, and in 2022 the Novo Nordic foundation price for Science Education as teacher educator. Her research field is teaching in the outdoors, with emphasis on regular Education Outside the Classroom. Karen Barfod is the corresponding author: ksba@via.dk.

Erik Mygind, Msc. and Ph.D. (1993) in sport and exercise science from Department of Nutrition Exercise and Sports (NEXS), Faculty of Science, University of Copenhagen (KU) and today associate Professor emeritus, affiliated Department of Geosciences and Nature Management (IGN), KU. Since 1982 developed and taught a number of outdoor education (OE) studies, programs and courses and since 2011 PhD OE courses. Since the turn of the millennium, his research has focused on the interaction between nature, people and udeskole/education outside the classroom (EOtC), with special focus on the role of teachers and students' health, motivation and physical activity in primary school. Erik was head of the Danish udeskole research project 'TEACHOUT' (2014–2018) with a total budget of 10 million DKR in partnership between University of Copenhagen (NEXS & IGN, KU), VIA UCC Aarhus, University of Southern Denmark and STENO Diabetes Centre). Board member of 9th International Outdoor Education Research Conference 2022.

International Perspectives and Case Studies

International Views on School-Based Outdoor Learning

Sue Waite

1 Introduction

There has been an acceleration in the decline in children's opportunities to be outdoors in formal or informal learning settings through an emphasis on academic attainment (Waite, 2010a, b), increased screen time, more supervised out-of-home activity (Mullan, 2018), and various pressures on family leisure time (McCabe, 2015) across the Western world. Concern about these reductions in children's exposure to natural environments (Louv, 2010) is gathering momentum internationally because it has been demonstrated that time spent outdoors impacts positively on physical and mental health (White et al., 2019), and "character capabilities" such as engagement with and self-regulation of learning, resilience, creativity, and empathy for others and the natural world (Malone, 2008). These so-called "soft skills" underpin success in learning and citizenship (Gutman & Schoon, 2016). However, despite a growth in school-based outdoor learning (OL), there are still few international comparisons to inform the development of this growth (Waite et al., 2016a) and little consensus about what outdoor learning signifies across cultures, even within nations.[1]

---

[1] For an attempt to change this, see PLaTO-Net Harmonization Project https://www.outdoorplayc anada.ca/plato-net/ (accessed 8/4/2021).

This chapter is an updated adaptation of a previously published article: Waite, S. (2020). Where are we going? International views on Purposes, Practices and Barriers in School-based Outdoor Learning. Special Issue: Outdoor Adventure Education: Trends and New Directions. *Education Sciences*, *10*, 311. https://doi.org/10.3390/educsci10110311, based on the report: Waite, S. (2017). *Purposeful Practice in School-Based Outdoor Learning*. Newark, UK: The Wildlife Trusts.

S. Waite (✉)
Church Road, Lympstone EX8 5JT, Devon, UK
e-mail: S.J.Waite@plymouth.ac.uk

© The Author(s) 2022
R. Jucker and J. von Au (eds.), *High-Quality Outdoor Learning*,
https://doi.org/10.1007/978-3-031-04108-2_17

To gain further insight into what the international picture of policy and practice might be, a survey funded by the UK Wildlife Trusts[2] was sent in September/October 2017 to expert commentators on OL through personal contacts and networks. School-based outdoor learning was defined as 'play, teaching, and learning that take place in natural environments for children in formal education and care settings.'

Literature that undertakes international comparisons of OL forms or policies or even adequately situates research in its material, cultural, and social context is still relatively rare (Passy et al., 2019), although research into OL across nations has exploded over recent years (Waite, 2019).

Several recent reviews conducted have usefully summarized the current field of knowledge and the evidence base for OL's effectiveness for educational outcomes as well as promoting health and wellbeing and education for sustainability is robust (see, for example, chapters "Outdoor Learning—Why It Should Be High up on the Agenda of Every Educator, A Coordinated Research Agenda for Nature-Based Learning, Do Experiences with Nature Promote Learning? Converging Evidence of a Cause-And–Effect Relationship, Refueling Students in Flight: Lessons in Nature May Boost Subsequent Classroom Engagement, Childhood Nature Connection and Constructive Hope Helping Young People Connect with Nature and Cope with Environmental Loss, How to Raise the Standards of Outdoor Learning and Its Research Summary of 'The Existing Evidence-Base About the Effectiveness of Outdoor Learning', by Fiennes et al." in this volume).

In their synthesis of research relevant to student outcomes and outdoor learning, Malone and Waite found five desired student outcomes that aligned with contemporary policy priorities, related to developing "a healthy and happy body and mind; a sociable confident person; a self-directed and creative learner; an effective contributor; an active global citizen" (2016, 5), echoing Article 29 of the United Nations Convention for the Rights of the Child (UNCRC) (1989). In the UK, these global policy aspirations have driven several preventative public health strategies (Marmot et al., 2020), social mobility campaigns for resilience (Paterson et al., 2014), a call for more creative and collaborative team workers (UKCES, 2014) and recognition of the interdependence of human and environmental well-being in the 25-year plan for improving the environment (HMG, 2018). In Scotland, educational policy supports these aims through the Curriculum for Excellence (Scottish Government, 2018). In some countries, such as Canada, the US, and Australia, policy adoption of outdoor learning to support these drivers tends to be at state level, although there is Australia-wide policy for Education for Sustainable Development (Australian Government, 2009). Sustainability is also the mainstay of policy support in Japan (Maruyama, 2010), while in Norway, Denmark, and Sweden (albeit the latter only at preschool level), it is primarily linked to curriculum educational objectives.

---

[2] The Wildlife Trusts comprise 46 individual Wildlife Trusts in the UK, charitable bodies formed by regional groups of people getting together to make a positive difference to wildlife and future generations, federated under the Royal Society of Wildlife Trusts, a registered charity founded in 1912. https://www.wildlifetrusts.org (accessed 8/4/2021).

However, Malone and Waite (2016) also noted that achieving these policy objectives (motivations for OL) requires greater clarity about what methods of OL are most likely to support distinct aims. We also need to be cautious as simply "borrowing" policies and practice can result in inappropriate translations from one context to another without attention to the particularities of cultural traditions and constraints affecting successful implementation elsewhere (Passy et al., 2019). Unfortunately, details of methods are rarely provided within articles. Waite, Bølling and Bentsen proposed a framework for comparing different forms of OL including "purpose, aims, content, pedagogy, outcome, and barriers" (Waite et al., 2016a, 871). Adopting a systematic process of comparison enables greater nuance in choosing distinct forms for specific desired purposes. In this chapter, through considering OL's drivers and motivations (why), and methods (how) in diverse contexts, I hope to promote understanding how movements to support outdoor learning can best be supported across different countries and help policy makers, practitioners, and researchers identify and consider where more effort in the future might be directed to maximize the positive impacts of time spent learning outside by children and young people in economically challenging times post COVID-19.

2 The Research

The aim of the research was to provide international contextualization for the Wildlife Trusts' work with schools and to support a clearer theory of change for their educational strategy development. Research questions included: What are the purposes and policy drivers for school-based outdoor learning across different nations? What forms of OL are used in various countries/areas? What barriers to OL are experienced in different countries/areas?

Invited experts possessed a high level of knowledge or skill in outdoor learning, identified through personal knowledge of their work or their membership of relevant academic and practitioner groups. They were asked to rate their capability of completing the survey from their knowledge and experience; 92% felt well or fairly well qualified to answer the questions posed. The networks approached included the International School Grounds Alliance, the Institute of Outdoor Learning research hub network; JISC discussion group OUTRES, the Economic and Social Research Council international partnership network on outdoor learning, and ERASMUS+collaborators, plus additional international contacts from conferences, projects, and previous correspondence, with further snowballing to obtain the widest sample achievable within a tightly defined period (three weeks). To comply with standard ethical practices, all those invited were free to participate or not without any penalty. Their identity was not revealed in the report unless with specific permission. The number of respondents was 80 from 19 countries (Table 1).

Not all questions were answered by all respondents, possibly left blank if beyond respondents' expertise. Some pointed out that policies and practice varied within

Table 1 Number of respondents by country

Asia	Australia	Europe	N. America	UK	Total
Indonesia 2 Japan 1 Nepal 1 Taiwan 1 Vietnam 1	13	Denmark 2 Finland 2 Germany 2 Ireland 1 Norway 2 Poland 1 Spain 1 Sweden 6 Switzerland 1	Canada 9 US 6	England 5 Scotland 16 UK-wide 7	
6	13	18	15	28	
					N = 80

their countries, and that their comments related to their regional situation or impressions of the wider national picture. For these reasons and because some places were represented by only one expert opinion, reports are merely indicative.

Descriptive analysis was used for both quantitative and qualitative data, and interpretive analysis about possible implications was based on this and extant literature. Three main themes are discussed below to show why different countries adopt outdoor learning, what types of outdoor learning are used and nuances of outdoor movements internationally.

3   Motivations

When asked what the main drivers for outdoor learning were in their country, between 61 and 64 respondents from 19 countries answered using a three-point Likert scale to indicate whether they agreed with the five desired twenty-first century student outcomes identified by Malone and Waite (2016). Participants also offered further comments. For example, effective delivery of the curriculum was mentioned as a driver in Scotland, while a Danish respondent noted,

> Giving meaningfulness to the topics being taught by connections between surroundings and the topic.

In Denmark, education policy advocates the relevance of learning in contexts other than the classroom, and although there is a grassroots movement for education outside the classroom, *udeskole*, this is further endorsed and promoted through top-down government investment and research encouraging this (Bentsen, 2013).

In the US, health promotion was a major influence.

> Physical Education and Physical Activity are the biggest drivers for outdoor learning, followed by nutrition and science education.

The respondents from Finland and Norway mentioned knowledge and skills in biology and ecology for "nature-friendly behaviour."

In Table 2, cells are shaded to show the pattern of response by country across the five policy drivers so that darker grey means respondents reported it as a main driver, light grey means they thought it was a main driver to a degree, and white means it was not considered a main driver. Where there was more than one respondent in the country, the response included was chosen by the most people. The number of respondents varied as shown.

Dominant drivers according to survey respondents were children's health and well-being, developing social, confident, and connected people, and care for others and the environment. Surprisingly, the driver that gained least traction across participating countries' respondents was supporting collaboration, yet this is a commonly

Table 2 Comparison of main drivers of outdoor learning in participating countries/areas

Countries / Purpose and Outcomes	Healthy Bodies and Positive Lifestyles	Social, Confident and Connected People	Creative and Self-Regulated Learners	Effective Contributions and Collaboration	Care for Others and the Environment	N
Indonesia						1
Japan						1
Nepal						1
Taiwan						1
Vietnam						1
Australia						9-11
Denmark						2
Finland						1
Ireland						1
Norway						2
Poland						1
Spain						1
Sweden						4
Switzerland						1
Canada						8
US						6
England						3
Scotland						13/14
UK-wide						4
N of countries reporting as main driver	11	11	7	6	10	

attributed outcome from outdoor learning (see chapter "How to Raise the Standards of Outdoor Learning and Its Research Summary of 'The Existing Evidence-Base About the Effectiveness of Outdoor Learning', by Fiennes et al." in this volume).

From responses received, Scotland, Indonesia, Japan, and parts of Australia indicated the strongest support through government policy for outdoor learning. As one respondent from Scotland reported:

> Teacher standards require use of outdoor learning and understanding of Learning for Sustainability within a values-based Professional Accreditation system. Curriculum for Excellence states, 'outdoors is often a better place than indoors to learn' and Outdoor Learning is a regular and progressive experience for all learners. ... We also have a requirement that all leadership support outdoor learning under new leadership qualifications, local authorities support school grounds to allow 'contact with nature on a daily basis' and 'green space suitable for teaching and learning' and Scotland's play policy and strategy also highlights our children's entitlement to 'free play opportunities, with daily contact with nature'.

Outdoor learning is also included within the state-wide curriculum in Victoria, Australia, where a government interdepartmental working group is tasked with exploring ways to embed outdoor learning in recognition of its potential to fulfil several wider policy aspirations. There are moves to include it within the nationwide Australian Curriculum. In parts of Australia, as in several other places, education for sustainability appears to be a strong motivation for outdoor learning recognized by individual teachers and in policy alike.

> For us, it is based on relationships with self, others and nature. With a foundational basis of sustainability.

In Japan, the Ministry of Education, Culture, Sports, Science and Technology is working with UNESCO to develop programs for Education for Sustainable Development through schools and communities, with some schools acting as hubs of good practice. This grounded method of expansion has also been used in the Natural Connections Demonstration project (Waite et al., 2016b), where 125 schools were supported in embedding sustainable curriculum-based outdoor learning through networks of schools with varying degrees of experience in outdoor learning (see chapter "Natural Connections: Learning About Outdoor-Based Learning" in this volume).

In Norway OL is part of the national curriculum, and it features in the early years, physical education, and biology curricula in Sweden. In England, educational policy support is mostly within early years provision, but recently the Department for the Environment Food and Rural Affairs (DEFRA) and the Department for Education have commissioned further trials to develop "nature-friendly schools" (The Wildlife Trusts, 2021). Amongst other drivers cited, connection to and knowledge about nature, risk awareness, and diverse and experiential learning environments for curriculum delivery were also mentioned. Nonetheless, as Waite (2010a) found in a survey in the southwest of England, respondents to the survey noted that motivations were often shaped at a local level according to teachers' or delivery organizations' interests.

4 Methods

Several forms of OL were suggested in the questionnaire and respondents indicated whether they were often, sometimes, or not used in their country. The methods were not defined in the questionnaire. Leaving the terms open maintained flexibility about interpretations. Respondents could explain further if they wished to do so and add other methods, including camps (Canada), visits to cultural places (Denmark), nature kindergarten, Bikeability and John Muir Award (Scotland), river, beach, mountain (Indonesia).

Forest School and Bushcraft

Forest School, which is a growing phenomenon globally (Knight, 2013), was reported as most prevalent in England, Scotland, and Canada and was not observed at all in Norway or Nepal. It sometimes or often occurred in 84% of the 19 countries, according to responses received. It is described by the Forest School Association (FSA) as:

> [A] child-centred inspirational learning process, that offers opportunities for holistic growth through regular sessions. It is a long-term program that supports play, exploration and supported risk taking. It develops confidence and self-esteem through learner inspired, hands-on experiences in a natural setting. (FSA, 2020)

The FSA proposes six principles that are supposed to characterize this form of outdoor learning, but in practice these are not always adhered to and a recent special issue on Forest School of the *Journal of Outdoor and Environmental Education* problematized the concept and its translation into different contexts (JOEE, 2018).

Interestingly, bushcraft was not recognized as a form of outdoor learning by respondents from Finland, Poland, Spain, or Nepal. Given its emphasis on the acquisition of practical skills, there may be some overlap with the concept of Forest Schools. For example, Australian early years providers that use nature-based play may describe themselves as bush kindergartens. Although rarely reported as often used (6%), bushcraft was reported as sometimes used in 65% of the countries.

Field Studies

Field studies were widely reported across the responding countries (98% often or sometimes). This is perhaps unsurprising as they are an established method within several academic subjects, such as geography and science. Field studies involve investigative work in the world beyond the classroom and therefore have some commonality with conceptualizations of Danish *udeskole* or learning outside the classroom in the UK.

Embedded On-Site Curricular Outdoor Learning

The most frequent use of this form was reported by respondents from Denmark, the US, and England. Alignment with the curriculum in countries with strong school performance agenda is understandable as teachers must meet given standards and therefore may need to cover curriculum objectives more directly (Waite, 2010b). In Denmark, the confluence of top-down policy and bottom-up teacher-led growth of *udeskole* likely contributed to its establishment as mainstream practice (Barfod et al., 2016). The respondent from Nepal noted that this form was not seen at all there.

Natural Environment Play and Early Years Outdoor Activities

These forms were reported as common across almost all nations with only the respondent from Nepal noting them absent. Norway, Switzerland, Indonesia, Japan, and Scotland were the countries where natural environment play was most reported as often occurring. Participants from Denmark, Norway, Spain, Sweden, Indonesia, and Japan reported early years outdoor activities as often occurring.

Outdoor and Adventure Education

This form of OL usually entails occasional trips far from the normal place of learning to residential or day centres specializing in outdoor activities that offer challenges, such as climbing, kayaking, and sailing. Frequently, special qualifications are required to lead such activities for health and safety reasons, and schoolteachers may not hold these additional qualifications, so it is common that they are provided by external organizations. This may explain the tendency for most countries to report that outdoor and adventure education took place sometimes rather than often. In Norway, the concept of *friluftsliv*, whereby outdoor living is highly valued and practiced within society, may account for its reported prevalence here (Gurholt-Pedersen, 2014). Nevertheless, it seems that many children across the participating nations experience the opportunity to engage in this sort of OL at least occasionally.

School Gardening and Wildlife Areas

School gardening appeared fairly well established as an OL method across many countries, but participants from Finland and Nepal did not report it, perhaps reflecting geographic or climatic barriers. Respondents from Ireland and Japan said it was often used. An advantage of this form is that the garden can be based on school grounds, obviating any need for travel time, costs to engage with nature, or requirements of risk assessments for every visit (Passy, 2014).

Wildlife areas may offer different sorts of affordances (Mawson, 2014) for children's learning; Wells and Lekies (2006) found both experiences positively affected subsequent pro-environmental attitudes, but only wild experiences influenced later pro-environmental behaviour. Providing wilder areas as part of the school grounds make biodiverse environments more easily accessible for learning purposes (Almers et al., 2020; Hammarsten et al., 2018). However, as one respondent in Australia commented, there might be safety reasons in some parts of the world that preclude leaving school grounds areas unmanaged. In others, the cultural importance of the appearance of a school site may favour tidier grounds.

Visits to Nature Reserves and National Parks

Nature reserves were reported as often visited for OL in Ireland, Spain, and Denmark and sometimes visited in 67% of responding countries. National parks were sometimes visited in 80% of countries represented in the survey. These special places offer a different experience from the nearby nature of school gardens (Carson, 1965). Maller (2009) suggests that a mixture of familiar places and progression to more remote highly valued natural environments may support children becoming connected to nature and engender later pro-environmental attitudes.

Movements

Respondents were also asked which forms of OL they considered were most appropriate for particular outcomes in order to determine how motivations for OL might best be supported by different methods. To indicate trends of association, the percentage of respondents choosing different options are shown in Table 3. The outcome most associated with each form is highlighted in darker grey, while the next perceived contribution of that form is highlighted in pale grey. We can see that encouraging healthy bodies and minds was considered by respondents as most supported by early years outdoor activities, outdoor and adventure education, and natural environment play; while developing social, confident, and connected people was regarded as most helped through outdoor and adventure education and early years outdoor activities. Embedded on-site curricular outdoor learning and Forest Schools together with early years activities were deemed important for stimulating creative self-regulated learners. In terms of supporting effective contributions and collaboration, school gardening was most selected, although embedded curricular outdoor learning was also associated with this outcome. Visits to national parks and nature reserves were very highly associated with underpinning care for others and the environment, although field studies and school gardening were also seen as linked with this outcome.

From this analysis, it appears that some methods of outdoor learning are more generalist in meeting various purposes, while others appear more specialist in their impact. Field studies, for example, seemed less associated with health and well-being outcomes; outdoor and adventure education appeared particularly aligned with healthy living and the development of some inter- and intra-personal skills. In all responding countries, early years outdoor activities appeared to be the most valued for achieving across all the desired outcomes.

Table 3 Aligning purposes and outcomes to forms of outdoor learning (across countries)

Forms of Out-door Learning / Outcomes	Healthy Bodies and Posi-tive Life-styles	Social, Confi-dent and Con-nected People	Creative and Self-Regu-lated Learners	Effective Contri-butions and Col-labora-tion	Care for Others and the Environ-ment	N
Forest Schools	48% 23	65% 31	73% 35	44% 21	67% 32	48
Field studies	17% 8	26% 12	39% 18	44% 20	70% 32	46
Embedded on-site curricular outdoor learning	57% 29	51% 26	61% 31	51% 26	41% 21	51
Natural environ-ment play	74% 37	60% 30	54% 27	38% 19	52% 26	50
Outdoor and ad-venture educa-tion	82% 40	86% 42	39% 19	45% 22	51% 25	49
School garden-ing	57% 28	41% 20	37% 18	61% 30	74% 36	49
Bushcraft	33% 13	64% 25	59% 23	36% 14	39% 15	39
Early years out-door activities	90% 44	74% 36	65% 32	45% 22	51% 25	49
Visits to nature reserves	38% 18	26% 12	30% 14	19% 9	87% 41	47
Visits to national parks	45% 21	21% 10	30% 14	23% 11	92% 43	47

Table cells give percentages of respondents ticking each option in response to the question: Which of these drivers do you think are mainly behind the use of the different forms of learning? (Tick as many as apply). The outcome most associated with each form is highlighted in darker grey, while the next perceived contribution of that form is highlighted in pale grey.

5 Obstacles to Outdoor Learning

Some barriers to outdoor learning were held in common across nations represented in the survey. The barriers suggested in the questionnaire were derived from the Natural Connections project findings (Waite et al., 2016b) and earlier scoping by Kings College, London (Natural England, 2011). Table 4 is a summary table that shows the combined assessment of barriers across participating countries, indicated by dark grey shading when the barrier was assessed as significant, light grey when it was considered significant to a degree, and white when it was not considered a barrier.

We can see that the most significant barriers internationally appeared to be linked to teacher training and how confident staff were in working outside and in linking the

Table 4 Assessment of significance of barriers by respondents for their countries/areas

Countries/ Barriers	Lacking Confidence in Working Outside	Uncertainty about Linking to Curriculum	Lack of Funding	Need for Volunteer Support	N
Indonesia					1
Japan					1
Taiwan					1
Vietnam					1
Australia					10
Denmark					1
Finland					1
Ireland					1
Poland					1
Spain					1
Sweden					4
Switzerland					1
Canada					6
US					6
England					2
Scotland					12
UK-wide					4
N responses / countries/areas	14	12	6	5	54/ 16

curriculum to outdoor activities. Lack of funding and the need for volunteer support were much less frequently regarded as significant barriers by respondents.

Staff Lacking in Confidence in Working Outside

Over three-quarters of respondents agreed this was a significant barrier indicating that attention was needed to train staff tasked with outdoor learning in appropriate pedagogies. About two-thirds of countries sometimes used external providers and these were expected to have expertise in the field. However, it was most common that teachers would lead outdoor learning across all countries. It seems many initial teacher training courses have limited input on how to teach outside the classroom (Prince, 2019), which is unfortunate as the inclusion of modules for outdoor teaching and continuing professional development courses might help to increase teacher confidence. As one respondent from Scotland noted, "Time of teachers to do CPD [continuing professional development] or something else in that area. Lack of resources and money, knowledge. No subject in school-based outdoor learning in teaching education/training" all potentially contribute to a lack of confidence. The Natural Connections project (Waite et al., 2016b, see chapter "Natural Connections: Learning About Outdoor-Based Learning" in this volume) found that an effective way of building teacher confidence in working outside was through practical sessions alongside more experienced colleagues.

However, there appeared little top-down support in the educational system for this in North America, where growth is attributed more to grassroots organizations' advocacy and support for schools. Even in Scotland, where policy promotes outdoor learning, one respondent commented that progress was happening,

> Very gradually via the policies mentioned ... and many committed NGOs and others 'chipping away' at schools, encouraging and supporting them to take learning outdoors (via blogs, evidence etc.) to justify the place of OL, training, networking etc.

In Nepal, it was reported that,

> School-based outdoor activities are still at infancy in Nepal thus leaving great possibilities in this field. Awareness workshops thus play a pivotal role in pushing the barrier to a great extent in the meanwhile.

The nations represented in the survey appeared at different points in their outdoor learning development. In Japan, creating natural infrastructure at schools was reported by the respondent as a priority:

> [S]chool biotope (wildlife area esp. natural pond) became movement to create in Japan, but because of grounds maintenance and lack of knowledge of using the area, in many cases the area became unused. School gardening is common since it is mentioned in National Curriculum.

School ground infrastructure development was mentioned by expert commentators in several other countries.

Staff Uncertainty About Linking Outdoor Learning to the Curriculum

A lack of ability to combine OL and unanticipated learning outcomes with teaching specific subject curriculum objectives was considered a barrier by many respondents. As discussed earlier, this may depend to some extent on whether there were strong pressures on delivery of curriculum content in that educational system.

Although teachers may well be capable of mapping outdoor activities and their outcomes to the curriculum if they have sufficient time to undertake the necessary planning, time is a commodity which is often in short supply in schools (Waite et al., 2016b). Providing teachers with suitable prepared resources was felt helpful by a respondent from Australia to relieve time and curriculum pressures, "There are a few structured programs such as school kitchen gardens, which are easier to implement as they come with teaching resources." In Switzerland, a suite of resources across the curriculum was available for teachers to improve outdoor learning provision,

> With our project 'Teaching Outdoors' which contains a manual for teaching all disciplines outdoors, with teacher training and a pilot study in coaching a few interested schools (www. draussenunterrichten.ch in German, www.enseignerdehors.ch in French).

One respondent from Scotland echoed comments from some Australian respondents about staff unwillingness, suggesting,

> Mindset—this is the key barrier. ... It is remarkable that early years practitioners can enable outdoor learning and play on a daily basis and that outdoor nurseries are springing up everywhere demonstrating that all areas of the curriculum can happen outside yet primary and secondary colleagues feel unable to do the same.

Respondents in Ireland and Vietnam pointed to cultural resistance by teachers,

> School-based outdoor learning is not so common in Vietnam due to curriculum and somehow difficult to change the traditional way of teaching and learning in the country (indoor learning). (respondent from Vietnam)

> Education has had a formal, structured emphasis from its inception here for cultural and historical reasons possibly as a result of the context being a previously agrarian society. To a lesser extent, there seems to be a historical/cultural barrier where many educationally progressive initiatives were seen as part of a colonial education. (respondent from Ireland)

Three respondents from the UK and Canada also mentioned risk and health and safety concerns. Other factors included time and a lack of awareness of the potential benefits. These comments illustrate how cultural factors influence possibilities for future development of OL (Bentsen et al., 2017).

Lack of Funding

According to most respondents, a lack of funding for OL was a barrier to some extent, but in some places, such as Indonesia, Taiwan, Poland, Canada, and the US, respondents considered it a significant one. The reasons for this are probably multiple. For example, if OL is provided by external providers or at remote sites, this entails extra expenditure by schools or parents to enable that. Where OL is more embedded within educational practice and happens on or near the school site, the additional costs of children participating is likely to be lower. However, providing progression from familiar to more remote and extraordinary natural environments with different learning possibilities will inevitably incur a financial cost.

Need for Volunteer Support

Not all countries involve volunteers in their OL provision; only some respondents in Australia, Canada, and the US reported that unpaid volunteers were usually involved in outdoor learning. In other countries, they were sometimes involved, but in Denmark, Poland, Spain, Switzerland, and Vietnam, they were never used, according to the survey respondents. However, requirements for high adult-to-children ratios to meet health and safety obligations for off-site visits and risk-averse societal attitudes may mean that parents and carers are needed to ensure compliance in many nations (ISGA, 2017). Community support can also extend possibilities for OL. In Indonesia, it was reported that parents and the society around the schools were also providers of OL; while in Finland, after-school clubs run by volunteers offered OL opportunities.

6   Discussion

In considering these responses from international expert commentators, we begin to appreciate how further work could contribute to addressing challenges associated with the development of school-based outdoor learning. The findings presented offer potential starting points for additional investigation. One possible method would be to develop a Delphi study, whereby ideas can be refined and contested within a panel of experts (Okoli & Pawlowski, 2004). Another fruitful avenue might be in-depth national surveys to test the resonance of the impressions that emerged from this study situated within greater detail of policy, practice, and barriers in various national contexts. Local studies that include the children's perspectives on how OL affects their lives will also provide valuable insight into how various offers are received.

These impressions and insights into the state of play internationally regarding school-based outdoor learning provide considerable food for thought. The number of expert commentators responding to the survey demonstrated that evidence for benefits from spending time in nature is in some respects well established. However, all described challenges in embedding OL within their educational systems, and countries appeared to be at different stages of development. For some, the challenge lay in cultural and material barriers, where the first steps may need to be awareness raising about the benefits to policy makers, practitioners, and the public (Learning & Teaching Scotland, 2010) or constructing infrastructure to support forms of outdoor learning that are accessible and affordable (Almers et al., 2020; Waite et al., 2016b). For others, dominant performativity culture meant that persuading school staff to make space for outdoor learning in busy content-driven curricular timetabling remained a hurdle (Waite, 2010a, b). Encouragingly, the main challenge seemed to be about changing mindsets rather than a lack of funding per se, and this cultural change can be achieved through on-the-job professional development training and experience (Waite et al., 2016b). At a national level, research and development efforts might profitably be directed towards identifying and understanding how to overcome specific challenges in a logical sequence appropriate to their context.

The alignment of methods of outdoor learning and motivations indicates how OL movements might be better tailored to address specific desired outcomes according to priorities, both at a national policy level and within schools themselves. Without regularity of curriculum-based learning outside the classroom, occasional forms of OL remain vulnerable to changes in priorities and external pressures (Waite, 2010a). Early years outdoor activities and on-site OL linked to the curriculum seemed to contribute to some degree to all desired outcomes and could comprise a minimum baseline of entitlement provision. A global priority to protect children's health and well-being and glaring inequalities in relation to this (UNCRC, 1989) also provide a compelling rationale for these methods to offer wider participation in the benefits of spending time in nature, and the additional provision of opportunities for outdoor and adventure education during schooling will make substantial contributions towards this goal. Sustainability agendas appeared to underpin strong motivation for promoting OL in many countries, whether at governmental or personal levels (Almers et al., 2020; HMG, 2018; Mawson, 2014). National parks and nature reserves were considered especially effective for inculcating care for others and the environment. Inclusion of visits to areas rich in biodiversity as part of children's experience at school will help to meet this aim. In short, increasing awareness of policy drivers and promoting the most effective forms of outdoor learning to achieve them can refine how OL is planned and operationalized at international, national, regional, and local levels.

Considering responses across countries and variation in emphases, it is apparent that explicit policy alignment would further facilitate designing outdoor learning programs to achieve desired goals. For teachers in some countries, having a policy directive to include more outdoor learning as an integrated element of curriculum delivery would give them permission to make room for it, although some teachers may still lack confidence and time to plan for this (Waite et al., 2016b). Having training and experiences in working outside is an effective tool to overcome personal resistance, and team teaching or on-site continuing professional development can be transformative (ibid.), but equally high-quality resources can provide a valuable springboard for local adaptations. Whether time, experience, or funds represent obstacles, the development of suitable OL environments within school grounds can enable a range of experiences on teachers' doorsteps, removing travel time and costs, the additional paperwork of repeated risk assessments, and external provider fees (ibid; Almers et al., 2020; Barfod et al., 2016; Passy, 2014).

Several commentators mentioned that inclusion of OL and its priority varied regionally and locally, so assessing patterns across whole nations is not clear cut. The interpretation of what OL might look like varied from macro-governmental and cultural influences through institutional expectations and affordances to the personal values and expertise of individuals within schools (Waite, 2010a, b). There was not agreement about every aspect within countries with multiple respondents, so findings derived from individual reports and small numbers obviously need to be interpreted with caution. Inevitably, local enactments and the position of the expert as policy maker, academic, or practitioner will shape opinions, but exploring such variation would support future collaborations to achieve greater consensus around intent, implementation, and impact (Ofsted, 2018) and clearer theories of change. An international project (PLaTO-Net Harmonization Project, see footnote 2 above) is currently underway to explore key terms, definitions, taxonomies, and ontologies related to outdoor experiences, based on a scoping literature review and collaboration of international experts in the field through analysis and discussion. This process is working towards conceptual models that can speak across nations. This ambition exceeds the possibilities of this small explorative study. Nonetheless, this research has highlighted some potential ways forward for the field.

Implications for the future

Suggestions that respondents made about how improvements could be made to school-based outdoor learning included the support of: grassroots teacher-led movements (Ireland); the Children in Nature network (US); continuing professional development, teacher education and collective provision (Australia, England, Scotland, Sweden, Switzerland); school grounds infrastructure development (Sweden, US, Japan); and outdoor learning being enshrined in educational policy, teachers' registration and professional recognition (Denmark, Norway, Scotland). To conclude,

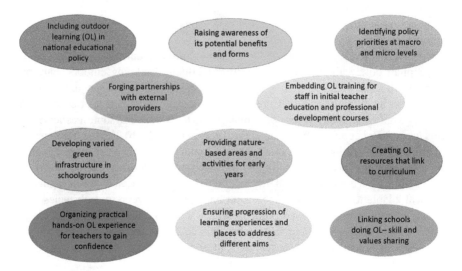

Fig. 1 Possible actions in developing school-based outdoor learning

Fig. 1 summarizes some possible actions that warrant consideration at national and local levels to support the further development of school-based outdoor learning.

Recommended further reading

1. Joyce, R. (2012) *Outdoor learning: Past and present.* Maidenhead: Open University Press.
2. Jeffs, T & Ord, J. (2018) *Rethinking Outdoor, Experiential and Informal Education.* Abingdon, Oxford: Routledge.
3. Alderslowe, L., Amus, G. & Devapriya, D.A. (2018) *Earth Care, People Care and Fair Share in Education: The Children in Permaculture Manual.* ERASMUS+project. https://issuu.com/childreninpermaculture/docs/cip_manual (accessed 01/09/2021).

Acknowledgements The Wildlife Trusts kindly gave permission for the publication of the original article arising from the results of the commissioned research and this summary chapter. Thanks are also due to all the experts in outdoor learning who contributed to the survey and to my colleagues in earlier contributory research projects referenced below.

Funding This research was funded by The Wildlife Trusts, UK, and informed by research funded by the Economic and Social Research Council, UK, grant number ES/J019445/1, and the Department for the Environment, Food and Rural Affairs, UK, Natural England and Historic England.

References

Almers, E., Askerlund, P., Samuelsson, T., & Waite, S. (2020). Children's preferences for school-yard features and understanding of ecosystem service innovations—A study in five Swedish preschools. *Journal of Adventure Education and Outdoor Learning.* https://doi.org/10.1080/147 29679.2020.1773879

Australian Government. (2009). *Living sustainably. The Australian government's national action plan for education for sustainability.* Canberra: Commonwealth of Australia. Retrieved April 8, 2021, from https://www.iau-hesd.net/sites/default/files/documents/2009_-_living_sustainably_the_australian_governments_national_action_plan_for_education_for_sustainability_fr.pdf.

Barfod, K., Ejbye, N., Mygind, L., & Bentsen, P. (2016). Increased provision of *udeskole* in Danish schools; An updated national population survey. *Urban Forestry Urban Greening, 20*, 277–281.

Bentsen, P. (2013). *Udeskole in Scandinavia.* Retrieved April 8, 2021, from https://www.childrenandnature.org/resources/udeskole-in-scandinavia-teaching-learning-in-natural-places/.

Bentsen, P., Ho, S., Gray, T., & Waite, S. (2017). A global view of learning outside the classroom. In S. Waite (Ed.), *Children learning outside the Classroom: From birth to eleven* (2nd ed., pp. 53–66). London: SAGE.

Carson, R. (1965). *The sense of wonder.* New York: HarperCollins.

FSA (Forest School Association). (2020). *What is forest school?* Retrieved April 8, 2021, from https://www.forestschoolassociation.org/what-is-forest-school/.

Gurholt, K. (2014). Joy of nature, *friluftsliv* education and self: Combining narrative and cultural-ecological approaches to environmental sustainability. *Journal of Adventure Education and Outdoor Learning, 14*, 233–246.

Gutman, L. M., & Schoon, I. (2016). A synthesis of causal evidence linking non-cognitive skills to later outcomes for children and adolescents. In M. S. Khine & S. Areepattamannil (Eds.), *Non-cognitive skills and factors in educational attainment* (pp. 171–198). Rotterdam: Sense Publishers.

Hammarsten, M., Askerlund, P., Almers, E., Avery, H., & Samuelsson, T. (2018). Developing ecological literacy in a forest garden: Children's perspectives. *Journal of Adventure Education and Outdoor Learning, 19*, 227–241.

HMG (Her Majesty's Government). (2018). *A green future: Our 25 year plan to improve the environment.* Retrieved April 8, 2021, https://www.gov.uk/government/publications/25-year-environment-plan.

ISGA (International School Grounds Alliance). (2017). *Risk in play and learning: Ubud-Höör declaration.* Retrieved April 8, 2021, https://www.internationalschoolgrounds.org/risk.

JOEE (Journal of Outdoor and Environmental Education). (2018). *Special issue: Forest school.* Retrieved April 8, 2021, from https://outdooreducationaustralia.org.au/library/march-2018-joee/.

Knight, S. (2013). *International perspectives on forest school: Natural spaces to play and learn.* London: SAGE.

Learning and Teaching Scotland. (2010). *Curriculum for excellence through outdoor learning.* Glasgow. Retrieved August 30, 2021, from https://education.gov.scot/Documents/cfe-through-outdoor-learning.pdf.

Louv, R. (2010). *Last child in the woods.* New York: Algonquin Books of Chapel Hill.

Maller, C. J. (2009). Promoting children's mental, emotional and social health through contact with nature: A model. *Health Education, 109*, 522–543.

Malone, K. (2008). *Every experience matters: An evidence based research report on the role of learning outside the classroom for children's whole development from birth to eighteen years.* Retrieved April 8, 2021, from https://www.researchgate.net/profile/Karen-Malone-3/publication/265231721_every_experience_matters_An_evidence_based_research_report_on_the_role_of_learning_outside_the_classroom_for_children%27s_whole_development_from_birth_to_eighteen_years/links/54414e170cf2a6a049a5704f/every-experience-matters-An-evidence-based-research-report-on-the-role-of-learning-outside-the-classroom-for-childrens-whole-development-from-birth-to-eighteen-years.pdf.

Malone, K., & Waite, S. (2016). *Student outcomes and natural schooling: Pathways from evidence to impact report*. https://doi.org/10.13140/RG.2.1.3327.7681. Retrieved April 8, 2021, from https://www.plymouth.ac.uk/uploads/production/document/path/6/6811/Student_o utcomes_and__natural_schooling_pathways_to_impact_2016.pdf.

Marmot, M., Allen, J., Boyce, T., Goldblatt, P., & Morrison, J. (2020). *Health equity in England: The Marmot review 10 years on*. London: Institute of Health Equity.

Maruyama, H. (2010). *Education for Sustainable Development (ESD) in Japan*. Retrieved April 8, 2021, from https://www.nier.go.jp/English/educationjapan/pdf/201103ESD.pdf.

Mawson, W. B. (2014). Experiencing the 'wild woods': The impact of pedagogy on children's experience of a natural environment. *European Early Childhood Education Research Journal, 22*, 513–524.

McCabe, S. (2015). Family leisure, opening a window on the meaning of family. *Annals of Leisure Research, 18*, 175–179.

Mullan, K. (2018). A child's day: Trends in time use in the UK from 1975 to 2015. *British Journal of Sociology, 70*, 997–1024.

Natural England. (2011). *Outdoor learning: Kings College London reports*. Retrieved April 8, 2021, from http://publications.naturalengland.org.uk/publication/4524600415223808.

Ofsted. (2018). *Curriculum research: Assessing intent, implementation and impact*. Retrieved April 8, 2021, from https://www.gov.uk/government/publications/curriculum-research-assessing-int ent-implementation-and-impact.

Okoli, C., & Pawlowski, S. D. (2004). The Delphi method as a research tool: An example, design considerations and applications. *Information & Management, 42*, 15–29.

Passy, R. (2014). School gardens: Teaching and learning outside the front door. *Education, 3–13*(42), 23–38.

Passy, R., Bentsen, P., Gray, T., & Ho, S. (2019). Integrating outdoor learning into the curriculum: An exploration in four nations. *Curriculum Perspectives, 39*, 73–78.

Paterson, C., Tyler, R., & Lexmond, J. (2014). *Character and resilience manifesto*. London: The All-Party Parliamentary Group (APPG) on Social Mobility. Retrieved April 8, 2021, from https://www.character-uk.org/wp-content/uploads/character-and-resilience.pdf.

Prince, H. E. (2019). Changes in outdoor learning in primary schools in England, 1995 and 2017: Lessons for good practice. *Journal of Adventure Education and Outdoor Learning, 19*, 329–342.

Scottish Government. (2018). Curriculum for excellence. Retrieved April 8, 2021, from https://edu cation.gov.scot/documents/All-experiencesoutcomes18.pdf.

The Wildlife Trusts. (2021). *Nature friendly schools*. Retrieved April 8, 2021, from https://www. naturefriendlyschools.co.uk/.

UKCES (UK Commission for Employment and Skills). (2014). *The future of work jobs and skills in 2030*. Retrieved April 8, 2021, from https://assets.publishing.service.gov.uk/government/upl oads/system/uploads/attachment_data/file/303335/the_future_of_work_key_findings_edit.pdf.

United Nations Convention on the Rights of the Child. (1989). Retrieved April 8, 2021, from https://downloads.unicef.org.uk/wp-content/uploads/2010/05/UNCRC_united_nat ions_convention_on_the_rights_of_the_child.pdf.

Waite, S. (2010a). Losing our way? Declining outdoor opportunities for learning for children aged between 2 and 11. *Journal of Adventure Education and Outdoor Learning, 10*, 111–126.

Waite, S. (2010b). Teaching and learning outside the classroom: Personal values, alternative pedagogies and standards. *Education, 3–13*(39), 65–82.

Waite, S. (2019). *Outdoor learning research: Insight into forms and functions*. Abingdon: Routledge.

Waite, S., Bølling, M., & Bentsen, P. (2016a). Comparing apples and pears? A conceptual framework for understanding forms of outdoor learning through comparison of English Forest Schools and Danish udeskole. *Environmental Education Research, 22*, 868–892.

Waite, S., Passy, R., Gilchrist, M., Hunt, A., & Blackwell, I. (2016b). *Natural connections demon-stration project 2012–2016b: Final report*; Natural England. Retrieved April 8, 2021, from http:// publications.naturalengland.org.uk/publication/6636651036540928.

Wells, N. M., & Lekies, K. S. (2006). Nature and the life course: Pathways from childhood nature experiences to adult environmentalism. *Children, Youth and Environments, 16,* 1–24.

White, M. P., Alcock, I., Grellier, J., Wheeler, B. W., Hartig, T., Warber, S. L., Bone, A., Depledge, M. H., & Fleming, L. E. (2019). Spending at least 120 minutes a week in nature is associated with good health and wellbeing. *Science and Reports, 9,* 7730.

Sue Waite is visiting Associate Professor at Jönköping University, Sweden, and former Reader in Outdoor Learning at the University of Plymouth, UK. She has researched and published widely regarding outdoor learning and health and wellbeing benefits from nature and is a member of Natural England's Strategic Research Group on Connecting People with Nature.

Natural Connections: Learning About Outdoor-Based Learning

Rowena Passy and Ian Blackwell

1 Introduction

In this chapter we introduce the Natural Connections Demonstration Project (NCDP) and discuss the evaluation methodology embedded in the project from its outset. We then draw on data from 24 case-study visits to describe the imaginative and innovative work undertaken by schools participating in the project. We conclude by discussing the importance of continuing professional development (CPD) for staff who are taking children's learning outside.

2 The Natural Connections Demonstration Project

The long-term aims underpinning the Natural Connections Demonstration Project were outlined in The Natural Choice White Paper (2011), produced by the UK Coalition Government of the time. This White Paper emerged in response to public and political concerns about a disconnection with nature across the population. Funding was set aside in the White Paper for a demonstration project, which would be large enough to enable testing of a variety of approaches to explore the most effective ways of enabling school-age children in England to benefit from learning experiences in their local natural environments. The resulting project—NCDP—was seen as the first phase in realising a long-term ambition of embedding outdoor curricular learning into schools: if successful in both stimulating and meeting the apparent

R. Passy (✉)
52 Baring St, Plymouth PL4 8NG, UK
e-mail: R.Passy@plymouth.ac.uk

I. Blackwell
2 Westonfields, Totnes, Devon TQ9 5QT, UK
e-mail: iblackwell@marjon.ac.uk

© The Author(s) 2022
R. Jucker and J. von Au (eds.), *High-Quality Outdoor Learning*,
https://doi.org/10.1007/978-3-031-04108-2_18

latent demand in schools, Natural Connections would be replicated and amplified more widely, with subsequent phases having different foci, such as outdoor play or health outcomes (an ambition, we feel a decade on, that is struggling to be realised due to current UK Government priorities that are focused elsewhere).

From the outset, therefore, the purpose of Natural Connections, being a *Demonstration* Project, was to investigate effective ways of engaging primary, secondary and special schools with learning outside the classroom in the natural environment (LINE). This was achieved by establishing NCDP as both a practical (delivery-focused) and as a research (evidence-focused) project. After a national tendering process, NCDP was awarded to the Plymouth Institute of Education, University of Plymouth and, as a consequence, the schools recruited to the project, the project management team, the research team, external providers and volunteers attached to the project were all based in the South West region of England. The project ran from 2012 to 2016, and was managed at the national level by Natural England, on behalf of the Department for the Environment, Food & Rural Affairs (DEFRA; the main funders). Other project funders were Natural England and English Heritage.

NCDP worked in areas of high multiple deprivation in the region, both urban (Plymouth, Torbay and Bristol) and rural (Cornwall and North Somerset), with the aim of supporting primary, secondary and special schools in these areas to investigate the potential of LINE for curriculum delivery. To overcome the acknowledged challenges of transport costs and time (Dillon & Dickie, 2012), NCDP focused on schools accessing green or spaces within walking distance of school, including (but not limited to) school grounds, municipal parks, nature reserves, food producers, 'blue' (i.e. water-related) spaces and local woodland.

While NCDP was a large-scale project involving 125 schools and 5,000 teaching staff, it was also important to work with each school to shape interventions and activities to meet individual needs and priorities, and to provide teachers with the most effective ways to offer inspiring and successful curricular learning in local green and/or blue spaces. In order to realise this targeted support, clusters of schools were provided with expert, independent advisers to help them access the range of quality LINE opportunities, resources, volunteers, community partners and outdoor providers that were available locally. These experts—called 'hub leaders' (see below) —offered face-to-face advice to build awareness, understanding and confidence in LINE, helped establish networks of teachers and schools, and supported volunteering opportunities in schools. This delivery model was designed to also embed a sustainable change in practice, both in how schools approached LINE and in the nature of the services available to them, to ensure a legacy beyond the life of the project.

In order to achieve these objectives, four core elements of the project were established:

- an independent brokerage model. This consisted of five 'hub leaders', one for each of the five geographic areas. These education experts were contracted by the central NCDP team (based at University of Plymouth) to manage relationship-building between schools, and between schools and providers, at the sub-regional level.

- a volunteer development programme was set up to test the role that volunteering might play in assisting schools initiate, diversify, extend and improve their LINE activities.
- a web service to publicise the services offered by outdoor providers and to distribute free LINE teaching resources.
- an evaluation programme to establish the effectiveness of the delivery model.

Overall, the purpose of the demonstration project, therefore, was to establish and test the effectiveness of these four elements in achieving the project's aims and objectives, and to provide clear recommendations for future activity and development.

The University of Plymouth devised a distributed model of responsibility that operated at four levels: the central team → hub leaders → beacon schools → cluster schools. The concept was to build local networks in which the local brokerage agencies ('hub leaders') would first recruit and enhance the work of schools that were already successful in LINE ('beacon schools'). These would, in turn, lead and support a local network of other schools ('cluster schools') in developing their LINE practices. The vision behind the model was a 'needs-led' approach, building sustainable LINE that was responsive to local circumstances, enabling participation, skills sharing and collaboration among schools, each of whom, to varying degrees, had both something to offer and to learn about outdoor learning. The ambition was that these networks of schools would become autonomous after project funding ceased.

The central team's initial task was to recruit hub leaders in five locations with areas of high multiple deprivation (Bristol, Cornwall, North Somerset, Plymouth and Torbay) who would undertake the work at the local level. Once recruited, the five hubs located beacon schools. A person—a LINE lead—was selected within each beacon school to become the main contact for the project. Each LINE lead aimed to build a 'LINE team' of up to seven people, including senior management, a governor, parent, teachers and other staff to ensure that LINE responsibility was shared and that, should the LINE lead leave the school, expertise and momentum would not be lost. Supported by the hub leader, the LINE team subsequently recruited four to eight cluster schools that had limited experience of LINE at the time of recruitment, and helped organise collaboration and sharing of expertise at the local level.

The intention was that the beacon schools would demonstrate success in and benefits from teaching and learning across the curriculum through LINE. This would then encourage other schools to take part and create mutually supportive communities focused on outdoor learning, which could be responsive to local priorities, needs and strengths. Over time, as cluster schools developed their own expertise, the aim was that they might become beacon schools and provide support for other local schools willing to engage with LINE. The intention, therefore, was that this approach would develop a sustainable, rhizomatic model that would expand both internally throughout each school and externally across schools as the clusters grew in confidence. Overall, the aim was to create an infrastructure that would, over three years, see a cultural shift in participating schools towards embedding LINE in their policies and embracing LINE as part of their everyday practice. The rhizome metaphor reflects the idea that support and growth were intended to be diverse, symbiotic and horizontal rather than top-down, leading to innovation and independent development of LINE at a local level, with transfer of information and learning across all levels.

3   Natural Connections Demonstration Project Evaluation

As this was a demonstration project, evaluation of Natural Connections was complex and wide-ranging. It was central to informing delivery and to capturing project outputs and outcomes, and was designed to:

- offer iterative feedback throughout the project to shape and inform the delivery model
- capture and report on outputs and outcomes
- evaluate the effectiveness of the structures and processes in meeting the aims of the project
- monitor the impact of the project on participating schools, organisations and individuals
- monitor the financial sustainability of the project model, including targets related to income generation
- make evidence-based recommendations for the design of future outdoor learning programmes.

In practical terms, it had two overarching aims: to evaluate whether and, if so, how the project was successful in stimulating LINE activity in project schools over three years; and to assess the impact of the project on participants. This would allow return of evidence-led conclusions about the model and its replication, and was balanced with the need for the evaluation to be manageable and realistic for schools. The research was embedded from the start of the project and designed around a framework of key evaluation questions that would enable the central team to monitor the key project processes, the relative success of each project element, and degrees of change in LINE activity at school level. These different elements would provide a comprehensive understanding of project development as a whole.

The evaluation framework enabled each of the four core project elements (brokerage, web service, volunteering and evaluation) to be systematically tested against a number of underpinning assumptions. The complexity of the project, that had three aims, four core elements and a distributed model of responsibility in five areas across the South West of England meant that a mixed method approach was most appropriate (Pommier et al., 2010). Mixed methods generated quantitative and qualitative data, thereby facilitating investigation and demonstration of the project's scale, scope, impact and processes (see Waite et al., 2016, 25).

Baseline surveys measured LINE activity levels at the start of the project, and activity logs (a subset of the surveys) captured a snapshot of activity in June and November to understand longitudinal and seasonal change. Other data collection instruments included reflective surveys (n = 3,083) which were employed with LINE leads, LINE providers, volunteers, pupils and parents to elicit their views of LINE activities, developments and impact. Semi-structured interviews were conducted with central team staff (n = 16) and hub leaders (n = 35), and 24 case-study visits involved semi-structured interviews with school staff (n = 119), volunteers (n = 11) and pupils (n = 167). The project's final report (Waite et al., 2016), which can be found on the Natural England website, includes full details of project organisation, implementation and evaluation.

Case study context

The 24 case-study visits were spread over the project lifetime and across the five hubs. The aim initially was to cover as wide a range of geographical, school and cluster-beacon models as possible in order to capture the full range of schools' experiences in the project. As NCDP progressed, however, these plans shifted to accommodate developments within the project; the Bristol and North Somerset hubs worked increasingly closely together and the distinction between beacon and cluster schools became blurred. All five hubs adopted a more democratic approach which meant that, rather than a hierarchical model of 'beacons' and 'cluster' schools, the hubs preferred to create a more horizontal, collaborative network system in which learning and expertise were pooled and shared. As a result, and following hub leader recommendations or through our own knowledge from the evaluation, schools at different stages of embedding LINE in their everyday curricular activity from across the region were invited to participate in the case-study phase of the research, regardless of their cluster/beacon status. The 24 case studies were divided across the hubs as follows: in Bristol and North Somerset, we visited six schools; in Plymouth six; in Cornwall five; in Torbay six. The final case-study visit was to a school in North Devon, which had joined NCDP through the Naturally Healthy Devon Schools project (see Waite et al., 2016, 30 for details). Altogether we visited 18 primary, two secondary and four special schools, reflecting the proportion of school sectors recruited to the project.

Schools generally responded positively to the invitation to participate as they felt that they had something positive to show, were committed to the idea and practice of promoting LINE, and were willing to share the ways in which they were trying to do this. Beyond this commonality we found that schools were motivated by different factors related to the community they served, and that they had a wide range of different approaches to LINE. The whole offered a rich tapestry of imaginative practices that provided inspiration at local, hub and project levels.

Researchers usually visited for a full school day, which enabled them to see a variety of LINE activities and talk to staff, pupils and, when possible, volunteers. Interviews with the headteacher or LINE lead set out the LINE vision for each school, and subsequent interviews with staff and pupils enabled us to discover the types of activities that were undertaken, their aims and perceived impact. Exploring the school grounds, sometimes with staff and at other times without, helped us to put the views expressed into context and to understand the affordances and/or limitations of each site. Following ethical clearance from the Plymouth Institute of Education for the project, all participants were assured of voluntary participation, their right to withdraw and secure data storage and management. Interviews were recorded with permission, and transcribed onto a template devised to facilitate evaluation against the project assumptions, aims and objectives. While case-study schools were named with permission in different fora (see, for instance, the Council for Learning Outside the Classroom blog https://learningoutsidetheclassroomblog.org/category/case-studies/), individual contributions remained anonymous.

The English education system

England has a fragmented educational system in which school choice, school autonomy and diversity of provision have been fundamental principles, aimed at raising standards, since the early 1990s. Some schools are obliged to follow the National Curriculum (see https://www.gov.uk/government/collections/national-curriculum), but others are not; some are managed by independent Multi-Academy Trusts (that have between three and 40 schools in their Trust) and others by the local authority (local education administration). In addition, there are special schools for pupils with special educational needs, although inclusion is part of mainstream education.

The common educational framework has three elements; the examination system, in which pupils take compulsory external examinations at the ages of seven, 11 and 16; the inspection system of Ofsted, which is scheduled to visit each school every three to four years; and the so-called 'league tables' in which schools are ranked according to their pupils' examination performance. This "tyranny of testing" (Mansell, 2007), in which pupil performance affects school recruitment and therefore funding levels, can have the effect of "compounding the disadvantages of the already socioeconomically disadvantaged" (Passy & Ovenden-Hope, 2020, 225) by failing to take into account the children's socioeconomic or familial background, or the efforts a school can make to support disadvantaged students in accessing their education. The testing regime can also have an inhibiting effect on teachers' willingness to experiment with new ideas and approaches. This was particularly the case with outdoor-based learning at the start of NCDP; taking learning outdoors was often regarded as a risky approach in which time might be 'wasted' outside rather than focusing on specific curricular requirements in a managed environment indoors (e.g. Passy, 2014). We therefore welcomed hub leaders' reports that LINE meetings generated both excitement and a sense of reassurance among project participants; there was excitement in the sense of discovering new approaches, and reassurance for participants who realised that there were others equally committed to LINE.

NDCP was, for all of us, a novel and exciting opportunity to learn about and to share the ways in which LINE and curricular learning were compatible. It was fundamentally an experimental project in which different approaches to LINE promotion and development were tried and tested at hub and school level, and in which we were finding ways of working with the grain of the educational system to offer children regular outdoor educational experiences. In schools that were confident or gaining confidence in their practice, we found that teachers were encouraged to experiment with different ways of engaging their pupils with curricular LINE. Those schools that lacked confidence learned from practices shared at network events and were supported by the hub leaders who found that continuing professional development (CPD) was central to the dynamic, rhizomatic process of learning and sharing across schools, clusters and hubs. The central team, too, engaged in this process by setting up CPD sessions as part of their delivery remit, and learned about new methods and approaches as part of their evaluation. As a result, the project was witness to much imaginative and innovative practice in participating schools.

In what follows, we draw on the qualitative data generated over two and a half years to discuss the types of outdoor-based learning that was undertaken in the case-study schools.

4   Imaginative and Innovative LINE Practice

Case-study visits showed that each school's vision for LINE was both active and reactive; it was partially constructed from staff members' ideas of what outdoor-based learning should or could provide, and partially made in response to the pupils' perceived needs. As the project progressed, we saw increasing numbers of teachers demonstrate their understanding of the importance of an holistic approach to learning that took account of children's physical, cognitive and socio-emotional development (e.g. Passy & Gilchrist, 2021) and that created a fuller educational experience than that prescribed by the cognitive-heavy National Curriculum demands of the time. As a result much LINE activity was aimed at fulfilling curricular requirements, but at the same time almost all case-study schools engaged with different types of investigation or experience that were designed to support different aspects of their pupils' development. Almost all case-study schools used variations of a Forest School approach with some or all of their children.

Below we have divided the case studies into three broad approaches to LINE that demonstrate the *whys* and *hows* of LINE in case-study NCDP schools. All quotations are unattributed to maintain interviewee anonymity.

Approach 1: the right to experience nature

The majority of case-study interviewees believed that today's children have less access to the natural environment than they had—a belief supported by research evidence (e.g. Hunt et al., 2016; Moss, 2012)—and were keen to offer children the chances to go outdoors. Often this was a form of nostalgia in which school staff regretted the increased use of electronic devices and/or wanted children to have similar experiences to their own childhoods, but several headteachers saw the lack of opportunity to engage with the natural world as a deeper issue. Knowledge that pupils lived in urban areas with little or no green space around them, and/or had little opportunity to visit green or blue spaces, fuelled these headteachers' argument that it was the school's responsibility to take children outdoors; as one commented, it is a "fundamental right for any child … [to] have that entitlement and opportunity …

for their spiritual growth, the personal growth ... [and] appreciation of the world".
He argued that being outdoors.

> connects children to something at a very deep human, almost animal level that being in the
> classroom may not ... it awakens the senses; fresh air, sunshine, blue sky ... Experiencing
> the elements, it's just a natural experience ... that is energising for anyone and particularly
> children.

Linked to this conviction was a belief that children should come to understand more
about the natural world and to become aware of their surroundings as they undertook
different tasks and activities. Examples of activities in these schools were:

- primary and secondary pupils working together to build hedgehog houses in the
  school grounds; making bat shelters
- making a squirrel 'assault course', in which squirrels jumped onto different ledges
  for food; pretending to be a squirrel and hiding conkers for winter 'food'
- having a carousel of pupil-led activities that included making bug hotels; making
  clay creatures; sketching; writing a poem inspired by listening to natural sounds
- appointing children as Wildlife Champions, whose task was to protect and
  encourage wildlife in and around the school grounds.

Participating in low-key activities such as these gave children the space to experience
the natural environment in their own time; to make discoveries, to explore links and to
have (often) new sensory experiences. But part of the reason for introducing children
to the natural world was to awaken an interest in and sense of responsibility for
the health of the planet or, as one headteacher put it, to learn about dealing with
'Mother Nature's Trustfund'. This idea of a bounteous but limited natural world is
close to that of One Health, an inter-disciplinary approach which contends that the
health of human, animal and planetary life is interconnected, and that we need to
work together to optimise the health of all (Stadtländer, 2015) if we are to avoid a
climate catastrophe. Here activities such as making bird boxes, composting, anti-
plastic pollution campaigns, digging out ponds and planting trees, in some schools
complemented by work on food production and food miles, were cited as activities
designed to support learning about the importance of the natural environment.

Approach 2: providing horizon-broadening experiences

Headteachers and teachers in particularly economically-deprived areas often spoke
of their pupils' narrow horizons, and of their school's responsibility for introducing
young people to the widest range of experiences possible. There were multiple
reasons given by interviewees for such an approach: that it enabled children to see
beyond the "present and the particular" (Bailey, 1984) and imagine a range of possible
interests, hobbies and/or occupations; that dealing with new situations encouraged
confidence and resilience; that it provoked children's curiosity; that children enjoyed
such outings. Here a teacher speaks about the effect that trips of all kinds can have
on literacy and vocabulary:

> Lots of these children are from quite deprived backgrounds and they don't get many opportu-
> nities to go to places. And that's really clear in their literacy ... A child from a family where

the adults would read to them and take them to places will have millions of ideas to relate to one word, 'forest', because they'll have seen it in so many different books, and they'll have been to the forest lots of times on different occasions, whereas a child that hasn't been read to and taken to those places won't … We did a beach topic last year and we spent loads of time at the beach, because that was the best thing for developing their language, because they had experience of that … [the writing afterwards was] hugely different and more inspired.

At least two schools initiated a form of 'experience passport', loosely based on the National Trust's idea of '50 things to do before you are 11¾' (see https://www.nat ionaltrust.org.uk/features/50-things-to-do-before-youre-11--activity-list) and that included such activities as local walks, building a shelter, exploring the outdoors on a wintery day, identifying ten wildflowers and visiting a farm.

Some teachers were more ambitious in the trips that they planned for their pupils, and two schools with secondary aged pupils (11–16) encouraged a team to participate in the annual Ten Tors walk across Dartmoor (see https://www.tentors.org.uk/), with one teacher commenting that this challenging walk had multiple aims and benefits:

> … to give an awareness and inspire of the beauty of Dartmoor and wilderness areas … To get children confident at walking in the outdoors. Those kinds of things … the survival, the map work, the compass, the team work. Organisation of equipment and looking after self.

Other outdoor-based learning trips included visiting farms, local woods, other schools, parks; orienteering on Dartmoor; camping trips on Dartmoor and other local places; and water-based activities such as sailing and kayaking.

Some schools, with perhaps less available funding, used imaginative ways to introduce new experiences in the school grounds, such as:

- Secondary-aged pupils undertaking a 'manhunt', with some hiding in the woods and others 'finding' them. Each then drew on this experience to write a story about what it would be like to be a spy, and this was followed by pupils bringing their work into the dance studio where they created movement material around their stories.
- Re-creating the Cornish rebellion of 1497. Pupils imagined participating in the rebellion and marched around the school grounds, shouting slogans. The aim was to encourage them to have a sense of and to question the historical accuracy of events; for instance, how long could they keep up the marching and chanting before becoming tired and disillusioned?

Approach 3: understanding others and making a contribution

A third approach was to encourage pupils to be aware of, develop empathy for and contribute to different local communities. There were three main rationales for this. The first was to encourage pupils to understand the challenges that individuals and/or communities could face during their lives, with examples such as:

- Carrying water from the bottom to the top of a steeply-sloping part of the school site to appreciate the practicalities of water shortages in some African villages.

- Building a refugee camp on the school site in an attempt to understand the challenges that follow natural disasters such as floods or volcanoes.
- Blindfolding pupils outdoors so that they could listen without distraction to an ex-marine telling the story of how he and some fellow marines were lost at sea for three days, and how finding a log saved their lives. The cold weather intensified the impact of the story, and both teachers and pupils described it as "very powerful".

The second rationale was to encourage pupils to see that their contribution mattered or made a visible difference, a perception reinforced possibly via newspaper articles or their own internal school newsletter. One school undertook an annual John Muir Award week (see https://www.johnmuirtrust.org/john-muir-award) in which Year 6 pupils (aged 10–11) worked with staff and student teachers on the four challenges of Discover, Explore, Conserve and Share in their school grounds. The 'Conserve' phase was used to repair, maintain and renew different parts of this extensive area that contained boardwalks near the river, a pond, different paths, bird boxes and vegetable-growing areas. This week was regarded as the highlight of the year for Year 6 pupils, and ensured that the grounds were maintained at minimum cost for all to enjoy during the rest of the year. Another school gave children the responsibility for developing projects on the school farm, and these included installing water pipes for the farm area, building a donkey shed, investigating the farm budget and selling farm-produced meat.

The third rationale was to have new experiences that would alert pupils to global issues outside of school. One headteacher argued that for some students school learning can be abstract and without a clear purpose, and suggested that learning "in real life allows some children to see that there is a greater purpose to what they are doing". Examples of such practical, community-based learning included:

- Growing vegetables in the school garden and donating them to local foodbanks
- Planting trees in collaboration with the Woodland Trust and the local council (municipal authority). The aim of this project was to commemorate fallen soldiers from the local area, and to involve their families in planting the trees and making and placing plaques in memory of their relatives. The school has pledged to look after the trees.
- Collecting rubbish from the beach, most of which was used later in an arts-based project.

These different projects and activities offered children a wide range of experiences, enabling them to engage in different ways with different topics while—as one head-teacher put it—"varying the diet" by taking the learning outside. In the final section, we discuss the challenges that undertaking these activities present for teachers and the importance of continuing professional development (CPD) for school staff.

5 Discussion: NCDP and Continuing Professional Development

These case studies have highlighted a number of innovative and creative LINE practices and for some readers the range, scale and scope of these ideas may seem daunting. In support of colleagues who want to initiate more outdoor learning activities in their setting, we now discuss practical ways to introduce Natural Connections approaches into everyday practice. As found in many other studies, teachers in the NCDP faced a number of challenges in making learning outside the classroom a more regular, embedded feature of school life. The main barriers tend to be teacher confidence, changing pedagogy (i.e. why, when and how to adapt teaching skills and approaches to the outdoor environment), integrating outdoor environments into the demands of the school curriculum, creating effective outdoor-indoor learning opportunities, and then demonstrating that learning is actually taking place and impacting on children's progression and attainment (Rickinson et al., 2012; Nicol et al., 2007; Thorburn & Allison, 2013; van Dijk-Wesselius et al., 2020). The Natural Connections central team and hub leaders were alert to these challenges and collated examples of good practice that highlighted ways to overcome these issues. These research and practice-based resources were made available to schools and guided the project's professional development strategy.

Studies of in-service teacher education have argued that professional development is an on-going process with, ideally, each teacher being supported with a personal "learning journey" (Guskey, 2002; Kennedy, 2005) where "change is primarily an experientially based learning process for teachers" (Guskey, 2002, 384). What the Natural Connections project set out to do, in response, was to overcome the varied barriers to LINE by offering diverse, enjoyable, blended and sustained professional development opportunities that not only enabled teaching staff to be more effective and comfortable when operating in outdoor environments, but were tailored to the needs of teachers and their desire to see a change in student learning outcomes. Establishing this, particularly at the start of a school's engagement in the project, took time. The hub leader needed to understand the needs of individual staff and LINE teams, and the priorities and ethos of each school in order to respond with an appropriate, engaging professional development plan for the individual schools. The central team, in line with its role of project strategic oversight, organised sub-regional or regional level professional development opportunities, as well as developing a web-site of teaching resources. Although time-consuming at first, this collective strategy was critical to the success of NCDP.

The CPD programme was core to the cultural change in schools we wanted to instigate and it was, therefore, important to base this programme on a thorough understanding of key elements of effective in-service professional development and the actual issues teachers face that thwart delivery of high-quality LINE. In response, NCDP created a range of informal and formal development opportunities. These included regular peer-to-peer sharing, in which network events saw teaching staff meeting to discuss a pre-agreed topic, such as 'Science in the School Garden' or

'Teach on the Beach', often led by a teacher who wanted to share their own practice. CPD events also involved external experts, such as marine biologists, garden designers, story-tellers or artists, who gave practical advice and low-cost ideas. The location of the events varied: sometimes they were held at a school so improvements to the school-grounds could be viewed or a class could be observed learning outside; at other times teaching staff met at a nearby natural location to explore its affordances for learning, such as a woodland, nature reserve, riverside walk or city farm. The emphasis throughout was on teachers physically being outside and learning through investigation, exploration, debate and 'hands-on' outdoor experiences—they were 'in the shoes' of children for a few hours and embodied the learning. Subsequently hub leaders facilitated group reflections on these experiences and teachers discussed how this learning could be implemented in practice (and at little cost) in the green spaces immediately around their school setting. In addition to these more informal approaches, more traditional training opportunities were made available to staff, such as having an experienced outdoor learning mentor, attending training days and conferences, taking Master's Level modules at Plymouth University, hearing from national and international outdoor learning practitioners, and having access to the latest research and best practice.

Taken together, this broad, dynamic approach to professional development aimed to increase the skills, confidence and 'can do' attitude of the participants as they came to recognise the multi-faceted and creative possibilities of LINE. Consequently, by seeing LINE in practice—seeing the enthusiasm of respected colleagues and observing pupils deeply engaged in and excited about curriculum learning—teachers' attitudes to outdoor learning shifted; they acknowledged LINE's potential value and they saw gains for their pupils from their successful implementation of the learning from the CPD activities. NCDP also acknowledged that professional development needs to be enjoyable, practical and should lead to greater professional satisfaction, and it was rewarding to hear that 79 per cent of teachers who benefitted from NCDP reported a positive impact on their teaching practice (Waite et al., 2016, 76). As part of a project that spanned three years, these structured, flexible, regular professional development opportunities had a cumulative, enduring effect on those involved which, we believe, has resulted in a sustained, transformative impact on their teaching and has led to cultural shifts in the schools well beyond the life-time of NCDP. To conclude, the importance of regular, high-quality, well-thought-out, varied and tailored continuing professional development (CPD) for embedding LINE into schools should not be underestimated.

Recommended further reading

1. Waite, S., Passy, R., Gilchrist, M., Hunt, A. & Blackwell, I. (2016). *Natural Connections Demonstration Project, 2012–2016: Final Report.* Natural England Commissioned Reports, NECR215. http://publications.natura lengland.org.uk/publication/6636651036540928

2. Passy, R. & Gilchrist, M. (2021). Child Development and Outdoor Learning. In: Maisey, D. & Campbell-Barr, V. (eds), *Why do teachers need to know about Child Development? Strengthening Professional Identity and Well-Being.* London: Bloomsbury, pp.43–57.
3. Cutting, R. and Passy, R. (eds.) (2022) *Contemporary Approaches to Outdoor Learning: Animals, the Environment and New Methods.* London: Palgrave Macmillan.

References

Bailey, C. (1984). *Beyond the present and the particular: A theory of liberal education.* London: Routledge and Kegan Paul.

Dillon, J., & Dickie. (2012). *Learning in the natural environment: Review of social and economic benefits and barriers. Natural England Commissioned Reports, NECR092.* Retrieved June 10, 2021, from http://publications.naturalengland.org.uk/publication/1321181.

Guskey, T. (2002). Professional development and teacher change. *Teachers and Teaching: Theory and Practice, 8*(3–4), 381–391.

HM Government. (2011). *The Natural Choice: Securing the value of nature.* Retrieved June 10, 2021, from https://www.gov.uk/government/uploads/system/uploads/attachment_data/file/228842/8082.pdf.

Hunt, A., Stewart, D., Burt, J., & Dillon, J. (2016). *Monitor of Engagement with the Natural Environment: a pilot to develop an indicator of visits to the natural environment by children—Results from years 1 and 2 (March 2013 to February 2015). Natural England Commissioned Reports, NECR208.* Retrieved June 10, 2021, from https://assets.publishing.service.gov.uk/government/uploads/system/uploads/attachment_data/file/498944/mene-childrens-report-years-1-2.pdf.

Kennedy, A. (2005). Models of continuing professional development: A framework for analysis. *Journal of in-Service Education, 31*(2), 235–250.

Mansell, W. (2007). *Education by numbers: The Tyranny of testing.* London: Politico's Publishing.

Moss, S. (2012). *Natural childhood.* National Trust. Retrieved June 10, 2021, from https://nt.global.ssl.fastly.net/documents/read-our-natural-childhood-report.pdf.

Nicol, R., Higgins, P., Ross, H., & Mannion, G. (2007). *Outdoor education in Scotland: A summary of recent research.* Perth: Scottish Natural Heritage.

Passy, R. (2014). School gardens: teaching and learning outside the front door. *Education 3–13, 42*(1), 23–38. Retrieved June 10, 2021, from https://doi.org/10.1080/03004279.2011.636371.

Passy, R., & Gilchrist, M. (2021). Child development and outdoor learning. In D. Maisey, & V. Campbell-Barr (Eds.), Why do teachers need to know about child development? Strengthening professional identity and well-being (pp.43–57). London: Bloomsbury.

Passy, R., & Ovenden-Hope, T. (2020). Exploring school leadership in coastal schools: 'Getting a fair deal' for students in disadvantaged communities. *Journal of Education Policy, 35*(2), 222–236. Retrieved June 10, 2021, from https://doi.org/10.1080/02680939.2019.1573382.

Pommier, J., Guevel, M.-R., & Jourdan, D. (2010). Evaluation of health promotion in schools: a realistic evaluation approach using mixed methods. *BMC Public Health, 10*(43).

Rickinson, M., Hunt, A., Rogers, J., & Dillon, J. (2012). *School leader and teacher insights into learning outside the classroom in natural environments. Natural England Commissioned Report NECR097.* Retrieved June 10, 2021, from http://publications.naturalengland.org.uk/file/1995820.

Stadtländer, C. (2015). One Health: People, animals, and the environment. *Infection Ecology & Epidemiology, 5*(1), 30514 Retrieved June 10, 2021, from https://doi.org/10.3402/iee.v5.30514.

Thorburn, M., & Allison, P. (2013). Analysing attempts to support outdoor learning in Scottish schools. *Journal of Curriculum Studies, 45*(3), 418–440.

van Dijk-Wesselius, J. E., van den Berg, A. E., Maas, J., & Hovinga, D. (2020). Green school-yards as outdoor learning environments: Barriers and solutions as experienced by primary school teachers. *Frontiers in Psychology, 10*, 2919. https://doi.org/10.3389/fpsyg.2019.02919 (accessed10/06/2021).

Waite, S., Passy, R., Gilchrist, M., Hunt, A., & Blackwell, I. (2016). *Natural connections demonstration project, 2012–2016: Final report. Natural England Commissioned Reports, NECR215.* Retireved June 10, 2021, from http://publications.naturalengland.org.uk/publication/663665103 6540928.

Rowena Passy has a long-standing interest in learning outdoors, at first through competitive horse-riding and teaching, and subsequently in academia. She was Evaluation Manager for the Natural Connections Demonstration project at the University of Plymouth; Recent projects include the cross-cultural Erasmus+ Go Out and Learn, and supporting Public Health Dorset with links between wellbeing and physical activity. Rowena Passy is the corresponding author: R.Passy@plymouth.ac.uk.

Ian Blackwell has worked in the learning outside the classroom sector for 25 years and was Project Manager for the Natural Connections Demonstration Project at the University of Plymouth. Ian is Forest School Programme Manager at Duchy College, Cornwall, and a Visiting Lecturer at Plymouth Marjon University (UK) where he teaches on outdoor learning and ESD modules. He is also the founder of Dangerous Dads CIC, a social enterprise that supports father figures and their children.

Outdoor School in Germany. Theoretical Considerations and Empirical Findings

Christian Armbrüster and Matthias D. Witte

1   Introduction

Outdoor school as an approach to schooling and the practice of teaching and learning is still in its infancy in Germany. This means that we as a team of researchers from the Johannes Gutenberg University Mainz were breaking new ground when we embarked upon a pilot project,[1] which involved teaching interdisciplinary material in line with the curriculum for one day a week to primary school children at locations outside the customary classroom context. This practical field project together with its scientific evaluation lasted from January 2014 to March 2017. Our work on the outdoor school is grounded in the thinking of the Scandinavian pioneers of *uteskole/udeskole* (Bentsen & Jensen, 2012; Jordet, 2007). Outdoor lessons were conducted in conjunction with the teaching content from within the classroom context. The outdoor days took place at nearby natural locations or spaces of cultural interest such as woods, parks, meadows, fields, museums or businesses. The classroom was the point of departure and return. The outdoor days were organised by the teachers, who were also occasionally accompanied by other professional experts including foresters,

---

[1] The project "Schulwandern—Draußen erleben. Vielfalt entdecken. Menschen bewegen " ["School Hiking—Experiencing the Outdoors. Discovering Diversity. Moving People"] was run in cooperation between the Johannes Gutenberg University Mainz (JGU) and the Deutscher Wanderverband (DWV) [German Hiking Association]. It was funded by the Bundesamt für Naturschutz [Federal Agency for Nature Conservation] as part of the Bundesprogramm Biologische Vielfalt [Federal Action Plan for Biodiversity]. Participants in the project included the authors as well as Robert Gräfe, Christian Gillessen, Marius Harring, Sarah Sahrakhiz and Daniela Schenk.

C. Armbrüster (✉) · M. D. Witte
Institut Für Erziehungswissenschaft, Johannes Gutenberg-Universität Mainz, Jakob-Welder-Weg 12, 55128 Mainz, Germany
e-mail: charmbru@uni-mainz.de

M. D. Witte
e-mail: matthias.witte@uni-mainz.de

© The Author(s) 2022
R. Jucker and J. von Au (eds.), *High-Quality Outdoor Learning*,
https://doi.org/10.1007/978-3-031-04108-2_19

environmental educators, geologists and others. The participating primary schools were selected in the early stages of the project using a tendering procedure. It was important for us that the schools differ socio-spatially and socio-structurally. The decision was ultimately taken in favour of a school in a primarily industrial district in a large city in southern Germany, a small, rural school in south-western Germany, and a medium-sized school in the new federal states in former East Germany which was located in a nature conservation area. The study used a longitudinal, multi-perspectival and triangulated research design. The research focus was on teachers, students, parents and teaching strategies associated with the three sample classes, which were initially in Year Two and subsequently in Year Three. The project team utilised qualitative and quantitative methods in the form of individual interviews, group conversations, semi-standardised questionnaires and participant observation. This data was collected in three phases. These took place at the beginning of outdoor teaching (t1, August/September 2014), after one year of school (t2, June/July 2015) and at the conclusion of the project after two years of school (t3, June/July 2016). The ethnographic observations at the schools took place on average once a month. The qualitative data, which will be dealt with forthwith, consisted of a sample of 12 guided expert interviews with teachers, 43 guided group conversations with children and 65 written logs from the ethnographic observations. The data were subsequently analysed using established evaluation procedures from qualitative social research. The variety of methods used to gather the data made it possible to correlate the findings, thereby providing a deeper insight into both the key aspects as well as particular characteristics of the classes being conducted outside on a regular basis. This article summarises for the first time, in a condensed way, the key empirical and theoretical findings of the qualitative research on outdoor school using the following four categories: the structural characteristics of the approach (Sect. 2), social, material and temporal changes in the schools and classes (Sect. 3), pedagogical concepts and action (Sect. 4) and children's agency (Sect. 5). It is due to the constraints of available space in the current volume that the article focuses more on the presentation of the central findings than on the presentation of the detailed analytical reconstructions. For the latter, reference must be made here to the existing publications from our project (e.g. Witte, 2015; Gräfe et al., 2016; Sahrakhiz et al., 2016; Armbrüster et al., 2016, 2019, 2021). If the readers are interested in a more in-depth discussion of individual results, they are very welcome to contact the authors.

2   Outdoor School as an Approach to Schooling

To date, there have been very few studies on outdoor school, which possess a solid grounding in theory. The reasons for this might lie in the nascence of outdoor school as a 'bottom up' movement, which was initiated by committed teachers. The founding generation of teachers was, in the first instance, more interested in the practice of outdoor school than in grounding the practice in (educational) theory (Bentsen, 2016). The first articles to look into outdoor school from the perspective of educational and teaching theory were those of Jordet (2002, 2003, 2007). He drew on John Dewey, Wolfgang Klafki, Oskar Negt and constructivist thought to define the concept of *udeskole* (outdoor school) as a form of "progressive outdoor experiential education" (Bentsen, 2016, 57), stressing the situational, experiential and holistic dimension of learning (ibid.). For the purposes of this study, we examined outdoor school using two theoretical approaches, which served us as sensitising concepts in the analysis of the empirical data. Both theories take first-hand experience and relationships (Adorno, 1959/2003, 103) as the starting point for the learning process. Firstly, we drew on Ulrich Oevermann's (2004a) concept of socialisation and education as an interplay between crisis and routine. At the heart of this theory lies the idea that new experience arises out of having to cope with crisis situations. Oevermann states that situations which are ideally conducive to learning are of the type he calls *crisis by leisure*; these give rise to *aesthetic experience* (ibid., 167). A crisis by leisure is something which is brought about by the subject themselves. The subject focuses on an "internal or external reality for its own sake" (ibid.). In this type of situation, in which the subject's experience of the world and the self is an end in itself—an aesthetic experience—the subject is open to perceiving the properties of objects that might otherwise have remained indistinct. Overcoming the crisis therefore consists of making the indistinct into something distinct and of learning something new in the process. The second approach is Hartmut Rosa's resonance theory. Here we were guided by a 'narrow' understanding of resonance. In this sense, the term in Rosa (2016) denotes a "kind of relationship to the world, formed through affect and emotion, intrinsic interest, and perceived self-efficacy, in which subject and world are mutually affected and transformed" (Rosa, 2016, 298). According to Rosa, successful learning processes—in the sense of "actively adaptively transforming parts of the world" (ibid., 58)—are heavily dependent on the formation of resonance relationships between students and teachers and/or between the learners and what they are learning (ibid.). Through case reconstruction and analysis, we succeeded in identifying resonance and aesthetic experience as two of the constitutive modes of outdoor education. We were then able to show that students developed an attitude outside in the natural environment that might—following on from Rosa—be termed *dispositional resonance*: "that could be interesting/exciting/fascinating" (Rosa, 2016, 418). Outdoor learning enables students to engage more intensively with phenomena in their natural environment. It gives rise to meaningful experiential crises for the children which are in turn tied to a high level of experienced resonance (Armbrüster, 2021). Herein lies the heightened learning potential of outdoor schooling.

3   Outdoor School and the Boundaries of School

Our analysis showed that outdoor schooling entails the dissolution of spatial, temporal and experiential boundaries. The removal of *spatial boundaries* makes itself felt in the outdoor school in two ways: firstly, insofar as the processes and structural patterns of schooling are transferred into (public) open spaces which previously have not functioned as pedagogical places of teaching and learning for the children (cf. on this topic Kolbe, 2006, 162), and secondly, insofar as novel socio-material settings outside the school can be integrated into the children's lessons. This means that the woods, for example, can suddenly turn into a place of learning which can be explored using the educational methods and research tools from inside the school. At the same time, the less constrained 'outside' world changes the role played by the participants' bodies and the way they see things. Objects become accessible. The removal of *temporal boundaries* becomes most visible in the greater flexibility accorded to the structuring of teaching time and non-teaching time outside the school context as well as on the way there and back again. Class times inside the school building are usually very clearly distinguishable from break times. These temporal boundaries are even regulated externally using acoustic or optical signals. In outdoor schooling, responsibility for this type of structuring falls on the teacher to a far greater degree. It is also observable that periods of 'class time' are far less clearly distinguishable from periods of free time. These periods of free time are frequently the times when the children have meaningful experiences. The dissolution of the boundaries between school and the children's real-world experience makes itself felt in two ways. Firstly, it is evident in the opening up of the school context to the children's everyday world. This leads to a softening of the typical characteristics of school life, especially fixed arrangements of times and spaces, subject specific approaches of teaching and a hierarchical sender-receiver setting concerning knowledge transfer. Instead, playful forms of learning, project-orientated, interdisciplinary and participatory ways of teaching and learning as well as real world experiences are explicitly taken into account (Fölling-Albers, 2000). Secondly, there is what might be termed the educational 'colonisation' of the experiential space outside school which the children usually associate with their free time and their family. Outdoor school transforms these into places of learning too (Armbrüster, 2021).

4   Pedagogical Concepts and Action in Outdoor Schooling

The research team approached the teaching staff involved in the outdoor days and conducted interviews with them on a variety of topics. Prior to the first outdoor school year commencing in 2014/15, the teachers were questioned using semi-standardised interviews (Flick, 2010), which were evaluated using qualitative content analysis (Mayring, 2010). Our guiding principle was to establish what motivated the teachers to engage in outdoor schooling. We sorted the results into five key categories:

1. *real-world learning*: teachers identified a child-friendly and sustainable approach to learning in the nexus between direct physical encounters and cognitive interaction with the (objects found at the) outdoor learning spaces;
2. *social learning*: teachers viewed outdoor school as an opportunity to change institutionalised role patterns and to use shared experience to impart important human values and social skills to the children;

3. *well-being*: teachers noticed an increase in the children's sense of well-being when participating in outdoor schooling, for example through the perceived slower pace of the school day as well as through the above-mentioned dimensions of sensory learning and shared experience;

4. *compensation*: teachers viewed outdoor schooling as a necessary counterbalance to social transformations which were alienating children from their environment and increasingly depriving them of opportunities to access and experience 'nature' first hand or as part of their education;

5. *broadening the definition of school*: teachers viewed outdoor school as a way to broaden the definition of school, thereby enabling them to forge connections with learning providers outside the traditional school context. They also mentioned that outdoor schooling could be used by schools to enhance their profiles in an increasingly competitive education system.

Overall, the data indicated a very positive attitude to outdoor schooling among teachers. At the same time, the data also indicated a link between the teachers' own deep-rooted biographical natural socialisation, and their motivations and attitudes towards outdoor schooling (Gräfe et al., 2016).

The next stage of the project focused on concrete pedagogical action in the outdoor school context. Conversations with groups of children (Heinzel, 2012; Nentwig-Gesemann, 2002; Vogl, 2005) which were subsequently evaluated based on an objective hermeneutical approach (Oevermann, 2000) were used to reconstruct the effects of softening the spatial, temporal and social boundaries of school (cf. Sect. 2) on the way lessons were organised in outdoor school locations. Structural changes were a particular obstacle to pedagogical action. It was possible to show, for example, that the move from the classroom to the outdoors gave rise to crises in customary classroom control. Teaching plans were disrupted by unforeseen distractions or natural circumstances largely beyond the teacher's control, for example when the teacher introduced the children to certain objects in class (e.g. plants, animals), but unforeseen weather conditions made it hard to find them outside. Situations such as these required the teachers to react quickly and introduce new learning activities. The time the teacher needed to adjust their lesson plan was frequently used as free time in which the children were mostly permitted to engage in activities they could choose themselves. It was noteworthy that the children actively used these phases to explore their learning environments. These phases of exploration as an end in themselves led to experiential crises for the children which then stimulated their learning processes (cf. Sect. 4). One key pedagogical challenge for the teachers was to capture these experiences which were so valuable to the children's learning processes and to then enrich them by providing additional knowledge. In many ways, the novel role of the body, objects and the children's way of looking at things made it much harder for the teacher to retain an overview of and control over what the children were doing. At the same time, the increased flexibility between class time and free time had an effect on the pedagogical action of the teacher. If, for example, a teacher was unable to put their teaching plan into practice because of unforeseen weather conditions (see above), the rest of the lesson depended to no small degree on how fast the teacher could find new learning material in the outdoor space and what kind of knowledge the teacher had acquired in preparation for their class and why (Armbrüster, 2021).

One of the study's key focal points in observing the actions of the teachers was the close analytical examination of speech acts during classes. Using participant observation in the classroom as well as outdoors, the study undertook a comparative conversation analysis of the teachers' speech acts. This made it possible to identify differences in the "language of immediacy and language of distance" (Koch & Österreicher, 1985). The findings showed that the teachers tended to use the language of immediacy in the outdoor school context to a greater degree than during lessons in the school classroom. This means that the teacher used more restrictive and directive language with greater emotional content in the outdoor school context. In the school classroom, however, the teacher tended to use language which was more in line with the conventions of written language. There were fewer interruptions and the teacher did not in general have to raise their voice as frequently to be heard. The reason behind these differences in the teachers' speech acts transpired to be the dissolution of spatial boundaries: in the natural spaces outside school, keeping to the lesson plan was harder due to the unaccustomed spatial situation and other unpredictable elements, which had a direct influence on the teacher's use of language. However, from the perspective of language-teaching methodology, the analysis cast a critical light on teachers' ability to teach children specialist education-related language skills during outdoor school lessons: the (spatial) dissolution of traditional school boundaries represented a serious challenge to the carefully considered and refined language of school and the classroom (Sahrakhiz et al., 2016).

5   Children as Participants in the Outdoor School

Another of the main focal points in the study was our analysis of the children's experiences of their environment in the outdoor school. We took an agency-orientated approach, which we used to examine the novel opportunities for action, learning and knowledge acquisition in the outdoor school as described by the children in their own first-hand narratives and as gleaned from participant observation. Initial contacts with the children dealt with the children's experience of outdoor school and how (in the context of school) they had dealt with the challenge of the new learning spaces. The group conversations with the children which were conducted in phase t1 were evaluated using qualitative content analysis. From the children's point of view, there was a clear difference between their normal school day and the dynamic, playful and research-based learning they experienced during their weekly outdoor day. The former was broadly characterised by them having to complete textbook tasks, a lack of physical movement, and the constrained role of the children's bodies, mostly inside the classroom. In contrast, the children embraced the natural spaces in the outdoor school by approaching them in a number of ways: by using an instrumental approach based on physical activity, for example through sporting activities, and by using a sensory-based aesthetic approach, for example through the slow and deliberate observation of natural phenomena. In addition, the children's narratives also included references to socially significant discourses which stressed the importance of sport and movement for fitness, health and the figure. Some of the children stated that the outdoor day was even a culinary highlight in the weekly school meal plan: the children's communal mealtime was often marked by ritualised, slow-food picnic events in the preparation of which even the children's own families became involved. Some children mentioned the risks, dangers and unknowns which went along with having lessons outside the secure classroom environment. For example, the fear of tics (a perennial topic in the media) was particularly pronounced among some children when classes were held in the woods (Sahrakhiz et al., 2018; Witte, 2015).

A subsequent section of our study examined how children appropriated the spaces used in outdoor schooling. Using the same empirical basis and following on from Martina Löw's (2001) relational space theory and Ulrich Deinet's (2014) concept of appropriation, we studied the practices the children used for spatial appropriation. We identified nine (sub-)categories of activity engaged in by the children in outdoor spaces: playing (1), investigating and discovering (2), moving (3), looking, observing and seeing (4), talking and telling (5), constructing, crafting, making (6), drawing (7), reading, writing and arithmetic (8), eating and drinking (9). In their narratives, the children gave most prominence to the first three categories. We therefore subjected these to closer scrutiny. We found that the activities that the children primarily associated with their out-of-school environment were often to be found in their school context. Similarly, structures from the school context were often transferred into the more open experiential spaces such as the woods, the park, the field, the ruins and the children's activities. In playing, investigating and discovering, and in moving, the children differentiated between types of action, which they were free to choose autonomously, and heteronomous forms of activity which were decided upon and initiated by others. These different types of action highlight the institutional potential as well as the limits of the children's spatial appropriation in the context of (outdoor) schooling. Finally, our study showed there was a novel interleaving of children's backstage and frontstage school life (Armbrüster et al., 2016). Backstage is understood here in the sense of a peer culture which is predominantly focused on the present; frontstage is understood in the sense of a more future-orientated learning culture (Deinet, 2014). We considered this finding deserving of greater scrutiny. We therefore embarked on a more in-depth study of the socio-material arrangements (Kalthoff, 2011; Röhl, 2013) at outdoor teaching locations and their connection with the children's agency in the outdoor school. This part of the study was based on group conversations with the children in the t2 and t3 phases of data collection as well as ethnographic observations which were conducted during the first year of the project. The analysis was based on relational theories (Emirbayer & Mische, 1998; Raithelhuber, 2012; Esser et al., 2016) and theories of practice (Hillebrandt, 2015; Reckwitz, 2003; Schatzki, 1996), and an evaluation was conducted on the basis of grounded theory (Breidenstein et al., 2015). This approach enabled us to reconstruct the children's agency in their performative creation of a common sphere of action through role-play and processes of subjectification. This indicated a close correlation between the children's actions and the materiality of space in the outdoor school. The children drew on their knowledge about the novel role of the body and way of seeing things in the outdoor environment to develop their own 'secret' way of playing. This allowed them to circumvent the school's disciplinary and control mechanisms and pursue their own interests. At the same time, the children also actively participated in creating a state of structure and order at the outdoor locations which was conducive to teaching and learning, for example by acknowledging the teachers' forms of address, accepting their instructional methods and by reacting to their prompting as they would have done in the school (Reh et al., 2011).

It was also clear that children were introduced to new objects under the direction of the teacher (Latour, 1994). The children appropriated the teacher's directions based on their own interests. This was evident in the children's role-play: when they were pretending to be Star Wars characters they transformed the sticks from the woods into pistols and swords and engaged in symbolic actions such as shooting and sword-fighting. A similar picture was observable in the children's library, which as a "locus of meaning" [*Bedeutungsanordnung*] (Hackl, 2015, 146) communicated with its visitors, addressed them and challenged them to attribute meaning, thereby opening up the potential for certain mental and physical actions. The children used this setting during the phases of free exploration for the competent exchange of knowledge with their peers. Using selected books, the children set up a performative sphere of action within which they addressed each other variously as boy, girl, layperson, expert, teacher and learner. In-depth analysis of these activities added granularity to our observations about the changed dynamics (see above) between the frontstage and backstage of the learning culture. Agency in the outdoor school context was less apparent in the children's creation of a school counterculture, and more apparent in them competently balancing peer-relationships and the demands of school (Armbrüster et al., 2019).

The objective hermeneutical analysis of the children's group conversations in phase t3 concluded with a closer examination of the children's processes of education and learning in the natural spaces of the outdoor school. We used detailed analysis to reconstruct the way the children had intense resonant experiences and established resonant relationships (Rosa, 2016) with objects in the outdoor learning context. These formed the basis for educationally relevant crises and discoveries as well as stimulating the children's interest in further engagement with the natural environment, on occasion even beyond the school day and involving their families. Stable resonant relationships often came into being through a concurrence of weak, desire-based affective judgements ('going outside and getting some fresh air is good for you') and strong, ethical-cognitive judgements ('being out in the fresh air means you don't fall ill so easily') (ibid., 230–235).

Overall, our empirical analysis demonstrated the high level of educational potential in outdoor school. Outdoor school facilitated children's autonomous engagement with their natural environment based on exploration through leisure. It encouraged their inquisitive appropriation of nature through resonant and aesthetic experiences. However, it also became apparent that successful processes of learning and education depend to no small degree upon the teachers' ability to relate the children's experiences to their taught knowledge (Armbrüster, 2021). This remains one of the key challenges facing the outdoor school.

6 Conclusion

Recent debates about school education have often been critical of the way current classroom practice at schools hinders the formation of vibrant relationships between teachers, children, and the learning material. This impedes educational processes at schools. Oevermann (2003, 2004b), for example, states that mandatory school attendance denies children their natural curiosity to learn from the outset. Rosa (2016, 419–420) is critical of the fact that school primarily opens up resonant spaces which bear the thumbprint of middle-class educational bias and are therefore a key contributor to social inequality. Even if outdoor school at the primary level is neither exempt from mandatory school attendance nor free from middle-class bias in its use of the natural environment, museums etc., it is nevertheless an approach which differs significantly from traditional classroom teaching. Our analysis showed that outdoor school repeatedly succeeds in creating open experiential spaces which the children appropriate at the peer and student level using practices they have chosen themselves. This is facilitated by the socio-material arrangements, the teacher's actions, and the dissolution of the boundaries between class time and free time. Our research points both to the potential offered by this concept as well as its limitations, for example in connection with the teachers' ability to equip the children with specialist education-related language skills during outdoor school lessons. Ultimately, however, it is clear that outdoor school creates more temporal spaces which give the children leisure time and resonant experiences, and allows them to engage autonomously with the places and objects of educational value outside the traditional school context (Armbrüster, 2021). If teachers can successfully incorporate the children's experiences into their teaching and augment these experiences with additional knowledge, then outdoor school can make a significant contribution to creating a versatile approach to school education.

Recommended Further Reading

1. Armbrüster, C., Harring, M., Sahrakhiz, S. & Witte, M. D. (2019). Materialitäten, Praktiken, Agency. Ein relationaler Zugang zum wöchentlichen Unterricht an außerschulischen Lernorten in der Grundschule. [Materialities, Practices, Agency. A Relational Approach to Weekly Lessons in Locations Outside School at Primary School]. *Zeitschrift für Soziologie der Erziehung und Sozialisation. 39*(1), 44–55.

2. Armbrüster, C. (2021). Naturerfahrung als Krise durch Muße? —Struktureigenschaften der Bildungspraxis der „Draußenschule" im Primarbereich. [Experiencing Nature as Crisis by Leisure?—Structural Characteristics of Educational Practice in 'Outdoor Schooling' at the Primary Level]. *Zeitschrift für Pädagogik*. *66*(1), 84–101.
3. Sahrakhiz, S., Harring, M. & Witte, M.D. (2018). Learning opportunities in the outdoor school—empirical findings on outdoor school in Germany from the children's perspective. *Journal of Adventure Education and Outdoor Learning*. *18*(3), 214–226.

References

Adorno, T. W. (1959/2003). Theorie der Halbbildung. (Theory of 'Halbbildung'). In R. Tiedemann (Ed.), *Theodor W. Adorno. Gesammelte Schriften. Band 8: Soziologische Schriften I (Complete works. Volume 8: Sociological essays I)* (pp. 93–121). Frankfurt/M.: Suhrkamp.

Armbrüster, C. (2021). Naturerfahrung als Krise durch Muße?—Struktureigenschaften der Bildungspraxis der „Draußenschule" im Primarbereich. (Experiencing nature as crisis by leisure?—Structural characteristics of educational practice in "Outdoor Schooling" at the primary level). *Zeitschrift für Pädagogik*, *66*(1), 84–101.

Armbrüster, C., Gräfe, R., Harring, M., Sahrakhiz, S., Schenk, D., & Witte, M. D. (2016). Spielen, Bewegen, Erkunden—Praktiken der Raumaneignung von Grundschulkindern in der Draußenschule. (Playing, moving, discovering—Practices of spatial appropriation used by primary school children in the outdopor school). *Diskurs Kindheits- und Jugendforschung*, *11*(4), 473–489.

Armbrüster, C., Harring, M., Sahrakhiz, S., & Witte, M. D. (2019). Materialitäten, Praktiken, Agency. Ein relationaler Zugang zum wöchentlichen Unterricht an außerschulischen Lernorten in der Grundschule. (Materialities, practices, agency. A relational approach to weekly lessons in locations outside school at primary school). *Zeitschrift für Soziologie der Erziehung und Sozialisation*, *39*(1), 44–55.

Bentsen, P. (2016). „Udeskole" in Dänemark. Von einer „Bottom-up-" zu einer „Top-Down-Bewegung". ("Udeskole" in Denmark. From a "Bottom-up" to a "Top-Down" movement). In J. von Au & U. Gade (Eds.), *„Raus aus dem Klassenzimmer". Outdoor Education als Unterrichtskonzept. ("Getting out of the Classroom". Outdoor education as a teaching method)* (pp. 50–69). Weinheim and Basel: Beltz Juventa.

Bentsen, P., & Jensen, F. J. (2012). The nature of udeskole: Outdoor learning theory and practice in Danish schools. *Journal of Adventure Education & Outdoor Learning, 12*(3), 199–219.

Breidenstein, G., Hirschauer, S., Kalthoff, H., & Nieswand, B. (2015). *Ethnografie. Die Praxis der Feldforschung. (Ethnography. The practice of field research)*. Stuttgart: UTB.

Deinet, U. (2014). *Vom Aneignungskonzept zur Activity Theory. Transfer des tätigkeitsorientierten Aneignungskonzepts der kulturhistorischen Schule auf heutige Lebenswelten von Kindern und Jugendlichen. (From the concept of appropriation to activity theory. Transferring the activity-orientated concept of the culturallly historical school to the modern-day lifeworlds of children and adolescents)*. Retrieved May 15, 2021, from http://www.socialnet.de/materialien/197.php.

Emirbayer, M., & Mische, A. (1998). What is agency? *The American Journal of Sociology, 103*(4), 962–1023.

Esser, F., Baader, M. S., Betz, T., & Hungerland, B. (2016). *Reconceptualising agency and childhood: New perspectives in childhood studies*. London and New York: Routledge.

Flick, U. (2010). *Qualitative Sozialforschung. Eine Einführung. (Qualitative social research. An introduction)*. Reinbek: Rowohlt.

Fölling-Albers, M. (2000). Entscholarisierung von Schule und Scholarisierung von Freizeit? Überlegungen zu Formen der Entgrenzung von Schule und Kindheit. (Descholastification of school and the scholastification of free time? Thoughts on ways to soften the boundaries between school and childhood). *Zeitschrift für Soziologie der Erziehung und Sozialisation, 20*(2), 118–131.

Gräfe, R., Gillessen, C., Harring, M., Sahrakhiz, S., & Witte, M. D. (2016). Einmal wöchentlich draußen unterrichten?! Eine qualitativ-empirische Studie zur Draußenschule aus der Perspektive von Grundschullehrerinnen. (Teaching outside once a week?! A qualitative-empirical study on outdoor school from the perspective of primary school teachers). In J. von Au & U. Gade (Eds.), *„Raus aus dem Klassenzimmer". Outdoor Education als Unterrichtskonzept. ("Getting out of the Classroom". Outdoor education as a teaching method)* (pp. 79–95). Weinheim and Basel: Beltz Juventa.

Hackl, B. (2015). Zimmer mit Aussicht. Räumlichkeiten als Medium von Bildungsprozessen. (Room with a view. Spaces as a medium for educational processes). In T. Alkemeyer, G. Kalthoff, & M. Rieger-Ladich (Eds.), *Bildungspraxis. Körper—Räume—Objekte. (Educational practice. Bodies—Rooms—Objects)* (pp. 131–158). Weilerswist-Metternich: Velbrueck.

Heinzel, F. (Ed.). (2012). *Methoden der Kindheitsforschung. Ein Überblick über Forschungszugänge zur kindlichen Perspektive. (Methods for childhood studies. An overview of research methods for accessing the children's perspective)*. Weinheim and Basel: Beltz Juventa.

Hillebrandt, F. (2015). Was ist der Gegenstand einer Soziologie der Praxis. (What does sociology of practice study?) In F. Schäfer, A. Daniel, & F. Hillebrandt (Eds.), *Methoden einer Soziologie der Praxis. (Methods of a sociology of practice)* (pp. 15–36). Berlin: De Gruyter. Retrieved May 15, 2021, from https://doi.org/10.14361/9783839427163.

Jordet, A. (2002). *Lutvann-undersøkelsen. En case-studie om uteskolens didaktikk. Delrapport 1* [The Lutvann study. A case study on the didactics of the Uteskole. Report Part 1]. Høgskolen i Hedmark.

Jordet, A. (2003). *Lutvann-undersøkelsen. En case-studie om uteskolens didaktikk. Delrapport 2* [The Lutvann study. A case study on the didactics of the Uteskole. Report Part 2]. Høgskolen i Hedmark.

Jordet, A. (2007). *Nærmiljøet som klasserom. En undersøkelse om uteskolens didaktikk i et danningsteoretisk og erfaringspedagogisk perspektiv [Die nähere Umgebung als Klassenzimmer. Eine Untersuchung zur Didaktik der Uteskole aus einer bildungstheoretischen und erfahrungspädagogischen Perspektive]*. Oslo: Unipub AS.

Kalthoff, H. (2011). Social studies of teaching and education. Skizze einer sozio-materiellen Bildungsforschung. (Social studies of teaching and education. Outline of a piece of socio-material research). In D. Šuber, H. Schäfer, & S. Prinz (Eds.), *Pierre Bourdieu und die Kulturwissenschaften. Zur Aktualität eines undisziplinierten Denkens. (Pierre bourdieu and the cultural sciences. On the currentness of undisciplined thinking)* (pp. 107–132). Konstanz: UVK Verlagsgesellschaft.

Koch, P., & Österreicher, W. (1985). Sprache der Nähe—Sprache der Distanz. Mündlichkeit und Schriftlichkeit im Spannungsfeld von Sprachtheorie und Sprachgeschichte. (Language of immediacy—Language of distance. Orality and textuality at the nexus of language theory and language history). *Romanistisches Jahrbuch, 36,* 15–43.

Kolbe, F. U. (2006). Institutionalisierung ganztägiger Schulangebote—eine Entgrenzung von Schule? (Institutionalisation of all-day schooling—The removal of school boundaries?) In H.-U. Otto & J. Oelkers (Eds.), *Zeitgemäße Bildung. Herausforderungen für Erziehungswissenschaft und Bildungspolitik. (Contemporary education. Challenges for educational science and education policy)* (pp. 161–177). München and Basel: Ernst Reinhardt Verlag.

Latour, B. (1994). Where are the missing masses? The sociology of a few mundane artefacts. In W. E. Bijker & J. Law (Eds.), *Shaping technology/building society. Studies in sociotechnical change* (pp. 225–258). Cambridge, MA: MIT Press.

Löw, M. (2001). *Raumsoziologie. (Sociology of space)*. Frankfurt/M.: Suhrkamp.

Mayring, P. (2010). *Qualitative Inhaltsanalyse. (Qualitative content analysis)*. Weinheim: Beltz.

Nentwig-Gesemann, I. (2002). Gruppendiskussionen mit Kindern: Die dokumentarische Interpretation von Spielpraxis und Diskursorganisation. (Group conversations with children: The documentary interpretation of play and discourse organisation). *Zeitschrift für qualitative Bildungs-, Beratungs- und Sozialforschung, 3*(1), 41–63.

Oevermann, U. (2000). Die Methode der Fallrekonstruktion in der Grundlagenforschung sowie der klinischen und pädagogischen Praxis. (The methods of case reconstruction in fundamental research and in clinical and pedagogical practice). In K. Kraimer (Ed.), *Die Fallrekonstruktion (The case reconstruction)* (pp. 58–153). Frankfurt/M.: Suhrkamp.

Oevermann, U. (2003). Brauchen wir heute noch eine gesetzliche Schulpflicht und welches wären die Vorzüge ihrer Abschaffung? (Do we still need mandatory school attendance and what would be the advantages of its abolition?). *Pädagogische Korrespondenz., 16*(1), 54–70.

Oevermann, U. (2004a). Sozialisation als Prozess der Krisenbewältigung. (Socialisation as a process of crisis management). In D. Geulen & H. Veith (Eds.), *Sozialisationstheorie interdisziplinär. Aktuelle Perspektiven. (Interdisciplinary socialisation theory. Current perspectives)* (pp. 155–181). Stuttgart: Lucius & Lucius.

Oevermann, U. (2004b). Über den Stellenwert der gesetzlichen Schulpflicht. Antwort auf meine Kritiker. (On the value of mandatory school attendance. A response to my critics). *Pädagogische Korrespondenz, 17*(1), 74–84.

Raithelhuber, E. (2012). Ein relationales Verständnis von Agency. Sozialtheoretische Überlegungen und Konsequenzen für empirische Analysen. (A Relational Understanding of Agency. Sociological Considerations and their Consequences for Empirical Studies). In S. Bethmann, C. Helfferich, H. Hoffmann, & D. Niermann (Eds.), *Agency. Qualitative Rekonstruktionen und gesellschaftstheoretische Bezüge von Handlungsmächtigkeit. (Agency. Qualitative reconstructions and the bearing of agency on social theory)* (pp. 122–153). Weinheim and Basel: Beltz Juventa.

Reckwitz, A. (2003). Grundelemente einer Soziologie sozialer Praktiken. Eine sozialtheoretische Perspektive. (Basic elements of a sociology of social practices. From the perspective of social theory). *Zeitschrift für Soziologie, 32*(4), 282–301.

Reh, S., Rabenstein, K., & Idel, T. S. (2011). Unterricht als pädagogische Ordnung. Eine praxistheoretische Perspektive. (Classes as pedagogical order. From the perspective of practice theory). In W. Meseth, M. Proske, & F. O. Radtke (Eds.), *Unterrichtstheorien in Forschung und Lehre. (Teaching theories in research and education)* (pp. 209–222). Bad Heilbrunn: Julius Klinkhardt.

Röhl, T. (2013). *Dinge des Wissens. Schulunterricht als sozio-materielle Praxis. (The things of knowledge. School teaching as socio-material practice)*. Stuttgart: Lucius & Lucius.

Rosa, H. (2016). *Resonanz. Eine Soziologie der Weltbeziehung. (Resonance. A sociology of worldly relations)*. Frankfurt/M.: Suhrkamp.

Schatzki, T. R. (1996). *Social practices. A Wittgensteinian approach to human activity and the social*. Cambridge: Cambridge University Press.

Sahrakhiz, S., Witte, M. D., & Harring, M. (2016). *Nähe und Distanz in der Lehrersprache. Eine Konversationsanalyse am Beispiel Draußenschule und Klassenzimmer. (Proximity and distance in teacher language. A conversation analysis based on outdoor school and classroom)*. Hohengehren: Schneider Verlag.

Sahrakhiz, S., Harring, M., & Witte, M. D. (2018). Learning opportunities in the outdoor school—Empirical findings on outdoor school in Germany from the children's perspective. *Journal of Adventure Education and Outdoor Learning., 18*(3), 214–226.

Vogl, S. (2005). Gruppendiskussionen mit Kindern: Methodische und methodologische Besonderheiten. (Group conversations with children: Methodical and methodological characteristics). *ZA-Information/Zentralarchiv für Empirische Sozialforschung, 57,* 28–60.

Witte, M. D. (2015). Draußenschule aus Kindersicht—Eine vernachlässigte Perspektive in der Udeskole-Forschung. (Outdoor School from the child's perspective—A neglected perspective in Udeskole research). *Die Grundschulzeitschrift, 29*(287), 22–27.

Christian Armbrüster is an academic member of staff at the Institute of Educational Science, Johannes Gutenberg University Mainz, Germany. He teaches theories of social education in an international context. His research interests are in childhood and youth studies and in qualitative social research. His specialisms are socialisation, biography, identity and agency.

Matthias D. Witte is professor of Educational Science specialising in Social Education and Social Work at the Johannes Gutenberg University Mainz, Germany. His research interests include child and youth welfare, outdoor education, transnational social support as well as flight and migration. He is an expert in biography research and life-world analytical ethnography using methods of qualitative social research. Matthias Witte is a visiting scholar at 'Eftimie Murgu' University of Reşiţa, Romania, and at University of Warsaw, Poland. He has held professorships at Phillips-Universität Marburg (Education with a focus on Adventure and Youth Research and Anthropology and Sociology of Sports) where he directed the Master's programmes 'Adventure and Experiential Education' and 'Transcultural European Outdoor Studies'.

Investigating Experiences of Nature: Challenges and Case-Analytical Approaches

Svantje Schumann

1 Introduction

Current trends show a decline in sensory experiences, physical activity and outdoor time for people in general and children in particular. The concerns associated with these trends are manifold and range from concerns about physical and mental health to fears of possible loss of empathy skills or a drop in educational attainment, including noticeable declines in the areas of problem-solving and innovative ability. Against this background, there is an increasing demand from practitioners and scientists to know more reliably, what the educational value of sensory-aesthetic experiences, outdoor-based learning and/or nature experiences really is.

The aim of this paper is to show what it takes to be able to make statements about the educational value of nature experiences (and thus also about outdoor-based learning) and to show why the study of nature experiences is so difficult. Using a case study, I show how accounts of nature experiences can be generated and which conclusions can be drawn from this with regard to settings that promote learning.

2 Theoretical Framework

2.1 Cognitive Processes as a "Crisis Through Leisure"

In the following, the theory of "cognitive processes as crisis through leisure" by Oevermann et al. (1996b), Oevermann (2004, 2008) serves as the theoretical framework.

S. Schumann (✉)
Institut Primarstufe, Pädagogische Hochschule der Fachhochschule Nordwestschweiz,
Hofackerstrasse 30, 4132 Muttenz, Switzerland
e-mail: svantje.schumann@fhnw.ch

© The Author(s) 2022   349
R. Jucker and J. von Au (eds.), *High-Quality Outdoor Learning*,
https://doi.org/10.1007/978-3-031-04108-2_20

A characteristic feature of experiencing and perceiving nature is that it has the inherent potential to trigger a "crisis" in the sense of Oevermann's crisis of knowledge. The sociologist Oevermann distinguishes between three different types of crisis, to which he has assigned different modes of constituting experience. According to Oevermann, experiences are constituted through the process of coping with a crisis: as long as one acts in a routine way, one does not make any new experiences, but draws on those already made (Oevermann, 2004, 160). Oevermann's three types of crisis are the traumatic crisis (i.e. the occurrence of surprising so-called "brute facts", cf. Peirce, 1877), the decision crisis ("The crisis of decision corresponds to the constitution of religious experience, because in it (…) it is a matter of finding a solution with a claim to justifiability, which, however, cannot be redeemed at the moment, which is to prove itself in the long term", Oevermann, 2004, 166) and the "crisis of leisure". This third type corresponds to the mode in which educational processes take place. A perception of leisure generates a crisis simply because the longer one perceives an object for its own sake, the greater the likelihood is that one becomes aware of something that one has never perceived before, even in an object that is in itself familiar and determined in tried and tested routines. This new perception takes one by surprise, so that at this stage the demand arises that one cannot *not* react to something that requires complete redefinition.

A confrontation with a natural phenomenon happens in such a way that problems or questions are posed by the phenomenon itself, which are quite difficult and whose solutions are not trivial. Everything that can be observed as a phenomenon or object has counterintuitive elements, contains surprising aspects or offers fascinating sensory stimuli in such a way that the viewers automatically poke at it or 'dig' into it.

According to Oevermann, the "learning process" which can be turned into a routine, stands in contrast to crisis-like experiences. Education can only be standardised to a very limited extent:

> In contrast, learning is a matter of routine. In it, a codified knowledge must be acquired through effective training. The typical form is memorising texts, committing vocabulary to memory. Mind you: education is not possible without the component of learning, and in this respect learning is unquestionably necessary. But to make it the dominant model, as in the principle of lifelong learning celebrated by modern educational science, educational processes need to be cut down to routines that can be standardised. (Oevermann, 2008, 60)

2.2 Experience of Nature

With regard to experiences of nature, a well-known example described by Oevermann is the following:

> Anyone who bivouacs on a high mountain at night cannot help but look up at the extraordinarily clear, starry sky. In doing so, even if he has a wealth of scientifically founded prior knowledge of astrophysics and should be able to subsume the visible in a differentiated way, he will not be able to avoid losing himself in a thoroughly crisis-like shivering over the

vastness of the cosmos and infinity in the truest sense of the word, or even disappearing into it with a feeling of tininess. (Oevermann, 1996b, 8)

For Oevermann, aesthetic experience is about

"an action that consists of nothing but perception, whose purposefulness is exhausted in the perception of something". (ibid., 1)

In this mere perception, in which aesthetic experience arises,

we allow an opposing other, a world, to have its entire effect on us, we curiously absorb it completely, we nestle ourselves completely close to the other, we open ourselves to something new, to something hitherto unthinkable, unimaginable, even when it concerns completely familiar objects. (ibid., 2)

According to Oevermann, aesthetic experience "as such forms the basis of all cognition, but above all of all expansion and modification of experience" (ibid., 15).

Experience of nature means the possibility that a process begins in which a transformation of "unarticulated raw experience" into "interpreted experience" (Oevermann, 1996a, v) takes place. Oevermann says that artistic action can be used "as a magnifying glass to study the general mechanism of the production of experience that is central to sociology" (Oevermann, 1996a, v). Since Oevermann repeatedly equates the reception of art with the process of experiencing nature in a variety of justified ways, it can be said that the study of experiences of nature also has the inherent potential to gain insights into this mechanism. A central question in education is how new things are generated, e.g. new knowledge, new patterns of action, new ways of thinking. At present, this central question is comparatively often asked in relation to sustainable behaviour.

The transformation from "unarticulated raw experience" into "interpreted experience" is reflected in the fact that processes of comprehension and deciphering can undergo a transformation from sensual-aesthetic perception to conceptual-mental comprehension, whereby these two paths of comprehension "enter into a natural dialectical connection in everyday practice" (Oevermann, 1996a, vi) and can lead to sensual and conceptual knowledge. In the course of the transformation process, one ideally progresses from the perception of what is sensually-aesthetically accessible to the decoding of what lies behind the visible.

3   Research Needs and Challenges for Research

Oevermann assumes that there is a "natural ability of appropriate reception" of natural and artistic objects in the subject (individual), which is to be attributed to him or her "independently of his or her specific previous education, solely on the basis of his or her perceptual organisation and epistemic genre equipment". The subject is capable of this reception solely "with the means of unclouded sensual cognitive ability" (Oevermann, 1996a, b, vii f.). Oevermann is of the opinion that the "constitutive structural characteristics and conditions" which determine such a reception, are still not sufficiently clarified (Oevermann, 1996a, viii).

Above all, there is a need for research with regard to the structures of perceptual organisation, including the structures in the process of indexing. In other words, it is an open question how these processes work, starting from the encounter with a phenomenon and leading up to the formulation of interpretations. It seems particularly interesting to investigate how children operate naturally and spontaneously when they have sensory experiences, because it can be assumed that the mode of operation is particularly "unadulterated" here and that a "truly authentic reception practice forms the object of investigation" (Oevermann, 1996a, x). However, this process or practice is difficult to grasp. On the one hand, even adults find it difficult to communicate sensory experiences verbally in a concise way, and on the other hand, verbal externalisation represents an artificial form that one would have to explicitly ask someone to do (e.g. to verbally communicate sensory experiences by means of 'thinking aloud'). Processes in which a subject progresses from encounter and sensual-aesthetic perception to, for example, asking questions and proposing interpretations can ultimately only be investigated by means of observation or questioning—and so only very indirect conclusions can be drawn about what actually happens during perception.

In an ideal situation for the study of experiences of nature we would have protocols of events in front of us in which children's attention is spontaneously attracted. Something in nature exerts such a high power of suggestion on them that they begin to focus their attention on this out of their own accord. These spontaneous moments can rarely be recorded for research purposes. However, it is extremely difficult to study the process of a natural, spontaneous reception "if one does not take a spontaneous reception practice as a basis for data collection" (Oevermann, 1996a, x).

One approach to the idea of externalising inner thought processes in relation to data logging is to create a constellation in which several children have a sensory experience together—in this way there is at least a higher probability that the children will enter into a dialogue with each other and thus externalise their thoughts. Another possibility is to enter into a dialogue as an adult with a child who is sensually perceiving a phenomenon. In both cases, the researcher is simultaneously moving in the research field of 'potentials of dialogical deciphering processes with regard to general educational processes'.

If one asks children to express themselves about a presented phenomenon—for the reasons mentioned above, one often cannot avoid resorting to the presentation of phenomena—the children's statements can be analysed with regard to various questions, such as the following: Are the primary school children interviewed in this study able to arrive at interpretations or readings based on their encounter with a phenomenon through sensory-aesthetic perception? What ideas and thoughts did they express? How did they go about 'reading' the phenomenon? Did they ask questions? Did they form hypotheses? Did they make suggestions about laws or concepts or connections related to the phenomenon? If so, how concrete or abstract were their hypotheses?

Here an interesting observation can be made. In various science modules/classes, students of primary education are often given the task of assessing children's pre-concepts. This approach honours, among other things, the concern of Scholz, who—from a professional point of view—regards thinking from the child's perspective as standing up for the children's demands (Scholz, 2005, 121). Understanding children's pre-concepts depends on using different methods to grasp the child's perspective and thus to get a better understanding of the child (cf. Heinzel, 2012, 23). In this context it is interesting that pre-concept surveys by students are regularly based on interviews. Their content is often not very rich and the children's ways of thinking remain strangely pale. It is noticeable that students often present a natural object to the children and then ask 'What do you know about it?' The children often respond very monosyllabically to these and other questions from the students. This behaviour of the children can be attributed, among other things, to the fact that the students use test-like questioning.

In order to find out something about children's thinking and perception processes, however, questioning that amounts to 'right' or 'wrong' answers inhibits dialogue. We only learn essential things in dialogues where the child can and wants to express itself as authentically and individually as possible. The best results are obtained when the child's counterpart in the conversation is genuinely curious and interested in the uniqueness of the other person. This also shows how demanding it is to conduct surveys in such a way that it is possible to gain insights into children's deciphering and interpretation processes.

The data collection form 'interview', which is often chosen in sociological research, is very demanding with regard to children and the collection and interpretation of their ways of thinking and educational processes (e.g. Fuhs, 2000; Heinzel, 1997; Krüger & Grunert, 2001; Scheid, 2012). Nevertheless, it should be pointed out that the resulting interview transcripts constitute at least a database for which there are research methods that allow us to arrive at interpretations. Frequently, however, we are dealing with 'silent processes of reflection' in the context of reception processes, especially during the first phases of experiencing nature, the phases of encounter and perception. Researchers therefore also try to generate data protocols by asking children to depict their experiences of nature in drawings and, if necessary, to explain them to the researcher afterwards. This is also not an easy way to obtain data from an uninfluenced situational-spontaneous event—the cases in which children begin to artistically record their nature experience on their own initiative and in which these drawings fall 'in front of one's feet' as data, so to speak, are rather rare and their occurrence is strongly left to chance. In addition, drawings by children can be counted among the very demanding data materials. There are still only comparatively few attempts to make children's drawings the starting point of educational research (cf. among others Neuss, 1999, 2005; Billmann-Mahecha, 1994, 2005; Peez, 2011; Scheid, 2012). At the same time, children's drawings are very interesting, as one can hope to gain access to children's perspectives through them (cf. Scheid, 2012).

Overall, the following can be said about the research field 'study of nature experience' (and also 'outdoor-based learning'): The well-founded assumption that primary experience of nature has great importance is disproportionate to the number of studies that deal with it in the sense of basic research.

4   Exemplary Case Study

Against the background described above, i.e. the manifold challenges in the study of educational processes related to experiences of nature, it is possible to consider how the potential of these educational processes can nevertheless be 'grasped' and studied.

For this purpose, a case is considered as an example. In pedagogy, working with case studies means using concrete individual examples to gain insights into educational processes in the broadest sense. In medicine, criminology, law and empirical social research, the term case refers to the object of investigation. A case can be used to illustrate the derivation of theses. In particular, case analyses make it possible to grasp the research object in its multi-dimensionality and complexity (Eisenhardt, 1989, 532; Mayring, 1993, 27).

The case presented here is a description of a planned encounter and educational situation in nature, implemented and described by a teacher (Czernoch, 2008). An excursion is presented in a reflective form. The purpose of the excursion was to convey knowledge of species and establish an appreciation of plants. In principle, a protocol recorded on equipment would be ideal since it is not overly influenced by subjective perceptions (cf. Oevermann et al., 1979). Nevertheless, this description of the educational situation is a protocol that seems to allow us to draw cautious conclusions about the nature and potential of nature experiences. The case is presented closely following the teacher's presentation.

4.1   The Case: Field Trips with Primary School Children

The teacher Andrea Czernoch designed an excursion with children of a second primary school class to the site of a disused railway yard, a ruined area with overgrown ruins of buildings and tracks (Czernoch, 2008). The teacher's intention was that the children should "expand and consolidate their knowledge of indigenous organisms by means of an active, explorative and project-oriented lesson at an extracurricular place of learning". Furthermore, "through the active handling of the plants (…) an appreciation should arise that should lead to the protection and preservation of the organisms in the long term". Finally, "the lesson aimed at introducing the children to scientific working methods, by means of which they should independently acquire and assess knowledge" (ibid., 4). The teacher claims to have been inspired by the didactics of teaching art derived from Martin Wagenschein (1896–1988), in particular the example by Susanne Wildhirt (cf. Wildhirt, 1995, 233–262), when preparing this excursion.

The teacher describes her own fears in relation to the excursion very impressively when she writes about her preliminary excursion:

> Overgrown tracks, ruined buildings and wilderness characterised the picture that opened up to me on my first visit. It was only when I took a closer look that I was able to recognise the diversity of the individual plants, and when I saw them, I was overcome by the first doubts and fear that I had set my sights too high with all the beauties I had never seen before. How was I supposed to explore biodiversity with the children when many of the species were also foreign to me at first glance? (Czernoch, 2008, 5)

She decided that it was her task to first explore and identify the plants herself, also with the help of experts.

The teacher talked to the children in advance about what a marshalling yard is, why it was closed down, how long the site has been abandoned, etc. The children began to think about how one would imagine such a site and what it might look like now.

The teacher then describes the first excursion—due to an untypically cold snap for the time of year, most of the flowering plants had not yet blossomed, as she noticed the day before. The teacher then had the children explore the grounds on their first excursion and catch and observe insects with glass jars. She also had the children look for signs of animal feeding, spider webs, birds' nests and feathers. Some dead insects were taken away and looked at with stereo magnifiers at school and the children were particularly fascinated by the compound eyes of a bumblebee. It was above all an "exciting experience" for the children how "the magnifying glasses (…) open up the discovery of an unknown dimension" and enabled the children to "see things that are commonplace but normally remain hidden from the human eye" (ibid., 6). The children made collages and woven pictures the next day at school with grasses they had brought with them as well as freshly picked the same day. They discovered that one has to be much more careful with the dry grasses than with the fresh grasses when weaving them in.

On the second visit to the site, many plants had opened their flowers. The teacher sent the children off in pairs to cut and collect flowers without pulling the plants out. The cut flowers were placed by the children on a large, white, spread-out cloth in small vases filled with water, and the same plants were to be placed in vases with the same plants. The teacher observed:

> I didn't have to worry about the correct sorting, because some of the girls quickly made it their business to monitor the assignment task and correct it if necessary. This was done on their own initiative and motivation without any outside help. While the girls in the class worked on the assigned task all the time, after a while some of the boys preferred to look for animals again, like the week before. I let them do it for a while, but then brought them back to the task at hand, which they continued to work on. (Czernoch, 2008, 7)

Afterwards, the teacher had planned for all the children to gather around the plants they had found, look at them closely, choose a plant and think of a suitable name for it. Due to the onset of rain, this part of the lesson was moved to a nearby clubhouse, which the teacher had reserved as a precaution. The children, as the teacher described, "started naming the plants, which mostly alluded to the specific appearance of the individual plants. There was now spiky flower, spiky king, cup flower, blue paintbrush or flag flower" (ibid., 8)—botanically speaking, it was the viper's bugloss. The teacher notes:

> All twelve species that the class had found on the site were given fantasy names in this way and the class was able to make their first acquaintance with the plants. They made precise observations for their work and soon special features of individual species were identified. (ibid.)

The teacher then also had the children draw an "original plant to sensitise them to details" (ibid.). She states: "The children's results showed an astonishing number of components of the individual plants" (ibid.).

The teacher's next goal is to design an identification key with which the children can reach their goal "without further help", namely to find out the botanical names of the plants and to "check their results in a self-directed way" (ibid., 9). She orients herself on a scientific identification key and considers which entry criterion "might work". She decides against the colour of the flower, on the one hand because some colours only occur once, and on the other hand because some plants change the colour of their flower, depending on the stage of flowering, or show a spectrum of colours. Therefore, the teacher studies the 12 plants again herself. She takes as the first criterion whether the stem of the plant is hairy or not, as the second criterion the shape of the leaf. In the identification key, the teacher also uses illustrations to indicate the various possibilities or uses analogue examples (e.g. grapefruit spoon to clarify the term 'toothed leaf edge'). At the beginning of the lesson, in which the children try to identify the plants with the identification key, the teacher first clarifies in conversation why it can make sense for everyone to use one and the same name for a plant. Then, also in dialogue, it is clarified how to work with an identification key. Children in groups of two then aim to identifying four to six different plants. To prevent the children from copying from each other, satchels are placed between the working teams. The teacher recognises the children's eagerness to continue working on the identification even during the break. She attributes the motivation of the children to the fact that there is an interest in the plants and an enjoyment of the newly learned method of identification as well as the possibility of working independently with the included chance to master the challenge. The teacher sees essential components of Deci and Ryan's (1993) self-determination theory at play and confirmed.

In order for the children to better retain the knowledge they had acquired, i.e. the plant names they had found out, the teacher looked for material in which, among other things, the origin of plant names, background information on plant names etc. was presented or in which exciting and unusual things about the individual plants were reported (e.g. the use of adder's head as a remedy against snake bites). With the help of various matching games, the teacher then repeated the plant names with the children. In addition, she gave the children the task of creating a description for a plant. This had to contain the scientific name as well as the essential characteristics (in drawings or in writing). A dried specimen was glued to the poster. The scientific names of the plants were written on the poster in such a way that they could be covered or folded over—this way the children could continue to practise the names with the posters.

At the end of the lesson, the class presented their work and knowledge to parents, other classes and the neighbouring kindergarten, among others. In doing so, the children "took on the role of teachers and knowers" (Czernoch, 2008, 13). Also in relation to this presentation, the teacher refers to Deci and Ryan's self-determination theory and emphasises the positive social experience and the positive emotional atmosphere as educationally effective components.

4.2 Reflection of the Case

Possible questions are: In the teacher's opinion, what is the potential of the nature experience in the present case and how does she determine this? Can further potential be identified beyond the teacher's assumptions? How does the teacher determine the educational gain? How can additional potential be identified?

4.2.1 The Teacher's View of the Potential of Experiencing Nature

Let us ask the question first: In the teacher's opinion, what is the potential of the nature experience in the present case?

The teacher attributes the lasting effect of the lessons "around the industrial waste-land" primarily to the fact that "this lesson was filled with so many emotional, direct and extremely appreciative and motivating moments" (Czernoch, 2008, 14). The teacher reports that one mother told her afterwards that her child now stops very often on excursions to look closely at plants. Another child stood in front of her door one day and brought her an armful of Stinking Cranesbill, sad that his father had carelessly uprooted it in the garden. Other parents reported that the children brought plants home from play that they wanted to look at more closely or that the children would ask more often for the names of plants.

The teacher herself conducted a questionnaire survey with the class out of interest—the children filled in the questionnaire once before and once after the implementation of the lesson. When the children were asked which plants they knew at the beginning, their answers were often very unspecific (e.g. tree, grasses, bushes, meadows) or they named very typical plants (dandelion, daisy, tulip, rose). In the second survey, they gave a total of 674 details, whereby girls named an average of 38 plants, boys 36. In the first survey, boys had given significantly fewer details. In the second survey, the gap between boys and girls had narrowed considerably. The question about appreciation was also included in the survey (How much do you like plants?)—here, an increase was noted. Overall, the teacher concluded that an

"awareness-raising with regard to the perception of plants and an increased appreciation" had been achieved (ibid., 17). She sees this as a basis for a later environmentally
protective approach to nature (ibid., 18).

In order to strengthen the educational potential, the teacher emphasises, outdoor
experiences do not require "a model meadow with many colourful flowers and many
insects", "a forest with an enormously high number of species and all kinds of
beetles", or "a clean park" and also no laid-out and labelled flower beds (ibid., 18).
Rather, teaching outdoors requires the "courage to develop lessons from what is
directly found in the children's living environment" (ibid.).

4.2.2 An Objective-Hermeneutic Reflection of the Case

If one tries to analyse the case even more deeply, based on Oevermann's theory of
objective hermeneutics, one can generate further theses beyond what has been said. In
contrast to a subsuming approach, the method of objective hermeneutics proceeds in
a reconstruction-logical way. It is particularly well suited to deciphering the typical,
i.e. characteristic structures of phenomena to be researched and to bringing to light
the "objective laws operating behind the phenomena" (Oevermann, 1996b, 1). With
the help of objective hermeneutics, an attempt is made to detect latent structures
of meaning and thus generate a case structure hypothesis. The procedure of objective hermeneutics can be practised by applying two evaluation procedures. One can
always consider a concrete case by asking: (a) How could the acting or speaking
person have behaved differently? (b) From which other contexts do we know what
is happening and what characterises these contexts? Thus, the following theses can
be generated for the present case.

The teacher is very clearly aware of the educational value of the emotional, social
and aesthetic experience. However, it seems as if she is controlling herself when
she addresses this dimension of education. Repeatedly she justifies her teaching
with references to, for example, the "consolidation and expansion of knowledge
of forms" (Czernoch, 2008, 14), or she makes use of terms such as "experiencing
competence" (ibid., 13) or "self-directed learning" (ibid., 12). It seems as if she feels
she has to activate generally accepted terms to justify her outdoor education approach.
At the same time, however, her underlying approach shows again and again, for
example when the teacher talks about the children making "acquaintance" with the
plants. This form of expression contains the social character of an in-relation setting.
Acquaintance means that a social relationship is entered into, whereby thinking,
acting and feeling are mutually related. Even though "acquaintance" is only a weak
form of social relationship, the expression contains the fact that two beings can
identify and recognise each other. The central educational concern of the teacher is
this in-relation setting. Nevertheless, she can only express this very indirectly or in
a protected way, for example when she says that it is important to "design lessons in
such a way that, in addition to the cognitive demands (…) they touch the heart a little"
(ibid., 18). This formulation shows how difficult it is for the teacher to openly express
what she intends with her teaching and has observed in the children. "Touches the

heart a little" is a very strongly controlled and withdrawn statement in comparison to the firm conviction that is repeatedly recognisable in the teacher regarding the importance of emotional and aesthetic experience.

The teacher is a very good observer. She registers the children's ability to perceive very accurately. It does not escape her that the children are enthusiastic about the task. She has a keen eye for what helps children in processes of indexing (e.g. illustrations, analogies, clarifying facts in dialogue). She also acts very authentically in relation to her own educational experiences. Thus, she can openly admit that she is afraid of not being able to identify plant species, or that some points in her planning get mixed up. In addition, she is able to be curious herself—she basically exhibits a research approach when, for example, she thinks about how to construct an identification key in a meaningful way. In doing so, she always has the educational object (plant) and the child equally in view. This is shown, for example, in the choice of the excursion location: a fallow land that is exciting and thrilling for children and that stimulates the child's imagination and feeds the curiosity of children. It is also significant that the teacher repeatedly appeals to the children's imagination and to their questioning. For example, she does not give the children an assignment such as researching the term industrial wasteland at the beginning. With such a research assignment, the actual question would have been erased and accordingly a crisis of meaning would have quickly arisen in the sense of "what use is it to me to have a definition of the term wasteland?" Instead, this teacher allows the children to explore for themselves what questions they have about a site they are told about and which feeds their curiosity and imagination. In this case, the teacher also describes very well the ways in which the children expressed themselves. Among other things, they assume that they would find "dead birds", "a falcon's nest", "horses", "old trains" or even "shooting stars" on such a site (ibid., 5).

So the question is: Why does the teacher, who has such good prerequisites for initiating social, dialogical, emotional and aesthetic educational processes, 'hide' behind 'common' constructs? Why does she often cite the factor "increase in knowledge", although the aspects of appreciation and lifelong positive experience are most important to her? Why does she resort to formulations such as "so that the class did not remain at the level of the imagined plant names, it was now a matter of (…)" (ibid., 11)? Or "this made memorising the plant names many times easier and more effective" (ibid.)? So why does she (indirectly) use vocabulary like performance or learning level or effectiveness? Yet at the same time she observes very precisely processes that run counter to this one-sided view of education, e.g. as follows:

> The tasks of naming or colouring set here allowed the division of the class into different 'performance levels' to be broken down. For here, it was not about reproduction or cognition, but about creativity and imagination. This was very clearly demonstrated by a child who had great problems with the acquisition of written language and the resulting consequential difficulties, but who was able to achieve excellent results in naming and especially in precise drawing and thus achieve a sense of achievement. The plant chosen by this child, the St. John's Wort, was clearly recognisable in the drawing, because both the typical flower shape, the distinctively dotted petals and the many stamens were precisely captured. (Czernoch, 2008, 8)

However, even here, she ultimately emphasises that the child carried out the task "correctly" and "exactly", with "excellent results"—whereas the focus is actually on the joy of the intensive and deepened creative work. Why does she not emphasise this 'mode' and 'process'? Why the correctness and the achievement of the goal (excellent results)? Elsewhere she writes that the children "made precise observations for their work". But at the same time, she observes the children as persons who are self-motivated and attentive for the sake of the thing, not for the sake of a work assignment. She also says that self-determination and open teaching are important to her. So why does she then always argue with assignments or tasks? It is almost as if the teacher doesn't dare to say that a discussion can also be a self-sufficient practice and that there doesn't always have to be a task. Or that it doesn't always have to be about a set task, but rather about the fact that something stimulates the children's reactions and actions, that questions are triggered, and that imagination and curiosity are stimulated.

This 'inner self-control' of the teacher is also evident in other places. For example, as most of the flowers are closed on the first excursion day, she writes: "My concept already got mixed up here" (ibid., 5). As if one should not deviate from a concept, as if one should immediately admit such changes of plan as a mistake. Alternatively, she could have presented and justified her ability here, namely that she is able to adapt lessons situationally-spontaneously to the needs and circumstances.

The most plausible assumption and thus the actual case structure hypothesis regarding all these observations is that the teacher doubts the acceptance or the significance of this form of education. She cannot imagine that her way of initiating educational processes would be accepted if she explicitly placed the emotional, aesthetic and social educational experience at the centre.

5 Argumentation Experience of Nature and Education

How can the potential of nature experiences for educational processes be presented argumentatively? Two levels are considered here: (a) the level of the individual educational process (b) the level of the institution school.

(a) **Experience of nature: educational processes at the level of the individual**
    Experiencing nature means that one can potentially experience what it is like to (a) start from the encounter with a natural phenomenon via (b) conscious perception with the chance that questions will arise, (c) via targeted observation and (d) the most diverse ways or modes of exploration up to (e) interpretations about the phenomenon and, if necessary, even up to (f) a reflection regarding higher-level questions of meaning attributions (cf. Fig. 1). According to the assumption, being able to witness such an educational process can be very formative if the process is embedded in successful, authentic interactions and is characterised by the greatest possible authenticity of all participants and if it

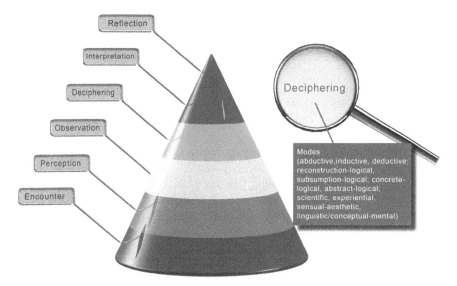

Fig. 1 Overview of possible phases of a deciphering and interpretation process (© Schumann)

is not burdened by pressure factors such as grading (selection pressure) or time-demanding specifications (time pressure). Such an experience of even a few exemplary educational processes potentially strengthens the self-confidence of those who are educating themselves. On the basis of an encounter with a natural phenomenon, one acquires a 'pattern' of the fact that and how it is possible to come to conclusions about the world and to be able to orient oneself so to speak by one's own strength.

More generally formulated: Experiences of nature that people gather will at some point be converted or transformed into knowledge, namely when they are opened up, i.e. as soon as the why-questions that arise from them (provided there is enough leisure for such questions to arise in the first place!) are answered. People can acquire objects and phenomena through deciphering and interpretation activities. This is the process of reconstruction. Successful reconstruction leads to structural knowledge. In reconstructing, one always establishes a reflexive reference to one's own experience; it is the reappraisal of an experience, the realisation of what constituted a solution to a crisis. In this way, the boundaries of an object are transcended or expanded. It does not remain merely a contemplation, but contemplation and reflection coincide. In the mental processing of experience, an already existing cognitive content undergoes a transformation in the sense of being newly created and reshaped, while retaining elements that are still viable—this is how new knowledge is created.

It becomes apparent how sensitive and how significant the first phase is in this entire process: the encounter with the natural phenomenon. The interaction needs to be created in such a way that children do not turn away from a natural phenomenon or object too quickly in the initial moment. Children need to be allowed to perceive it in leisure. Then, the probability increases that the children can be fully enthralled by the phenomenon, becoming aware of something they think is striking. If this is happening, an educational process is initiated, e.g. by questions arising. The design or facilitation of such interactions requires an awareness on the part of the educational facilitators of the importance of initial moments and perception in leisure. A challenge for educators is to enable the emergence of moments of aesthetic experience—of encountering and perceiving an object or phenomenon in leisure, of relating to the object, of silence, of wonder, of forming hunches, analogies and questions—without hastily intervening or 'directing' the processes. Mastering this challenge can be successful if there is an awareness of the structure of deciphering and interpretation processes, including the importance of leisure. This awareness is a possible result of experiencing nature.

(b)   **Experiencing nature: educational processes and the role of schools**

The possibility of lived experience is in principle open to all people. However, in the institution of school, it is apparently no longer kept in mind as a normal case (cf. Oevermann, 1996a, b, xiv). Especially the lessons at primary level, for example, take place predominantly in classrooms, so phenomena are not visited outside and at their place and in the habitat of their existence. Phenomena are often only 'transported' into the classroom on the worksheet or by means of the medium 'film'. In addition, the mode of—in Adorno's sense—"semi-educated standardisation of receptions" dominates in school—that one thus tries to approach phenomena in science education by 'investigating' them, e.g. with the help of a list of given technical terms or linguistic formulation aids as well as given experimental set-ups (standardised production of 'knowledge' and 'problem solving'). If the encounter with natural phenomena takes place in this way from the very first encounter and, if necessary, always in a standardised way, this means a considerable reduction of aesthetic experience as lived experience. The danger is that school, if it is structured in this way, contributes itself to the institutionalisation of semi-education. However, schools should succeed in counteracting the forces currently at work, which (can) lead to a decline in the facilitation of lived experience, in a compensatory way. It would be fatal if half-education, e.g. in the form of reciting misunderstood technical terms, is rewarded by school and if those who do not have that half-education and thus cannot shine rhetorically, perceive precisely this as a lack of education and are ashamed of this lack (cf. Oevermann, 1996a, b, xii). School must be a place where it is possible, in case of doubt, to start from very cautious and uncertain expressions and questions, and to recognise these as authentic and adequate engagement with the world. The case study selected and presented is an example of the possibility of the success of educational processes that point in such an authentic and thoughtful direction.

6 Outlook

The above thoughts on requirements and challenges in relation to research on nature experiences as well as the case study presented as an example make it clear that it is extremely challenging to analyse nature experiences and their educational value or potential. Against the background described and the complexity of factors, is it possible to find out objectively whether real encounters have a decisive, positive effect on educational processes? There is still a lack of long-term studies and of high-quality data protocols.

However, if we look at the potential of nature experiences alone in the theoretical and empirical approach presented here, one central thesis crystallises: Experiencing nature holds great potential in terms of personal development. However, in order for this effect to unfold and also become demonstrable, moments of experiencing nature must, on the one hand, take place at all, and on the other hand, they must take place in such a way that they can form authentic encounters in leisure. They must be combined with dialogues that do justice to both child and subject, under conditions that do not allow for any semi-educational tendencies, but on the contrary, allow for "authentic personal development and vivid experience" (cf. Oevermann, 1996a, b, ix ff.).

Recommended further reading

1. Schumann, Svantje (2017). *Reading Nature.* Handreichungen—Kultusministerium Hessen, bsj, In M. Vollmar, P. Becker & J. Schirp (eds.), *Handreichungen für die naturpädagogische Praxis von Kindertagesstätten.* https://www.bsj-marburg.de/fileadmin/user_upload/downloads/6_wege_in_die_Natur/handre ichungen-fuer-naturpaedagogische-praxis.pdf (accessed 20/12/2020).
2. Wildhirt, Susanne (1995). Bouquets of flowers, after Rousseau. In H. Ch. Berg & Th. Schulze (eds.), *Lehrkunst—Lehrbuch der Didaktik.* Neuwied: Luchterhand, 233–262.
3. Wohlleben, Peter (2012). *Kranichflug und Blumenuhr: Naturphänomene im Garten beobachten, verstehen und nutzen [Crane flight and flower clock. Observing, understanding and using natural phenomena in the garden].* Darmstadt: pala-verlag.

References

Billmann-Mahecha, E. (1994). Über die Interpretation von Kinderzeichnungen. L.O.G.O.S. *Interdisziplinär* 2(1):28–35.
Billmann-Mahecha, E. (2005). The interpretation of children's drawings. In G. Mey (Ed.), *Handbook of Qualitative Developmental Psychology* (pp. 435–453). Köln: Kölner Studienverlag.

Czernoch, A. (2008). Der alte Rangierbahnhof und die Selbstbestimmungstheorie der Motivation. In E. Gläser, L. Jäkel, & H. Weidmann (Eds.), *Sachunterricht planen und reflektieren. Ein Studienbuch zur Analyse unterrichtlichen Handelns* (pp. 4–18). Baltmannsweiler: Schneider Verlag Hohengehren.

Deci, E., & Ryan, R. M. (1993). The self-determination theory of motivation and its relevance to pedagogy. *Journal of Pedagogy, 29*, 223–228.

Eisenhardt, K. M. (1989). Building theories from case study research. *Management Review, 14*(4), 532–550.

Fuhs, B. (2000). Qualitative interviews with children. Reflections on a difficult method. In F. Heinzel (Ed.), *Methods of Childhood Research. An overview of research approaches to the child perspective* (pp. 87–103). Weinheim: Juventa.

Heinzel, F. (1997). Qualitative interviews with children. In B. Friebertshäuser & A. Prengel (Eds.), *Handbuch Qualitative Forschungsmethoden in der Erziehungswissenschaft* (pp. 396–413). Weinheim: Juventa.

Heinzel, F. (Ed.). (2012). *Methods of childhood research: An overview of research approaches to the child perspective* (2nd ed.). Weinheim: Beltz Juventa.

Krüger, H.-H. & Grunert, C. (2001). Biographical interviews with children. In I. Behnken & J. Zinnecker (Eds.), *Kinder, Kindheit, Lebensgeschichte. Ein Handbuch* (pp. 129–142). Seelze-Velber: Kallmeyer.

Mayring, P. (1993). *Qualitative content analysis. Fundamentals and techniques* (4th expanded ed.). Weinheim: Deutscher Studienverlag.

Neuss, N. (1999). *Symbolische Verarbeitung von Fernseherlebnissen in Kinderzeichnungen. Eine empirische Studie mit Vorschulkindern.* München: KoPäd-Verlag.

Neuss, N. (2005). Children's drawing. In L. Mikos & C. Wegener (Eds.), *Qualitative media research* (pp. 333–342). Konstanz: UVK Verlagsgesellschaft.

Oevermann, U. (1996a). Vorwort. In Th. Loer (Ed.), *Halbbildung und Autonomie. Über Struktureigenschaften der Rezeption bildender Kunst* (pp. v–xiv). Opladen: Westdeutscher Verlag.

Oevermann, U. (1996b). Theoretische Skizze einer revidierten Theorie professionalisierten Handelns. In A. Combe & W. Helsper (Eds.), *Pädagogische Professionalität. Untersuchungen zum Typus pädagogischen Handelns* (pp. 70–182). Frankfurt am Main: Suhrkamp.

Oevermann, U. (2004). Sozialisation als Prozess der Krisenbewältigung. In D. Geulen & H. Veith (Eds.), *Sozialisationstheorie interdisziplinär. Aktuelle Perspektiven.* Bd. 20 der Reihe "Der Mensch als soziales und personales Wesen" (pp. 155–182). Stuttgart: Lucius und Lucius.

Oevermann, U. (2008). 'Crisis and Routine' as an analytical paradigm in the social sciences. Retrieved May 05, 2021, from https://archive.org/details/AbschiedsvorlesungOevermannVideo. Furthermore In: R. Becker-Lenz, A. Franzmann, A. Jansen, & M. Jung (Eds.), *The Methodological School of Objective Hermeneutics. A stocktaking* (pp. 43–114). Wiesbaden: Springer Fachmedien.

Oevermann, U., Allert, T., Konau, E., & Krambeck, J. (1979). Die Methodologie einer „objektiven Hermeneutik" und ihre allgemeine forschungslogische Bedeutung in den Sozialwissenschaften. In H. G. Soeffner (Ed.), *Interpretative Verfahren in den Sozial- und Textwissenschaften* (pp. 352–434). Stuttgart: J. B. Metzlersche Verlagsbuchhandlung.

Peez, G. (2011). Kinder kritzeln, zeichnen und malen—Warum eigentlich? *Forschung Frankfurt, 29*(2), 45–48.

Peirce, C. S. (1877). The fixation of belief. In Chr. J. W. Kloesel, M. H. Fish, L. A. Ziegler, D. Roberts, N. Houser, A. Houser, U. Niklas, & E. C. Moore (Eds.), *Writings of Charles Sanders Peirce: A chronological edition* (Vol. 3, pp. 1872–1878). Bloomington: Indiana University Press.

Scheid, C. M. (2012). An exploration of the methodology of social scientific analyses of drawn and painted images through the analysis of two children's drawings. *FQS 14*(1), art. 3.

Scholz, G. (2005). Anschlussfähige Bildungsprozesse gestalten aus der Perspektive Kindergarten und Grundschule. Vortrag am 06.10.2005 in Trier. In G. Scholz (Ed.), *Bildungsarbeit mit Kindern. Lernen ja—Verschulung nein. Thema 6.* Mülheim: Verlag an der Ruhr. Retrieved July 10, 2020, from http://grundschulforschung.de/GSA/Bildungsarbeit_6.pdf.

Wildhirt, S. (1995). Bouquets of flowers, after Rousseau. In H. Ch. Berg & Th. Schulze (Eds.), *Lehrkunst—Lehrbuch der Didaktik* (pp. 233–262). Neuwied: Luchterhand.

Svantje Schumann is head of the Chair of Didactics of Science Education at the School of Education FHNW, Institute of Primary Education. Her work focuses on case analyses, research into learning processes in the field of science learning and teaching—including primary experience of nature, technical education and learning processes at extracurricular learning sites—and the analysis of the significance of interactions for learning processes. Correspondence address: svantje. schumann@fhnw.ch.

Creating a Forest for Learning

How the National Forest in the UK has developed an Outdoor-Based Learning Project

Carol Rowntree Jones, Caroline Scothern, Heather Gilbert, and Sue Anderson

1 Twenty five Years of Groundwork

> The National Forest has the potential to be one of the biggest and most exciting open-air classrooms in the country. With increasing emphasis now being placed upon the natural world through the national curriculum … it will also be a dynamic, practical demonstration of how local, national and global environmental issues interact with one another. (Countryside Commission, 1994)

This prescient paragraph was written not in 2020 in the midst of the global pandemic, but in 1994, when the UK's National Forest published its first strategy document.

The concept of the National Forest had been developed in the mid-1980s by a visionary team in the Countryside Commission. They identified the potential for bringing multi-purpose forestry (that is, forestry for both commercial and environmental benefit as well as for recreation and leisure) near to where people live and work in lowland England. It was a radical concept. At that time, 'forestry' in the UK had a poor reputation (Aldhous, 1997). There was a widely held perception that decades of government-funded national planting of fast-growing non-native conifers had been done unsympathetically, doing little for native biodiversity. Planting mixed native woodlands nearer to people could maximise the social, environmental and economic benefits that a modern forest could offer, where trees would be part of a living landscape and part of the fabric of people's lives. The English Midlands, a distinctly non-forested part of the UK, was selected as the location for this ambitious project. It was to be called the 'national' forest as it was to be an example to the

C. Rowntree Jones (✉) · C. Scothern · H. Gilbert · S. Anderson
The National Forest Company, Bath Yard, Moira, Swadlincote, Derbyshire DE12 6BA, UK
e-mail: crowntreejones@nationalforest.org

H. Gilbert
e-mail: hgilbert@nationalforest.org

S. Anderson
e-mail: sanderson@nationalforest.org

© The Author(s) 2022
R. Jucker and J. von Au (eds.), *High-Quality Outdoor Learning*,
https://doi.org/10.1007/978-3-031-04108-2_21

367

Fig. 1 Coal mining in the heart of what has become the National Forest. Forest cover in this area has more than tripled. Photo credit: The Magic Attic

country: if this could work here, it could work anywhere. Trees and forestry would be shown to be a driver for regeneration and transformation even in one of the most unlikely of places.

An area of 200 square miles bordered by the cities of Leicester, Derby and Birmingham was chosen, with support from local communities being a crucial part of the decision to place it here.

Before the National Forest began, forest cover in this area stood around 6%, one of the lowest in the country. The central part of the Forest area was the former Midland Coalfield, where deep and open cast coal mining and clay extraction had employed thousands of people. The closure of the pits in the 1980s had left generations of families unemployed and the landscape damaged and scarred (Fig. 1). To their credit, they welcomed the opportunity to repair this by creating a forest.

It has been a forest grown from the ground up, in all senses.

2 Developing Environmental Education in the Forest

The small team at the National Forest Company (NFC), the organisation established in 1995 by the UK government to lead the creation and development of the National

Forest, began to work with passion, persuasion and a tight budget[1] to cultivate relationships with both local landowners and communities to create the Forest. One of the first tasks of the newly appointed Community Liaison Officer was to establish "environmental education to help foster understanding and appreciation of the Forest." (Countryside Commission, 1994).

The drive for environmental education in the Forest came from a commitment to ensure that the next generation growing up here would have a true connection to their surroundings. In a place where trees, woodland and the concept of 'forest' were not previously part of the culture, giving young people an understanding of the Forest, and empowering them to care for and defend it, would give the best chance for the Forest to survive and thrive over generations to come.

These young people did not come from families of foresters. Individuals were more likely to have a heritage of mining, brick making or farming; many other things than looking after trees.

By the time the first strategic plans for the Forest were being drawn up in 1994, activities with young people already included tree planting, developing nature areas in school grounds, promoting growing trees from seed, giving talks to schools and student groups and developing teachers' packs.

It was also identified early on that for the full potential of this work to be realised, long-term partnerships would have to be developed with education authorities, policy makers and funders, teacher training colleges, arts boards and other specialist organisations.

Between 1994 and 2001, two visitor centres in the Forest opened and became the main hubs for activity to deliver environmental education: Rosliston Forestry Centre near Burton upon Trent and Conkers Discovery Centre near Ashby de la Zouch. Along with planting trees (often in the wind, rain and mud—tree planting taking place between November and March each year), children had fun as they learnt about bug hunting in dead wood piles, animals preparing for winter, the tough life of a tree and more.

By 2015, 500,000 children in and around the National Forest had taken part in environmental education activities such as these. They came from local rural and urban schools within the Forest itself and, when funds were available, from inner city schools in the surrounding cities of Derby, Leicester and Birmingham. This work was made possible by generous support over many years from committed partners such as Derby-based Rolls-Royce, demonstrating another aspect of the longstanding work to grow and embed the National Forest in the local consciousness with businesses and communities.

However, at the National Forest we still faced the same problems as the rest of the country for outdoor learning in our primary schools. Delivering the standard curriculum was seen as a very indoors matter at this time and a trip outdoors was an

---

[1] £60 m of public money was spent on creating and developing the National Forest in the first 25 years, "equivalent to two miles of three-lane motorway." https://www.theguardian.com/enviro nment/2016/aug/07/national-forest-woodland-midlands-regeneration.

exception, a treat, a day out. Our goal was to truly embed time spent in the outdoors and outdoor learning within children's everyday activities.

The early findings of the Natural Connections Demonstration Project (Waite et al., 2016, see chapter "Natural Connections: Learning About Outdoor-Based Learning" in this volume) reinforced the importance of tackling barriers and providing supportive networks for schools, and there was growing discussion and interest throughout the sector in the holistic benefits of learning outdoors (Department for Education and Skills, 2006).

What better for the aspirations of this growing teenage forest? To become a space not only for bug hunting and shelter building, but also somewhere where children could grow with the intrinsic benefits of being out in nature, showing how an outdoor classroom can free up a child's imagination and engagement. Outdoor learning in woodland offers very special advantages: shade, a wonderful quality of light, variety of tactile experiences as well as the chance to climb trees, make things from trees, and forage from the woodland floor. A woodland is truly immersive and engaging, not just a backdrop.

By 2016 more than 8 million trees had been planted in the National Forest, forest cover had increased from 6 to 20% and hundreds of new woodlands had been created, the majority of which had public access. We had also started to bring together our thinking about how to reach all the children in the Forest, and how this would help us develop an intrinsic forest culture and help our communities feel at ease out in the woods. We realised that the most effective way to do this was to use the existing schools' infrastructure. After all, we had 25 years of experience in building up partnerships with schools.

Our understanding was that nearly a third of all primary schools in the Forest were doing no outdoor learning activity at all and the majority of those that were, offered it on an ad hoc basis and were not maximising the use of their own school grounds or staff resources.

We then had a breakthrough moment when we discovered the Audemars Piguet Foundation—a corporate foundation with a mission "to support worldwide forest conservation through environmental protection and youth awareness-raising endeavours" (Foundation Audemars Piguet, 2021). We could hardly believe our eyes. It was the perfect funder for the work we hoped to do and a great opportunity to join forces with a philanthropic partner.[2]

---

[2] Many organisations trying to encourage outdoor learning are faced with the reality that without the support of philanthropic foundations, these important projects cannot be run, given that dedicated state funding for this is limited.

3   2016 Creating a Forest for Learning: Funding Opportunity

Our proposal was to build on our substantial experience of environmental education work and bring about a step change in provision across the whole Forest—to challenge and support every primary school in the National Forest to achieve a minimum level of regular provision for outdoor learning, 'regular' meaning at least once a month.

Our experience had shown that, although popular, outdoor learning was often considered specialist teaching and was presented in different ways by different external providers. Although there was some very good learning being delivered, this model was not helping to engage schoolteachers, or the school itself, to fully embrace an outdoor learning culture.

When we asked schools what was holding them back, the same barriers cropped up repeatedly: the cost of transport to take children off-site, the lack of specialist expertise of teachers within schools, the perceived risk and time of arranging out of classroom sessions, and the absence of facilities within the school grounds.

We found that schools that offered regular provision were most likely those with extensive grounds or who could afford transport, and that funding was available for others, but was often sporadic.

Costs associated with the activity were in many cases being met by the parents, and this inevitably meant that outdoor learning was a one-off treat rather than a regular part of the curriculum. We wanted to ensure that all children in the Forest could have access to outdoor learning, regardless of their background or their school.

Our approach was designed to address these barriers by focusing on building capacity within the schools themselves by funding training for teachers and infrastructure improvements to ensure every primary school could provide regular outdoor learning provision within the school grounds or within walking distance. The ultimate goal was to embed outdoor learning within each School Plan so that it became an accepted and expected part of school life for children, staff and parents.

We had some experience of facilitating teacher training over the previous years in the form of a series of one-day training sessions for teachers, covering Forest School[3] activities, woodland crafts, music, arts and literacy. They were often over-subscribed, and we had increasing demand from teachers wanting to develop their skills and gain confidence.

We had also worked with dozens of schools in the early days of the Forest offering tree planting days on site to encourage them to feel part of this exciting new initiative to create a Forest (Fig. 2). We therefore knew there were many school grounds throughout the Forest with young trees. These just needed a bit of tender loving

---

[3] Forest School is a developmental ethos shared by thousands of trained practitioners throughout the world. It is a child-centred holistic learning process, developing confidence and self-esteem through learner inspired, hands on experiences in a natural, forest setting. Creating a Forest for Learning in the National Forest follows this philosophy, but layered with the desire to develop young citizens of the National Forest.

Fig. 2 Pupils creating future outdoor learning spaces. Photo credit: Steve Baker/National Forest Company

care to be able to create little glades that could offer space for shelters to be rigged up under the branches, provide ample material for kindling, whittling and artwork, and give inspiration for creative writing and exciting spaces for science and maths studies.

For those schools without such spaces within their grounds, we knew the majority had woodlands and green spaces nearby. Our proposed funding model would make it possible for a school to work with a neighbouring woodland owner who could apply for funding to cover any necessary adaptions to make the space suitable as an outdoor classroom, giving the school access to outdoor learning within walking distance.

We wanted to make it as easy and seamless as possible for teaching and learning to take place outdoors in a wooded setting on a systematic and regular basis. Audemars Piguet Foundation approved of our plan and provided the funding that enabled us to embark on a substantial three-year programme.

4   2017—The Start of Creating a Forest for Learning (CF4L)

We appointed a dedicated Education Officer, and the project was launched formally in June 2017 with an event where policy makers and leaders were invited to walk in the woods and join children from two schools in the Forest to take part in various activities from fire lighting to leaf printing, natural art to insect study. Our goals for the first three years were:

- To ensure half of all primary schools in the Forest were using an outdoor wooded space within easy walking distance, year-round. The remaining schools to be aware of the opportunities and support available and making plans.
- To create a vibrant and active network of mutually supportive Forest Schools practitioners and outdoor educators.
- To develop a network of teachers who were confident in their knowledge and understanding of the Forest, liaising with landowners and being part of an active network.
- To devise relevant training and determine programmes of support with established demand for delivery of these resources, including a single point of contact at NFC and visits to each school to meet with grounds staff, teaching staff and leadership.
- To establish an awards scheme with at least 30 schools aspiring to achieve the award.
- To create a record of current education provision in the Forest that would provide a benchmark against which future progress could be measured and a clear strategy to support, guide and advocate the development of sustainable outdoor learning provision into the future.

We were also working towards outcomes of the project beyond these three years to ensure that:

- Every primary school in the Forest has access to a woodland setting as a regular learning space for teaching within school grounds or within walking distance.
- Every primary school has teaching staff trained in Forest School and/or environmental education techniques.
- A sustainable network of support for teachers with a financially sustainable training programme is in place.
- Partner organisations in the Forest are coordinating outdoor learning delivery, sharing best practice, and supporting each other.
- Outdoor learning is beginning to be embedded into each primary school's ethos and culture.
- An exemplar model of sustainable outdoor learning provision would exist and could be replicated nationally and internationally.

5   The National Landscape and Our Five Point Plan for Outdoor Learning

Midway through the project we presented an interim report at a National Forest event at the Houses of Parliament (National Forest Company, 2018). The national landscape was developing by this time: people were talking more about children's mental health and recognising the challenges they faced in the 21st century. Public Health England had found that 28% of children aged two to 15 were overweight or obese (Public Health England, 2017) and a 2017 survey showed one in eight 5- to 19-year-olds had suffered at least one mental health disorder (NHS Digital, 2018). The government was also taking notice, embedding aims based on connecting people with nature specifically for mental health benefits into their 2018 25-year plan (HM Government, 2018). The importance of creating a connection with nature for young people was becoming increasingly apparent. Creating a Forest for Learning felt increasingly like core work for our vision of the National Forest—transforming lives as well as the landscape.

We summarised our ambition in a Five Point Plan for Outdoor Learning in the National Forest, and used it in communications with schools, parents, funders and partners. It set out our aims to encourage every primary school in the National Forest to have:

1. A monthly programme of outdoor learning sessions all year round
2. At least one Forest School trained teacher/teaching assistant
3. An outdoor wooded learning space within the school grounds or within walking distance
4. Outdoor learning included as a key part of the school improvement plan
5. Access to a supportive network of outdoor learning professionals and high quality off-site outdoor learning provision.

We saw this five-point plan as an expression of our exemplar role as the 'national' forest: it could provide a template to be rolled out across the country as a simple cost-effective approach to reconnecting the next generation with the natural world, creating positive change for learning, wellbeing and the environment.

The simplicity of our approach demonstrated that relatively straightforward activities and modest funding could make a real and lasting difference: training teaching staff, creating outdoor learning areas and supporting schools to build their confidence and experience. Resources invested in improving school facilities and the expertise of teaching staff were helping to build their commitment to ongoing provision of outdoor learning. Our investment to this point had been hundreds rather than thousands of pounds per school per year and yet was having a dramatic impact on outdoor learning provision in schools throughout the Forest.

Our approach showed that affordable outdoor learning could be undertaken regularly by primary schools with all their children. It was also evidence that outdoor learning could be used for any lessons—literacy, numeracy or science as much as for particular environmental themes—and could happen all year round, changing with the seasons and weather conditions (Fig. 3).

We were also beginning to work towards taking this approach to other stages of education, looking to develop new programmes for secondary schools based on the increased confidence and wellbeing that outdoor learning can bring to older students, and work with pre-schools to provide early experiences of fun and learning through play in the outdoors.

Fig. 3 Outdoor learning in the National Forest. Photo credit: Darren Cresswell/National Forest Company

We were learning more about the needs of schools and barriers they faced to taking up outdoor learning. We took time to map the gaps in provision and gaps in woodlands within easy reach of schools. We facilitated a specialist network of outdoor learning professionals that schools could approach for advice as well as ourselves, and were beginning to develop plans for creating champion schools to foster confidence in those schools who were just starting out. We also realised that we had to identify champions within the schools themselves: teachers or governors with a passion for outdoor learning who could advocate for it within the school's management.

Once expertise within the school developed, more advanced sessions would begin to take place and where limited wooded learning space was available in school grounds off-site visits would follow, making the most of the proximity of diverse woodland throughout the Forest.

6   Examples of Success in First Stage: Champion Schools

We developed a number of champion schools who embodied our five-point plan and who were already sharing their best practice with others.

Woodstone

This school had an enthusiastic headteacher and one Forest School trained teacher in 2017 but they were unsure where to go next. CF4L helped to train further staff in Forest School and provided Continued Professional Development training in outdoor learning for all the staff, including the site manager.

In 2018 they successfully hosted woodland management training for 14 other schools. Woodstone showcased the project in a news item for regional television and featured in our Forest for Learning Five Point Plan document and National Forest campaign video.

Funders Audemars Piguet Foundation visited the school in October 2018 as an outstanding example of how established outdoor learning is in the school, and how the funding has enabled this. They also saw the huge value for children in outdoor learning through building the teaching staff's confidence and skills. Woodstone has even added an outdoor learning question to their interviews for teachers, to ensure they appoint people with interest and enthusiasm for the work.

Woodstone has reported extraordinary benefits for the children who have been learning outdoors:

> We have seen a huge positive impact on the children who have been taking part in our Forest School programme; in particular the children's confidence, communication and team working skills have greatly developed. It has also impacted positively on the children's mental health, which is a key focus on our school development plan this year. We have seen a big impact in the classroom; the children are making accelerated progress due to them building on and developing these important positive learning behaviours. *Patrick Mullins (Headteacher) Woodstone Primary School*

Fountains

Fountains is a special school for children with a range of learning and physical difficulties. Fountains is committed to giving pupils the opportunity to learn in an outdoor environment and believe that taking learning outside is good for promoting self-esteem, wellbeing, sociable behaviour, co-operative learning and problem solving.

CF4L supported and helped fund an enthusiastic teacher from Fountains in their Forest School training. The school has now seen how these skills feed positively back into classroom work and other settings, and the positive impact it is having on the children.

Throughout the project, Fountains have remained engaged, attending woodland management training, attending the FEN (Forest Education Network) Conference held in the Forest in 2019 and currently running a National Forest schools' network for schools to meet and share outdoor learning ideas and successes. With support from CF4L the primary school is now supporting the secondary school in developing their outdoor learning.

Awards Programme

We introduced Forest for Learning Awards covering four categories:

- Inspirational beginnings
- Creative use of space
- Use of local woodlands
- Sharing best practice.

We presented 52 schools with an award matching their particular achievements and celebrated all the schools at an event at the National Forest's Timber festival. We invited key outdoor learning partners to the event leading to a great sharing of ideas, contacts and making plans for the future.

7 Funding Extended 2019–2024

After successfully achieving our goals set out in 2016, we were delighted to have our funding extended from 2019 to 2024. We had achieved 50% of all primary schools in the Forest offering regular outdoor learning sessions. We had created a vibrant network of supportive teachers and practitioners, with 12 champion schools, and had set up an awards scheme with at least 30 schools aspiring to achieve the award. Senior and head teachers were becoming advocates for outdoor learning in their schools and with other schools locally, having seen the positive impact on children's behaviour.

We developed our exemplar role further by establishing new partnerships to secure additional funding from UK central government to work with schools in disadvantaged areas beyond the immediate Forest boundary. Forest Foxes, a partnership between the NFC, Leicester City in the Community (the community foundation of English Premier League football club Leicester City) and the Forest School Association, was set up as one of five Community Forest and Woodland Outreach projects under the national Children and Nature programme, working to foster opportunities for children to spend time in nature, with the benefits this can have for their health and wellbeing and how they engage with their education.

> I would also like to thank you for going beyond planting, by continuing to improve engagement with local authorities, local businesses and local communities. Your successful bid to the National Lottery Heritage Fund for £2.7 million, and £0.5 million from Audemars Piguet Foundation, Morrisons Foundation and Defra/Natural England in partnership with Leicester City Football Club Community Trust are great examples of this. *The Rt Hon Lord Goldsmith of Richmond Park, Minister of State*

We were poised to make such good progress and then the Covid-19 pandemic hit.

8 Creating a Forest for Learning—Progress by April 2021

The pandemic had a huge impact on the project due to the restrictions placed on schools, the NFC and the Forest itself. However, the NFC Education Officer remained in contact with schools and local outdoor learning practitioners to enable school staff to receive support in re-thinking their activities in the light of the pandemic. Funding for essential grounds maintenance, the production of online training videos and the development of virtual networks and digital conferencing meant that engagement with primary schools developed exceptionally well through this challenging time.

Despite the difficulties, by April 2021 the project had achieved:

- Over 90% of all primary schools in the Forest taking part in some outdoor learning.
- 59% of all primary schools taking part in regular outdoor learning.
- All primary schools within the National Forest aware of opportunities to engage in outdoor learning (Fig. 4).

In addition to the headline success in working with primary schools, the aspiration to extend the work into secondary schools continues. This has been massively compromised by the pandemic, but five secondary schools are engaged in the project and have helped to give insight into how the work could progress. It is often the children who struggle in the classroom who benefit most from outdoor learning, which means our initial focus will be to work with teacher-selected cohorts, pupil referral units and special schools to ensure we are offering opportunities to those who need them most.

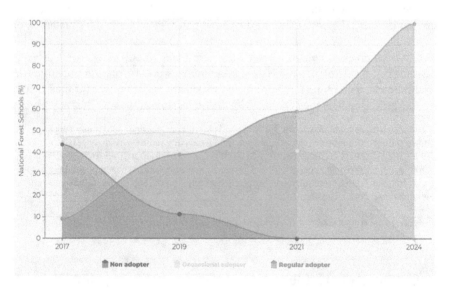

Fig. 4 Percentage of schools within the National Forest that had never undertaken outdoor learning (orange), adopted outdoor learning occasionally (yellow) or at least one a month (green). The darker colours representing data prior to 2021 show the actual progress of the CF4L programme. The lighter colours representing post-2021 data are a projection of outcomes based on the goals of the 2019–2024 project

Case Study: John Taylor Free School (Secondary School)
John Taylor Free School was grant aided through CF4L to support staff training and capital works to the school grounds. The improvements to the site have meant more pupils can engage in outdoor learning, as well as improving the biodiversity of the site. They've created an outdoor classroom and purchased equipment to ensure sessions are accessible to all. The students currently involved are from the Special Educational Needs and Disabilities (SEND) group and are known as the OWL cohort, due to their Outdoor Wild Learning.

Case Study: Ivanhoe College Middle School
"We intend to train two staff to run sessions for targeted groups of students based on additional needs (e.g. disengaged learners and SEND students) so that we can offer lessons such as Drama in the Forest and other projects with a nature focus. We are hugely excited by the potential this opportunity offers."

9 Developing the Project into the Future

Funding

Since long-term sustainability is at the heart of what we are trying to achieve, we have modified our funding model slightly to support this. The new model requires that any school reapplying for funding from the project identifies how they will share their learning and best practice with other schools across the Forest. This could include supporting twilight sessions for teachers from local schools, supporting training at Inset days, or inviting local schools to take part in outdoor learning sessions on their site.

Identifying how schools can support the long-term sustainability of outdoor learning within the Forest will allow for continued learning across a variety of schools, developing a strong supportive and sharing culture. The grant process supports the creation of champion schools, identifying how each applicant can offer support and share their learning. Over time, the increased number of champion schools will support a sustainable network of outdoor learning across the Forest. The grants on offer have also been increased to up to 70% of costs of training and capital improvement work on site.

Online activity

The pandemic has increased reliance on online support and activity for us all, but three of our champion schools shared their learning on the Forest Foxes project Facebook page, enabling them to share vital learning with other school staff across the Forest and the Leicester city area. One school also joined online resilience training delivered through the Forest Foxes project, enabling them to share learning from their own activities with other schools who are new to delivering outdoor learning.

10 Looking Forward: What We have Learnt and Key Objectives for Creating a Forest for Learning

Networking and Sharing Best Practice

We have learnt that the schools prefer to engage and network at a local level to share and develop their outdoor learning practice, in preference to a central hub.

> We could offer opportunities for other schools within the vicinity to take part in our Forest schools programme. We would like to think that we could offer training and CPD opportunities for teachers in the future. *Sarah Rowe (Headteacher) Walton on Trent Primary School*

However, there is still a need for the National Forest to raise awareness of the importance of outdoor learning, celebrate best practice and help signpost teaching staff and volunteers to the support and training they need.

Harder to Reach Schools

Networking between teachers, schools and professional networks can open up communication with harder to reach schools since word-of-mouth recommendation of CF4L from valued colleagues is very effective in encouraging engagement. These networks can also be beneficial in sharing best practice, experiences, successes and challenges. As well as our Forest Foxes project, we secured funding from the Morrisons' Foundation to work with six schools close to their supermarkets in the towns of Coalville, Swadlincote and Burton upon Trent. Both Forest Foxes and the Morrisons funded work have proved particularly helpful in building relationships with harder to reach primary schools in some of the poorest areas of the Forest.

We also use our wider work and partnerships to help us reach reticent schools. For example, we sent every primary school in the Forest a copy of Robert Macfarlane and Jackie Morris's award-winning book *The Lost Words* (2017), with its stunning illustrations and poetic vocabulary of the natural world. We invited the schools to tell us of the children's reaction when they opened the package (it is a big, beautiful book). The excitement was clear and generated a response from 17 schools. Four of these were new contacts which we followed up with a visit to offer advice on the use of their school grounds.

Limited Use of Training for Woodland Owners

We expected some private woodland owners may have applied for funding to train in risk assessment, drawing up agreements for educational use etc., but the main interest has come from public landowners or other charities (see point 4 below), who already have expertise and policies in place for engaging with the public. When private landowners have been involved, they have appreciated continued facilitation by NFC. However, schools themselves have benefited from woodland management training alongside landowners and it featured as a workshop as part of the Forest Education Network National Conference held in the National Forest in 2019.

Limited Development of Woodland Beyond School Grounds

CF4L has facilitated a few schools in developing relationships with local landowners to use their woodland for regular Forest School activity, such as Forestry England, the Woodland Trust and a few local private woodland owners. Both private and public landowners have valued how CF4L has been able to extend the use and enjoyment of their woodland.

Overall, schools are prioritising establishing outdoor learning spaces on their own grounds for ease of regular use. However, as schools become established in delivering outdoor learning with trained and confident staff it is envisaged that interest in using local woodlands will grow as larger spaces will enhance what the staff can offer and the children can experience.

Training

Face to face training became impossible during the pandemic. However, skills and resources developed at this time of emergency will stand in good stead going forward, as training videos and online platforms will continue to be of use—although there is nothing to beat being out in the woods together!

Networking

Similarly, in person networking was impossible for much of 2020 and 2021. Virtual networks that were established as a matter of need will continue to have their place, as well as social media and digital conferencing helping to engage people and share best practice in a wider arena.

Key Objectives up to 2024

- Embed outdoor learning in all primary schools in the Forest by 2024.
- Better understand current activity, aspirations, barriers and gaps in provision and to establish new activity in 40% of secondary schools.
- Look at gaps in pre-school provision, encouraging the youngest learners to interact with nature.
- Further develop the role of champion host schools, a training programme to provide support for more advanced activities, and refinement of our grant scheme

to ensure it continues to incentivise schools to engage in outdoor learning. At the time of publication, we have made arrangements for our nine Forest Foxes schools to each visit a champion school in the Forest. This will be an exciting opportunity to widen the impact of the work that has been established at 'exemplar' schools, but also to share what is important in the work of both participant schools in each encounter.

- To influence our schools and partners to use outdoor learning as a catalyst to embed environmental awareness across the curriculum.
- To create a sustainable framework to support outdoor learning beyond 2024, including a self-sustaining training programme, grant funding embedded within NFC core budget and a well-developed virtual hub to provide advice and support and signpost other services.

11   Conclusion

We believe Creating a Forest for Learning has given us a successful model for widening engagement in outdoor learning—both within the National Forest and beyond. Our strategy to build capacity within the schools themselves by funding staff training and capital works in school grounds has proved effective.

In a wider way, the project has taken forward our work in embedding a forest culture throughout this 200 square mile area of the Midlands. The occurrence of the global pandemic during the progress of the work has only bolstered our belief in the value of outdoor learning. The natural world became a solace for so many people, during months when personal human contact was unavailable. The National Forest, with hundreds of woodlands near where people live, felt like it had come into its own—woodlands and green spaces available on people's doorstep, just when they needed them.

> It is peaceful and magical in the woods. It is amazing listening to all the sounds. *Child attending Forest School session*

But as far as specifically young people are concerned, it is increasingly clear that it is important for them to spend time in nature for the sake of their mental wellbeing, their physical health, social skills and academic achievement (Harvey et al., 2020; Otte et al., 2019). Outdoor learning is essential in the National Forest; it is vital to ensure that more children and young people are engaged with nature throughout their learning career and develop crucial understanding and engagement in the National Forest for future generations.

It is essential that young people feel connected to the natural world to fully engage in working positively to help grow the future together. At the National Forest we believe that tackling climate change is urgent, and that sustainability is achievable. We have spent the last 30 years transforming the landscape, using trees and forest to recover from our industrial past. We need to spend the next 25 years mitigating and adapting to climate change to create a greener future that promotes sustainable lifestyles.

We have a strong background story in the National Forest, and examples of young people who grew up in the Forest and are now actively engaged in making this their professional lives too. One young woman delivers Forest School for a day nursery in the Forest and says it was taking part in tree dressing activities with NFC while at primary school that made her certain that one day she would work with trees.

Our aspirations are that:

- generations of children grow up fully aware of the benefits of woodland and able to realise the potential of the Forest for their education, wellbeing, creativity, employment or enterprise.
- pupils, teachers and their families feel a better connection to their local trees and woodlands, understanding the natural world and being empowered to take informed decisions as active citizens helping our responses to Covid-19 and the climate crisis.
- schools will begin to recruit their staff based on an expectation that they will be able to deliver outdoor learning.
- there will be so much outdoor learning delivery across the Forest that teachers changing jobs will simply result in more sharing of skills rather than a loss in overall capacity for outdoor learning.
- parents will select education settings based on the quality and availability of outdoor learning.

Furthermore, we look towards

- Active travel—walking to school through the woods
- Mental health and resilience strengthened through learning outdoors
- Local field trips (instead of boarding coaches to National Parks), with more residential opportunities within the Forest (linking with our wider work to grow sustainable tourism in the National Forest)
- "Generation Forest" will be equipped to change the world!

As was declared in the early days of the Forest in 1994, we want to fulfil the National Forest's potential to be one of the biggest and most exciting open-air classrooms in the world. Creating a Forest for Learning has set us on this path, and opened up a positive, creative way to engage our young people in truly sustainable living.

Recommended further reading

1. Dr Seuss (1971). *The Lorax*. London: Random House.
2. Sinden, Neil (1990). *In A Nutshell*. London: Common Ground.
3. The Forest School Association (2020). *Full Nature Premium Proposal Briefing Documents*. https://naturepremium.squarespace.com/nature-premium-briefing-documents (accessed 11/09/2021).

References

Aldhous, J. R. (1997). British forestry: 70 years of achievement. *Forestry, 70*(4), 283–291. https://doi.org/10.1093/forestry/70.4.283

Department for Education and Skills. (2006). *Learning outside the classroom manifesto.* DfES Publications. https://www.lotc.org.uk/wp-content/uploads/2011/03/G1.-LOtC-Manifesto.pdf

Foundation Audemars Piguet. (2021, August 3). About Foundation Audemars Piguet. https://www.audemarspiguet.com/com/en/about/foundation.html.

Harvey, D. J., Montgomery, L. N., Harvey, H., Hall, F., Gange, A. C., & Watling, D. (2020). Psychological benefits of a biodiversity-focussed outdoor learning program for primary school children. *Journal of Environmental Psychology, 67*, 101381. https://doi.org/10.1016/j.jenvp.2019.101381

HM Government. (2018). *A green future: Our 25 year plan to improve the environment.* Defra Publications. https://www.gov.uk/government/publications/25-year-environment-plan.

Macfarlane, R., & Morris, J. (2017). *The lost words.* London: Hamish Hamilton.

National Forest Company. (2018). *A forest for learning.* https://www.nationalforest.org/sites/default/files/components/downloads/files/144%20TWD%20NF%20Report%20v4_3.pdf.

Countryside Commission. (1994). *National forest: The strategy—The forest vision.* Countryside Agency Publications.

NHS Digital. (2018). *The mental health of children and young people in England 2017.* https://digital.nhs.uk/data-and-information/publications/statistical/mental-health-of-children-and-young-people-in-england/2017/2017.

Otte, C. R., Bølling, M., Stevenson, M. P., Ejbye-Ernst, N., Nielsen, G., & Bentsen, P. (2019). Education outside the classroom increases children's reading performance: Results from a one-year quasi-experimental study. *International Journal of Educational Research, 94*, 42–51. https://doi.org/10.1016/j.ijer.2019.01.009

Public Health England. (2017). *Health matters: obesity and the food environment.* https://www.gov.uk/government/publications/health-matters-obesity-and-the-food-environment/health-matters-obesity-and-the-food-environment--2.

Waite, S., Passy, R., Gilchrist, M., Hunt, A., & Blackwell, I. (2016). *Natural connections demonstration project, 2012–2016: Final report. Natural England Commissioned Reports, NECR215.* http://publications.naturalengland.org.uk/publication/6636651036540928.

Carol Rowntree Jones is Media Relations Officer at the National Forest Company. She has seen the National Forest grow over nearly two decades and is passionate about communicating the unique nature of this forest growing in and among where people live and work. A writer and poet, Carol is working on a book about the National Forest. Correspondence address: crowntreejones@nationalforest.org.

Caroline Scothern is Education Officer at the National Forest Company, working to build the capacity of schools to deliver Outdoor Learning in their everyday curriculum. She is passionate about ensuring young people care for and have fun in the woodlands on their doorstep, with all the benefits this offers for their education, health and wellbeing. Caroline is a qualified social worker and experienced teacher and Forest School practitioner. In her spare time, she can often be found walking or cycling on Forest trails.

Heather Gilbert is the Research and Evidence Manager for the National Forest Company. After completing her PhD at the University of Nottingham, Heather undertook several years' fieldwork studying biodiversity trends around the world. In recent years, Heather has worked with students of all ages to engage them with biodiversity research and the conservation issues it informs. Heather now works with National Forest teams to support a diverse range of programmes encompassing environmental, societal and economic research into building a sustainable future.

Sue Anderson is Community Engagement Manager at the National Forest Company. Since its inception she has sought to engage communities in the National Forest and realise its potential to transform lives, whether by improving health and wellbeing, creativity, skills, aspirations or careers.

Printed in the USA
CPSIA information can be obtained
at www.ICGtesting.com
LVHW011032151023
761135LV00001B/1

9 783031 041105